Grade 2

School Day Skills

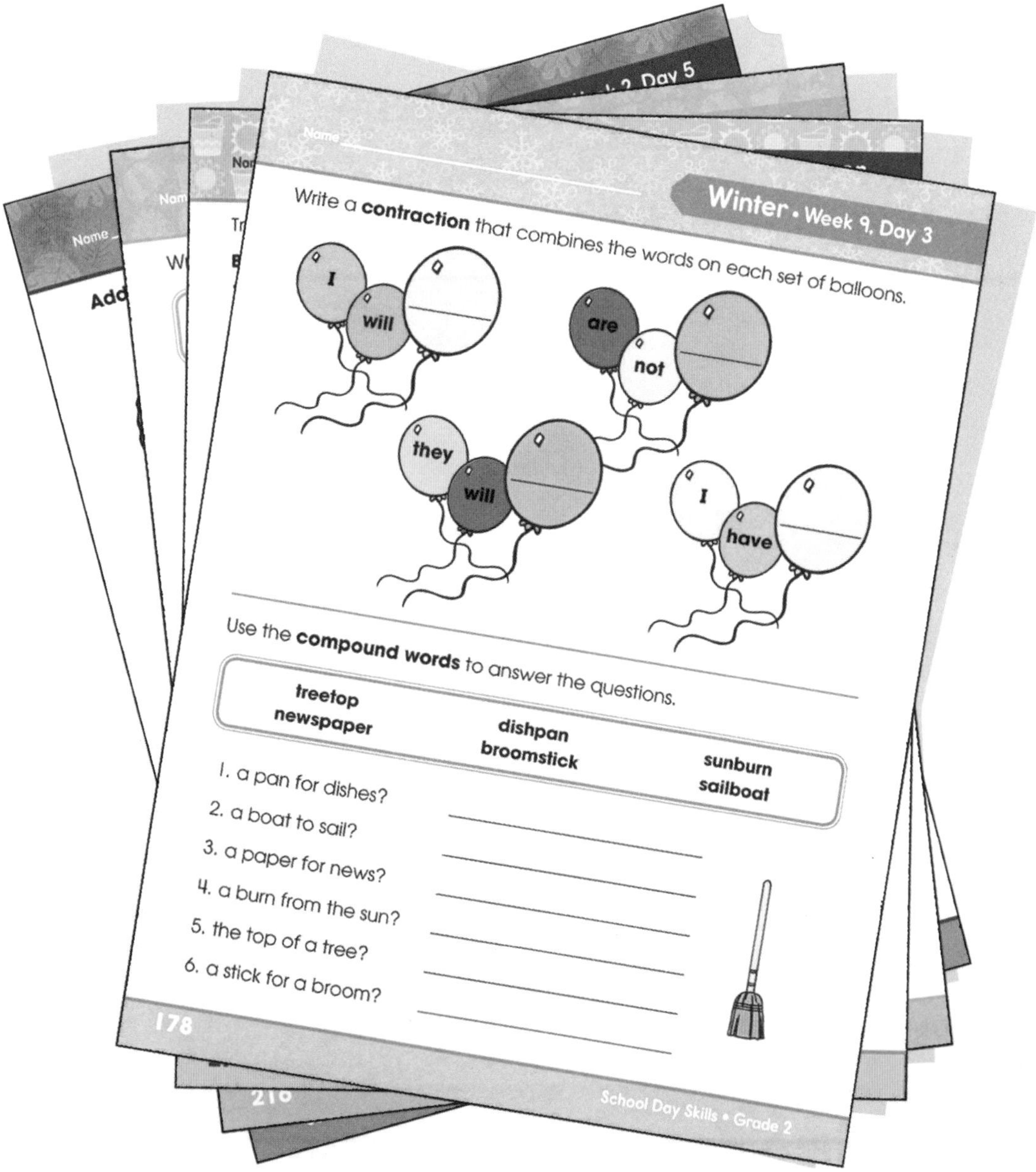

Thinking Kids™
An imprint of Carson-Dellosa Publishing LLC
P.O. Box 35665
Greensboro, NC 27425 USA

Thinking Kids™
Carson-Dellosa Publishing LLC
P.O. Box 35665
Greensboro, NC 27425 USA

ISBN 978-1-4838-3114-5
01-157161151

Table of Contents

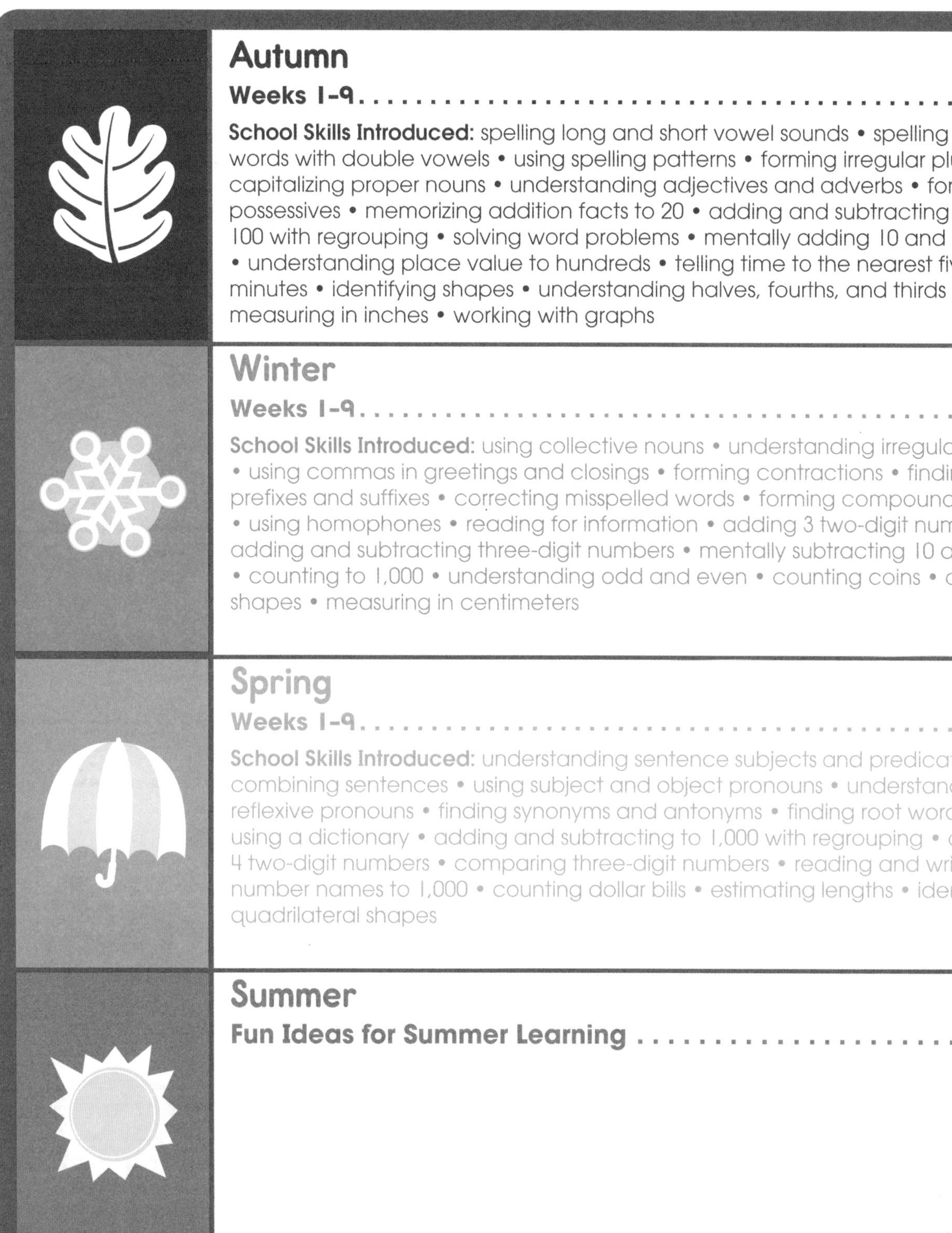

Write a letter to complete each **short vowel** word.

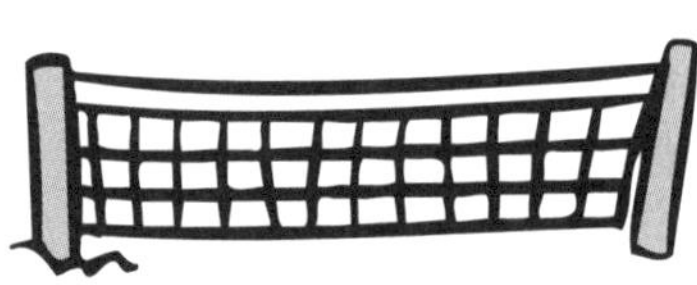

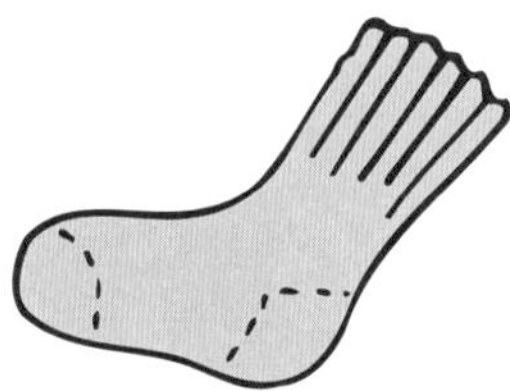

p___p

n___t

s___ck

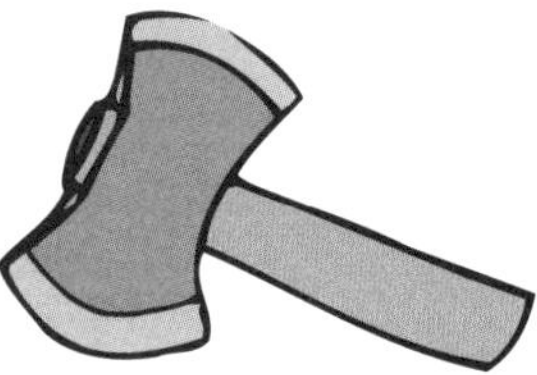

___x

l___ps

t___nt

Roll dice to find two addends. Write them on the first two lines. **Add** to find the sum.

1. ________ + ________ = ________

2. ________ + ________ = ________

3. ________ + ________ = ________

4. ________ + ________ = ________

5. ________ + ________ = ________

A clock face has numbers from 1 to 12. There are 60 minutes in one hour. Fill in the numbers. Count by **ones** on the clock face. Count by **fives** around the clock.

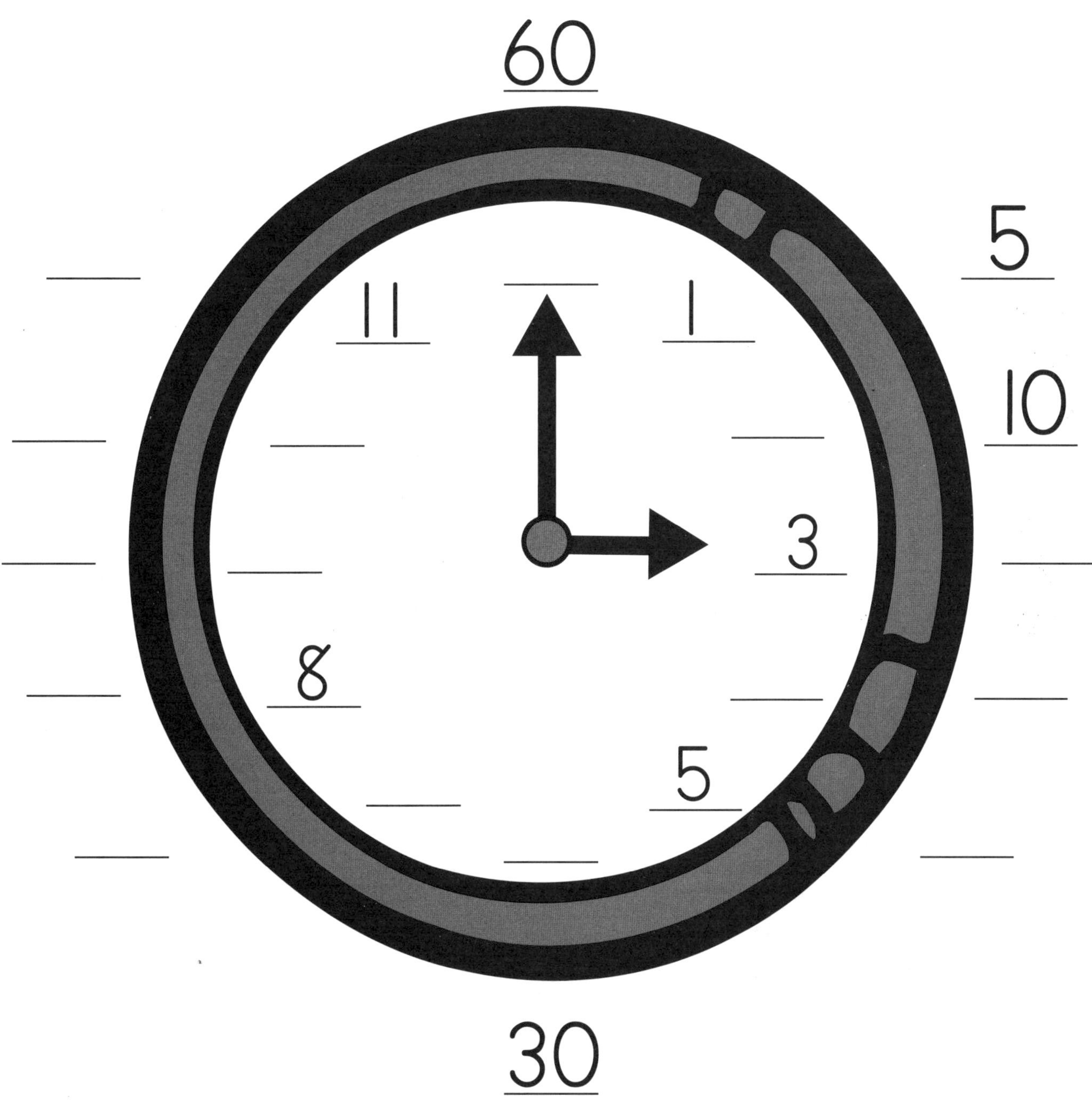

Write the words that rhyme with each word below. Circle the letters in each word that spell the **long e** sound.

neat	**read**	**team**	**eat**	**seat**
sea	**mean**	**meat**	**beam**	**lean**

wheat ______________________ **seam** ______________________

______________________ ______________________

______________________ **bead** ______________________

______________________ **bean** ______________________

tea ______________________ ______________________

Add numbers with two digits. Add the **ones**. Then, add the **tens**. Follow the example.

Step 1: Add the ones.

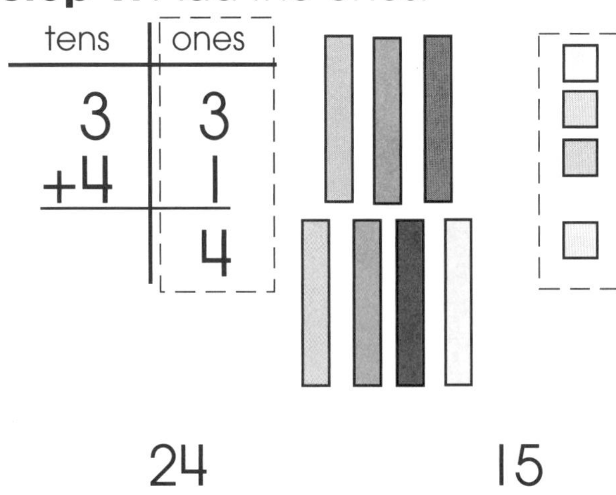

Step 2: Add the tens.

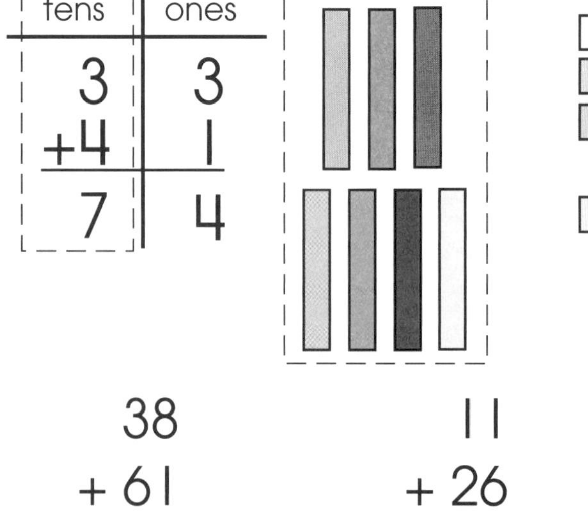

$$\begin{array}{r} 24 \\ +\ 62 \\ \hline \end{array} \qquad \begin{array}{r} 15 \\ +\ 23 \\ \hline \end{array} \qquad \begin{array}{r} 38 \\ +\ 61 \\ \hline \end{array} \qquad \begin{array}{r} 11 \\ +\ 26 \\ \hline \end{array}$$

The names of places, products, and holidays are **proper nouns** that begin with a capital letter. Rewrite each sentence, capitalizing all the proper nouns.

1. Aunt Frances lives in detroit, michigan.

   ____

2. We celebrate valentine's day in february.

   ____

3. I chose yumtime muffins for our snack.

   ____

4. We live in the united states of america.

   ____

An **inch** is a unit of measurement. A ruler shows 12 inches. Use a ruler to measure each object to the nearest inch.

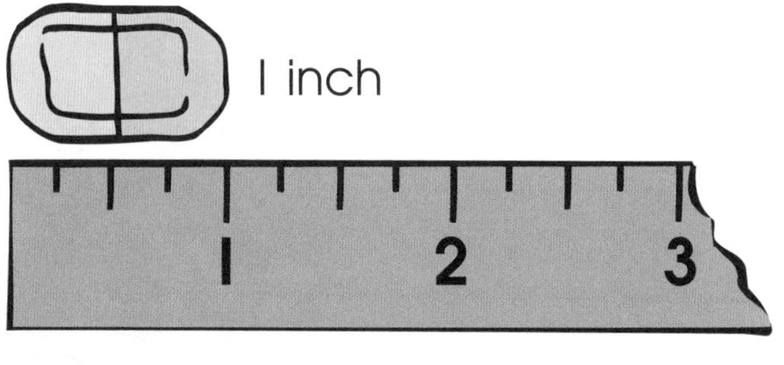

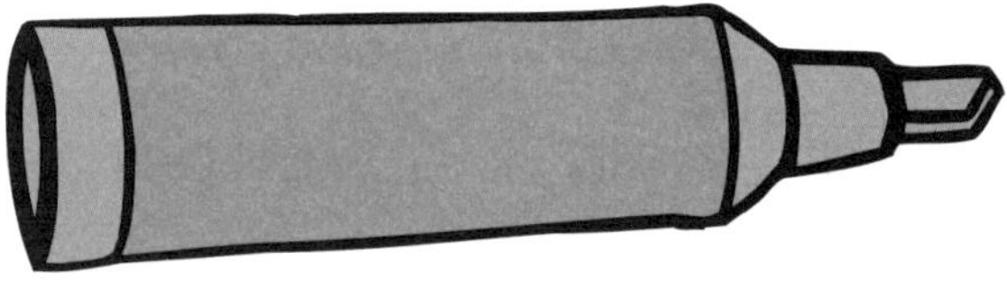

_______ inches

_______ inches

_______ inch

How much longer is the marker than the paper clip? _______ inches

Subtract numbers with two digits. Subtract the **ones**. Then, subtract the **tens**. Follow the example.

Step 1: Subtract the ones.

	tens	ones
	2	8
−	1	4
		4

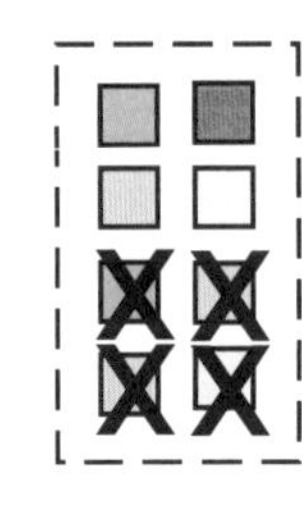

Step 2: Subtract the tens.

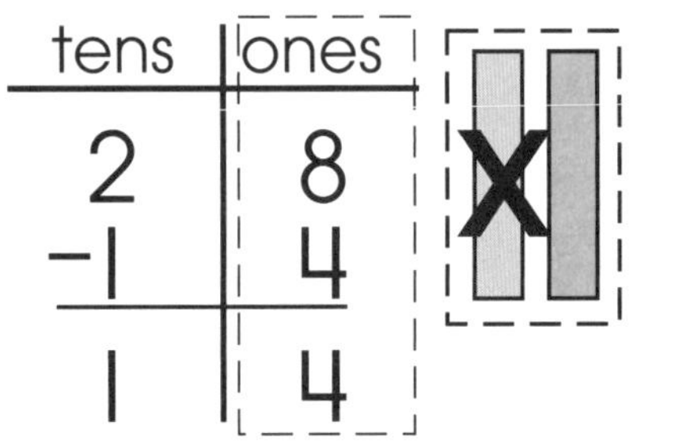

	tens	ones
	2	8
−	1	4
	1	4

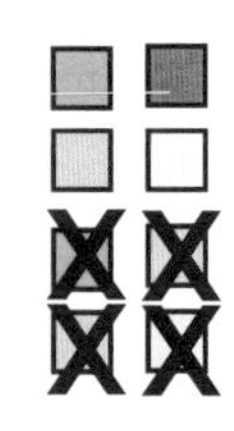

```
  24      61      77      85
- 12    - 30    - 44    - 24
----    ----    ----    ----
```

Add an **apostrophe** and the letter **s ('s)** to the noun in each sentence to show who owns something.

1. That is Holly ___ flower garden.

2. Mark ___ new skates are black and green.

3. Mom threw away Dad ___ old shoes.

4. Buster ___ food dish was lost in the snowstorm.

Color the picture. Then, color spaces to make a **bar graph** that shows how many of each item you count.

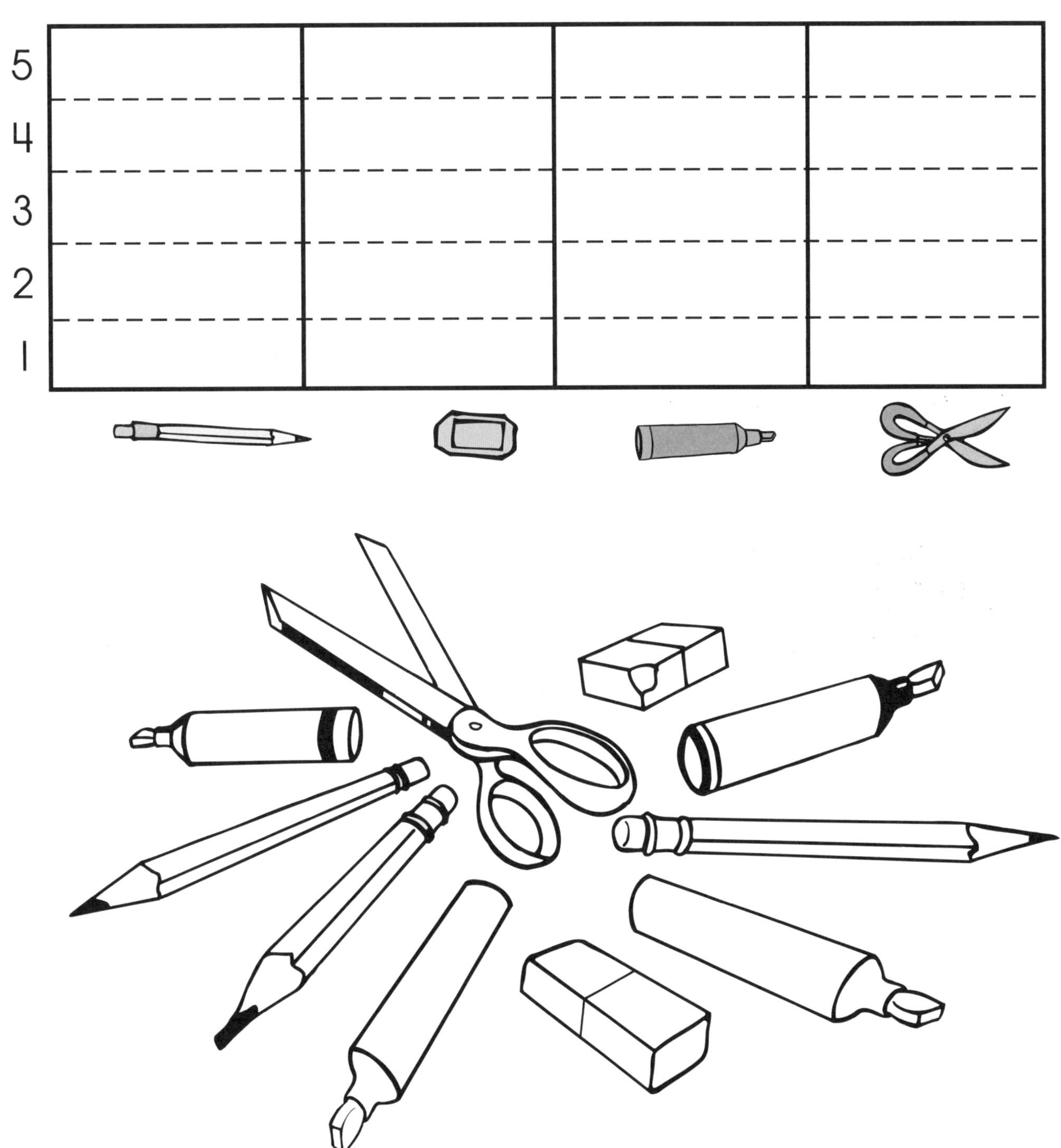

Write a letter to complete each **short vowel** word.

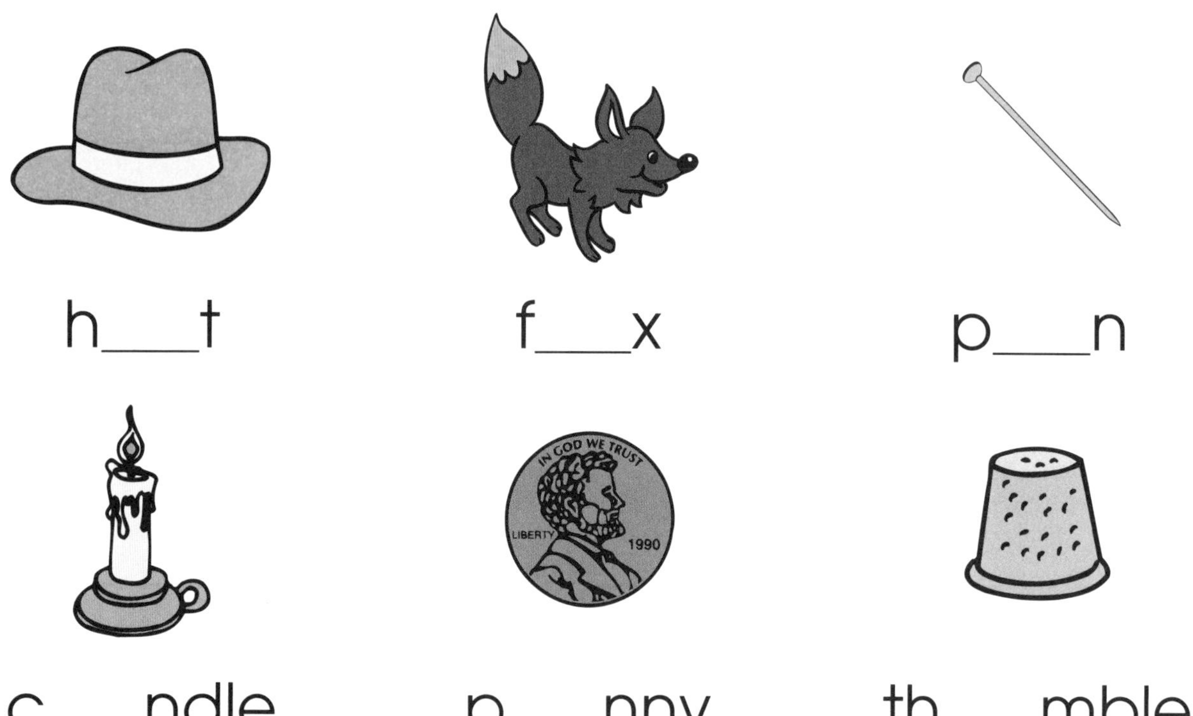

h___t   f___x   p___n

c___ndle   p___nny   th___mble

An **adverb** is a word that describes a verb. It can tell where, how, or when. Adverbs often end with **ly**. Circle the adverb in each sentence. The first one is done for you.

1. The skateboarder landed (smoothly.)
2. Their call was returned quickly.
3. We easily learned the new words.
4. He did the work perfectly.
5. She lost her purse somewhere.

Add the **ones**. Then, add the **tens**. Write the sum.

2 tens and 6 ones
+ 1 ten and 3 ones

___ tens and ___ ones = ____

1 ten and 4 ones
+ 3 tens and 3 ones

___ tens and ___ ones = ____

2 tens and 5 ones
+ 2 tens and 3 ones

___ tens and ___ ones = ____

1 ten and 6 ones
+ 5 tens and 1 one

___ tens and ___ ones = ____

There are 60 minutes in one hour. The short hand shows the **hour**. The long hand shows the **minutes**. Write the time shown on each clock. The first one is done for you.

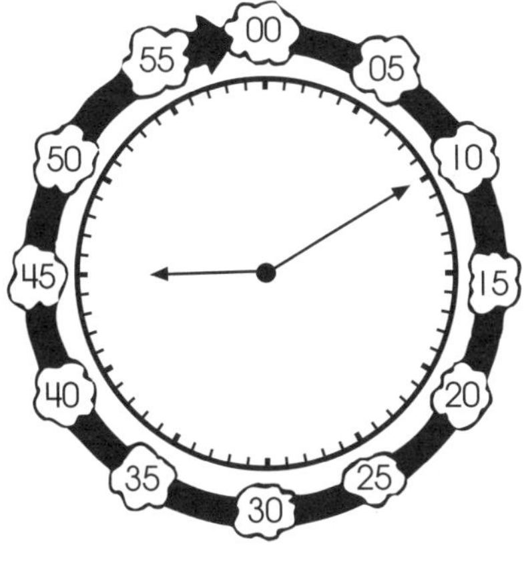

9 : 10

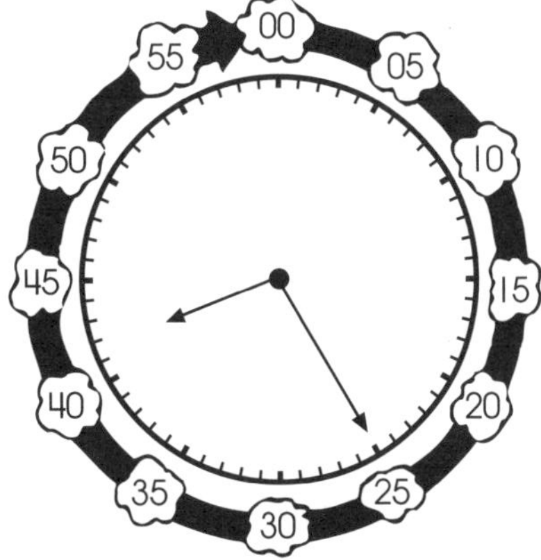

____ : ____

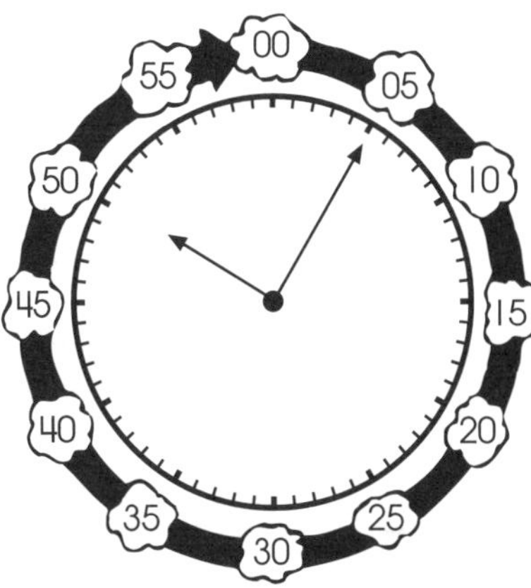

____ : ____

Add in one minute or less.

8 + 8	2 + 3	7 + 1	2 + 8	5 + 7
9 + 10	4 + 10	6 + 0	9 + 5	8 + 6

Adjectives describe nouns. They can tell what kind, how many, or which one. Color each space that has an adjective.

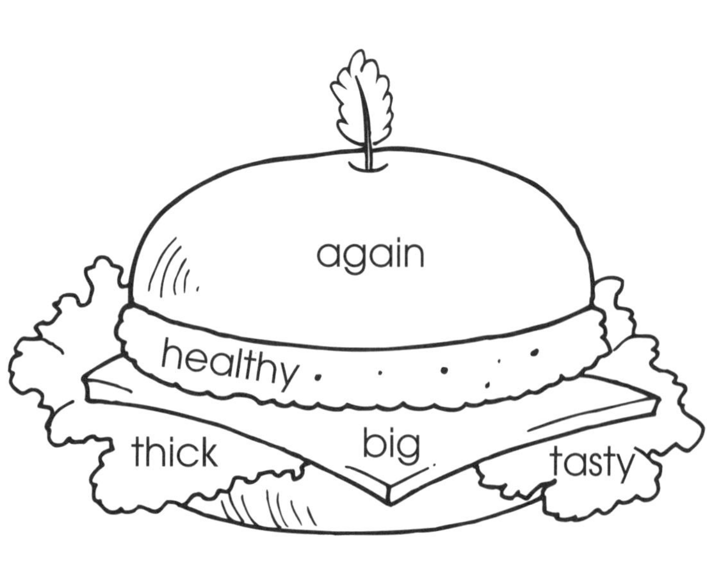

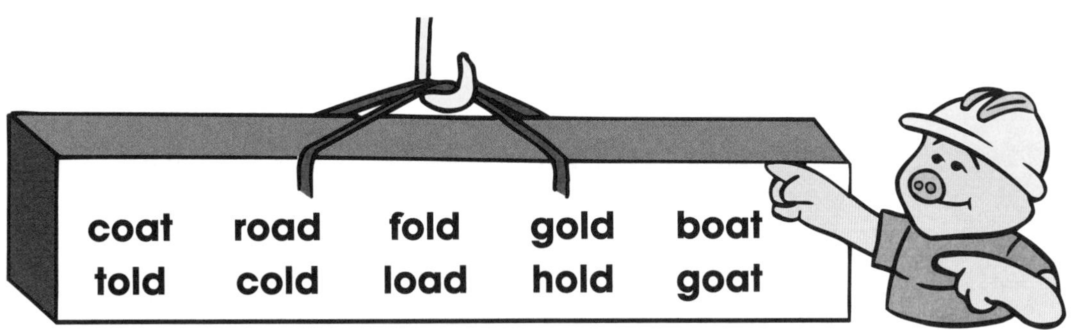

coat road fold gold boat
told cold load hold goat

Write the words with **o** followed by **ld** that make the **long o** sound.

______ ______ ______

______ ______

Write the **oa** words that make the **long o** sound.

______ ______ ______

______ ______

Use a ruler to measure each object to the nearest **inch**.

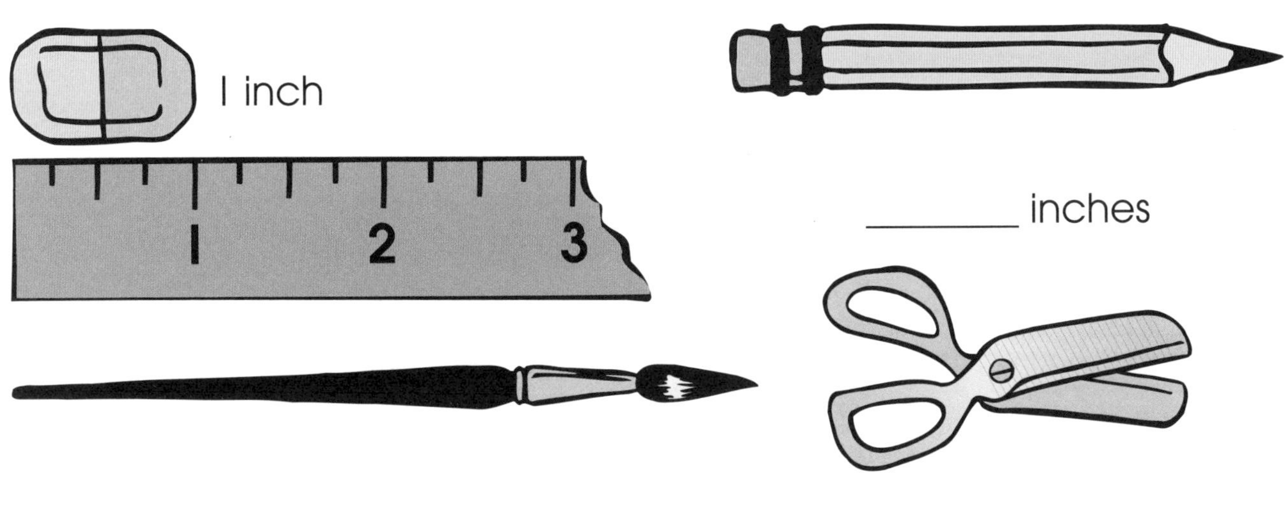

How many inches longer is the paintbrush than the pair of scissors? ______ inches

Circle the correct answer.

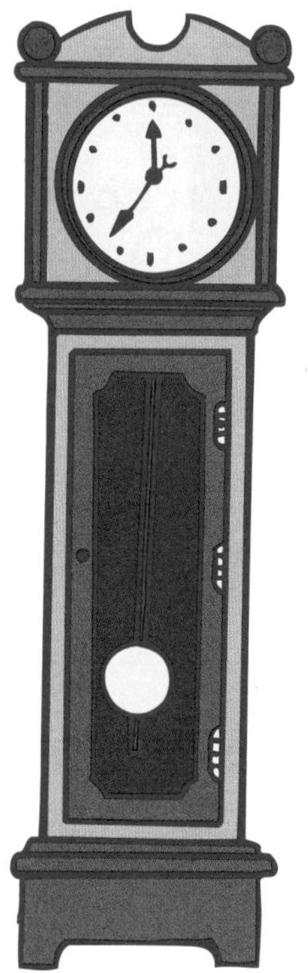

1. There are 60 seconds in a (minute, year).
2. There are 60 minutes in an (second, hour).
3. There are 24 hours in a (minute, day).
4. There are 365 days in a (year, week).
5. There are 7 days in a (week, hour).
6. There are 12 months in a (year, week).

When two vowels appear together, the first vowel often makes a **long vowel sound**. The second vowel is **silent**. Unscramble the double-vowel words.

 teas ____________

 otab ____________

 ogat ____________

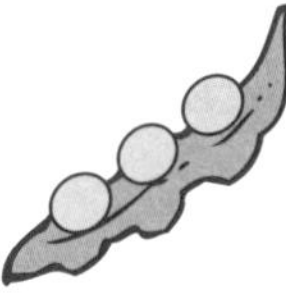 spea ____________

 atli ____________

 apil ____________

Subtract to find out how many of each exercise the players should do. Subtract the **ones**. Then, subtract the **tens**.

Write the **plurals**. Follow the examples.

Example: dog + s = dogs

cat ____________________

boot ____________________

house ____________________

Example: peach + es = peaches

lunch ____________________

bunch ____________________

punch ____________________

Example: ax + es = axes

fox ____________________

tax ____________________

box ____________________

Example: glass + es = glasses

mess ____________________

guess ____________________

class ____________________

Add the **ones**. Then, add the **tens**. Write the sum.

1 ten and 3 ones + 1 ten and 1 one	2 tens and 5 ones + 2 tens and 0 ones
___ tens and ___ ones = ____	___ tens and ___ ones = ____

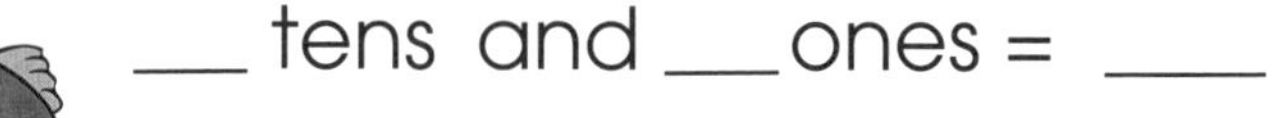

1 ten and 5 ones + 2 tens and 4 ones	7 tens and 6 ones + 2 tens and 2 ones
___ tens and ___ ones = ____	___ tens and ___ ones = ____

Write the time shown on each clock. The first one is done for you.

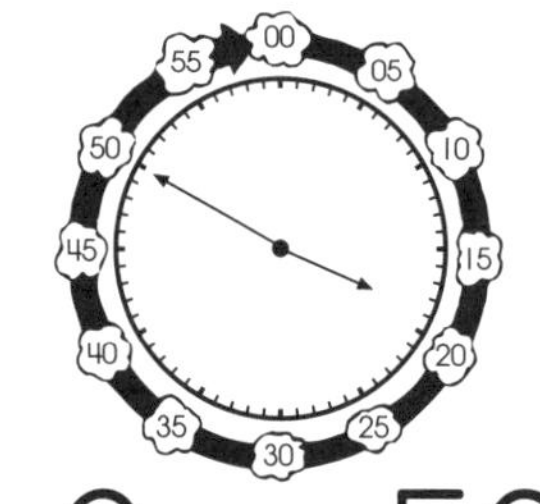

3 : 50

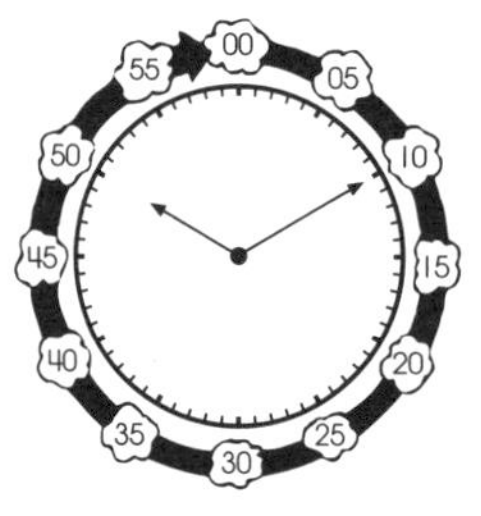

_____ : _____

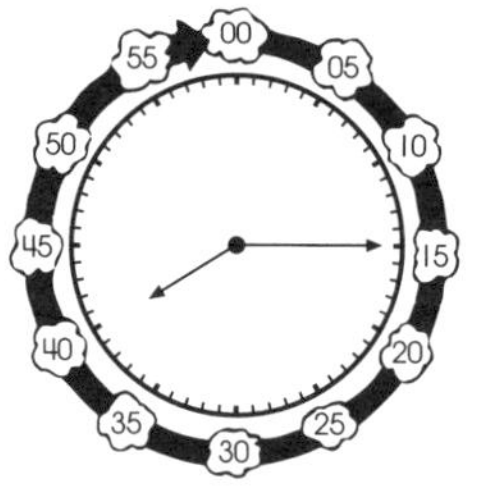

_____ : _____

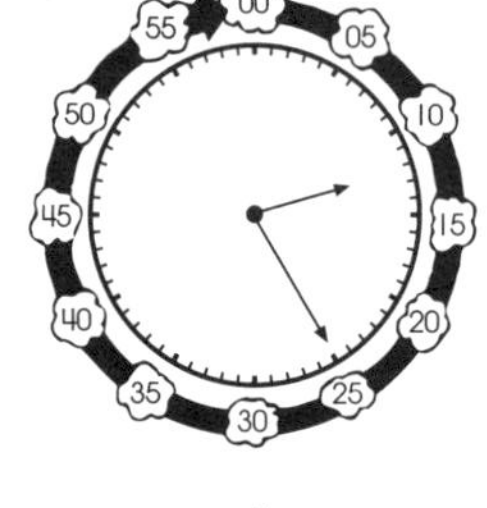

_____ : _____

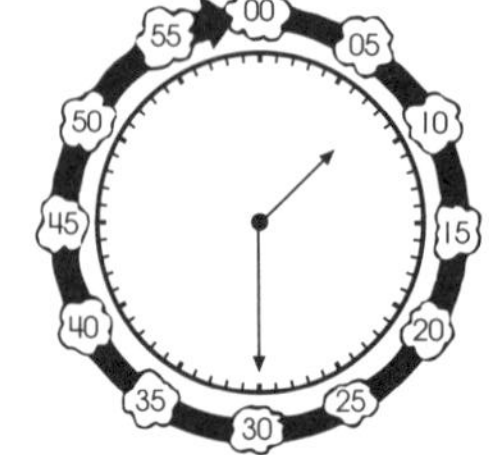

_____ : _____

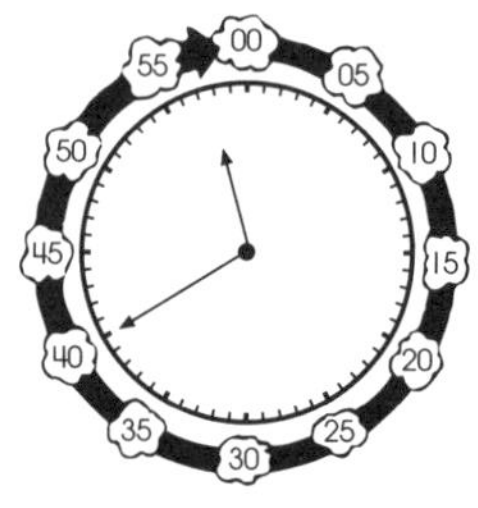

_____ : _____

The names of places, products, and holidays are **proper nouns** that begin with a capital letter. Rewrite each sentence, capitalizing all the proper nouns.

1. We will have a family picnic on memorial day.

____

2. I want a roadways bike for my birthday.

____

3. The mall of america is in minneapolis, minnesota.

____

4. Can you believe we drove from florida to maine?

____

Write letters to complete the words with **short vowel sounds**.

l___dder

p___pcorn

p___pp___t

h___mmer

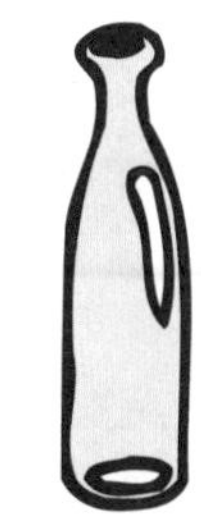

b___ttle

b___tt___n

Find each item. Use a ruler to measure it to the nearest **inch**.

a stack of blocks ________ inches

a toy car ________ inches

your foot ________ inches

a spoon ________ inches

the length of a book ________ inches

a toothbrush ________ inches

Which item was shortest? ____________________

Which item was longest? ____________________

Add **'s** to the noun in **bold** in the first sentence. Use the new word to complete the second sentence.

1. **Dad** is charging his phone.

   ____________________ phone is charging.

2. **Isa** has a blue backpack.

   Have you seen ____________________ blue backpack?

3. **Jake** got a new video game.

   Let's play ____________________ new video game.

4. **Mrs. Allen** has wilted plants.

   We helped water ____________________ plants.

Add in one minute or less.

9 + 10	2 + 5	4 + 6	9 + 9	3 + 4
0 + 8	3 + 7	1 + 11	7 + 10	2 + 5

---

way	**sail**	**pain**	**say**	**rain**
wait	**day**	**pay**	**nail**	**lay**

Write the **ai** words that make the **long a** sound.

______________ ______________ ______________

______________ ______________

Write the **ay** words that make the **long a** sound.

______________ ______________ ______________

______________ ______________

Write **ou**, **ow**, or **aw** to complete each word.

h_______se

fl_______er

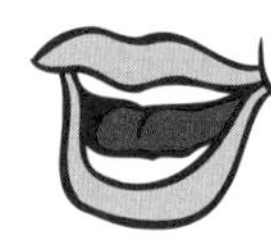

m_______th

p_______

_______l

s_______

cl_______d

p_______der

j_______

Subtract. Circle the answers. Then, color the cookies with differences that are greater than 30.

20 25 35

67 86 65

12 26 16

31 33 32

56 36 37

34 43 39

Color the pots to make a **bar graph** that shows the number of flowers.

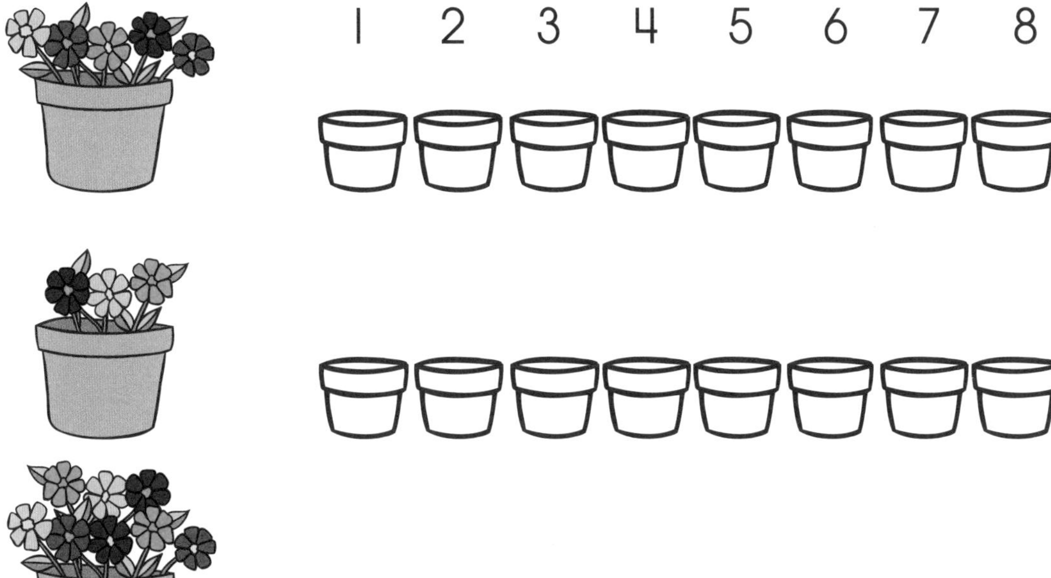

Write an **adjective** in each blank. Then, draw a picture to match the sentence.

The __________ flag waved over the __________ building.

A __________ lion searched for food in the __________ jungle.

Color part of each clock face to show the number of **minutes**. The first two are done for you.

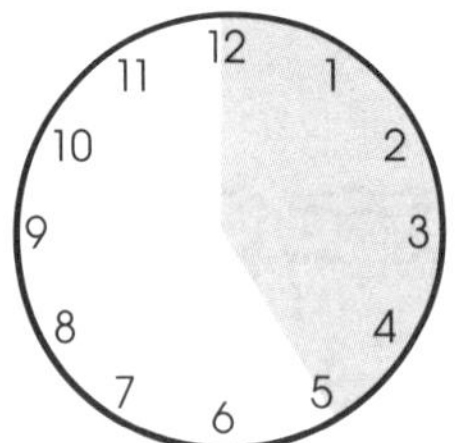

25 minutes

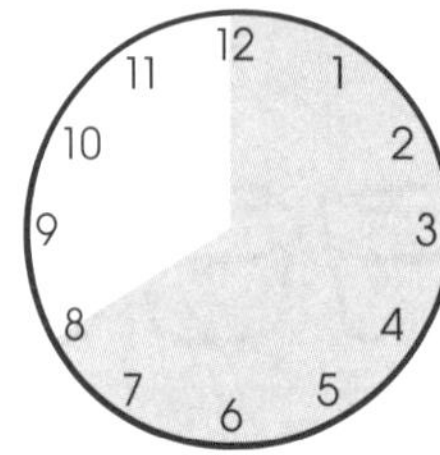

40 minutes

30 minutes

15 minutes

45 minutes

55 minutes

Many words that end with **silent e** have a **long vowel** sound. Complete each word with a letter that helps make the long vowel sound.

___pe

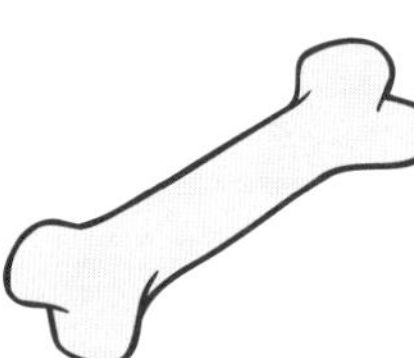

b___ne

c___be

k___te

r___ke

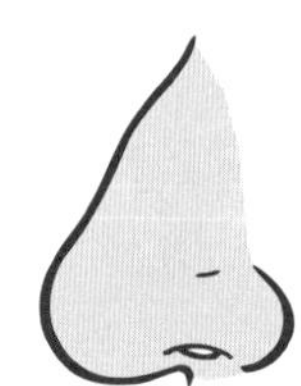

n___se

Add. First, add the **ones**. Then, add the **tens**. Write the sum.

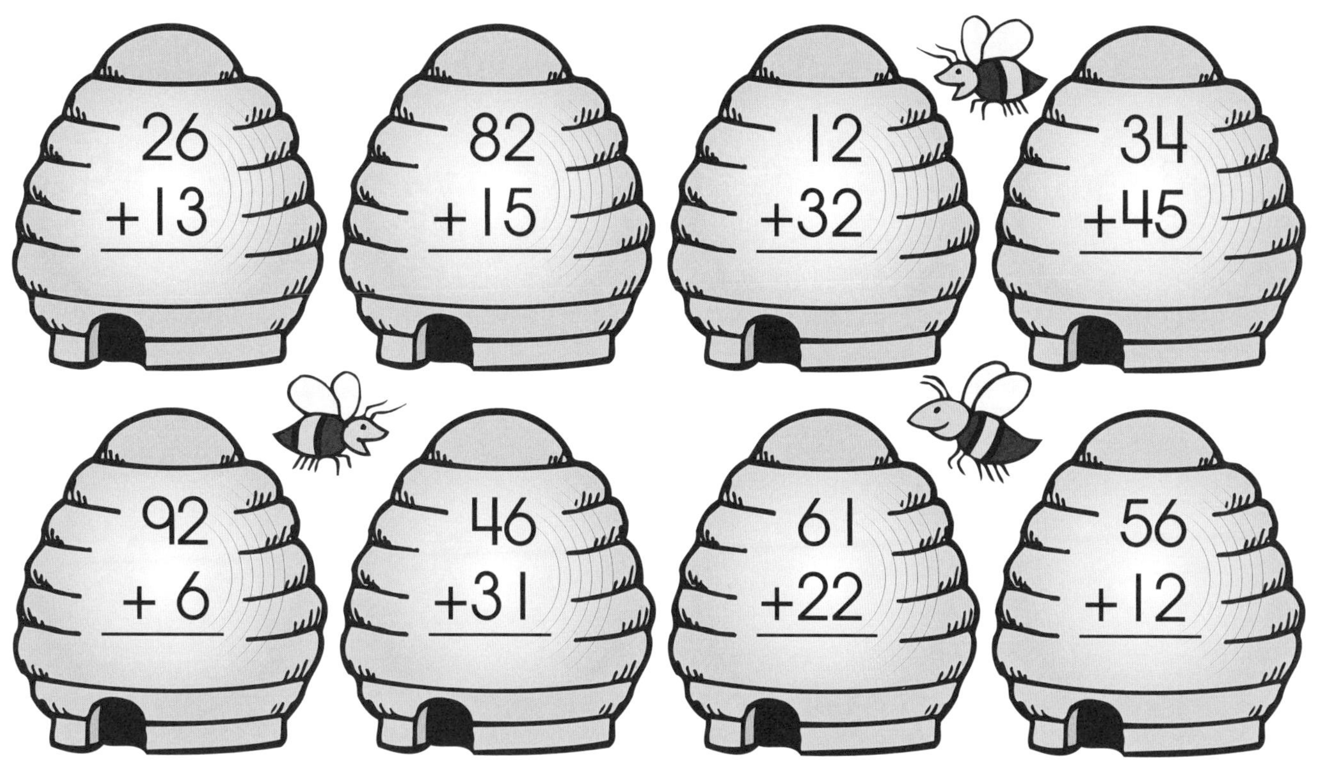

Write **how**, **when**, or **where** to explain what each **adverb** tells.

1. I run **today**. ____________
2. I run **outside**. ____________
3. I will run **tomorrow**. ____________
4. I run **around**. ____________
5. I run **nearby**. ____________
6. I run **sometimes**. ____________
7. I run **there**. ____________
8. I run **far**. ____________
9. I run **happily**. ____________
10. I run **weekly**. ____________
11. I run **swiftly**. ____________
12. I run **first**. ____________
13. I run **next**. ____________
14. I run **gracefully**. ____________

Add in one minute or less.

9	5	3	0	7
+ 3	+ 6	+ 3	+ 1	+ 9

8	6	6	7	5
+ 2	+ 10	+ 3	+ 1	+ 9

Use a ruler to measure the line segments to the nearest **inch**. Write the number of inches on each candy jar.

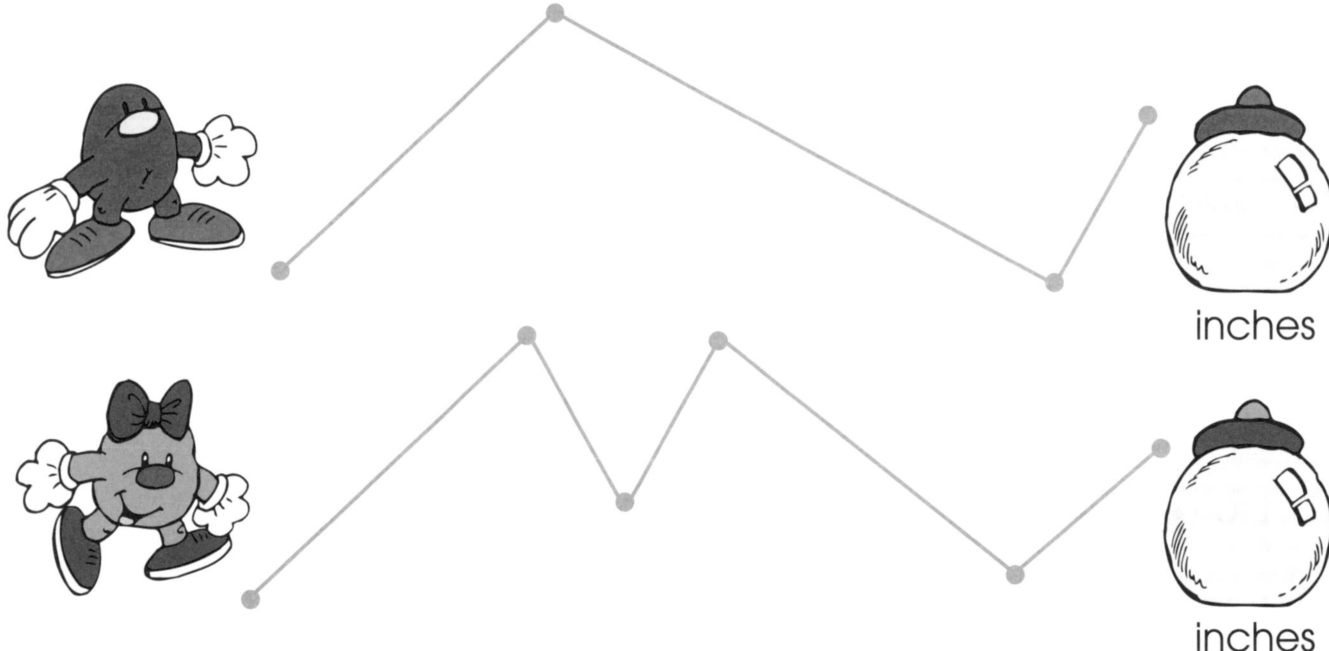

sky	**might**	**dry**	**by**	**night**
sight	**cry**	**light**	**right**	**fly**

Write the **igh** words that make the **long i** sound.

____________________ ____________________ ____________________

____________________ ____________________

Write the words ending in **y** that make the **long i** sound.

____________________ ____________________ ____________________

____________________ ____________________

In each sentence, circle an **adjective**. Then, draw an arrow from it to the noun it describes. The first one is done for you.

1. A platypus is a furry animal that lives in Australia.
2. This interesting animal lays eggs.
3. Its strange nose looks like a duck's bill.
4. It has a broad tail like a beaver.
5. Platypuses are great swimmers.
6. They have webbed feet which help them swim.

Write the **plural** of each noun. In each word, change **y** to **ie** before adding **s**.

berry ______________________

cherry ______________________

bunny ______________________

penny ______________________

family ______________________

candy ______________________

party ______________________

Add the **ones**. Then, add the **tens**. Write the sum.

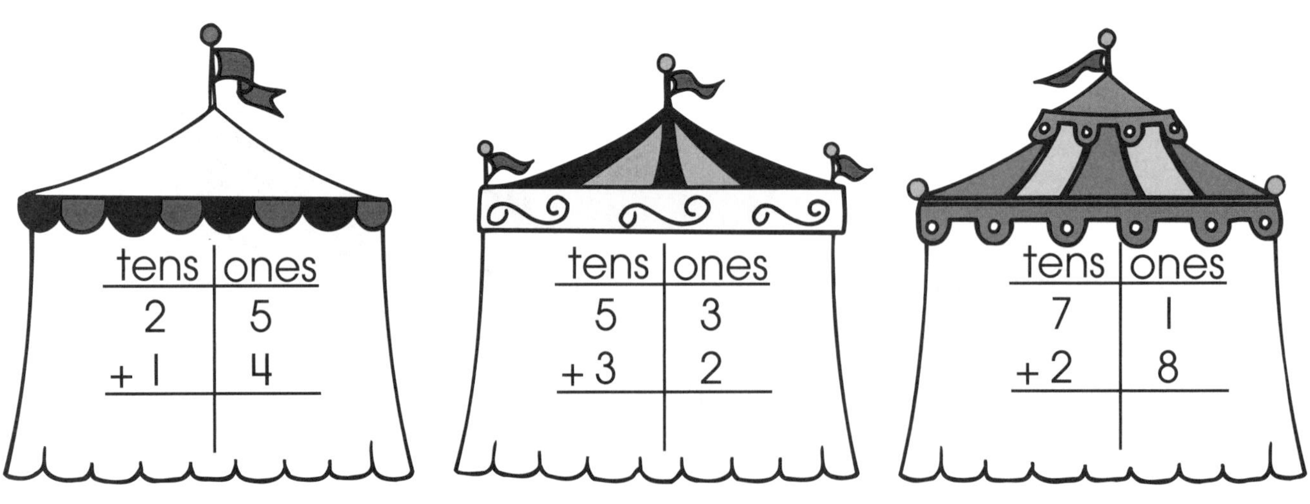

The letters **ea** can spell a **short vowel sound** (as in **head**), a **long vowel sound** (as in **bead**), or a vowel sound followed by **r** (as in **heard**). Write each **bold** word from the story in the correct column.

Have you ever **read** a book or **heard** a story about a **bear**? You might have **learned** that bears sleep through the winter. Some bears may sleep the whole **season**. Sometimes, they look almost **dead**! But they are very much alive. As the cold winter passes and the spring **weather** comes **near**, they wake up. After such a nice rest, they must be **ready** to **eat** a **really** big **meal**!

words with short ea	words with long ea	ea followed by r
____________	____________	____________
____________	____________	____________
____________	____________	____________
____________	____________	____________

Add or **subtract**. Circle the answer on the number line.

20 − 13 = ____

0 1 2 3 4 5 6 7 8 9 10 11 12 13 14 15 16 17 18 19 20

20 + 19 = ____

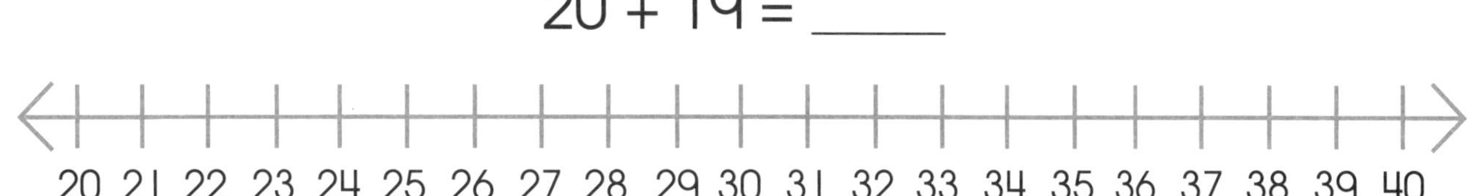

Count the **tens** and **ones** and write the numbers. Then, **subtract**. The first one is done for you.

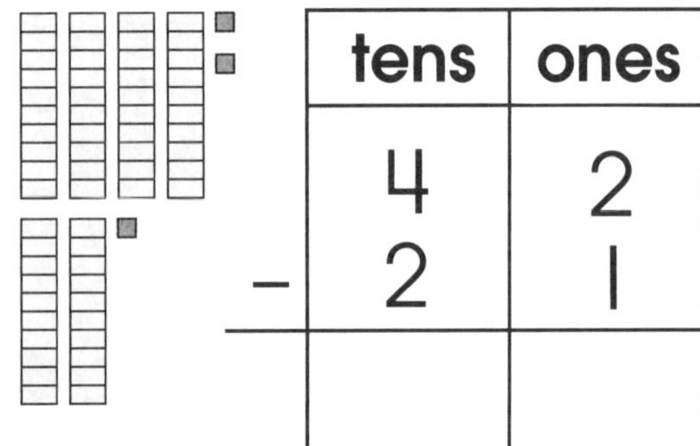

	tens	ones
	4	2
−	2	1

	tens	ones
−		

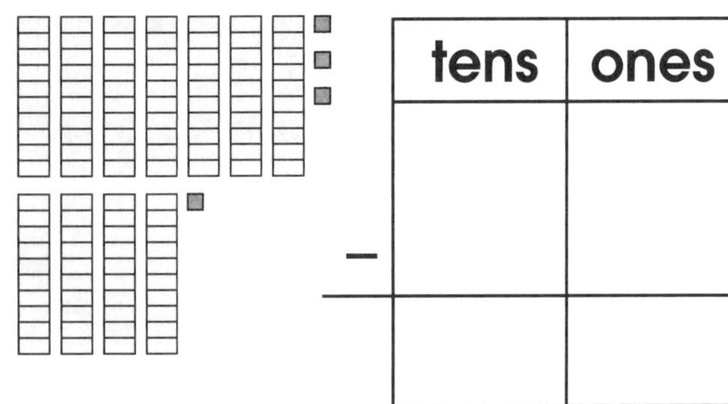

	tens	ones
−		

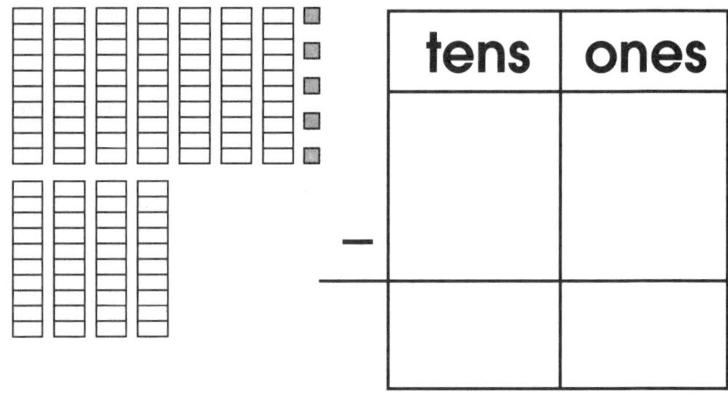

	tens	ones
−		

Color the pictures whose names have a **short vowel sound blue**. Color the pictures whose names have a **long vowel sound orange**.

frog

queen

nine

drum

stamp

bell

rope

rain

The proofreading mark ≡ means "capitalize." Write ≡ under each letter that should be a capital.

1. At arrowhead elementary, there is no school on presidents' day.
2. When I was seven, our family moved from des moines, iowa, to phoenix, arizona.
3. Reggie loves dog days dog food, but Mitzy will only eat pet choice.
4. Grandma and Grandpa will make brunch for the whole family on easter sunday.
5. Eric went to college in pittsburgh, pennsylvania.

The hours between 12:00 midnight and 12:00 noon are **A.M.** hours. The hours between 12:00 noon and 12:00 midnight are **P.M.** hours. Draw a line between times that are the same.

six o'clock in the evening	8:00 A.M.
3:30 A.M.	6:00 P.M.
4:15 P.M.	three thirty in the morning
eight o'clock in the morning	four fifteen in the afternoon
quarter past five in the evening	5:15 P.M.

Write the words on the correct road.

sleepy	many	dry	shy	penny	fly	why	funny

y sounds like long e | **y sounds like long i**

______________ ______________

______________ ______________

______________ ______________

______________ ______________

Y

Add **'s** to the noun in **bold** in the first sentence. Use the new word to complete the second sentence.

1. The **turtle** has green and brown spots on its shell.

   Did you see the pattern on the ______________ shell?

2. I live two doors down from **Malia**.

   My house is close to ______________ house.

3. **Nana** makes minestrone soup.

   ______________ minestrone soup is the best!

4. **Coach Tom** is our soccer coach.

   I work hard during ______________ practices.

Add in one minute or less.

9 + 5	7 + 7	2 + 10	5 + 6	3 + 5
1 + 4	9 + 4	10 + 6	2 + 2	4 + 8

Color: **one half** **red**	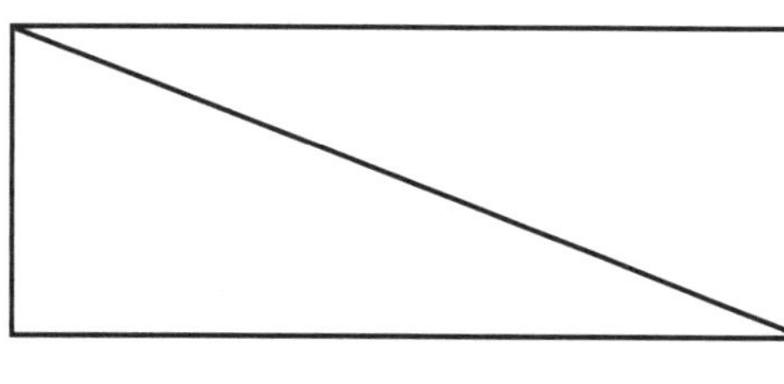 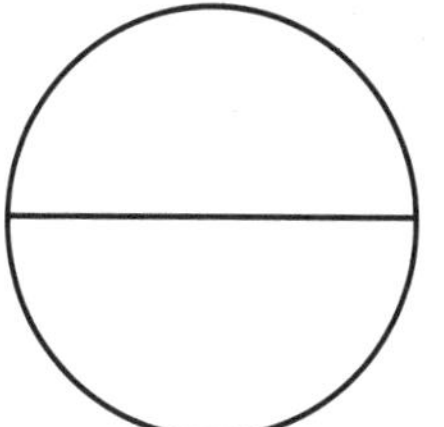
Color: **one fourth blue**	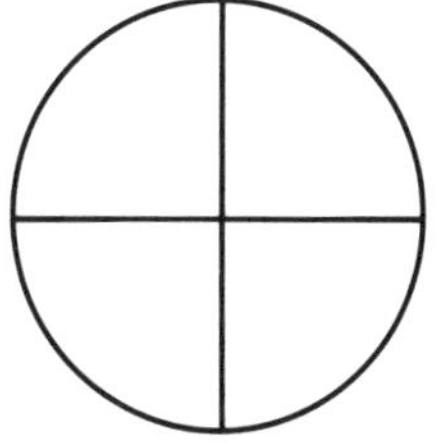 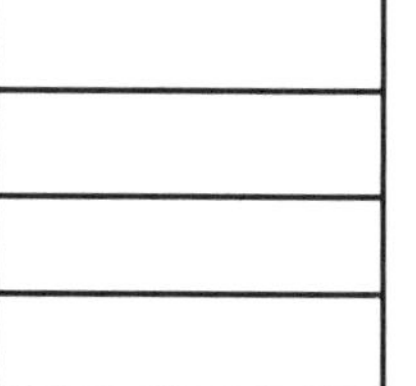 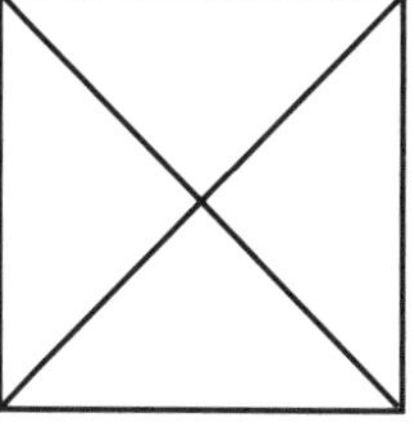
Color: **one third orange**	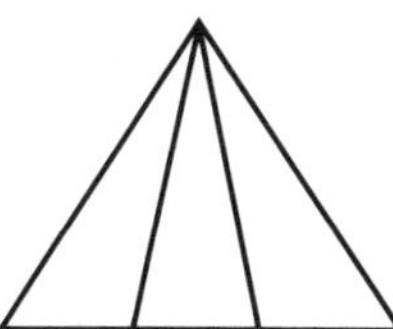  

Add the points scored in each game. Add the **ones**. Then, add the **tens**.

Total __________

Total __________

Total __________

Total __________

Total __________

Total __________

An **adverb** describes an action. Circle the adverb in each pair of words.

1. soon, supper
2. neatly, nine
3. proudly, prove
4. help, easily
5. warmly, wonder
6. quilt, quickly
7. finally, feather
8. quietly, quacks
9. sail, safely
10. later, laugh

Write **inch**, **foot**, or **mile** to show the unit that best measures each item.

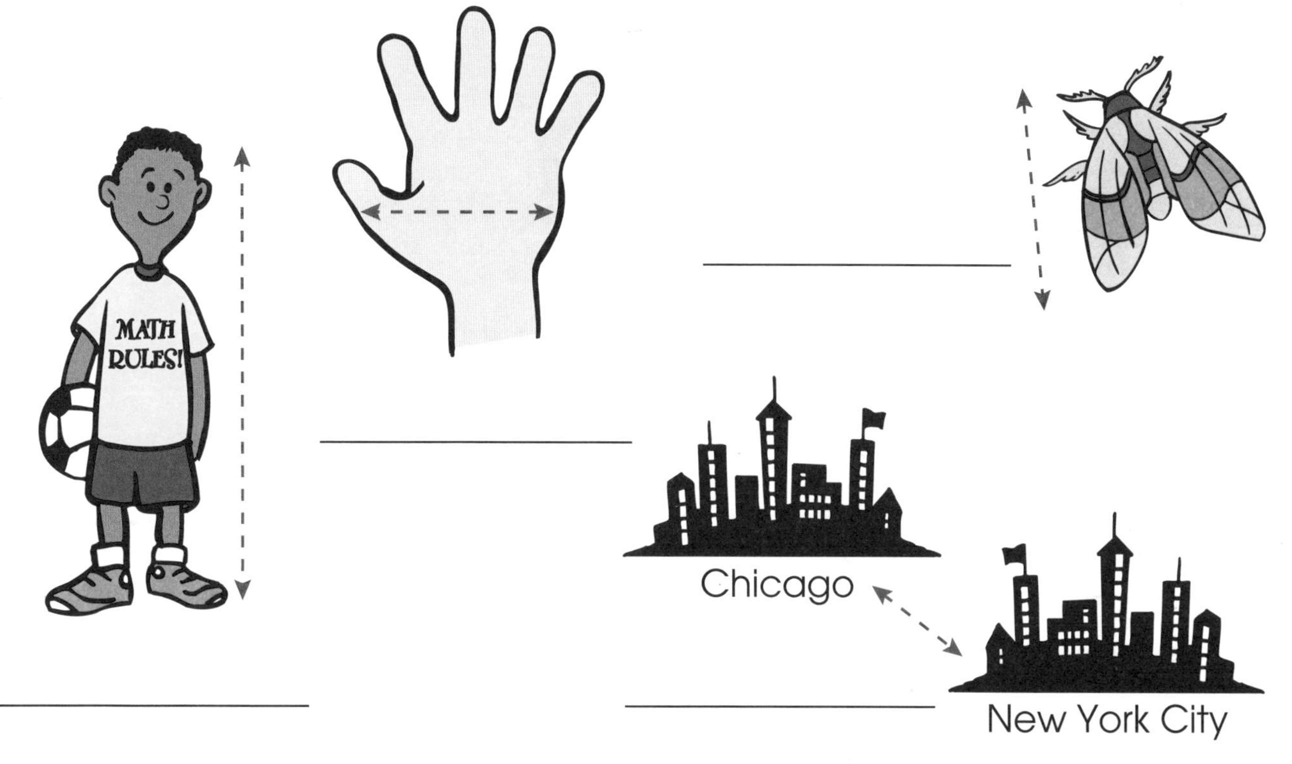

If the letters **ie** or **ei** spell the **long e sound**, color the box **green**. If the letters **ei** spell the **long a sound**, color the box **blue**.

neighbor	either	eight
ceiling	reindeer	believe

Subtract to find out how many of each exercise the players should do. Subtract the **ones**. Then, subtract the **tens**.

Color the pictures whose names have a **short vowel sound blue**. Color the pictures whose names have a **long vowel sound orange**.

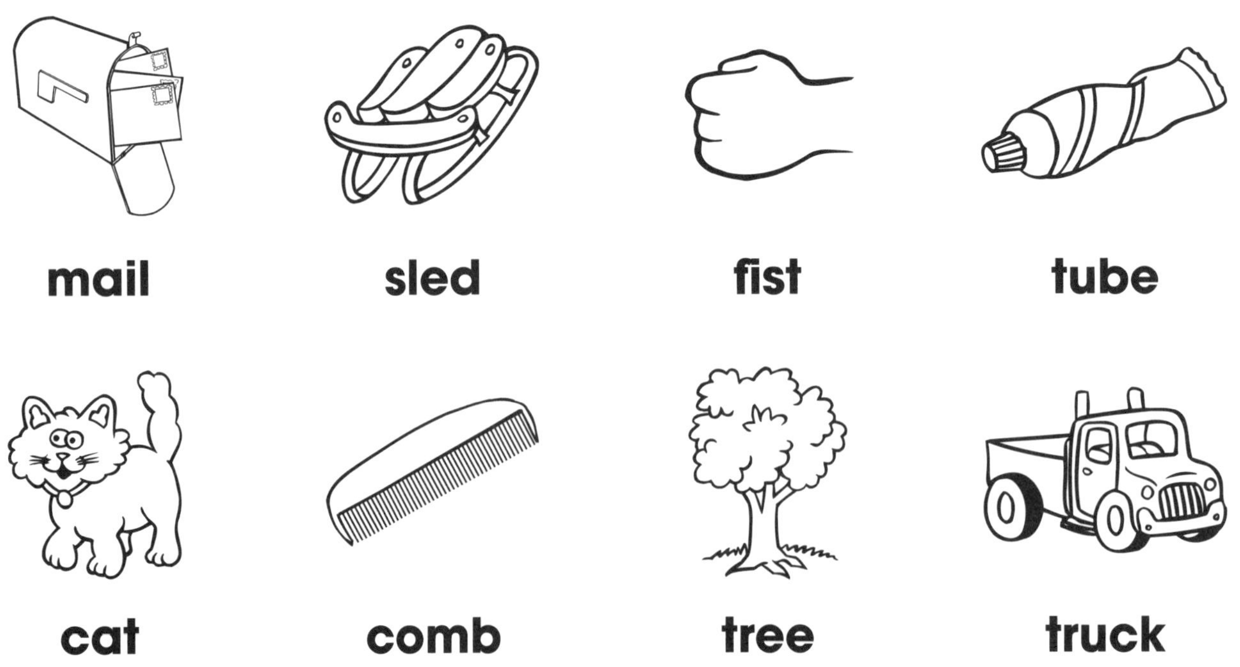

Look at the **bold** noun in each sentence. Circle an **adjective** that describes the noun.

1. Wild **animals** do not make good pets.
2. These animals eat special **diets**.
3. These **animals** want to be free.
4. Even small **animals** can be difficult if they are wild.
5. Raccoons and squirrels are not tame **pets**.
6. Never touch a baby **animal** in the wild.

Draw lines to connect times that are the same.

Add in one minute or less.

10	4	1	5	7
+ 2	+ 6	+ 8	+ 8	+ 6

9	4	3	5	8
+ 6	+ 4	+ 9	+ 4	+ 5

Decide whether each sentence needs a **plural noun** or a **possessive noun**. Circle a noun to complete each sentence.

1. The ________________ played in the cage. gerbil's gerbils
2. The ________________ ran in the field. horse's horses
3. My ________________ coat is torn. sister's sisters
4. Three ________________ flew past our window. birds bird's
5. The ________________ paws are muddy. dogs dog's

Say the name of the first picture in the row. Circle the pictures that have the same vowel sound.

Write **half**, **fourth**, or **third** to tell what part of each shape is colored.

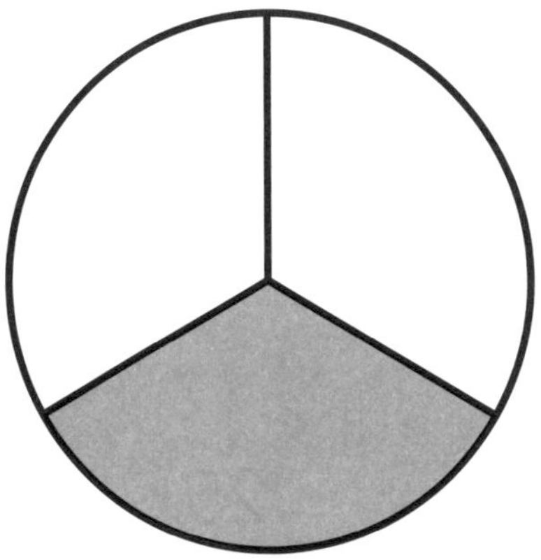

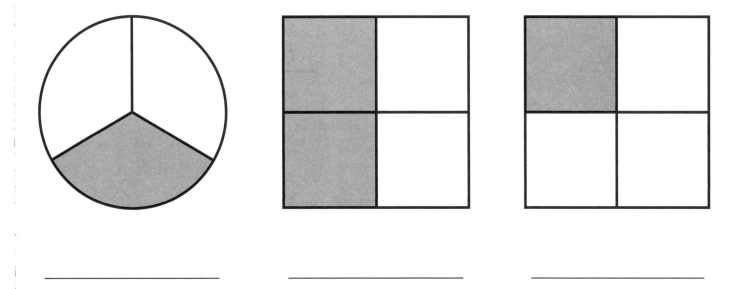

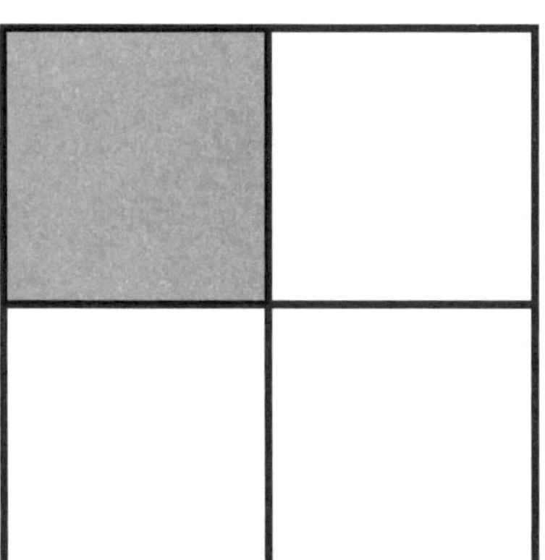

______________ ______________ ______________

Write a **consonant blend** to complete each word.

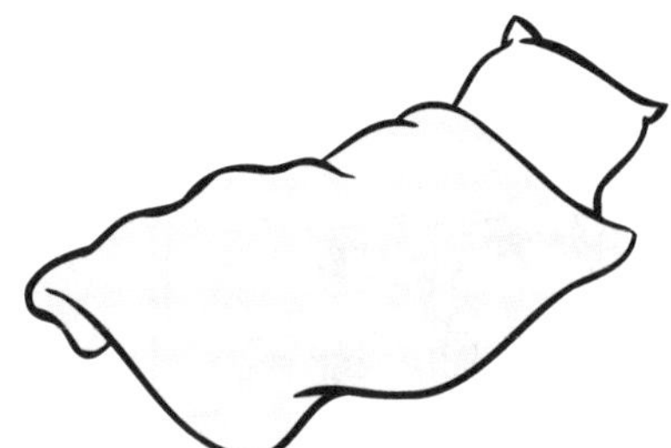

______anket

______ayon

______ock

______uck

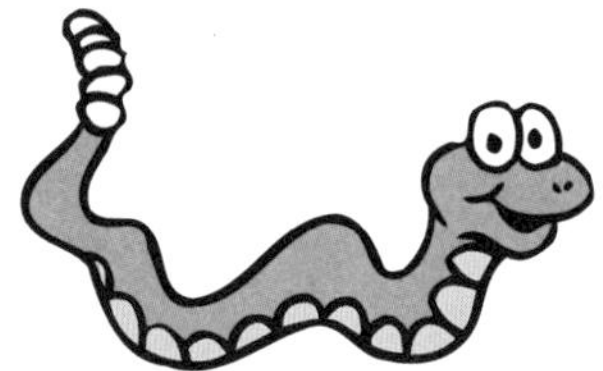

______ake

______ag

Add.

$$\begin{array}{r} 37 \\ +\ 42 \\ \hline \end{array} \qquad \begin{array}{r} 72 \\ +\ 11 \\ \hline \end{array} \qquad \begin{array}{r} 33 \\ +\ 51 \\ \hline \end{array} \qquad \begin{array}{r} 10 \\ +\ 30 \\ \hline \end{array}$$

$$\begin{array}{r} 25 \\ +\ 42 \\ \hline \end{array} \qquad \begin{array}{r} 62 \\ +\ 14 \\ \hline \end{array} \qquad \begin{array}{r} 32 \\ +\ 44 \\ \hline \end{array} \qquad \begin{array}{r} 25 \\ +\ 13 \\ \hline \end{array}$$

Write the **plural** of each noun to complete the sentence. In each word, change **y** to **ie** before adding **s**.

1. I am going to two birthday ____________ this week.
(party)

2. Sandy picked some ____________ for Mom's pie.
(cherry)

3. At the store, we saw lots of ____________.
(bunny)

4. My change at the candy store was three ____________.
(penny)

Use a ruler to measure each fish to the nearest **inch**.

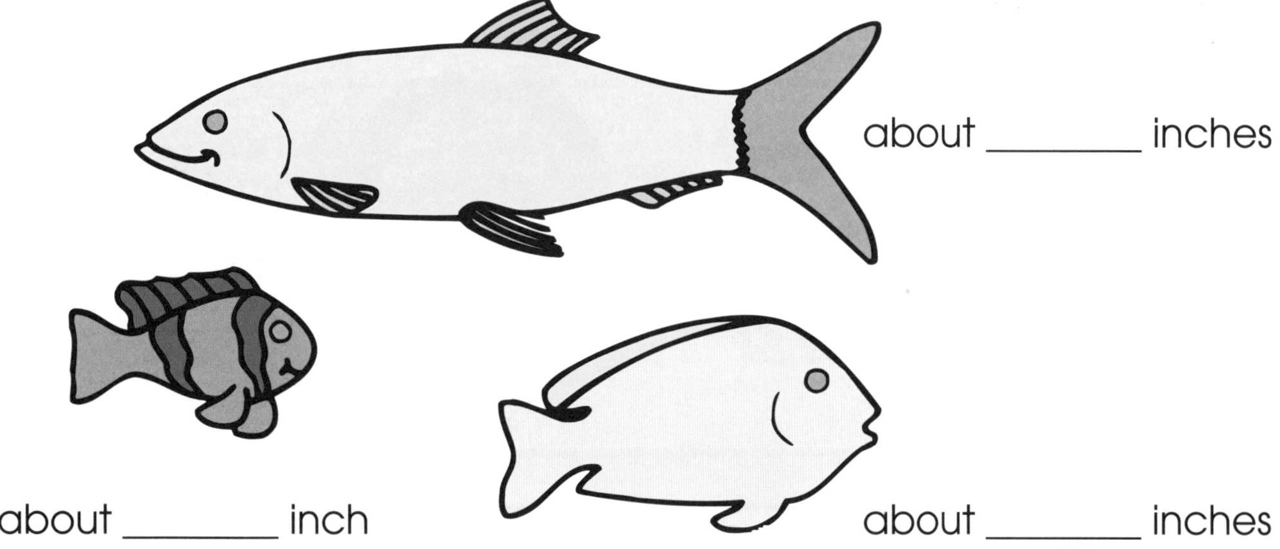

about ______ inches

about ______ inch

about ______ inches

What is the difference between the shortest fish and the longest fish? about ______ inches

Write words with **short vowel sounds** under the doll. Write words with **long vowel sounds** under the bone.

soft	most	wild	lost	blind	blink	odd	toast

Short Vowel Sound **Long Vowel Sound**

Short Vowel Sound	Long Vowel Sound
____________	____________
____________	____________
____________	____________
____________	____________

Write the time shown on each clock.

________ ________ ________ ________

The proofreading mark ≡ means "capitalize." Write ≡ under each letter that should be a capital.

1. Our class will perform a thanksgiving play.

2. I think suntime orange juice tastes the best.

3. We will change planes in toronto, canada.

4. Have you played the new game starquests?

5. The city of alameda, california, has a big independence day parade.

Subtract.

57 − 23	87 − 33	59 − 34	96 − 16
29 − 15	74 − 51	46 − 32	69 − 35

An **adverb** describes a verb. It can tell how, when, or where an action takes place. Circle the adverbs in the story. Then, write each one in the correct column to complete the chart.

The snow began early in the day. Huge snowflakes floated gracefully to the ground. Soon, the ground was covered with a blanket of white. Later, the wind began to blow briskly. Outside, the snow drifted into huge mounds. Suddenly, the snow stopped and the children went outdoors. Then, they played in the snow there. They went sledding nearby. Others happily built snow forts. Joyfully, the boys and girls ran around. They certainly enjoyed the snow.

How	When	Where

Add in one minute or less.

3 + 1	8 + 6	10 + 4	6 + 7	3 + 6
8 + 4	4 + 7	10 + 7	1 + 6	6 + 6

Add or **subtract**. Circle the answer on the number line.

49 – 17 = _____

42 + 17 = _____

When the sum of the **ones** is more than 10, **regroup** the **tens**. Follow the example. Trace the gray numbers.

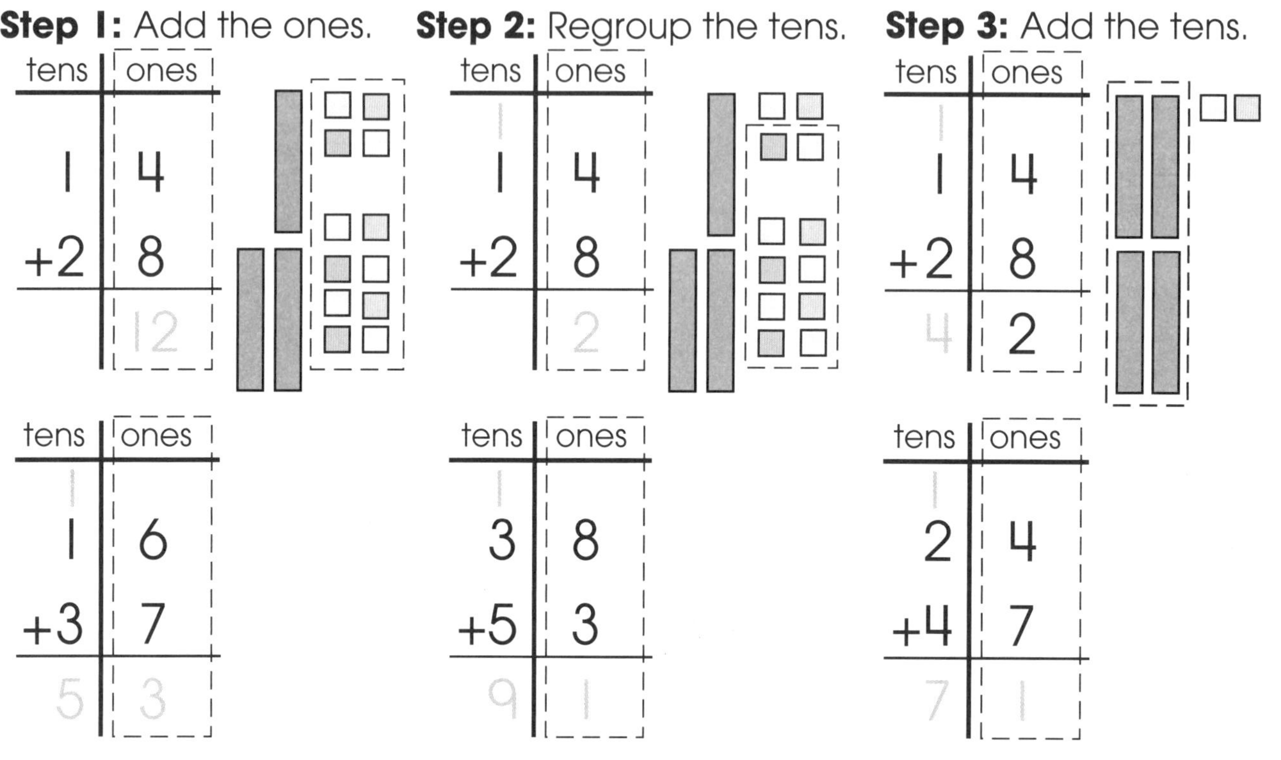

To show ownership, add **'s** to a singular noun (**dog's**). For a plural noun, add just an apostrophe after the **s** (**dogs'**). For a plural noun that does not end in **s**, add **'s** (**children's**). Circle the answers.

1. Our class's pet show was last Friday.
   How many classes had a pet show? **one** **more than one**

2. The students' pets were interesting.
   How many students had pets? **one** **more than one**

3. The snake's meal was a mouse.
   How many snakes were there? **one** **more than one**

4. The mice's cage was next to the snakes.
   How many mice were there? **one** **more than one**

Write the words on the correct road.

baby	**sky**	**my**	**candy**	**sly**	**fuzzy**	**cry**	**lazy**

y sounds like long e | **y sounds like long i**

______________________ ______________________

______________________ ______________________

______________________ ______________________

______________________ ______________________

One **hundred** is 10 **tens**. Count the groups of crayons and **add**. The first one is done for you.

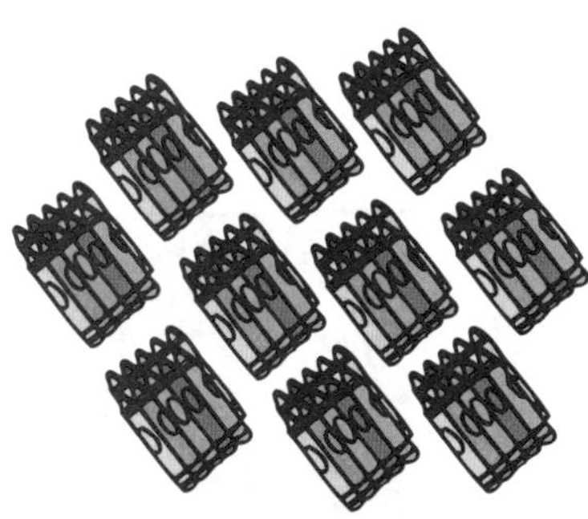 + + = | Hundreds | Tens | Ones |
|---|---|---|
| 1 | 1 | 3 |

1 Hundred + 1 Ten + 3 Ones

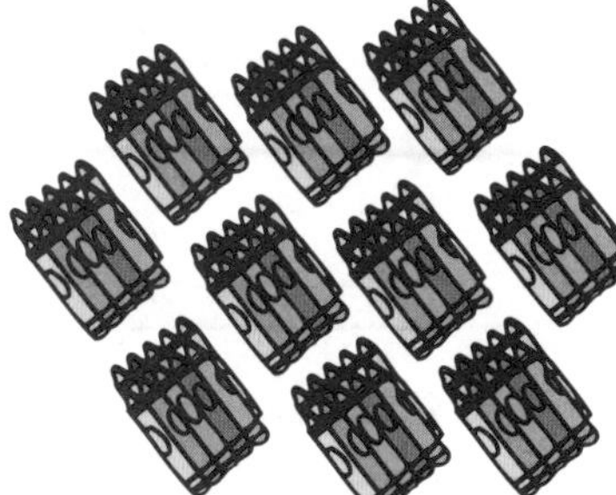 + + = ___ ___ ___

jump	kind	land	bump	camp
pond	hand	stamp	send	ramp

Write the words that end with the same consonants as **sand**.

____________ ____________ ____________

____________ ____________

Write the words that end with the same consonants as **stump**.

____________ ____________ ____________

____________ ____________

Write the time shown on each clock.

____________ ____________ ____________ ____________

When there are not enough **ones** to subtract from, **regroup** the **tens**. Follow the example. Trace the gray numbers.

Step 1: Regroup. **Step 2:** Subtract the ones. **Step 3:** Subtract the tens.

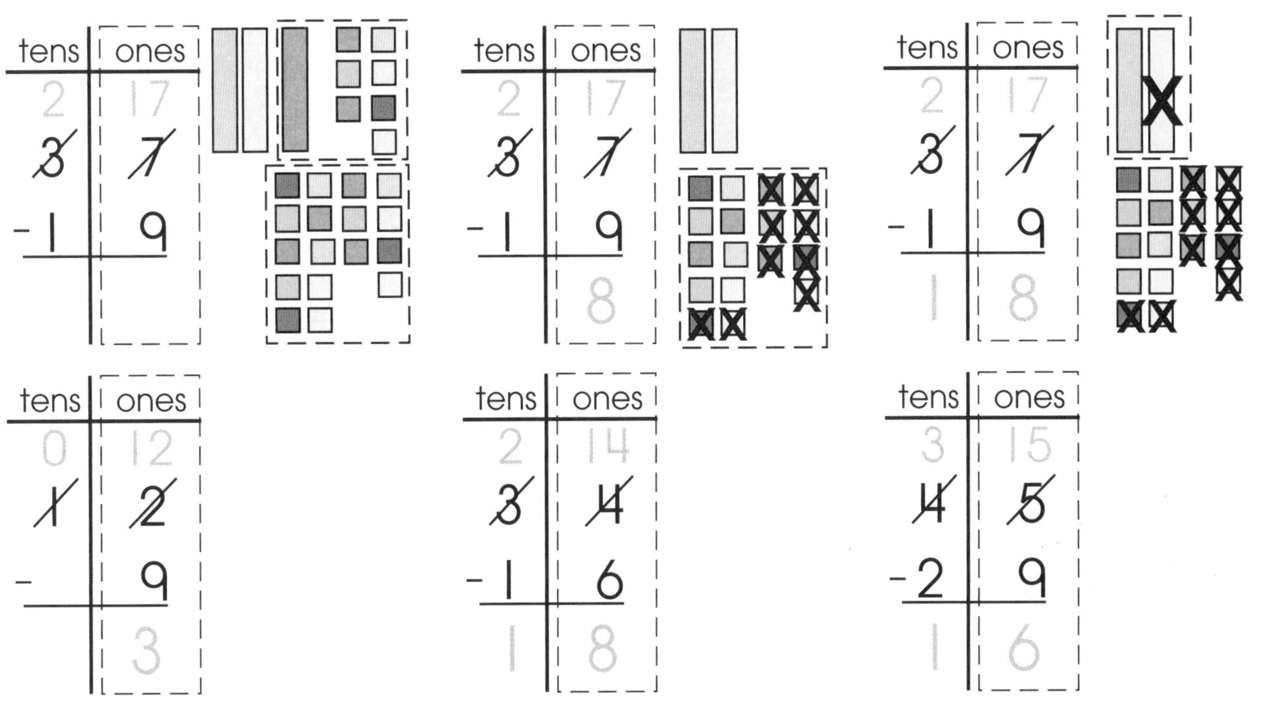

Capitalize each **proper noun** and write it under the correct category.

christmas	tastee cereal	safefirst helmets
denver, colorado	lake michigan	earth day
rhode island	chinese new year	funtime theaters

Holidays	**Product Names**	**Place Names**
______________	______________	______________
______________	______________	______________
______________	______________	______________

Add in one minute or less.

7	4	10	5	2
+ 4	+ 9	+ 8	+ 5	+ 6

5	10	3	3	4
+ 7	+ 3	+ 8	+ 4	+ 5

Say the name of the first picture in the row. Circle the pictures that have the same vowel sound.

couch

howl

A number with three digits has **place values** for **hundreds**, **tens**, and **ones**. Write the missing numbers in the blanks. Follow the example.

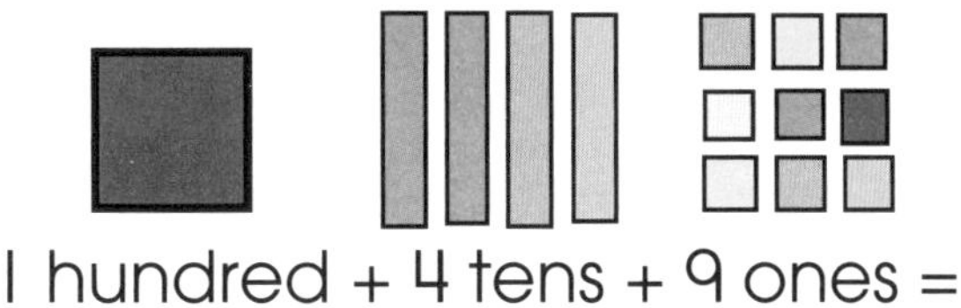

1 hundred + 4 tens + 9 ones =

hundreds	tens	ones	
1	4	9	= 149

	hundreds	tens	ones	total
3 hundreds + 4 tens + 8 ones =	3	4	8	= ____
___ hundreds + ___ ten + ___ ones =	2	1	7	= ____
___ hundreds + ___ tens + ___ ones =	4	7	9	= ____
___ hundreds + 5 tens + 6 ones =	4	____	____	= ____
3 hundreds + 1 ten + 3 ones =	____	____	____	= ____

The **k** sound can be spelled **c**, **k**, **ch**, or **ck**. Read the words. Circle the letters that spell the **k** sound. The first one is done for you.

ache	school	comb	camera
deck	darkness	Christmas	necklace
doctor	stomach	thick	escape

Use a ruler to measure the line segments to the nearest **inch**. Write the number of inches on each candy jar.

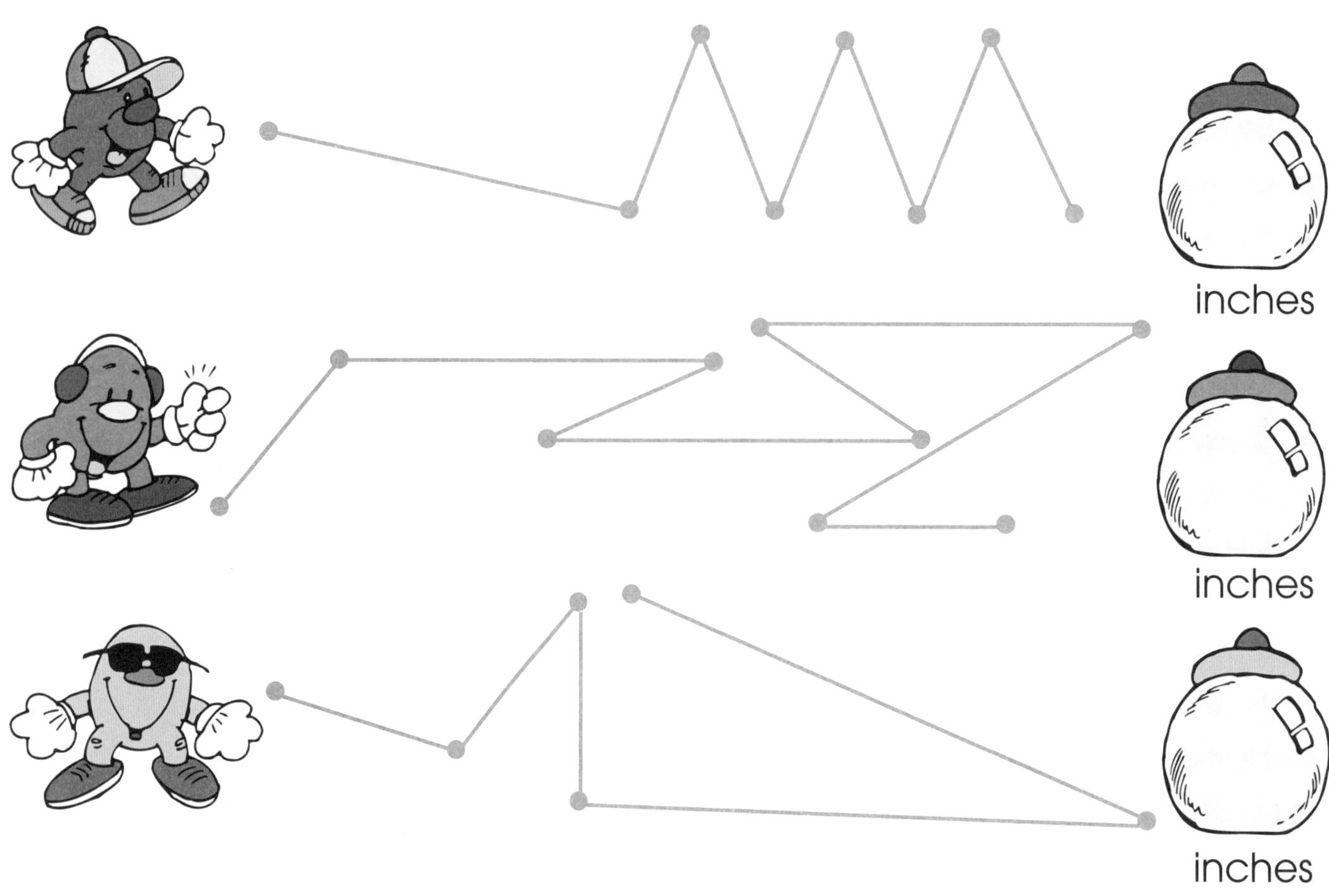

Add. **Regroup** as needed. The first one is done for you.

tens	ones
1	
3	8
+ 4	6
8	4

tens	ones
5	4
+ 2	7

tens	ones
4	9
+ 1	3

tens	ones
2	6
+ 1	7

Write words with **short vowel sounds** under the doll. Write words with **long vowel sounds** under the bone.

run	men	mild	sand	hope	clock	say	seed

Short Vowel Sound	Long Vowel Sound
______________________	______________________
______________________	______________________
______________________	______________________
______________________	______________________

Circle words in the puzzle going up and down that have the hard **g** sound (as in **goat**). Circle words going across and backward that have the soft **g** sound (as in **giraffe**). Write the words in the columns.

g

Hard ↓								Soft ➡
	t	s	g	e	m	n	r	
__________	e	l	t	n	e	g	p	__________
__________	g	n	s	g	e	r	m	__________
__________	i	t	o	a	h	o	f	__________
__________	r	i	h	p	r	a	o	__________
__________	l	e	g	i	a	n	t	__________

Subtract by **regrouping** if needed. The first one is done for you.

	Tens	Ones
	4	14
	~~5~~	~~4~~
−	1	7
	3	7

	Tens	Ones
	3	3
−	1	5

	Tens	Ones
	6	1
−	3	3

	Tens	Ones
	2	7
−	1	6

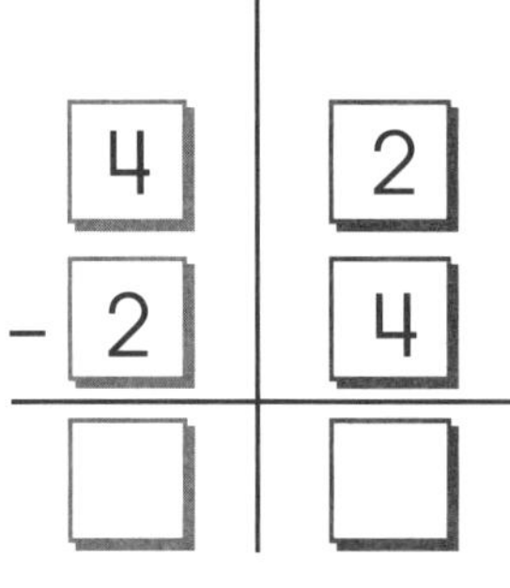

	Tens	Ones
	4	2
−	2	4

	Tens	Ones
	5	2
−	2	6

One **hundred** is 10 **tens**. Count the groups of crayons and **add**.

Hundreds Tens Ones

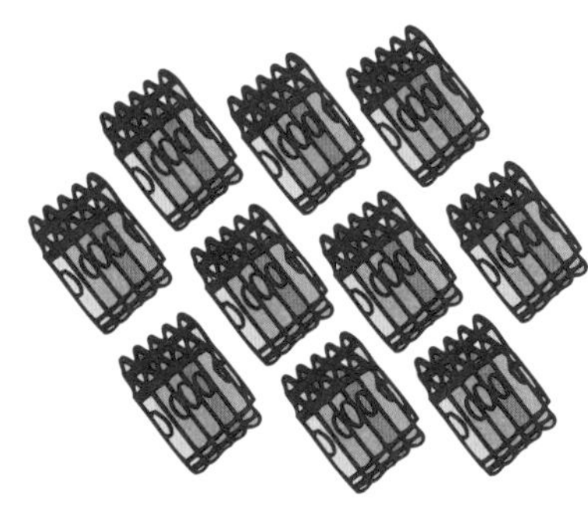 + 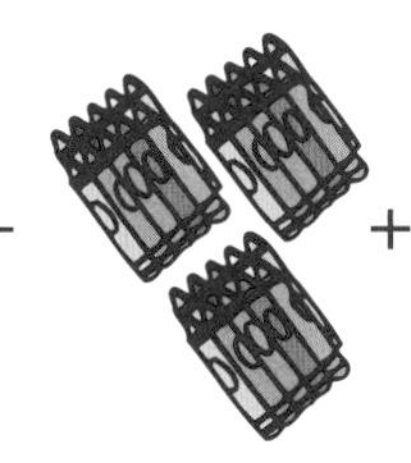 +  = _____ _____ _____

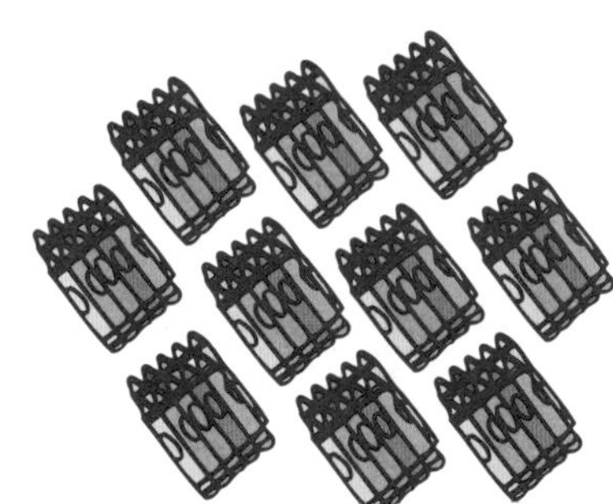 + 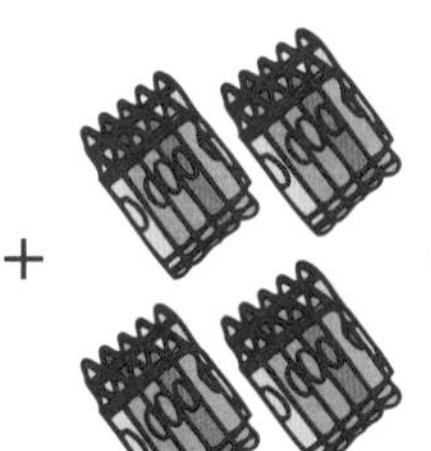 + 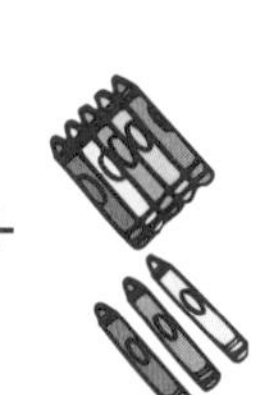 = _____ _____ _____

The **plurals** of some nouns do not follow the rule you know. Their plurals do not end with **s**. Complete each sentence with a special plural. Then, write the letters from the boxes in the blanks to answer the riddle.

tooth	**mouse**	**teeth**	**mice**
child	**woman**	**children**	**women**
foot	**man**	**feet**	**men**

1. I lost my two front ___ ___ ___ [___] ___ !

2. My sister has two pet ___ ___ ___ [___].

3. Her favorite book is Little ___ ___ ___ [___] ___.

4. The circus clown had big ___ ___ ___ [___].

5. The teacher played a game with the

___ [___] ___ ___ ___ ___ ___ ___.

Take good care of this pearly plural!

___ ___ ___ ___ ___.
1 2 3 4 5

Name ______________________________

Color the **bar graph** to show how many of each bakery treat.

Number of Bakery Treats

12						
11						
10						
9						
8						
7						
6						
5						
4						
3						
2						
1						

Add in one minute or less.

6 + 9	8 + 7	9 + 2	5 + 3	10 + 0
7 + 3	9 + 8	2 + 4	4 + 0	7 + 8

Write your own **adverb** to complete each sentence. The first one is done for you.

1. The bees worked busily.
2. The dog barked ______________.
3. The baby smiled ______________.
4. She wrote her name ______________.
5. The horse ran ______________.

A number with three digits has **place values** for **hundreds**, **tens**, and **ones**. Write the missing numbers in the blanks. Follow the example.

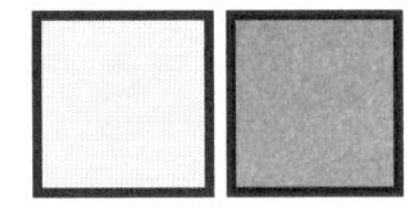 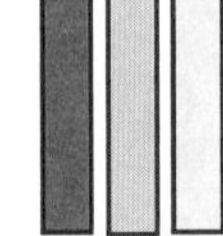 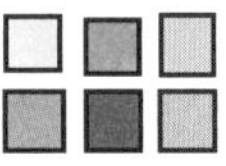

2 hundreds + 3 tens + 6 ones =

hundreds	tens	ones	
2	3	6	= 236

	hundreds	tens	ones	total
___ hundreds + ___ tens + ___ ones =	2	9	4	= ______
3 hundreds + ___ tens + 7 ones =	____	5	____	= ______
6 hundreds + 2 tens + ___ ones =	____	____	8	= ______
___ hundreds + 8 tens + 3 ones =	4	____	____	= ______
9 hundreds + ___ tens + ___ one =	____	0	1	= ______

Add or **subtract**. **Regroup** when needed.

tens	ones
9	3
− 2	5

tens	ones
3	0
+ 2	7

tens	ones
6	5
+ 1	7

tens	ones
7	1
− 3	6

tens	ones
7	6
− 2	8

tens	ones
7	2
+ 1	9

tens	ones
5	6
− 2	8

tens	ones
2	5
− 1	6

Say each word. If **y** sounds like **long i**, color the space **purple**. If **y** sounds like **long e**, color the space **yellow**.

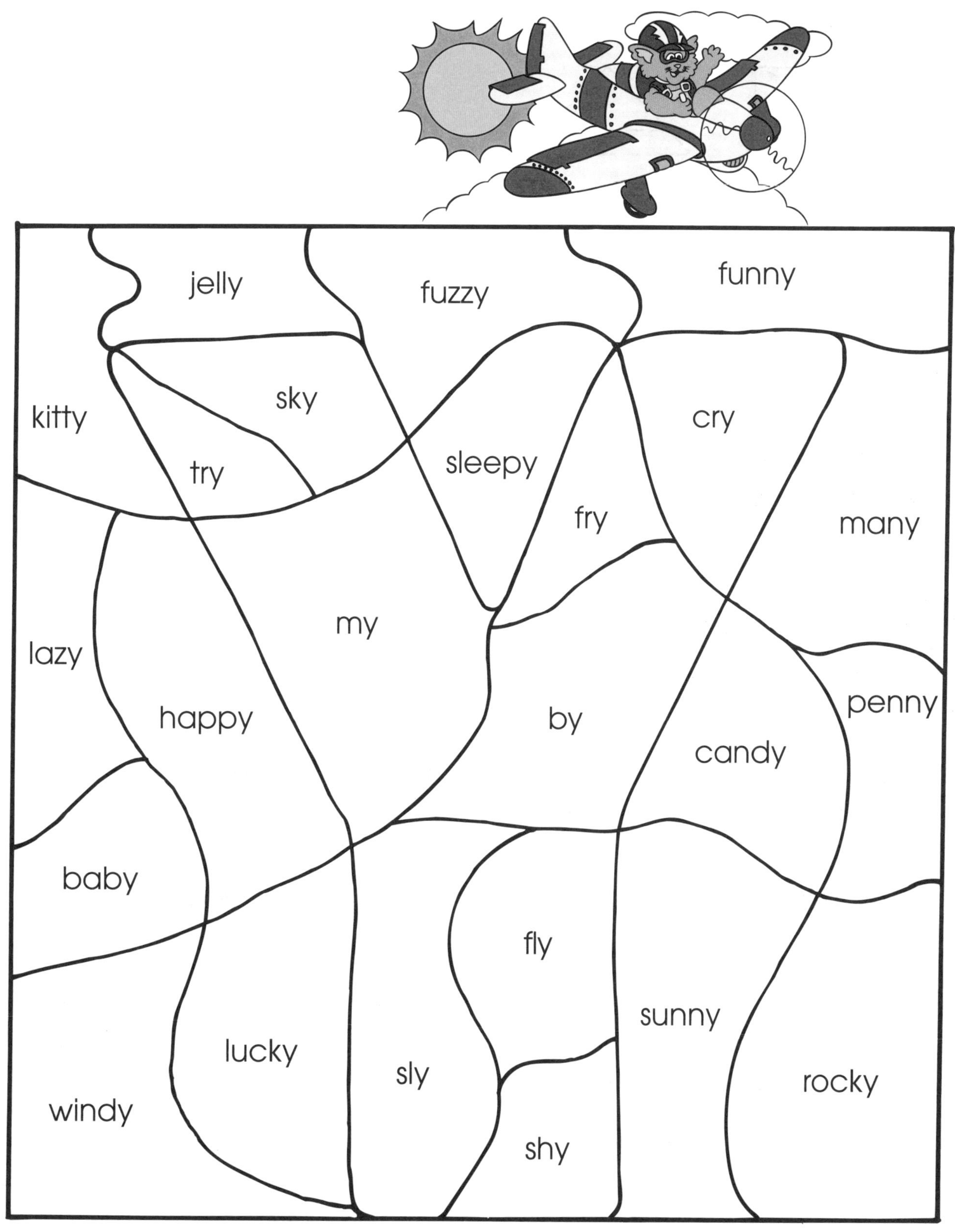

Color the shapes that show equal **halves red**. Color the shapes that show equal **fourths blue**. Color the shapes that show equal **thirds green**.

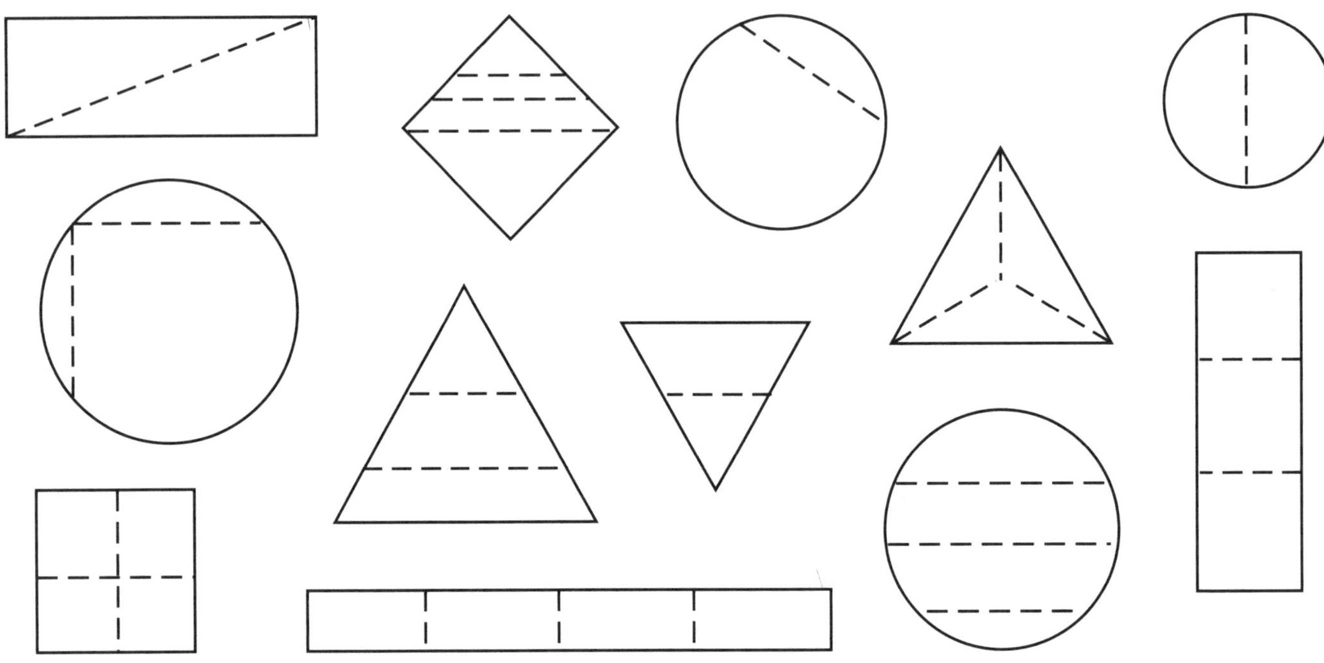

Capitalize each **proper noun** and write it under the correct category.

labor day	**walk-on shoes**	**halloween**
health pure snacks	**rosh hashanah**	**my choice gum**
new york	**dallas, texas**	**mexico**

Holidays	**Product Names**	**Place Names**
______________	______________	______________
______________	______________	______________
______________	______________	______________

Subtract. Regroup as needed.

Color spaces with differences of:

10–19 **red**	20–29 **blue**	30–39 **green**
40–49 **yellow**	50–59 **brown**	60–69 **orange**

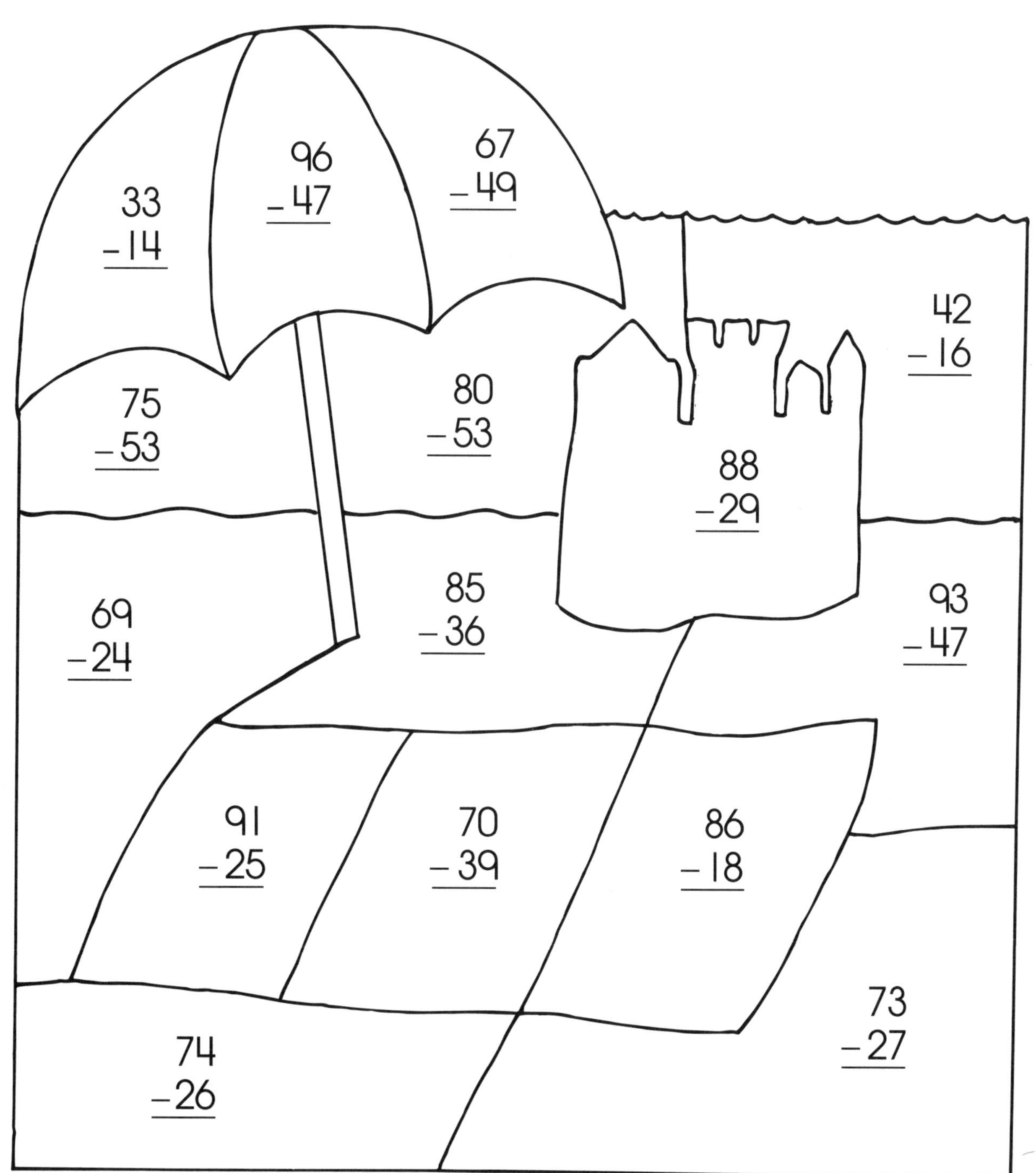

Write the time shown on each clock.

______ ______ ______

______ ______ ______

Add in one minute or less.

2 + 9	7 + 9	2 + 7	1 + 5	3 + 10
6 + 2	5 + 10	7 + 2	8 + 9	3 + 2

kite	sick	key	pick	king
back	call	cake	duck	candy

Write the words beginning with **c** that make the **k** sound.

__________ __________ __________

Write the words beginning with **k** that make the **k** sound.

__________ __________ __________

Write the words ending with **ck** that make the **k** sound.

__________ __________

__________ __________

To show ownership, add **'s** to a singular noun (**dog's**). For a plural noun, add just an apostrophe after the **s** (**dogs'**). For a plural noun that does not end in **s**, add **'s** (**children's**). Circle the answers.

1. The girl's hamster got out of the cage.
   How many girls had hamsters? **one** **more than one**

2. The puppies' barking was disturbing.
   How many puppies were there? **one** **more than one**

3. The chickens' clucking was noisy.
   How many chickens were there? **one** **more than one**

4. The box turtle's shell protected it well.
   How many box turtles were there? **one** **more than one**

Add by **regrouping**. Connect the sums of 83 to make a road for the truck.

			17 + 66	48 + 26	42 + 19
28 + 38	64 + 19	26 + 57	58 + 25	17 + 75	65 + 29
37 + 39	48 + 35	58 + 37	65 + 16	38 + 25	39 + 59
59 + 27	55 + 28	39 + 44			

Write the words in the correct column.

mice	foot	children	teeth	feet	mouse	child	tooth

______________	______________
______________	______________
______________	______________
______________	______________

Use a ruler to measure each fish to the nearest **inch**.

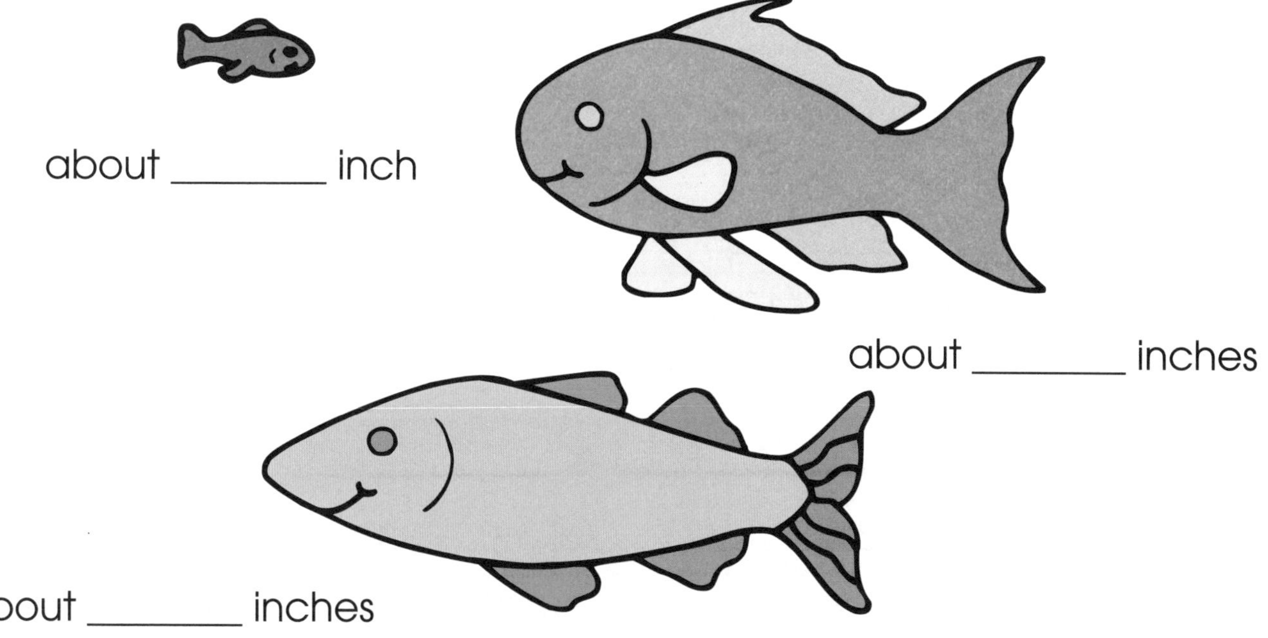

about ________ inch

about ________ inches

about ________ inches

Circle words in the puzzle going up and down that have the hard **c** sound (as in **cat**). Circle words going across and backward that have the soft **c** sound (as in **celery**). Two words going diagonally have both sounds. Write the words in the columns.

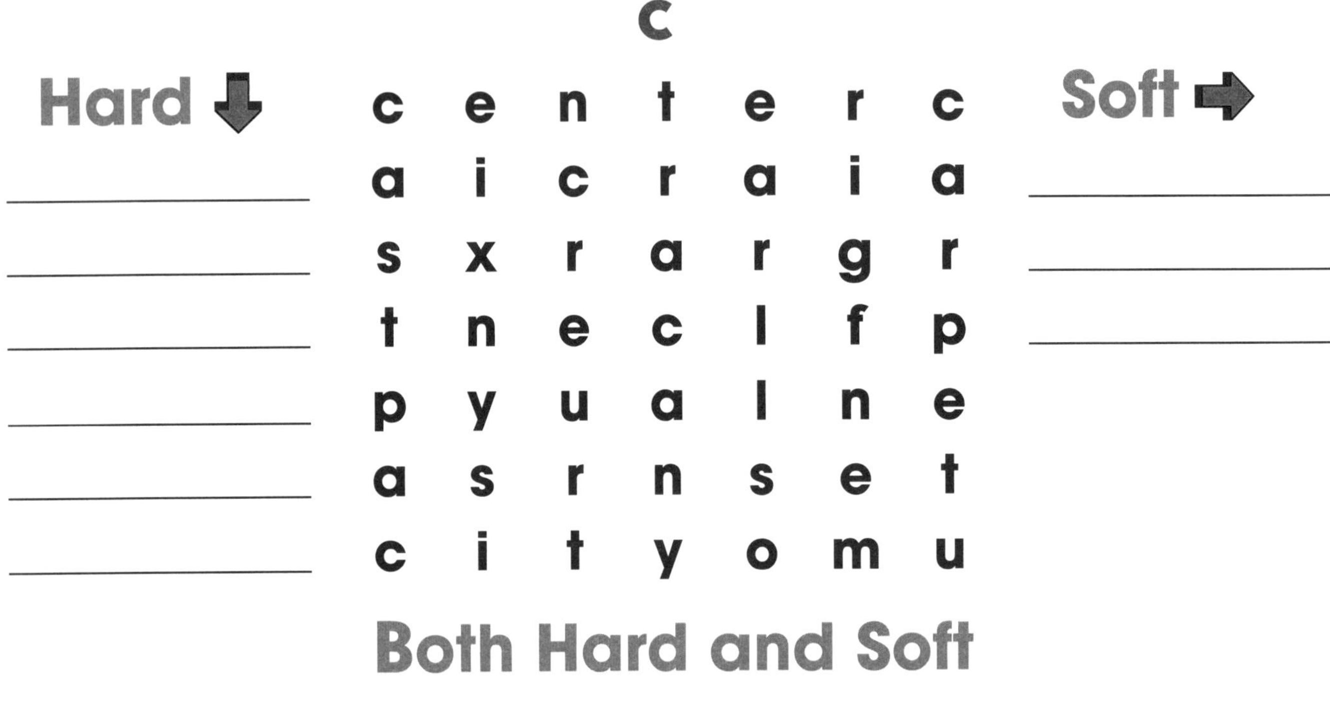

Add or **subtract**. Circle the answer on the number line.

65 − 12 = _____

50 51 52 53 54 55 56 57 58 59 60 61 62 63 64 65 66 67 68 69 70

27 + 13 = _____

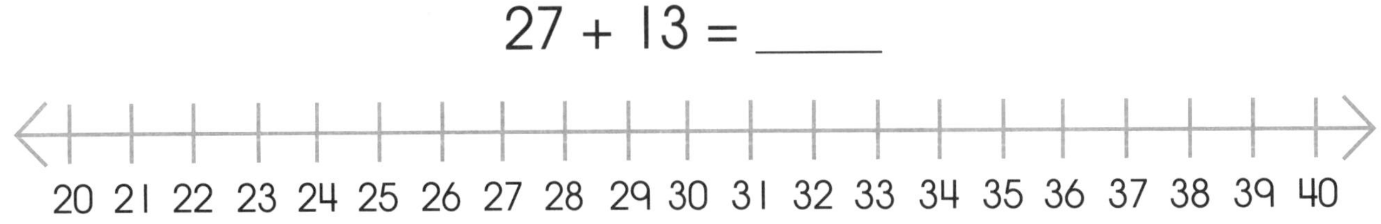

Write a **proper noun** to answer each question.

1. What is the name of your city and state?

   ____

2. What is your favorite restaurant?

   ____

3. What is your favorite brand of breakfast cereal?

   ____

4. What is your favorite holiday?

   ____

5. What city would you like to visit?

   ____

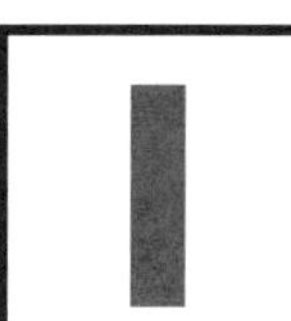

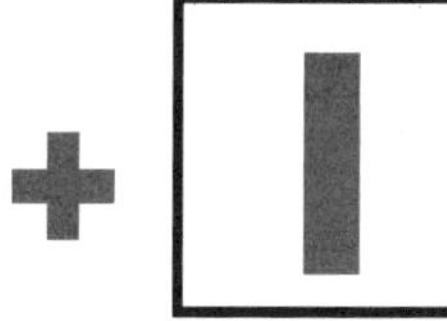

What is 10 more than the number?

48, ______ 8, ______ 89, ______ 121, ______

What is 100 more than the number?

2, ______ 47, ______ 156, ______ 782, ______

wood	book	push	foot	cook
put	pull	took	full	look

Write the words with double **o** that make the sound you hear in the middle of **hook**.

______________ ______________ ______________

______________ ______________ ______________

Write the words with **u** that make the sound you hear in the middle of **foot**.

______________ ______________

______________ ______________

Look at the **bold** verb in each sentence. Circle an **adverb** that describes the verb. Then, check a box to tell if the adverb explains how, when, or where.

	How	When	Where
1. She can **come** over later.	☐	☐	☐
2. The baby **clapped** happily.	☐	☐	☐
3. We will **watch** the movie downstairs.	☐	☐	☐
4. I **finished** the book quickly.	☐	☐	☐
5. The elevator **will stop** soon.	☐	☐	☐

Add in one minute or less.

4 + 2	9 + 10	8 + 1	10 + 10	1 + 9
8 + 10	10 + 5	2 + 1	8 + 3	5 + 0

Use a ruler to measure each object to the nearest **inch**.

about ________ inch

about ________ inches

about ________ inches

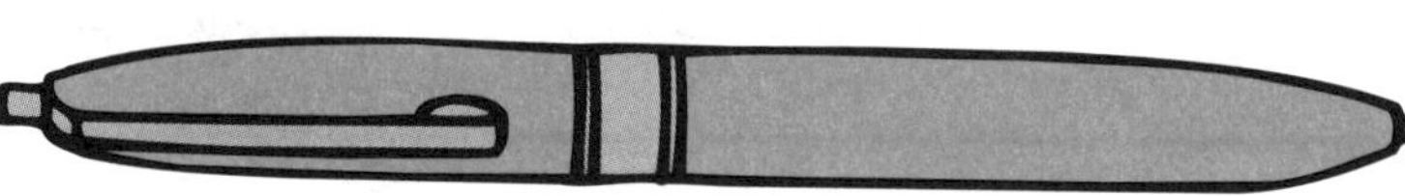

about ________ inches

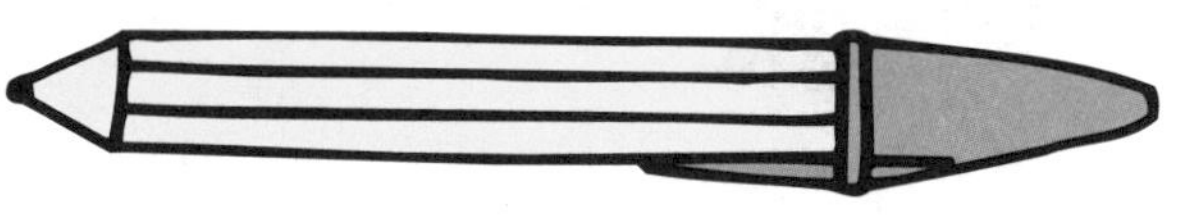

about ________ inches

Write the numbers for **hundreds**, **tens**, and **ones**. Then, **add**. The first one is done for you.

To show one owner, write **'s** after the singular noun. To show two or more owners, write an apostrophe (**'**) after **s** at the end of the plural noun. Circle a word to complete each sentence. Write it in the blank.

1. My five ______________________ uniforms are dirty.
   brother's   brothers'

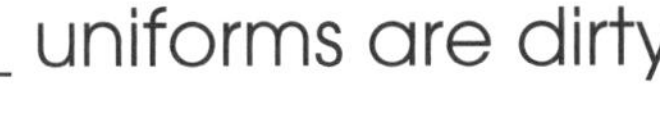

2. The ______________________ doll is pretty.
   child's   childs'

3. These ______________________ collars are different colors.
   dog's   dogs'

4. The ______________________ tail is short.
   cow's   cows'

Write **1** or **2** to tell how many syllables each word has. If a word has two syllables, draw a line between the syllables. The first one is done for you.

tim|ber	2	blanket	________
brush	________	chair	________
bedroom	________	slipper	________
street	________	tree	________

Solve the word problems.

1. Maddy rode the bus 26 times in October and 19 times in November. How many times did she ride in all? ________ times

2. Ollie did 21 math problems on Monday and 14 math problems on Tuesday. How many more problems did he do on Monday? ________ problems

Write the **singular form** of each plural.

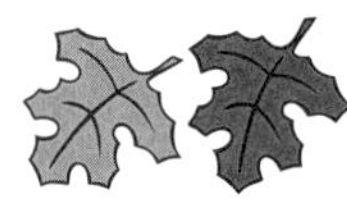 leaves ______________________

 men ______________________

 cities ______________________

 tomatoes ______________________

 fish ______________________

 people ______________________

What is 10 more than the number?

135, ______ 19, ______ 309, ______ 422, ______

What is 100 more than the number?

16, ______ 140, ______ 555, ______ 841, ______

clown	down	how	house	now
our	count	town	about	out

Write the **ou** words that make the vowel sound you hear in **mouse**.

____________________ ____________________ ____________________

____________________ ____________________

Write the **ow** words that make the vowel sound you hear in **cow**.

____________________ ____________________ ____________________

____________________ ____________________

Divide the apple into two equal **halves**. Divide the pizza into four equal **fourths**. Divide the cake into three equal **thirds**. Color the pictures.

Write two **adjectives** to describe each noun. Then, write a sentence using all three words.

marshmallows ______________ ______________

____

____

airplane ______________ ______________

____

____

beach ______________ ______________

____

____

How many **sides** does each shape have? Write the number in the shape.

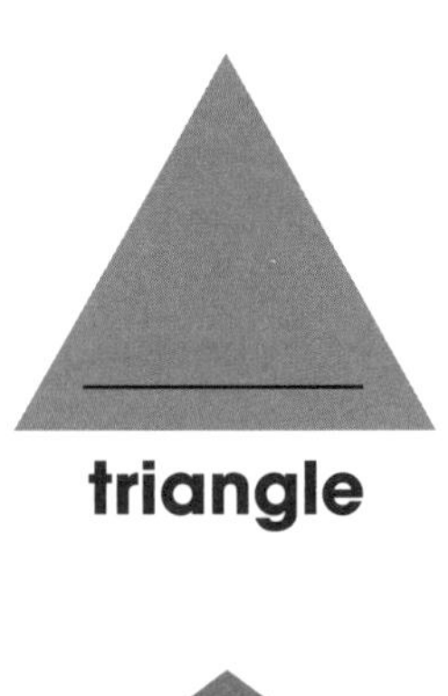

triangle

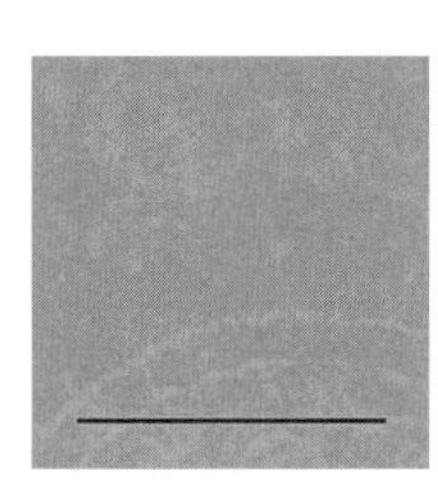

square

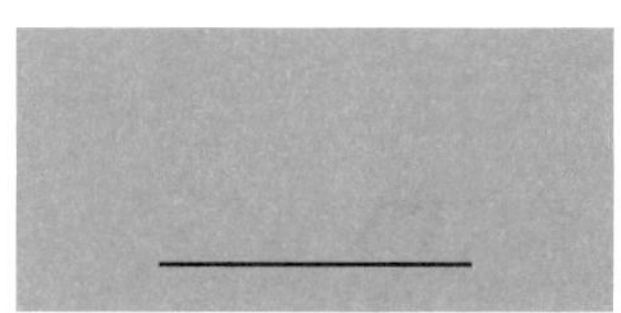

rectangle

pentagon

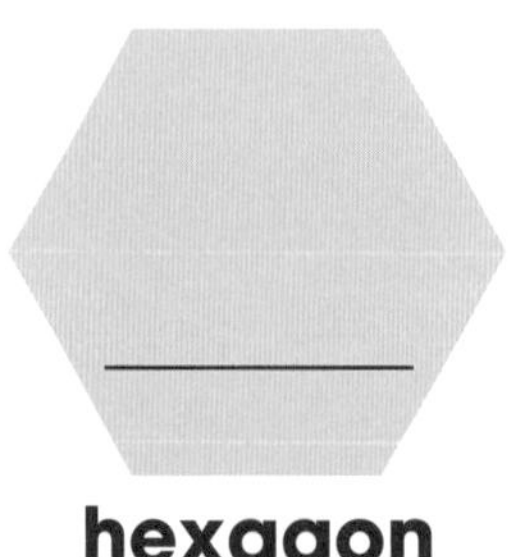

hexagon

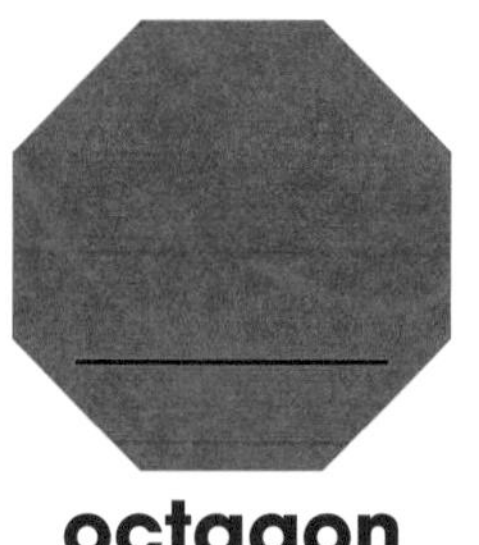

octagon

Add. **Regroup** when needed. Use the key to color the fish according to their sums.

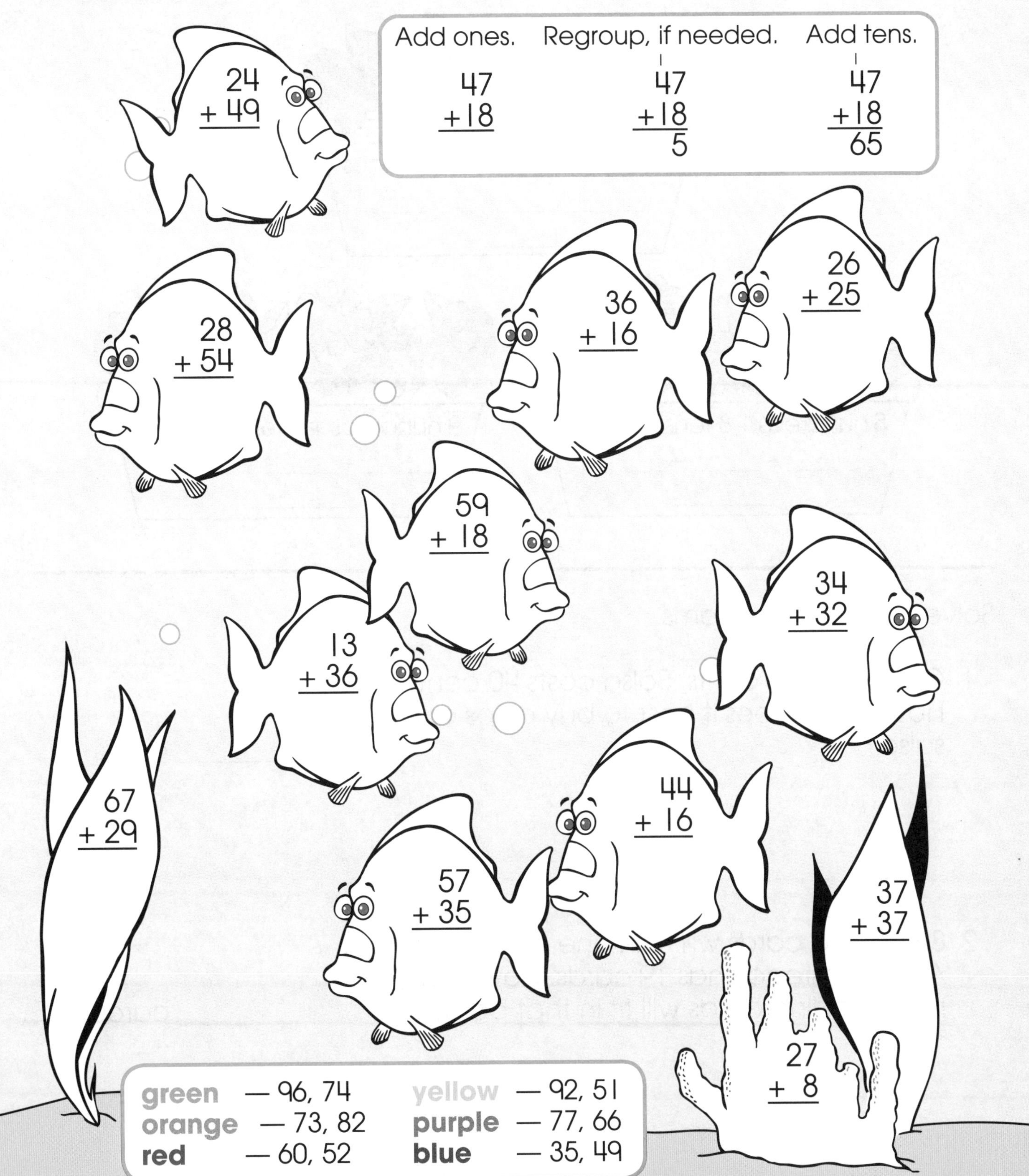

Write the numbers for **hundreds**, **tens**, and **ones**. Then, **add**.

Solve the word problems.

1. Chips cost 60 cents. Salsa costs 40 cents. How much does it cost to buy chips and salsa? _______ cents

2. 36 trading cards will fit in one album page. A page already has 19 cards. How many more trading cards will fit in that page? _______ cards

food	huge	room	soon	zoo
school	use	cute	rude	moon

Write the double **o** words that make the **oo** sound.

______________ ______________ ______________

______________ ______________ ______________

Write the words ending with **e** that make the **oo** sound.

______________ ______________

______________ ______________

A **helping verb** is often used with an action verb. Write a helping verb to complete each sentence.

were	does	might	will	am

1. Mom ______________ buy my new soccer shoes tonight.
2. Yesterday, my old soccer shoes ______________ ripped by the cat.
3. I ______________ going to ask my brother to go to the game.
4. He usually ______________ not like soccer.
5. But, he ______________ go with me because I am his sister.

Count the number of squares inside each rectangle. Write the number.

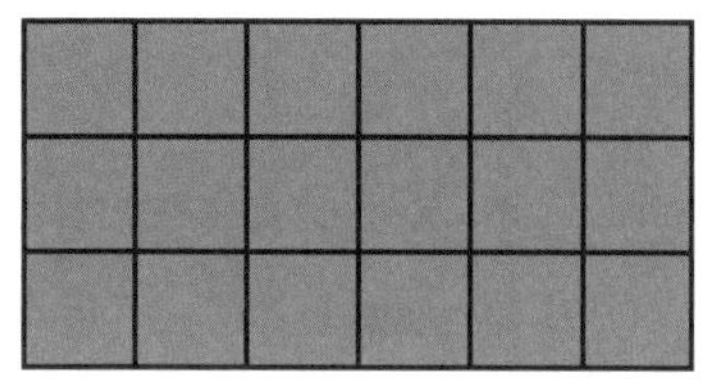
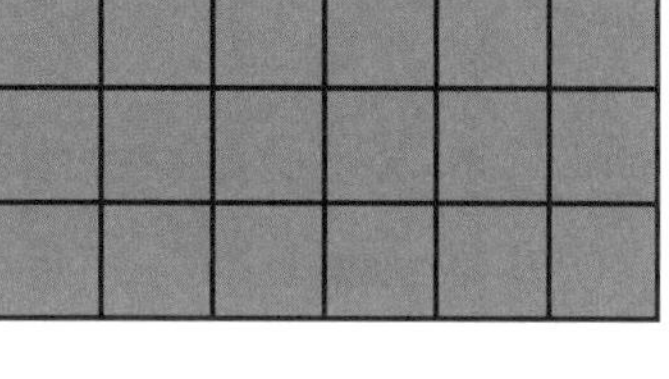

______

______

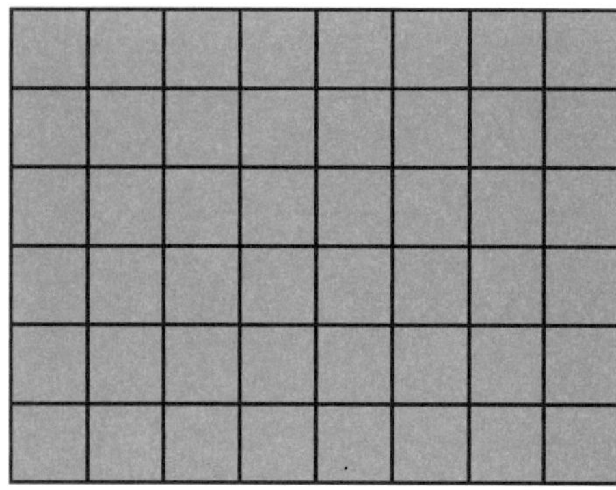

______

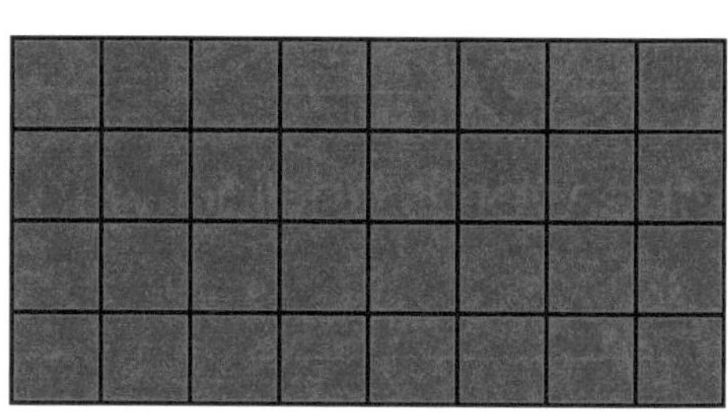

______

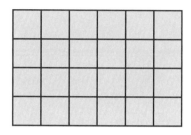

Circle the word that means the same or nearly the same as the **bold** word.

The flowers are **lovely**.
pretty green

The baby was very **tired**.
sleepy hurt

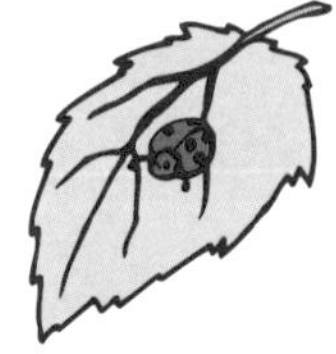

The ladybug is so **tiny**.
small red

We saw a **scary** tiger.
frightening ugly

Does the missing word show one owner or two? Circle a word to complete each sentence.

The __________ noses are big.

clowns   clown's   clowns'

The __________ hat is pretty.

girls   girl's   girls'

Our __________ hat is blue.

coaches   coach's   coaches'

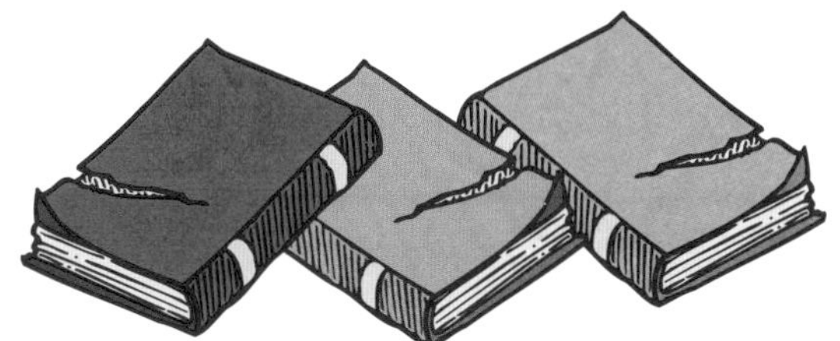

The __________ covers are torn.

books   book's   books'

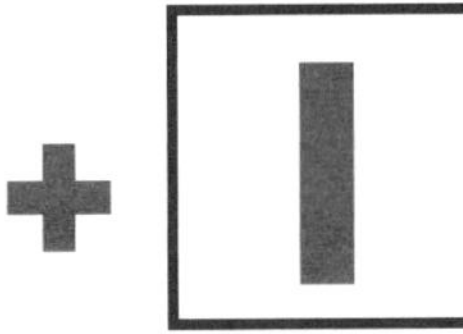

What is 10 more than the number?

88, ______   13, ______   624, ______   101, ______

What is 100 more than the number?

204, ______   431, ______   89, ______   717, ______

Subtract by **regrouping**.

Use the answers and the letter on each lamp to solve the code.

___ ___ ___ ___   ___ ___ ___ ___
58 39 45 33   14 66 72 28

___ ___   ___ ___   ___ ___ ___ ___ ___ ___ ___ !
66 72   47 58   43 39 47 47 37 54 26

Look at the **bold** verb in each sentence. Circle an **adverb** that describes the verb. Then, check a box to tell if the adverb explains how, when, or where.

	How	When	Where
1. My cousin **leaves** for Michigan today.	☐	☐	☐
2. Luke **laughed** loudly at the joke.	☐	☐	☐
3. Sasha **added** carefully to solve the problem.	☐	☐	☐
4. We **played** tag yesterday.	☐	☐	☐
5. My cat usually **sleeps** there.	☐	☐	☐

Color the shapes that have four **sides**.

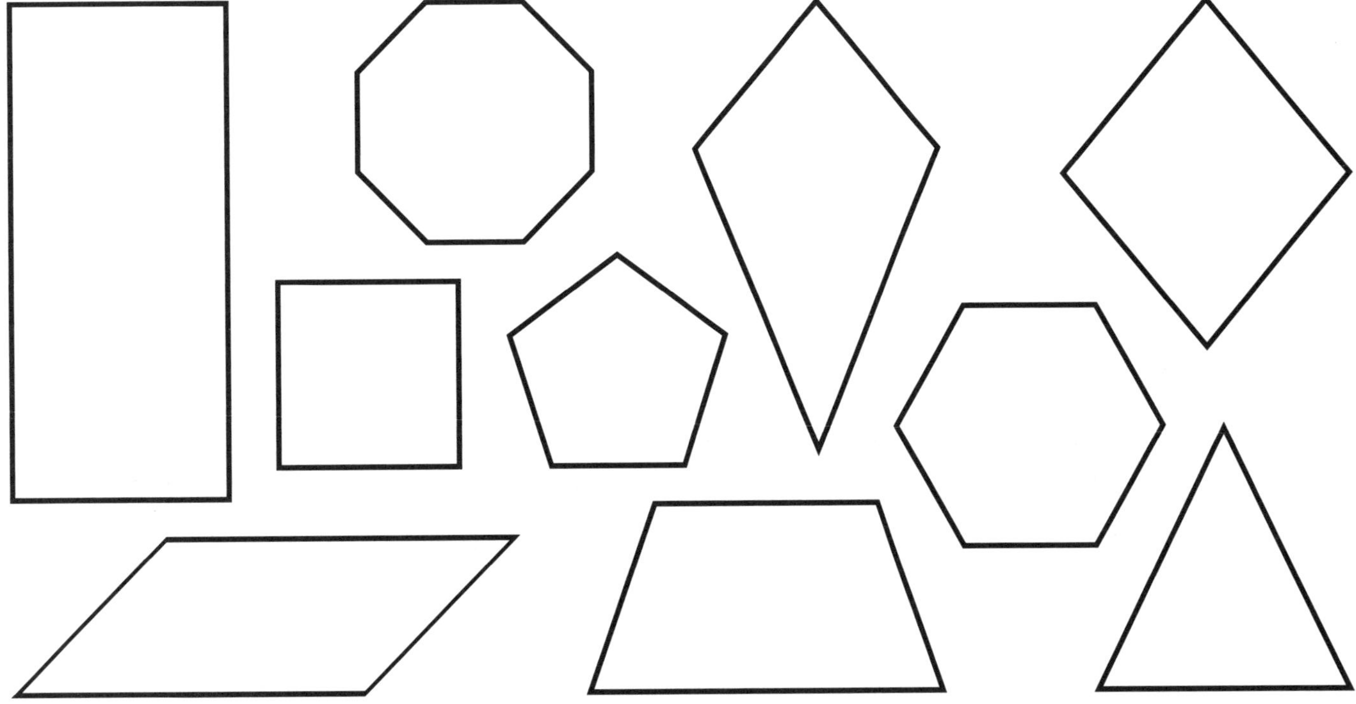

Write the **plural form** for each singular noun.

country ______________________

potato ______________________

deer ______________________

wife ______________________

half ______________________

foot ______________________

Solve the word problems.

1. Colby swings 75 times at the playground. She pumps her legs 52 times. For how many swings does she not pump her legs? ________ swings

2. A family on vacation traveled 49 miles in the morning and 46 miles in the afternoon. How many miles did the family travel in all? ________ miles

stir	herd	her	girl	clerk
skirt	first	bird	verb	jerk

Write the words with **er** that make the sound you hear in the middle of **fern**.

______________ ______________ ______________

______________ ______________

Write the words with **ir** that make the sound you hear in the middle of **shirt**.

______________ ______________ ______________

______________ ______________

Divide the shapes into equal **halves**.

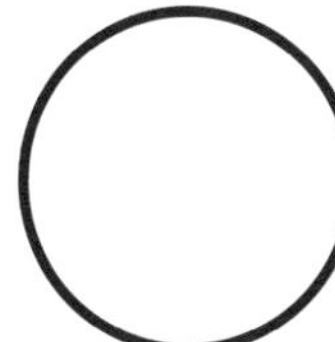  

Divide the shapes into equal **fourths**.

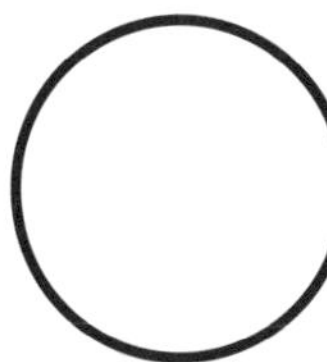  

Divide the shapes into equal **thirds**.

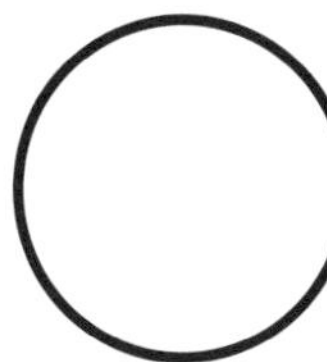  

Draw lines to match words that have similar meanings.

delight •	• discover
speak •	• tidy
lovely •	• start
find •	• talk
nearly •	• beautiful
neat •	• almost
big •	• joy
sad •	• unhappy
begin •	• large

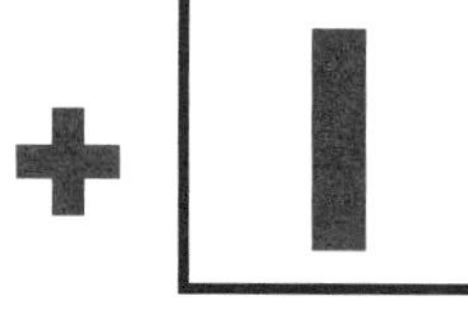

What is 10 more than the number?

5, ______ 856, ______ 311, ______ 62, ______

What is 100 more than the number?

333, ______ 610, ______ 403, ______ 679, ______

Write the time shown on each clock to the nearest five minutes.

__________ __________ __________

__________ __________ __________

The words **am, is, are, was,** and **were** are **linking verbs**. They link the noun in a sentence with words that describe it. Underline a linking verb in each sentence.

1. I am happy.
2. Toy collecting is a nice hobby.
3. Itsy and Bitsy are stuffed mice.
4. I was excited.
5. The elephants were gray.

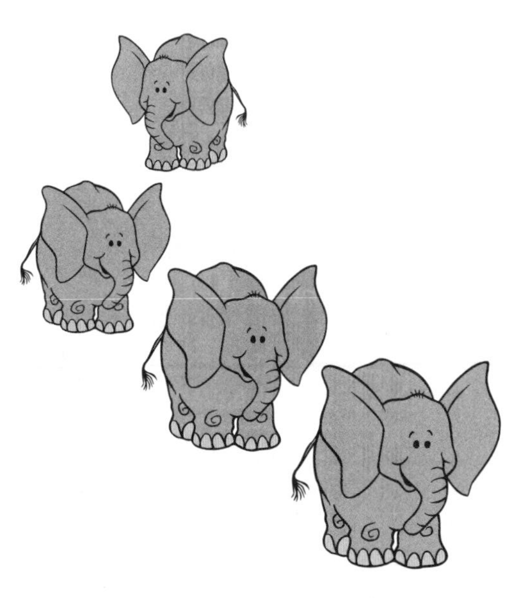

Add **ed** or **d** to the **present-tense verb** shown in bold in the first sentence. Use the new **past-tense verb** to complete the second sentence.

1. You **enter** through the middle door.

   We ________________ that way last week.

2. Please **add** this for me.

   I already ________________ it twice.

3. Will you **share** your cookie with me?

   I ________________ my apple with you yesterday.

4. It's your turn to **fold** the clothes.

   I ______________ them yesterday.

5. May I **taste** another one?

   I already ________________ one.

Add or **subtract**. Circle the answer on the number line.

100 − 15 = _____

80 81 82 83 84 85 86 87 88 89 90 91 92 93 94 95 96 97 98 99 100

31 + 9 = _____

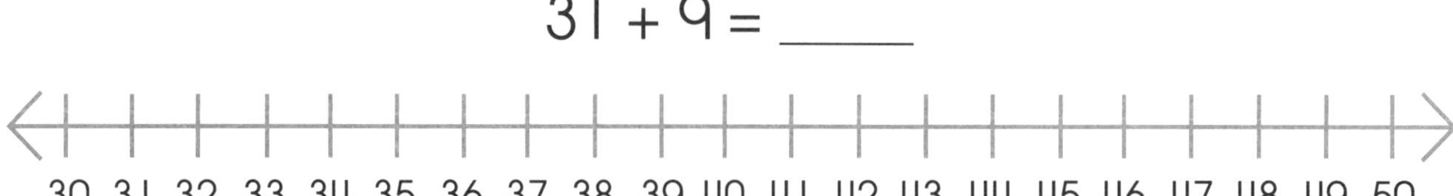

30 31 32 33 34 35 36 37 38 39 40 41 42 43 44 45 46 47 48 49 50

Add. **Regroup** when needed.

58	63	31	67	72
+ 26	+ 18	+ 42	+ 33	+ 19

54	37	26	51	37
+ 27	+ 72	+ 67	+ 16	+ 55

In each sentence, find two words that have **opposite** meanings. Write them in the boxes.

I thought I lost my dog, but someone found him.

The teacher will ask questions for the students to answer.

Airplanes arrive and depart at the airport.

story	park	corn	part	north
horse	far	farm	hard	start

Write the words with the same vowel sound you hear in **horn**. Then, circle the letters that make that sound.

____________________ ____________________

____________________ ____________________

Write the words with the same vowel sound you hear in **jar**. Then, circle the letters that make that sound.

____________________ ____________________ ____________________

____________________ ____________________ ____________________

Solve the word problems.

1. A book about pandas has 92 pages. A book about alligators has 46 pages. How much longer is the book about pandas? ________ pages

2. At the school carnival, a game ticket costs 35 cents. A face-painting ticket costs 55 cents. How much are the two tickets together? ________ cents

Change the **present-tense verb** in the first sentence to a **past-tense verb** to complete the second sentence. Double the consonant at the end of each verb before adding **ed**. The first one is done for you.

1. We skip to school. Yesterday, we skipped the whole way.
2. It's not nice to grab things. When you ______________ my cookie, I felt angry.
3. Did Dad hug you today? Dad ______________ me this morning.
4. We plan our vacations every year. Last year, we ______________ to go to the beach.
5. Is it my turn to stir the pot? You ______________ it last time.

Write the name of each shape.

cube	triangle	rectangle	pentagon	hexagon

______________ ______________ ______________

______________ ______________

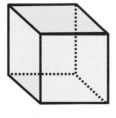

Subtract. **Regroup** when needed.

56	83	43	75	91
– 27	– 47	– 39	– 53	– 18

73	35	67	26	68
– 66	– 14	– 58	– 7	– 45

Rewrite the **bold** noun from each sentence as a possessive noun. To show one owner, end it with **'s**. To show two or more owners, end with **s'**.

1. Two **bears** costumes were purple. ____________________
2. One **boys** laughing was very loud. ____________________
3. The **mans** popcorn was tasty. ____________________
4. Three **girls** balloons burst in the air. ____________________

Count the number of squares inside each rectangle. Write the number.

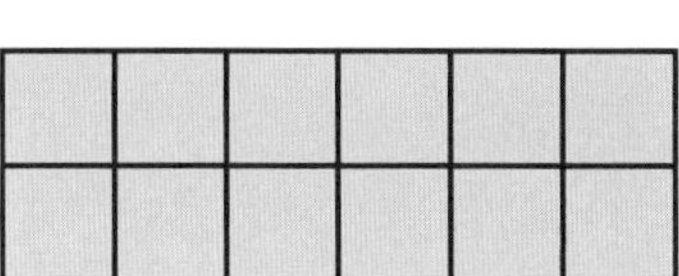

______

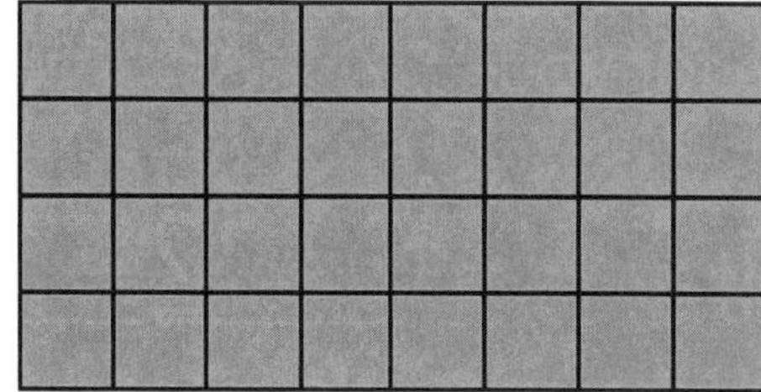

______

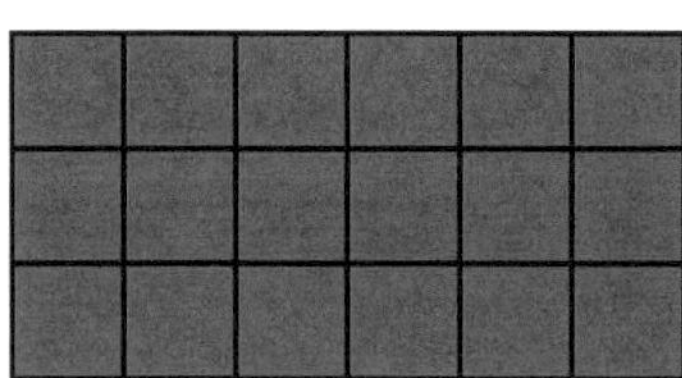

______

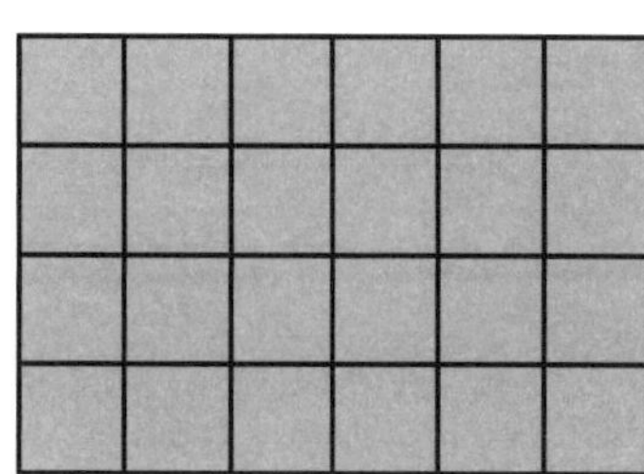

______

Read the passage. Write to complete the list of directions about how to treat a ladybug.

Ladybugs are shy. If you see a ladybug, sit very still. Hold out your arm. Maybe the ladybug will fly to you. If it does, talk softly. Do not touch it. It will fly away when it is ready.

1. Sit very still.
2. ______________________________
3. Talk softly.
4. ______________________________

Write **1**, **2**, or **3** to tell how many syllables each word has. If a word has more than one syllable, draw a line between the syllables. The first one is done for you.

rab|bit	2	elephant	______
understand	______	yellow	______
wind	______	basketball	______
open	______	popcorn	______

Like a corner, an **angle** is where two lines meet. Use the key to color the shapes according to the number of angles they have.

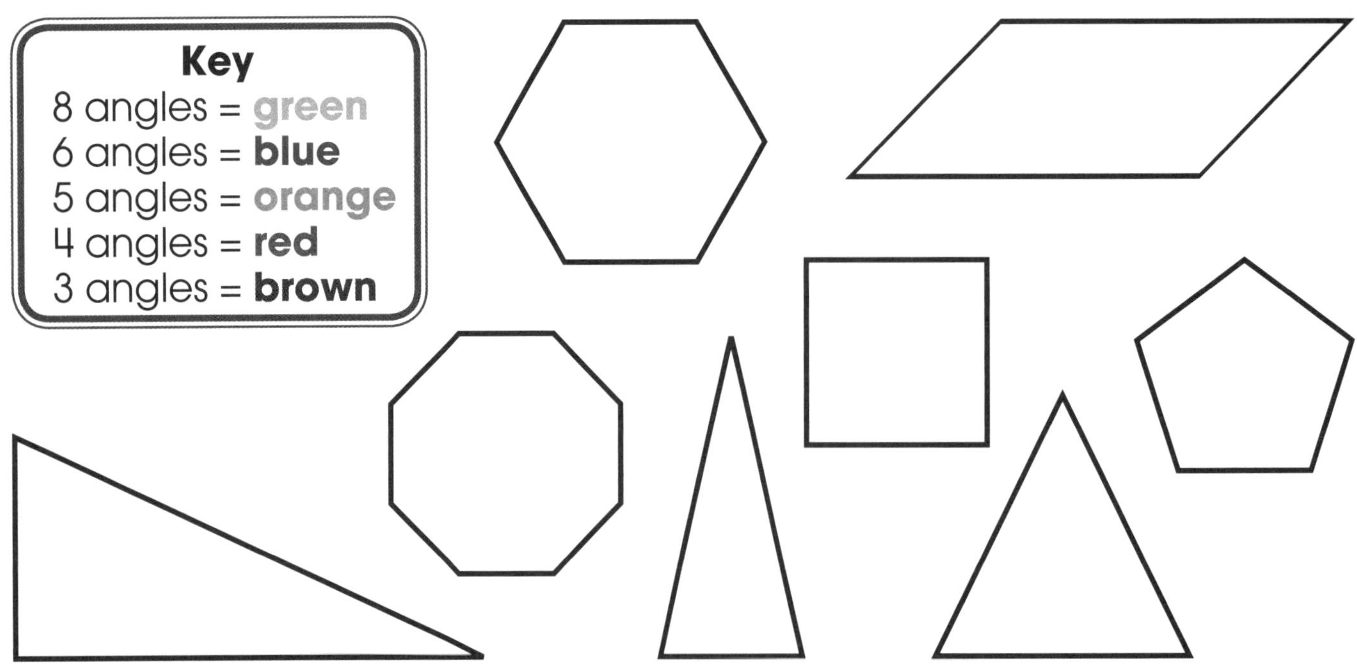

Write an **adverb** to complete each sentence.

next	smoothly	here	loudly

1. The band is scheduled to play ____________________.

2. They will set up their instruments over ____________________.

3. Carlos plays the saxophone ____________________.

4. Lila beats the drums ____________________.

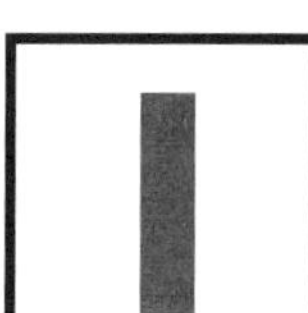

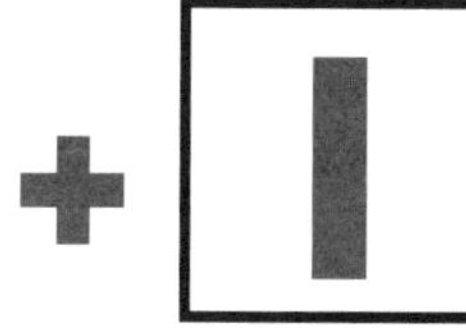

What is 10 more than the number?

13, ______ 512, ______ 100, ______ 990, ______

What is 100 more than the number?

44, ______ 86, ______ 299, ______ 426, ______

Write each number. The first one is done for you.

Hundreds	Tens	Ones
■	|||	●●

_1_ hundred
_3_ tens
_2_ ones = _132_

Hundreds	Tens	Ones
■	||||	●●●●●●●

___ hundred
___ tens
___ ones = ______

Hundreds	Tens	Ones
■■■	|||	●●●●●●●●●

___ hundreds
___ tens
___ ones = ______

Hundreds	Tens	Ones
■■■■■	|	●

___ hundreds
___ ten
___ one = ______

Form the **past tense** of most verbs by adding **ed**. Sometimes, you only need to add **d**. Other times, you need to double the final consonant before adding **ed**. Write the past tense of each verb.

stir ______________ smile ______________

search ______________ load ______________

clap ______________ decide ______________

dance ______________ plan ______________

Homophones sound alike, but they have different spellings and meanings. Write the letter of the best definition for each homophone.

_______ 1. hare — A. a mass of unbaked bread

_______ 2. hair — B. an animal related to the rabbit

_______ 3. peer — C. to look closely; to gaze

_______ 4. pier — D. a female deer, hare, or rabbit

_______ 5. doe — E. a platform built out over water

_______ 6. dough — F. growth that covers the scalp of a person or the body of a mammal

---

Solve the word problems.

1. A stairway at the library has 37 steps. A stairway at the museum has 28 steps. How many more steps are in the stairway at the library? _______ steps

2. Max did 38 jumping jacks. He did 23 squats. How many exercises did he do in all? _______ exercises

Add or **subtract**.

61 − 53	54 + 28	80 − 9	59 + 22	25 + 29
88 − 49	36 + 45	84 − 36	74 + 17	90 − 59

Compound words are two words put together to make one new word. Complete each sentence with a compound word made up of the two **bold** words.

1. A **box** with **sand** is a ______________________.
2. The **way** through a **hall** is a ______________________.

3. A **box** for **lunch** is a ______________________.
4. A **coat** for the **rain** is a ______________________.

5. A **room** with a **bed** is a ______________________.

To be is a special verb that does not follow the patterns you know. We say I **am**, he **is**, we **are**, and you **are**. Use **is**, **are**, or **am** to complete the sentences.

1. My friends ______________ helping me build a tree house.

2. It ______________ in my backyard.

3. We ______________ using hammers, wood, and nails.

4. It ______________ a very hard job.

5. I ______________ lucky to have good friends.

In a group with an **even** number of objects, the items can be evenly matched in groups of two. In a group with an **odd** number of objects, the items cannot be evenly matched. Circle the group with an odd number of items.

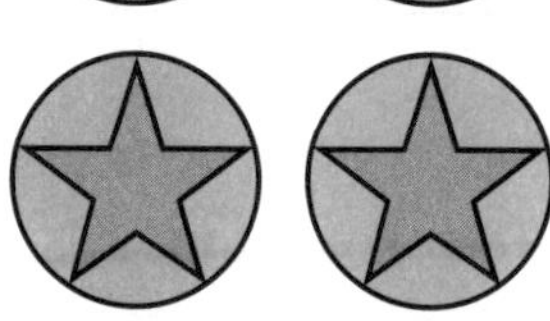

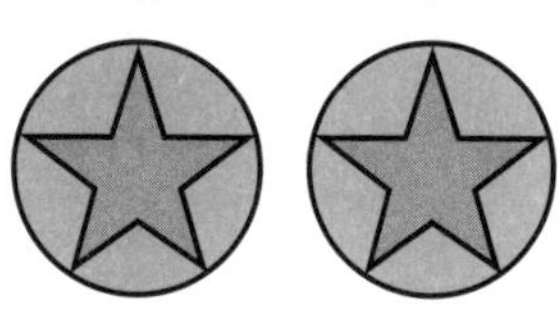

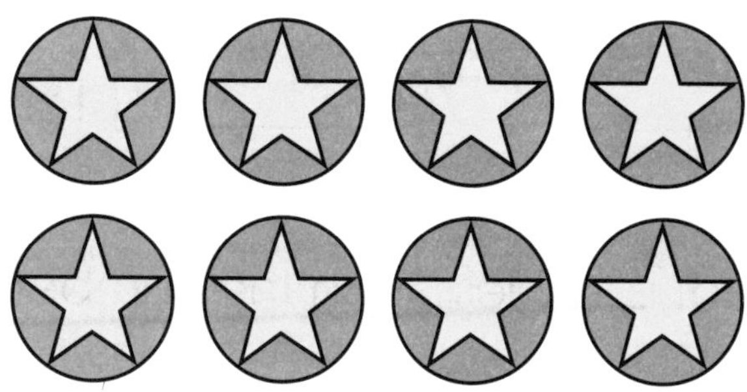

Write the **homophones** in the blanks to complete the sentences.

eye **I** He hurt his left ______________ playing ball.

______________ like to learn new things.

see **sea** Can you ______________ the winning runner from here?

He goes diving for pearls under the ______________.

eight **ate** The baby ______________ the banana.

Jane was ______________ years old last year.

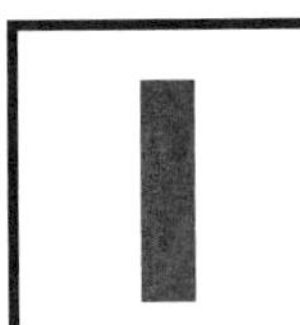

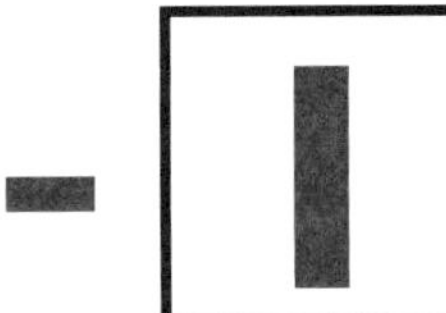

What is 10 less than the number?

22, ______ 79, ______ 119, ______ 385, ______

What is 100 less than the number?

111, ______ 209, ______ 700, ______ 599, ______

Use a ruler to measure the logs to the nearest **centimeter**.

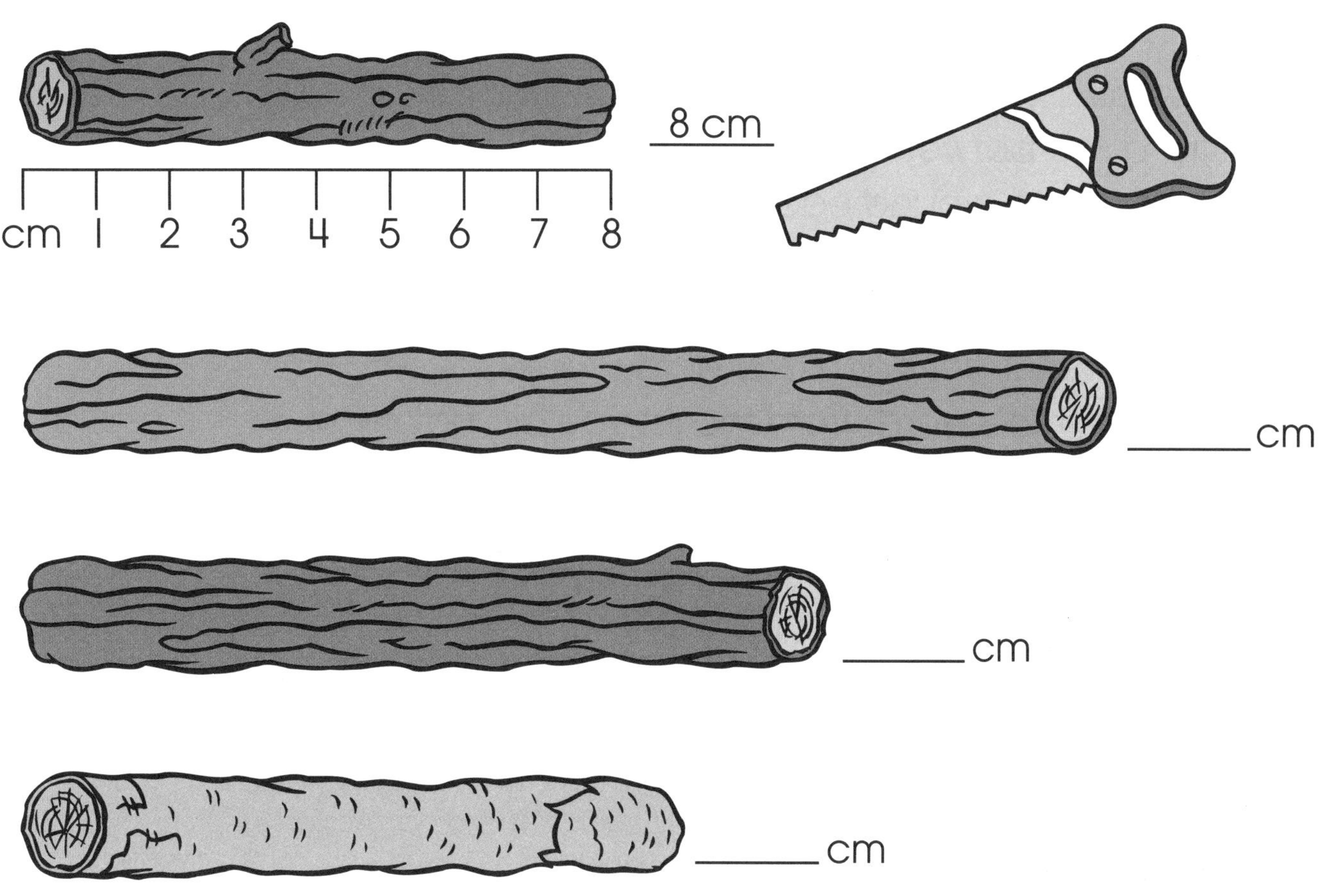

Collective nouns name an entire group. In a sentence, collective nouns are treated the same as singular nouns such as **she** or **he**. In each sentence, circle a collective noun. Underline the verb.

1. My family hikes together on Sundays.
2. Our group presents first on Friday.
3. This school has its own garden.
4. My team plays eight games in April.
5. The audience claps loudly.

Read each sentence and do what it says to do.

1. Count the syllables in each word. Write the number on the line by the word.
2. Draw a line between the two words in each compound word.
3. Draw a circle around each name of a month.
4. Draw a box around each food word.
5. Draw an X on each noise word.
6. Draw a line under each day of the week.
7. Write the three words from the list you did not mark. Draw a picture of each of those words.

______ April	______ vegetable	______ tablecloth
______ bang	______ June	______ meat
______ sidewalk	______ Saturday	______ crash
______ astronaut	______ March	______ jingle
______ moon	______ cardboard	______ rocket
______ Friday	______ fruit	______ Monday

____________ ____________ ____________

Write each number.

Hundreds	Tens	Ones
■ ■		●●● ●●● ●●●

___ hundreds
___ tens
___ ones = _______

Hundreds	Tens	Ones
■ ■ ■ ■ ■ ■	||||| |	●●●

___ hundreds
___ tens
___ ones = _______

Hundreds	Tens	Ones
■ ■ ■	||||	●●● ●●

___ hundreds
___ tens
___ ones = _______

Hundreds	Tens	Ones
■ ■	||||| |||	●●● ●●● ●

___ hundreds
___ tens
___ ones = _______

Solve the word problems.

1. 100 kids came to science camp in the morning. 10 kids left at lunch. How many kids stayed for the afternoon? _______ kids

2. In a game, the kids tossed 90 eggs. 38 eggs broke. How many eggs did not break? _______ eggs

In a **contraction**, two words are joined together. Some letters are left out. The missing letters are replaced by an **apostrophe** (**'**). Draw a line from each pair of words to the matching contraction.

I am	she's
it is	they're
you are	we're
we are	he's
they are	I'm
she is	it's
he is	you're

Change the meaning of the sentences by adding the **prefixes** to the **bold** words.

The boy was **lucky** because he guessed the answer **correctly**.

The boy was (un) ______________________ because he guessed

the answer (in) ______________________.

When Maya **behaved**, she felt **happy**.

When Maya (mis) ______________________, she felt

(un) ______________________.

Connect the dots to make each shape. Not all dots will be used.

a rectangle

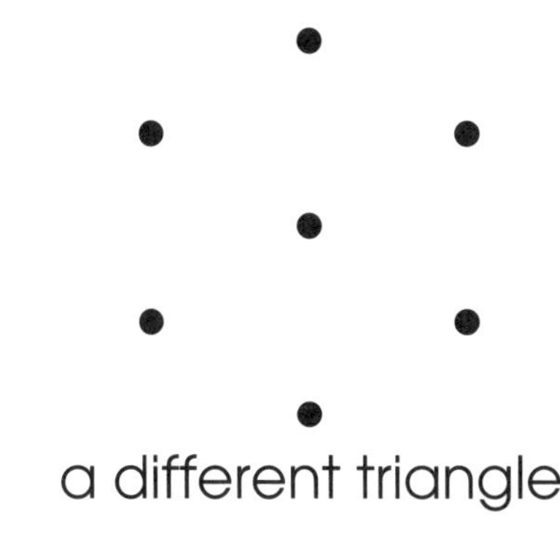

a triangle

a different triangle

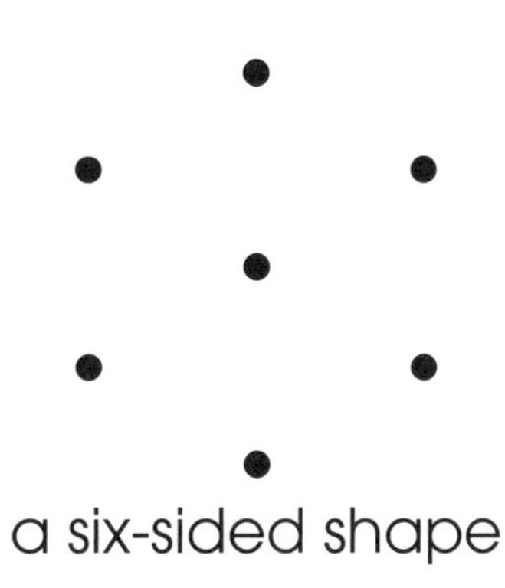

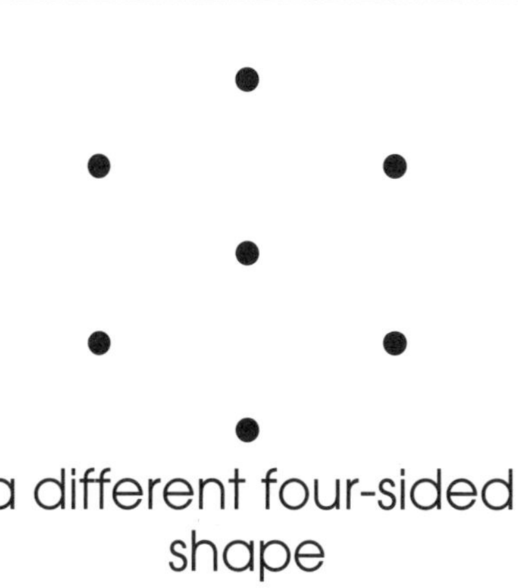

a four-sided shape

a six-sided shape

a different four-sided shape

Add or **subtract**.

54	90	55	63	59
+ 28	− 42	− 22	− 33	+ 25

71	48	24	17	53
− 52	+ 38	+ 67	+ 18	− 44

Rewrite each sentence, replacing **nice** or **good** with a better **adjective** from the box.

sturdy	new	great	chocolate	delicious	special

1. Father baked a good cake.

____

2. David made a good wish.

____

3. Mom served good soup.

____

4. Carly got a nice scooter as a gift.

____

Write the total amount for each group of coins.

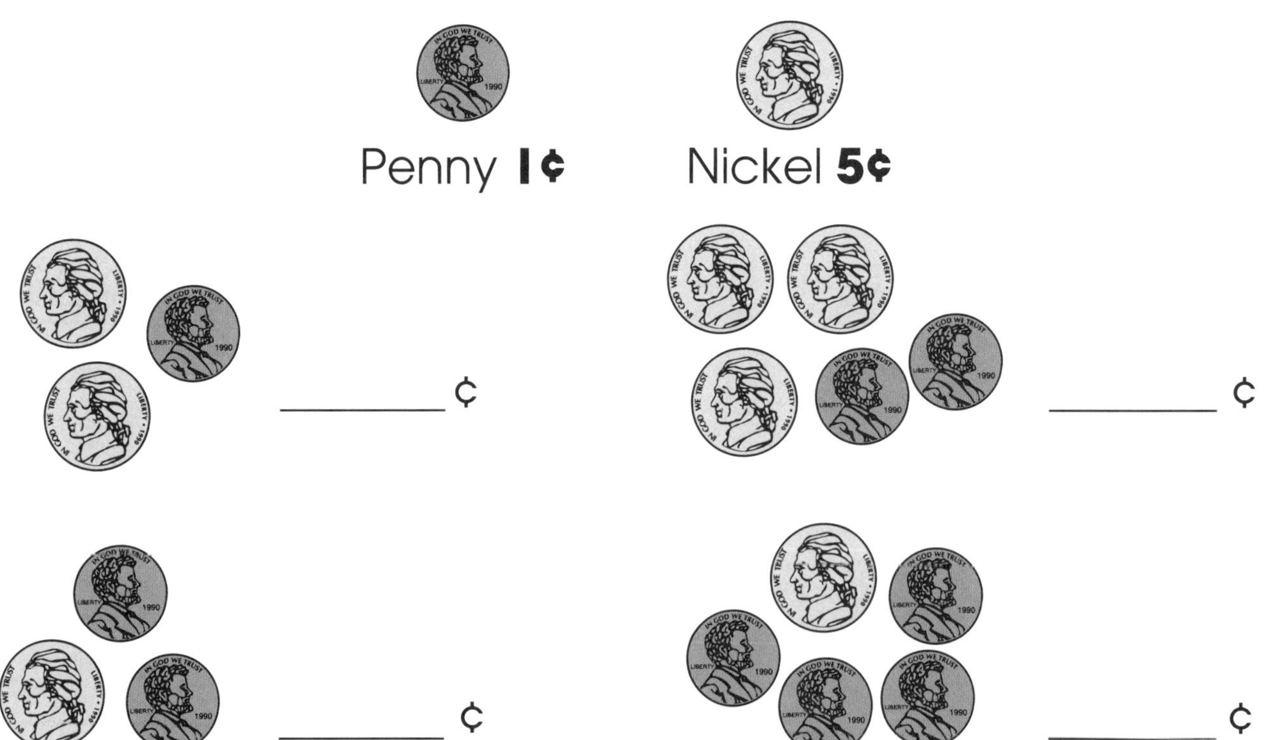

Add three numbers together. Write numbers from the balloons in the blanks. Then, write the sums.

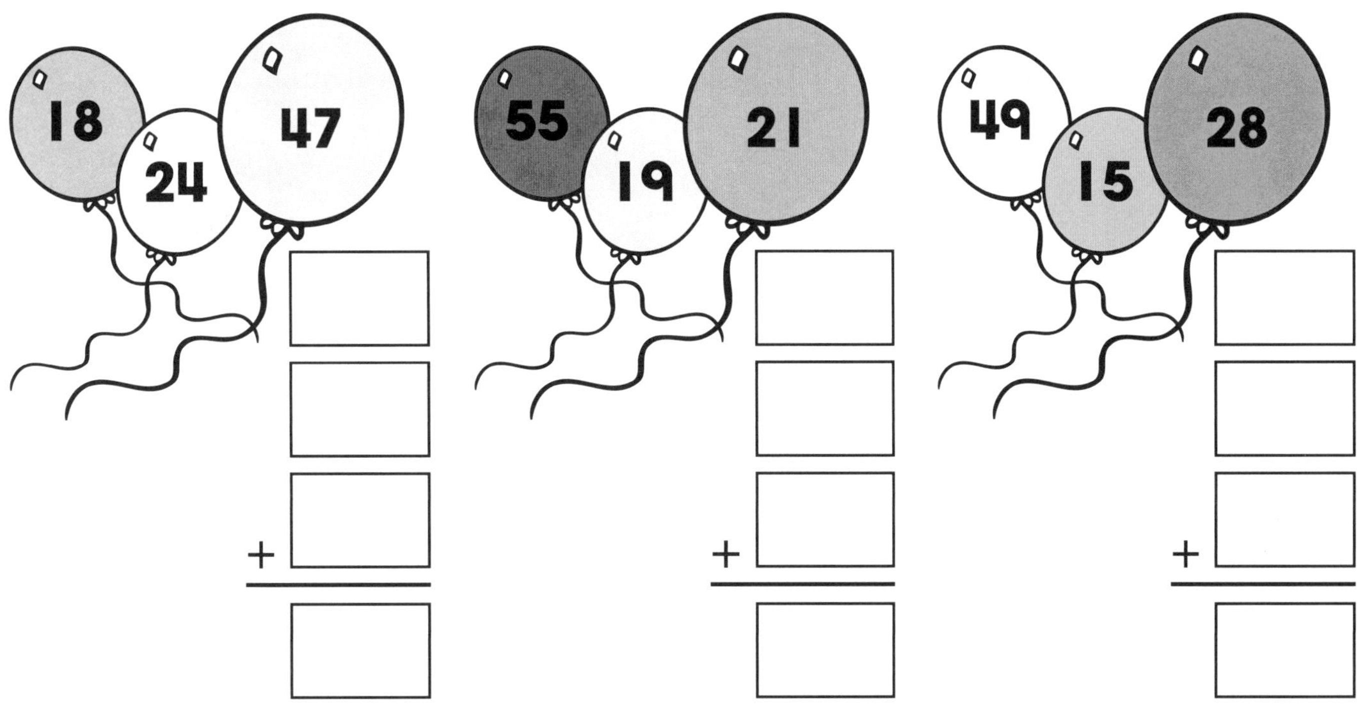

Read all the sentences. Then, choose the best **adjective** to complete each sentence.

happy	**glad**	**joyful**	**thrilled**

1. Playing with my dog makes me ______________.
2. The ______________ dancers leaped and twirled.
3. Dad was ______________ that I remembered to clean up.
4. The little boy was ______________ by his first roller coaster ride.

In a group with an **even** number of objects, the items can be evenly matched in groups of two. In a group with an **odd** number of objects, the items cannot be evenly matched. Circle the group with an even number of items.

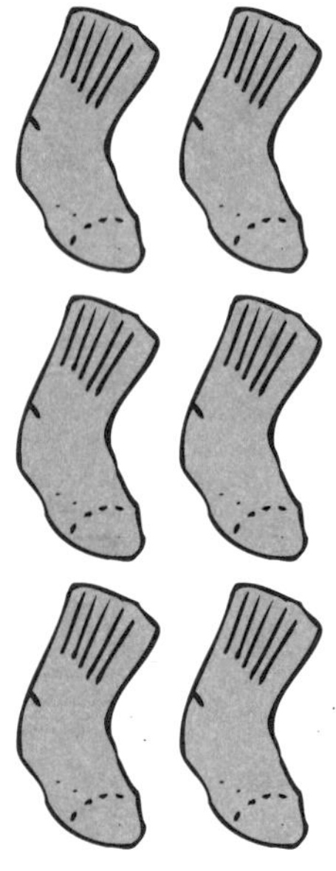

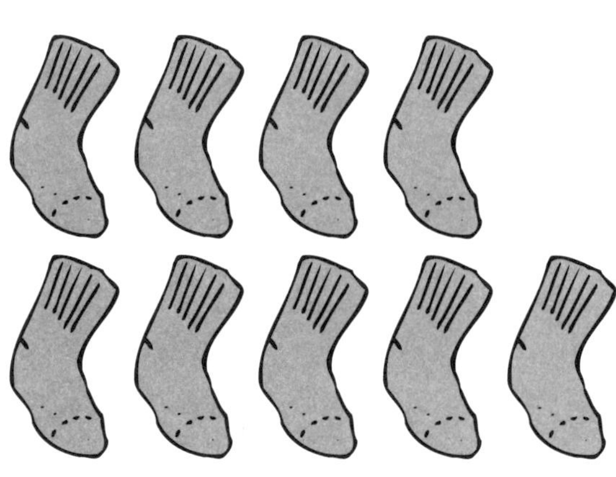

Solve the word problems.

1. The library displayed 37 mystery books and 18 nonfiction books. How many books were displayed in all? ________ books

2. In a video game, Roberto scored 65 points on Saturday and 35 points on Sunday. How many points did he score in all? ________ points

Read the story. Answer the questions.

Hercules was born in the warm Atlantic Ocean. He was a very small and weak baby. He wanted to be the strongest hurricane in the world. But he had one problem. He couldn't blow 75-mile-per-hour winds. Hercules blew and blew in the ocean, until one day, his sister, Hola, told him it would be more fun to be a breeze than a hurricane. Hercules agreed. It was a breeze to be a breeze!

1. What is the setting of the story? ______________________
2. Who are the characters? ______________________
3. What is the problem? ______________________
4. How does Hercules solve his problem? ______________________

   ____
5. How are a hurricane and a breeze alike? ______________________

   ____

   ____

To be is a special verb that does not follow the patterns you know. In the past tense, we say I **was** and you **were**. Use **was** or **were** to complete the sentences.

1. Lily ____________________ eight years old on her birthday.

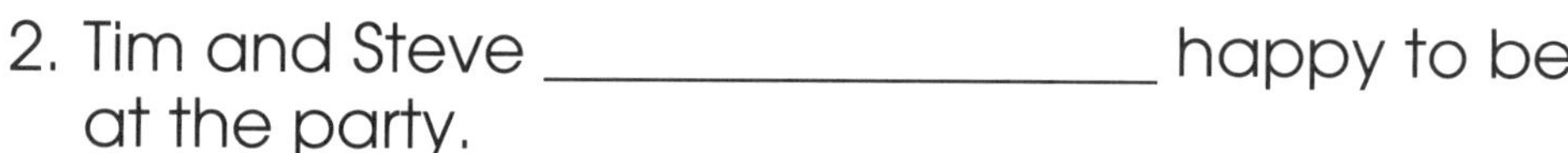

2. Tim and Steve ____________________ happy to be at the party.

3. Megan ____________________ too shy to sing "Happy Birthday."

4. Ben ____________________ sorry he dropped his cake.

5. All of the children ____________________ happy to be invited.

Write the total amount for each group of coins.

Penny **1¢**

Nickel **5¢**

Dime **10¢**

__________ ¢

__________ ¢

__________ ¢

__________ ¢

Add or **subtract**.

52 − 37	45 − 24	45 + 36	74 − 30	82 − 43
59 + 15	18 + 52	76 − 26	48 + 46	35 + 25

Underline the **compound word** in each sentence. On the line, write the two smaller words that make up the compound word.

1. A firetruck came to help put out the fire. ____________________
2. I will be nine years old on my next birthday. ____________________
3. We built a treehouse last summer. ____________________
4. Dad put a scarecrow in his garden. ____________________
5. It is fun to make footprints in the snow. ____________________

Circle the misspelled word in each sentence. Write the correct spelling on the line.

1. Be sure to stopp at the red light. ______________

2. The train goes down the trak. ______________

3. Please put the bred in the toaster. ______________

4. I need another blok to finish. ______________

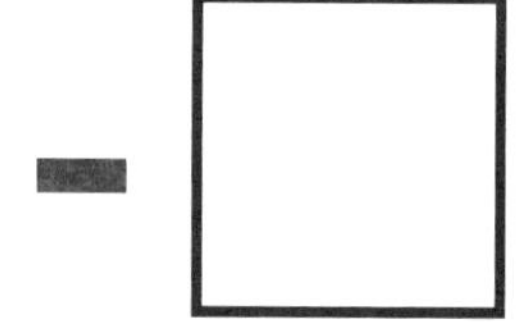   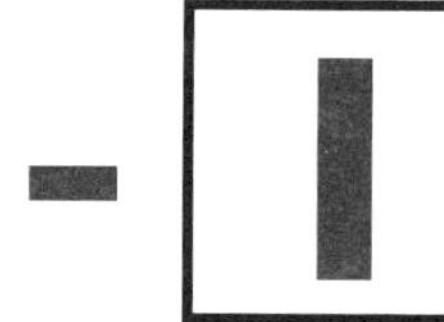  

What is 10 less than the number?

154, ______ 312, ______ 615, ______ 947, ______

What is 100 less than the number?

368, ______ 904, ______ 133, ______ 505, ______

Write an **adjective** in each blank to make the sentences more interesting.

1. The airplane flew through the storm.

   The ______________ airplane flew through the ______________ storm.

2. A firefighter rushed into the house.

   A ______________ firefighter rushed into the ______________ house.

3. The detective hid behind the tree.

   The ______________ detective hid behind the ______________ tree.

How many **halves** make one **whole**?

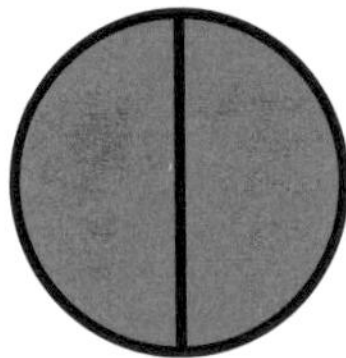

________ halves

How many **thirds** make one **whole**?

________ thirds

How many **fourths** make one **whole**?

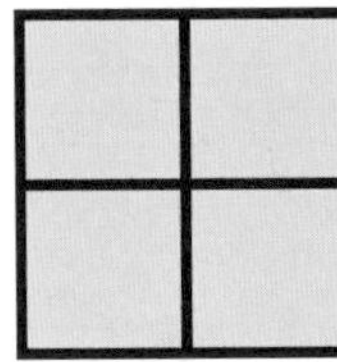

________ fourths

Read each sentence. Look at the word in **bold**. Circle the **prefix**. Write the **root word** on the line.

1. The **preview** of the movie was funny. ____________
2. We will have to **reschedule** the trip. ____________
3. I have **outgrown** my new shoes already. ____________
4. Police **enforce** the laws of the city. ____________
5. The boy **distrusted** the big dog. ____________
6. That song is total **nonsense**! ____________

Write the missing numbers. Count by **tens**.

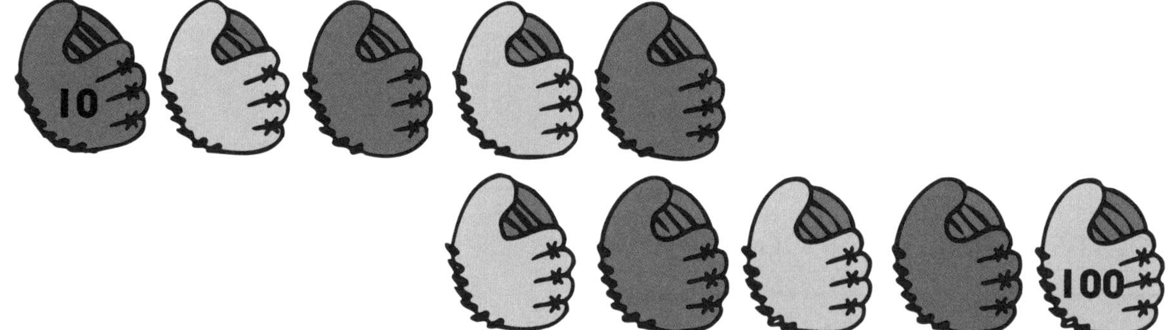

Count by **hundreds**.

Add the three numbers shown on each flower. Write the sum in the center.

In a **contraction**, two words are joined together. Some letters are left out. The missing letters are replaced by an **apostrophe** (**'**). Draw a line from each pair of words to the matching contraction.

would not	I've
was not	he'll
he will	wouldn't
could not	wasn't
I have	couldn't

Add or **subtract**.

73	63	38	33	80
− 44	− 33	+ 24	+ 37	− 42

30	42	26	25	97
+ 59	− 26	+ 33	+ 18	− 9

Draw lines to match the amounts of money.

Find and correct three misspelled words in the letter. Write **commas** inside the boxes to complete the **greeting** and **closing**.

Dear Grandma☐

I hope you come two visit soon. We can go to the museum together. I have sumthing to show you. It is something I made miself. I think you will like it.

Love☐
Marc

Circle words that would best describe the ocean.

tiny **salty** **vast** **still** **wavy**

Circle words that would best describe a taco.

sweet **hot** **spicy** **frozen** **crunchy**

Circle words that would best describe a playground at recess.

noisy **serious** **colorful** **dull** **active**

How many **columns** of four squares are in the rectangle? ________

How many **rows** of five squares are in the rectangle? ________

How many squares are in the rectangle? ________

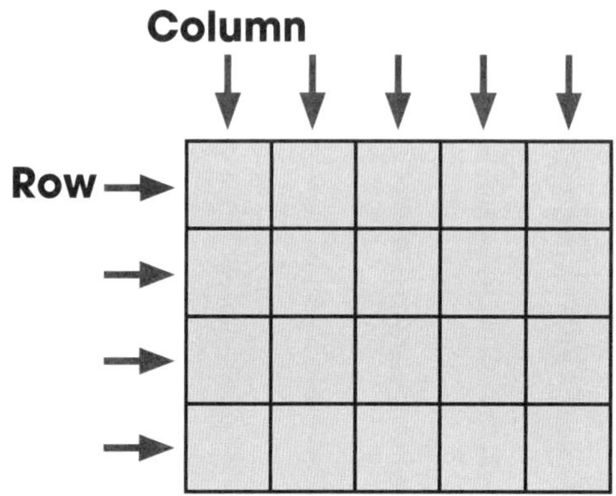

Use columns and rows to divide the rectangle into 12 squares.

Go is a special verb that does not follow the patterns you know. Its **past-tense form** does not end with **ed**. The past tense of **go** is **went**. Write **go** or **went** to complete the sentences.

1. Today, I will ____________________ to the store.

2. Yesterday, we ____________________ shopping.

3. Juan and Seth will ____________________ to the party soon.

Write the **homophones** in the blanks to complete the sentences.

one **won** Jill ______________ first prize at the science fair.

I am the only ______________ in my family with red hair.

be **bee** Jenny cried when a ______________ stung her.

I have to ______________ in bed every night at eight o'clock.

two **to** **too** My father likes ______________ play tennis.

I like to play, ______________.

It takes at least ______________ people to play.

Jace, Jade, and Joy are triplets. How many cents will it cost to buy each of the triplets:

a toy car? ________¢

an ice cream cone? ________¢

a puzzle? ________¢

Circle the group with an **even** number of items.

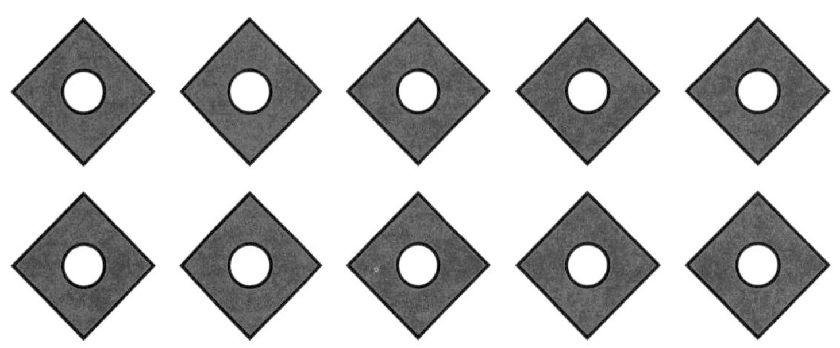

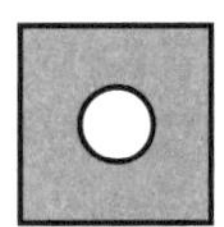 

Solve the word problems.

1. A park had 88 visitors on Thursday and 100 visitors on Friday. How many more visitors came on Friday? ________ visitors

2. Room 114 donated 35 cans of food. Room 120 donated 28 cans of food. How many cans of food were donated in all? ________ cans

Circle the word that begins with a **prefix**. Then, write the prefix and the **root word**.

1. The dog was unfriendly. ________ + ____________
2. The movie preview was interesting. ________ + ____________
3. The referee called an unfair penalty. ________ + ____________
4. Please do not misbehave. ________ + ____________
5. My parents disapprove of that show. ________ + ____________
6. I had to redo the assignment. ________ + ____________

Circle the **contraction** that replaces the underlined words.

1. The boy <u>was not</u> sad.
   wasn't weren't

2. We <u>were not</u> working.
   wasn't weren't

3. Jen and Caleb <u>have not</u> eaten lunch yet.
   haven't hasn't

4. The mouse <u>has not</u> been here.
   haven't hasn't

Combine the words to make **compound words**. Write the compound words on the lines.

sun	**foot**	**air**	**bath**	**mail**	**class**	**ball**	**flower**
box	**plane**	**basket**	**room**	**water**	**melon**	**guard**	**body**

______________________ ______________________

______________________ ______________________

______________________ ______________________

______________________ ______________________

______________________ ______________________

______________________ ______________________

______________________ ______________________

Draw lines to match the amounts of money.

Add or **subtract**.

33 + 46	73 − 14	29 + 68	66 − 28	72 − 34
33 + 37	44 + 28	76 − 13	84 + 9	81 − 68

Collective nouns name an entire group. In a sentence, collective nouns are treated the same as singular nouns such as **she** or **he**. In each sentence, circle a collective noun. Underline the verb.

1. Our school collects cans and papers to recycle.
2. The winning team shouts for joy!
3. The audience cheers for each new act.
4. The family has two sets of twins.
5. My group is reading a book about Africa.

Add three numbers together. Write numbers from the balloons in the blanks. Then, write the sums.

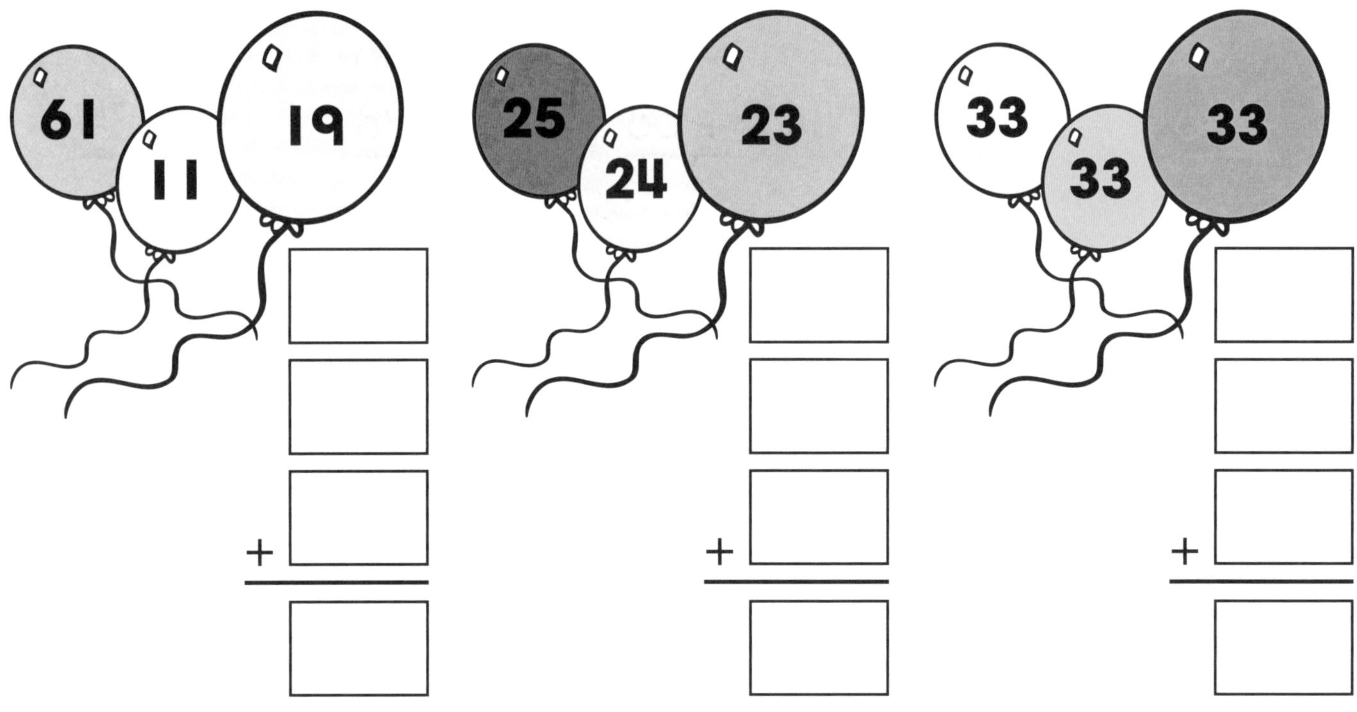

Read all the sentences. Then, choose the best **verb** to complete each sentence.

tiptoed	**walked**	**marched**	**trudged**

1. On Tuesday, we ____________________ to the library.
2. The farmer ____________________ through mud to get to the barn.
3. We ____________________ past the sleeping baby's crib.
4. The proud girl ____________________ up to get her prize.

Use a ruler to measure the logs to the nearest **centimeter**.

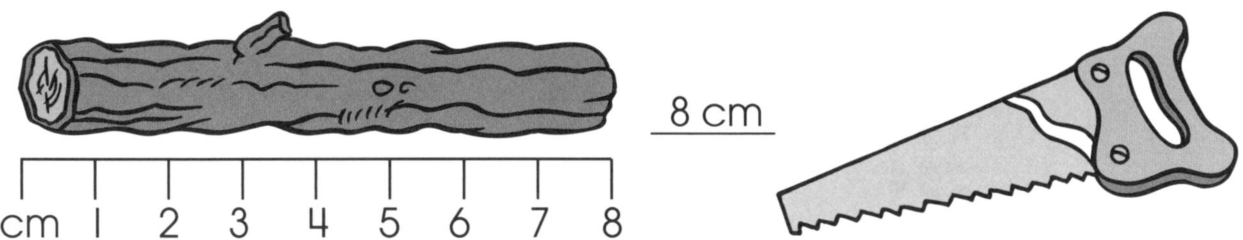

8 cm

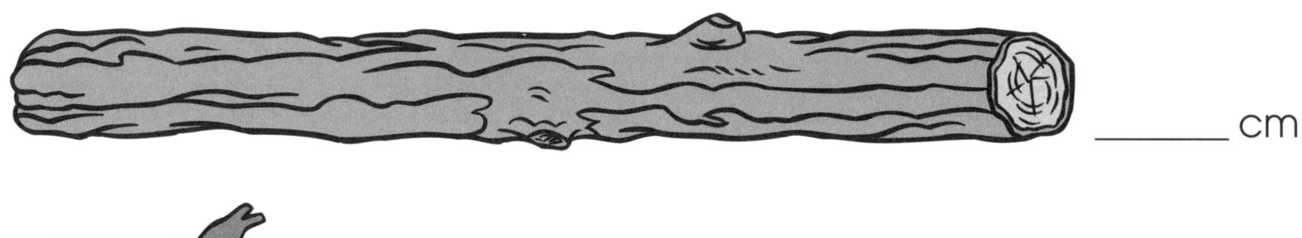

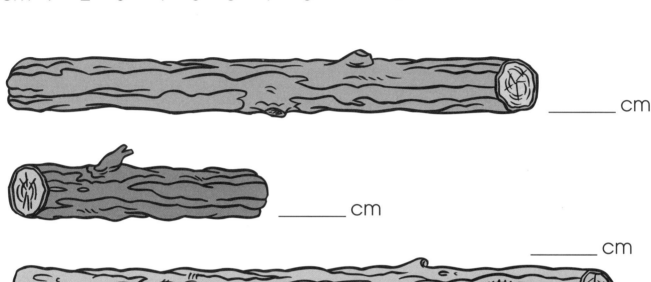

______ cm

______ cm

______ cm

Write words that tell **who** or **when** to expand the sentences.

1. Mary's little ____________________ is starting her first day at school ____________________.

2. Aunt ____________________ is moving to Florida ____________________.

3. It was almost ____________________ when ____________________ arrived at the party.

Write the total amount for each group of coins.

25¢ 10¢ 5¢ 1¢

_______ ¢ _______ ¢

_______ ¢ _______ ¢

What is 10 less than the number?

26, _____ 84, _____ 714, _____ 588, _____

What is 100 less than the number?

247, _____ 987, _____ 325, _____ 411, _____

Circle the misspelled word in each sentence. Write the correct spelling on the line.

1. The beasst player won a trophy. ____________________

2. Blow out the candles and make a wiish. ____________________

3. The truk blew its horn. ____________________

4. Watch the kite flie! ____________________

The words name different **parts of speech**. Use them to label the words in the sentence.

noun	**verb**	**preposition**	**article**	**pronoun**

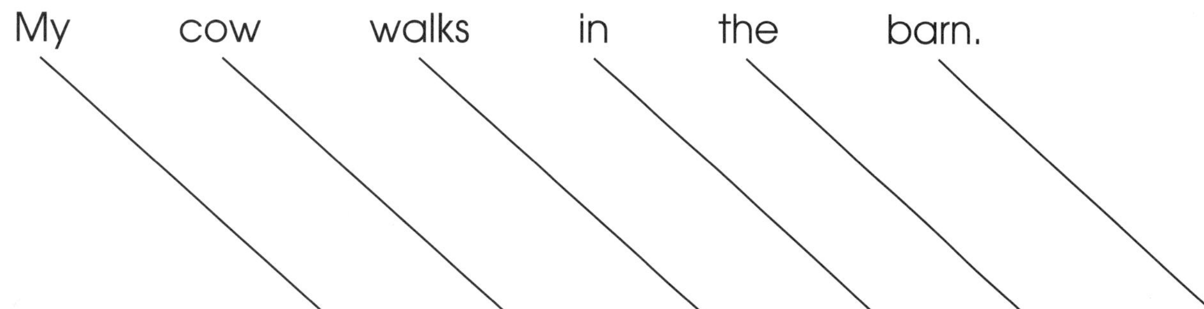

Read the meaning on each treasure chest. Write the matching word. Then, underline the **prefix** in each word.

disagree	**input**	**redo**	**unable**

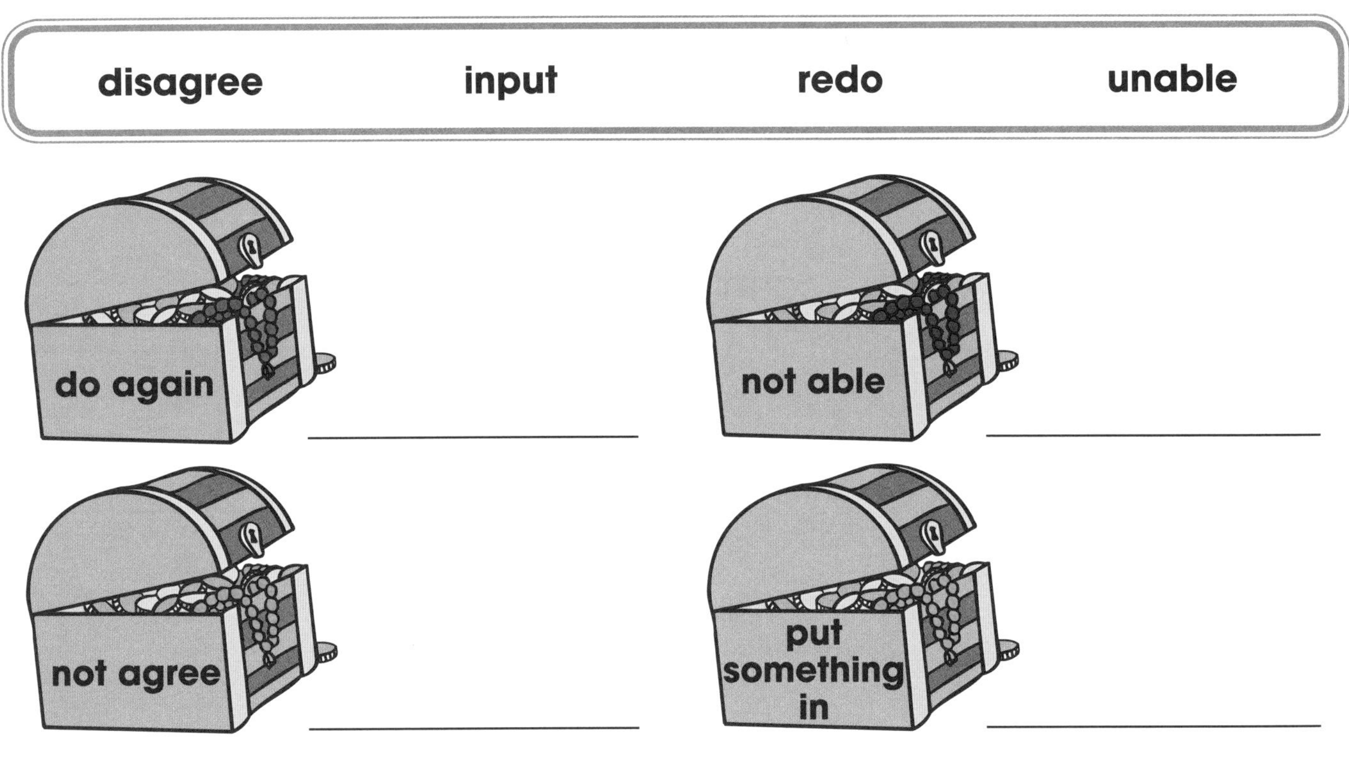

Color one **half** of each shape.

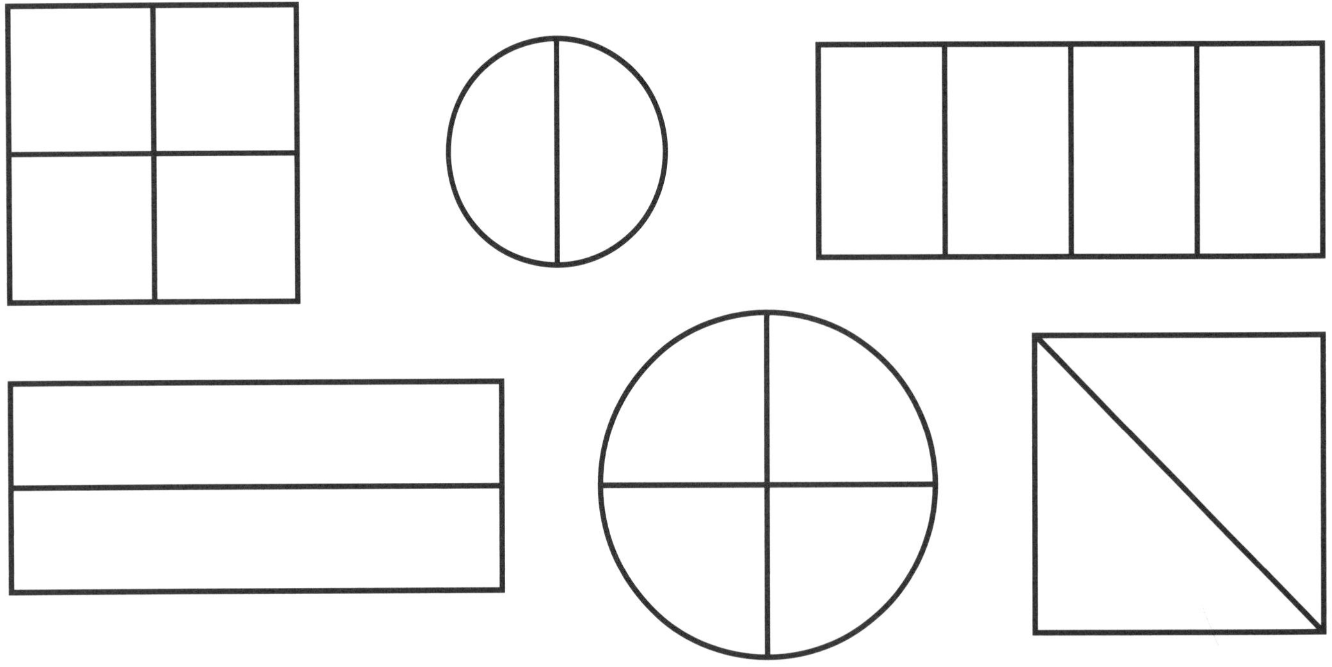

Add or **subtract**.

42 − 35	92 − 53	41 + 49	73 + 19	24 − 15
83 − 56	32 + 59	63 + 17	55 − 42	69 + 13

Have is a special verb that does not follow the patterns you know. Its **past-tense form** does not end with **ed**. The past tense of **have** is **had**. Write **have** or **had** to complete the sentences.

1. We ____________________ three cats at home.
2. Bucky and Charlie ____________________ gray fur.
3. When I was little, we ____________________ only one cat.
4. I ____________________ to ask my parents for more!

Combine the words to make a **compound word** to describe each picture.

shoe	lace	cup	cake	mail	ball
stool	box	foot	basket	bell	door

______________________ ______________________ ______________________

______________________ ______________________ ______________________

Circle the group with an **odd** number of items.

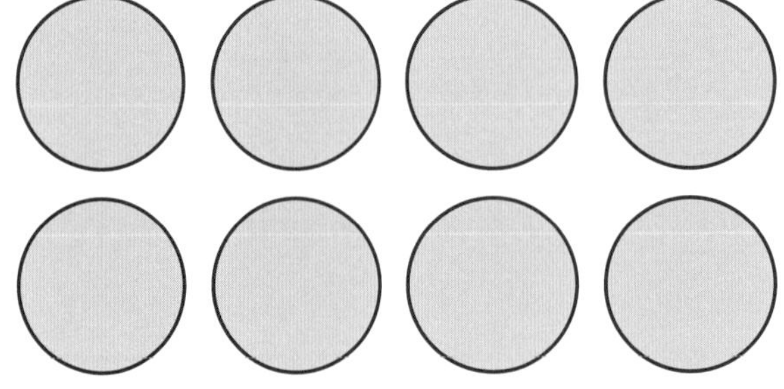

Find and correct three misspelled words in the letter. Write **commas** inside the boxes to complete the **greeting** and **closing**.

Dear Room 22☐

Thank you for the nyce cards and drawings. They cheered me up when I wuz sick. My surgery went well. I will be bak to school in two weeks. I will be happy to see you all.

Your friend☐
Aggie

Solve the word problems.

1. Group A wrote 16 words on the word wall. Group B wrote 24 words on the word wall. How many words were written in all? ________ words

2. A bakery sold 78 cheese bagels and 53 plain bagels. How many more cheese bagels were sold? ________ bagels

Read the play. Answer the questions.

Pip: Hey, Pep. What kind of turkey eats very fast?

Pep: Uh, I don't know.

Pip: A gobbler!

Pep: I have a good joke for you, Pip. What kind of burger does a polar bear eat?

Pip: Uh, a cold burger?

Pep: No, an iceberg-er!

Pip: Hey, that was a great joke!

1. Who are the characters in the play? ___

___

2. What are the jokes about? ___

___

3. What are the characters in the play doing? ___

___

4. What does it mean to gobble your food? ___

___

5. What is an iceberg? ___

___

Write the total amount for each group of coins.

 ______ ¢

   ______ ¢

  ______ ¢

   ______ ¢

- [ ] [1] [0]

- [1] [0] [0]

What is 10 less than the number?

522, ______ 18, ______ 99, ______ 100, ______

What is 100 less than the number?

100, ______ 399, ______ 802, ______ 664, ______

Add or **subtract**.

21	30	47	80	92
+ 29	− 27	+ 37	− 22	− 43

72	58	41	22	64
+ 19	− 44	+ 29	+ 28	− 29

Circle two misspelled words in each sentence. Write the correct spellings on the lines.

1. Are you goeing to shere your cookie with me?

______________________ ______________________

2. We planed a long time, but we still wur not ready.

______________________ ______________________

3. My pensil has not brokken yet today. 

______________________ ______________________

4. We need to fynd the rite address.

______________________ ______________________

Count the number of sunny days. Draw one sun in the box for every five sunny days in June. This kind of graph is called a **picture graph**.

June						
		☀	☀	☁	☂	☀
☀	☀	☁	☀	☀	☀	☀
☀	☀	☀	☀	☁	☁	☂
☀	☁	☁	☂	☀	☀	☀
☀	☀	☁	☀			

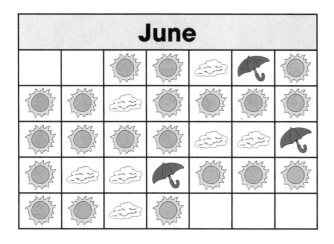

Sunny Days in June

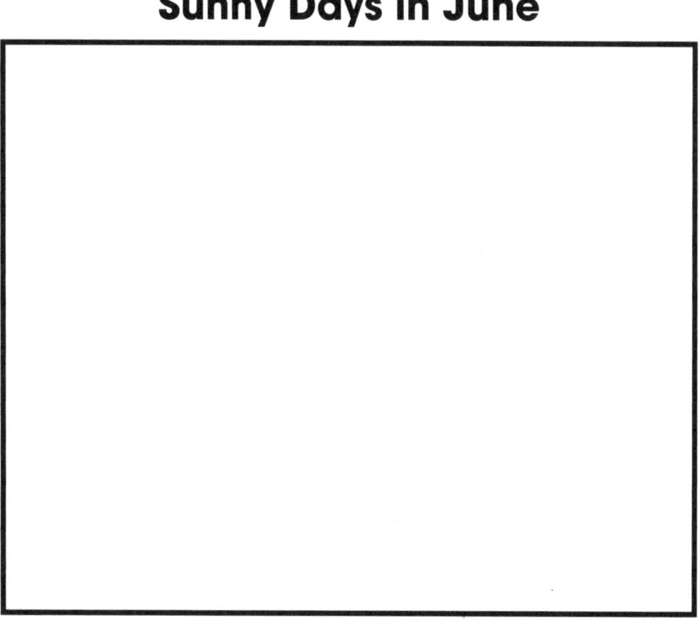

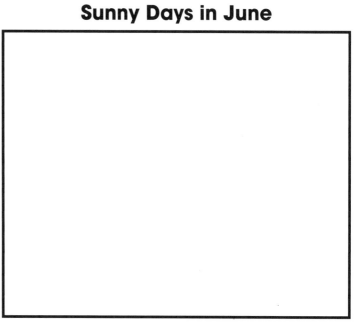

☀ **= 5 sunny days**

Draw a line from each pair of words to the matching **contraction**.

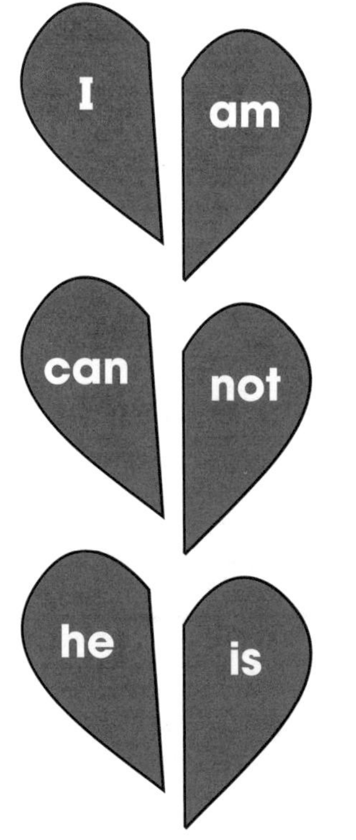

Add the three numbers shown on each flower. Write the sum in the center.

Write the total amount for each group of coins.

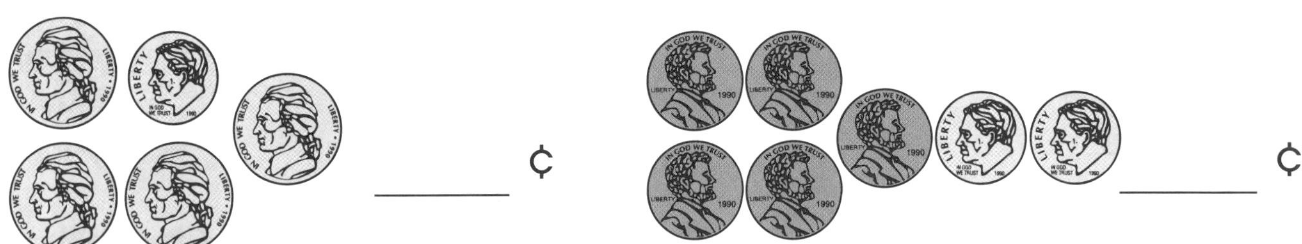

_______ ¢

_______ ¢

_______ ¢

_______ ¢

Circle the correct **homophone** to complete each sentence. Write the word on the line.

1. I am going to ____________________ a letter to my grandmother. right write

2. Draw a circle around the ____________________ answer. right write

3. Wait an ____________________ before going swimming. our hour

4. This is ____________________ house. our hour

5. He got a ____________________ from his garden. beat beet

Rewrite each sentence, adding at least two **adjectives** to provide more information and details.

1. The girl dropped her coat.

____

2. The boy played with cars.

____

3. The boy put books away.

____

See is a special verb that does not follow the patterns you know. Its **past-tense form** does not end with **ed**. The past tense of **see** is **saw**. Write **see** or **saw** to complete the sentences.

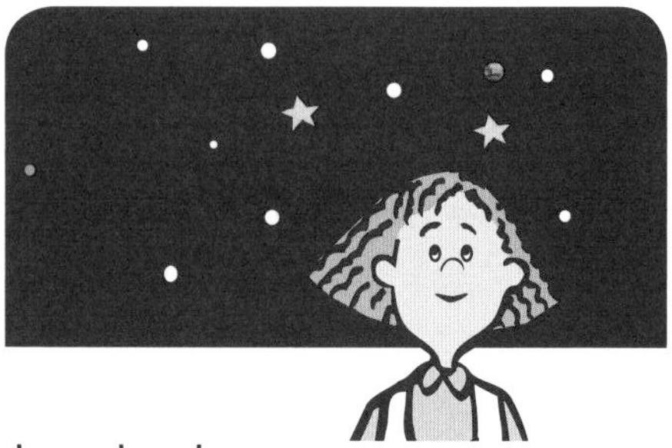

1. Last night, we ________________ the stars.

2. John can ________________ the stars from his window.

3. Last week, he ________________ the Big Dipper.

4. Can you ________________ it in the night sky, too?

Circle the group with an **even** number of items.

Read the meaning on each treasure chest. Write the matching word. Then, underline the **prefix** in each word.

discover	**inside**	**unhappy**	**replay**

play again ______________

find or uncover ______________

within the sides ______________

not happy ______________

Win the tic-tac-toe game by drawing an X through equations that are not true.

51 + 13 = 73	45 − 22 = 23	72 − 17 = 55
21 + 19 = 40	82 − 36 = 53	39 + 47 = 86
73 − 26 = 47	53 + 29 = 82	75 − 29 = 50

Add or **subtract**.

90 − 59	42 + 18	72 − 44	60 − 36	48 + 19
82 − 53	62 + 18	13 + 37	75 − 42	22 + 58

Draw a line from each pair of words to the matching **contraction**.

Write the missing amounts.

10¢ + ______¢ = ______¢

______¢ + ______¢ + ______¢ = ______¢

______¢ + ______¢ = ______¢

Circle words that would best describe a thunderstorm.

sunny **soggy** **calm** **booming** **cloudy**

Circle words that would best describe a snow cone.

icy **fruity** **steaming** **drippy** **meaty**

Circle words that would best describe a bumblebee.

buzzing **gigantic** **cuddly** **flying** **striped**

Combine words from the box to make a **compound word** to describe each picture.

rain	**fish**	**light**	**sun**	**tail**
shirt	**book**	**worm**	**bow**	**star**

______________ ______________ ______________

______________ ______________

The words name different **parts of speech**. Use them to label the words in the sentence.

article	**adjective**	**noun**	**verb**

The large dog was excited.

Count by **fives**. Write the missing numbers.

Count by **tens**. Write the missing numbers.

Count by **hundreds**. Write the missing numbers.

Solve the word problems.

1. 82 people saw the movie. 37 people did not like it. How many people liked the movie? ________ people

2. The baby napped in the car for 29 minutes and at home for 49 minutes. How many minutes did the baby nap in all? ________ minutes

Use a ruler to measure each item to the nearest **centimeter**. Answer the questions.

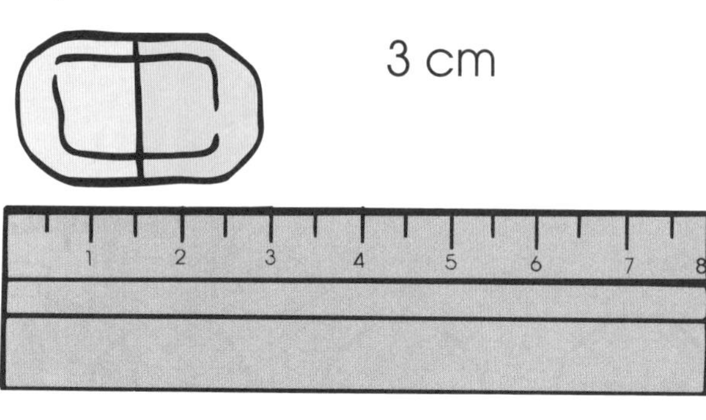

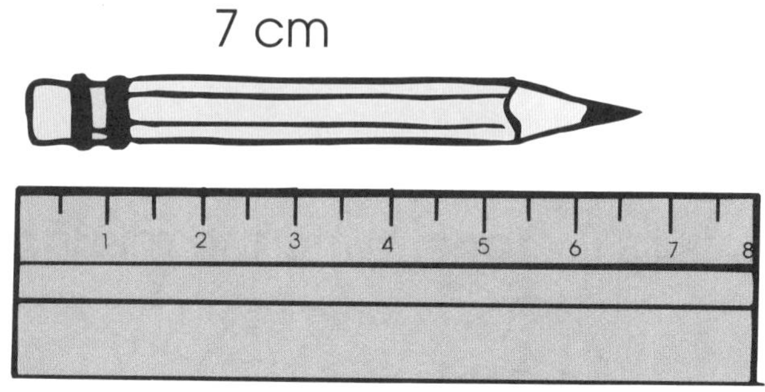

 ________ cm

 ________ cm

How much longer is the paintbrush than the crayon? ________ cm

How much longer is the paintbrush than the pencil? ________ cm

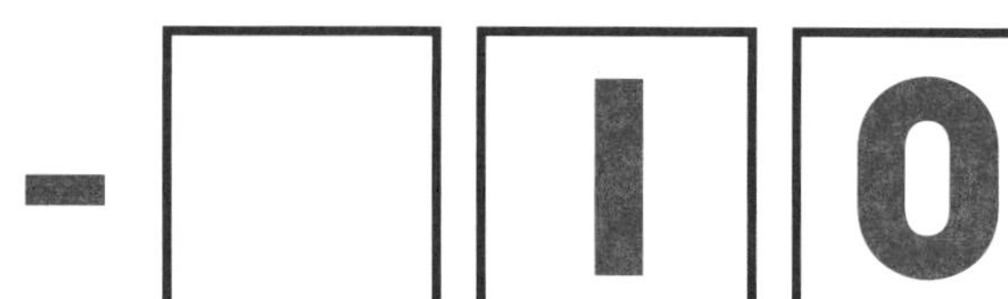

What is 10 less than the number?

36, ______ 10, ______ 892, ______ 70, ______

What is 100 less than the number?

444, ______ 768, ______ 132, ______ 319, ______

Write the **part of speech** of each underlined word.

NOUN PRONOUN VERB ADJECTIVE ADVERB PREPOSITION

There (1) are many (2) different kinds of animals. Some animals live in the wild. Some animals live in the (3) zoo. And still others live in homes. The animals that (4) live in homes are called pets.

There are many types of pets. Some pets without fur are fish, turtles, snakes, and hermit crabs. Trained birds can fly (5) around (6) your house. Some (7) furry animals are cats, dogs, rabbits, ferrets, gerbils, and hamsters. Some animals can (8) successfully learn tricks that (9) you teach them. Whatever your favorite animal is, animals can be (10) special friends!

1. ______________
2. ______________
3. ______________
4. ______________
5. ______________
6. ______________
7. ______________
8. ______________
9. ______________
10. ______________

How many **columns** of four squares are in the rectangle? ________

How many **rows** of six squares are in the rectangle? ________

How many squares are in the rectangle? ________

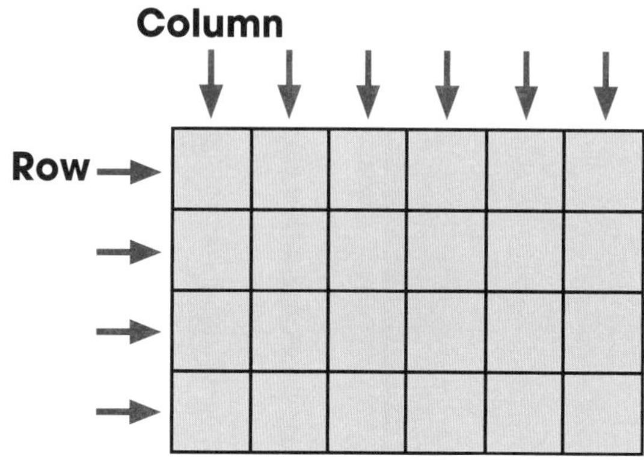

Use columns and rows to divide the rectangle into 15 squares.

Choose the correct verb to complete each sentence. Write it in the blank.

1. My family ______________________ together as often as we can.
   (eat/eats)
2. This group ______________________ new games to play at recess.
   (invent/invents)
3. Our class ______________________ our pet hamsters.
   (love/loves)
4. My team ______________________ two coaches.
   (has/have)

Add three numbers together. Write numbers from the balloons in the blanks. Then, write the sums.

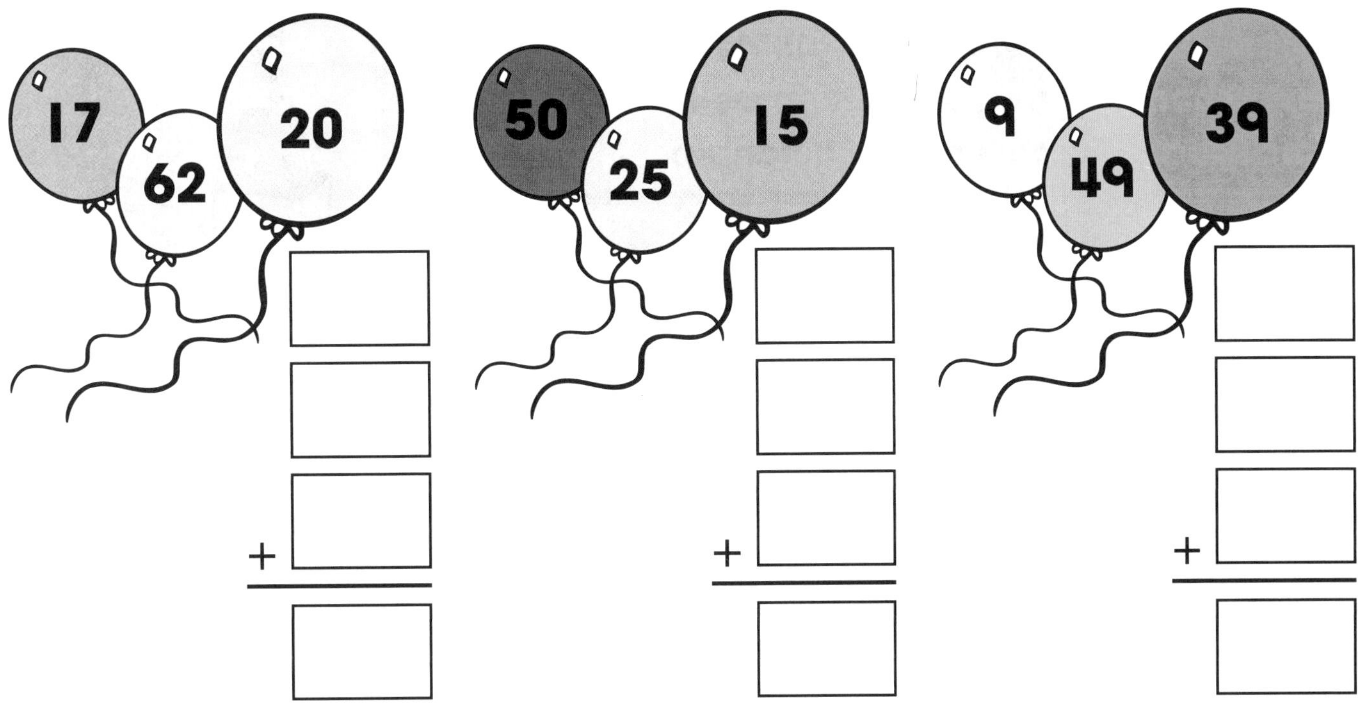

Write an **adjective** or an **adverb** on each line to describe the **bold** word.

Adjectives		
adorable	many	best

Adverbs		
excitedly	straight	pitifully

1. Dad and I **went** ________________ to the back of the store.
2. We saw ________________ animal **cages**.
3. The ________________ **puppies** interested me most.
4. One little beagle **wiggled** ________________.
5. He **whined** ________________.
6. A puppy would be the ________________ **present** I could have.

Write the correct **compound word** on the line. Then, use the numbered letters to solve the code.

sometimes	**downtown**	**girlfriend**	**today**
everybody	**maybe**	**myself**	
baseball	**outside**	**lunchbox**	

1. Opposite of **inside** ___ ___ ___ ___ ___ ___ ___ (1)
2. Another word for **me** ___ ___ ___ ___ ___ ___ (2, 3)
3. A girl who is a friend ___ ___ ___ ___ ___ ___ ___ ___ ___ ___ (4, 5)
4. Not yesterday or tomorrow, but . . . ___ ___ ___ ___ ___ (6)
5. All of the people ___ ___ ___ ___ ___ ___ ___ ___ ___ (7, 8)
6. A sport ___ ___ ___ ___ ___ ___ ___ ___ (9)
7. The main part of a town ___ ___ ___ ___ ___ ___ ___ ___ (10, 11)
8. Not always, just . . . ___ ___ ___ ___ ___ ___ ___ ___ ___ (12, 13)
9. A box for carrying your lunch ___ ___ ___ ___ ___ ___ ___ ___ (14)
10. Perhaps or might ___ ___ ___ ___ ___ (15)

___ ___ ___ ___ ___ ___ ___ ___ ___ ! ___ ___ ___
10 8 11 6 15 7 3 1 9 2 8 1

___ ___ ___ ___ ___ ___ ___ ___
3 8 1 11 6 13 14 15

___ ___ ___ ___ ___ ___ ___ ___ ___ ___ ___ ___ ___ !
7 5 4 14 13 12 8 9 1 13 5 8 11

Add numbers with three digits. First, add the **ones**. Next, add the **tens**. Then, add the **hundreds**. The first one is done for you.

hundreds (3)	tens (2)	ones (1)
1	3	2
+ 6	5	2
7	8	4

hundreds	tens	ones
4	5	3
+ 2	2	6

hundreds	tens	ones
8	2	5
+ 1	1	1

hundreds	tens	ones
1	2	7
+ 1	7	1

hundreds	tens	ones
5	5	5
+ 2	3	4

hundreds	tens	ones
	4	3
+ 2	3	5

Match the correct amount of money with the price of the object.

Write a word in each blank to answer the question and make the sentence tell more.

Mrs. ____________ bought a sweater and two ____________
Who? What?

before leaving the ____________ to pick up ____________
Where? Who?

at ____________.
When?

Divide the shape into equal **thirds**.

Divide the shape into equal **halves**.

Divide the shape into equal **fourths**.

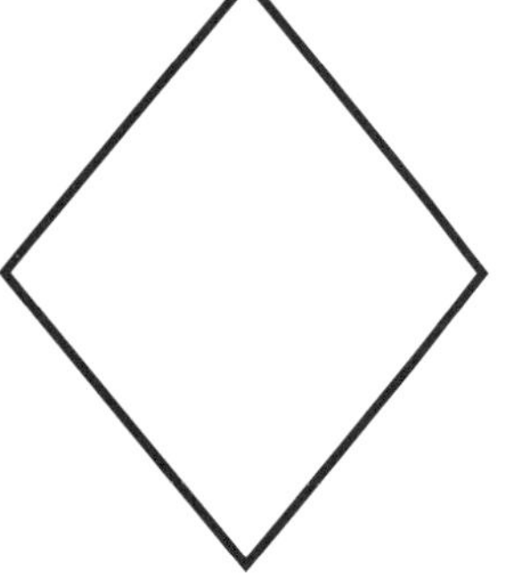

Color one **whole** shape.

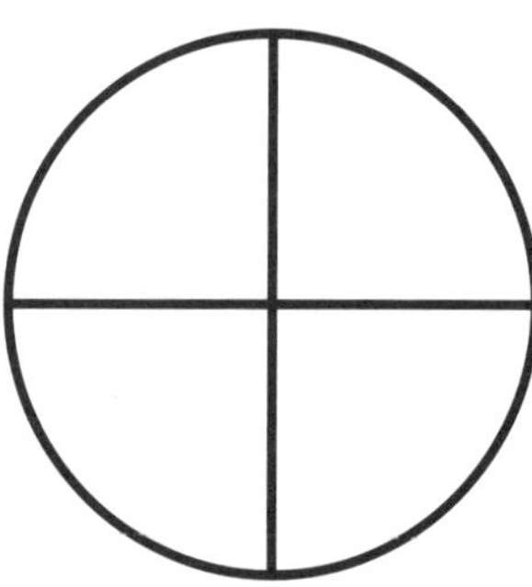

Add. First, add the **ones**. Next, add the **tens**. Then, add the **hundreds**.

hundreds (3)	tens (2)	ones (1)	hundreds	tens	ones	hundreds	tens	ones
4	4	3	1	5	4	2	1	4
+ 3	2	6	+ 6	3	3	+ 4	3	5

hundreds	tens	ones	hundreds	tens	ones	hundreds	tens	ones
1	7	5	3	3	3	2	3	4
+	2	4	+ 5	6	6	+ 1	2	3

Eat is a special verb that does not follow the patterns you know. Its **past-tense form** does not end with **ed**. The past tense of **eat** is **ate**. Write **eat** or **ate** to complete the sentences.

1. We like to ________________ in the lunchroom.

2. Last week, our teacher ________________ in a different room.

3. Yesterday, we ________________ pizza, pears, and peas.

4. Today, we will ________________ turkey and potatoes.

Subtract from numbers with three digits. First, subtract the **ones**. Next, subtract the **tens**. Then, subtract the **hundreds**.

hundreds (3)	tens (2)	ones (1)
9	8	6
−5	3	2

hundreds	tens	ones
5	8	2
−3	5	0

hundreds	tens	ones
7	4	9
−2	2	7

hundreds	tens	ones
7	6	4
−7	4	1

hundreds	tens	ones
9	1	8
−8	0	2

hundreds	tens	ones
1	5	7
−	3	5

Circle the group with an **odd** number of items.

Circle the correct **homophone** to complete each sentence. Write the word on the line.

1. Our football team ____________________ that team.
   beat   beet

2. Go to the store and ____________________ a loaf of bread.
   by   buy

3. We will drive ____________________ our house.
   by   buy

4. It will be trouble if the dog ____________________ the cat.
   seas   sees

5. They sailed the seven ____________________.
   seas   sees

Choose the correct verb to complete each sentence. Write it in the blank.

1. Our family ____________________ to the beach every summer.
   (go/goes)

2. My sister's school ____________________ delicious black bean chili.
   (serve/serves)

3. The baseball team ____________________ new uniforms.
   (have/has)

4. Mom's neighborhood group ____________________ a parade every year.
   (plan/plans)

Read the story. Answer the questions.

Sean really likes to play basketball. One sunny day, he decided to ask his friends to play basketball at the park, but there were six people—Sean, Aki, Lance, Kate, Zac, and Oralia. A basketball team only allows five to play at a time. So, Sean decided to be the coach. Sean and his friends had fun.

1. How many kids wanted to play basketball? ____________________

2. Write their names in ABC order:

   ________________ ________________ ________________

   ________________ ________________ ________________

3. How many players can play on a basketball team at a time? ________________

4. Where did they play basketball? ____________________________

5. Who decided to be the coach? ____________________________

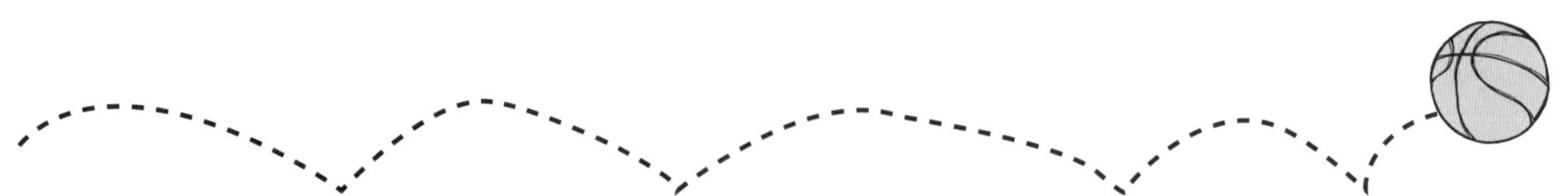

Subtract. First, subtract the **ones**. Next, subtract the **tens**. Then, subtract the **hundreds**.

3 ↓ 2 ↓ 1 ↓

hundreds	tens	ones	hundreds	tens	ones	hundreds	tens	ones
5	8	7	9	2	8	5	7	4
- 3	2	0	- 8	0	6	- 3	5	0

hundreds	tens	ones	hundreds	tens	ones	hundreds	tens	ones
3	6	5	4	2	6	5	5	0
- 3	4	2	- 1	1	4	- 2	3	0

Write the amount for each group of coins.

_________ ¢

_________ ¢

_________ ¢

_________ ¢

When the sum of **ones** is more than 10, regroup the **tens**. When the sum of tens is more than 100, regroup the **hundreds**. Follow the example. Trace the numbers for each step.

Step 1: Add the ones.

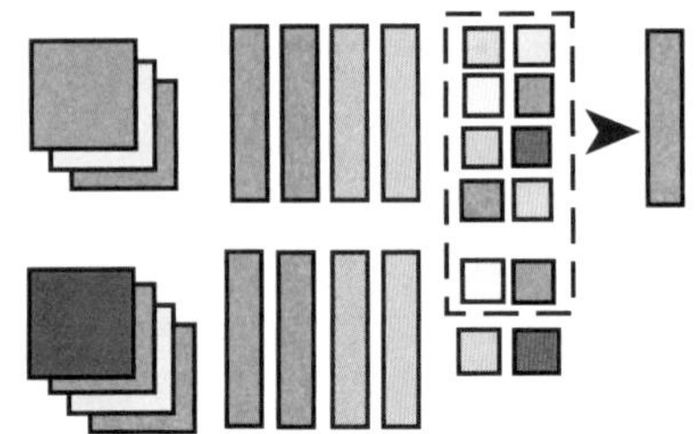

Do you regroup? Yes

Step 2: Add the tens.

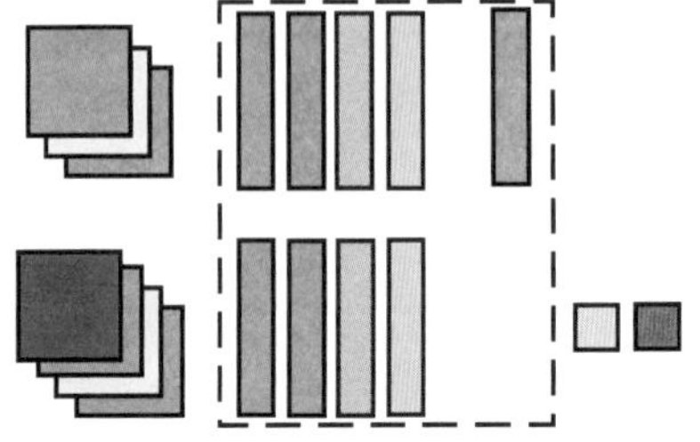

Do you regroup? No

Step 3: Add the hundreds.

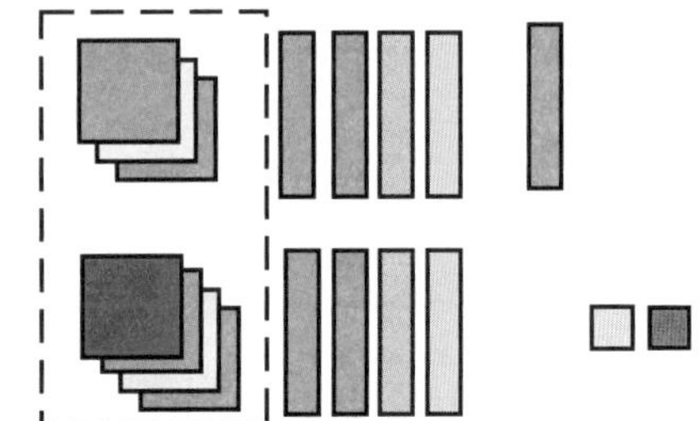

hundreds	tens	ones	hundreds	tens	ones	hundreds	tens	ones
	1			1			1	
3	4	8	3	4	8	3	4	8
+ 4	4	4	+ 4	4	4	+ 4	4	4
		2		9	2	7	9	2

Write the value of the underlined digit. The first three are done for you.

258 50   875 ______   470 ______

305 300   58 ______   562 ______

699 9   325 ______   989 ______

Write the **contraction** for each pair of words. Use an **apostrophe** (') to replace the letters you leave out.

1. you are ____________
2. does not ____________
3. do not ____________
4. would not ____________
5. she is ____________
6. we have ____________
7. has not ____________
8. did not ____________

Circle the **suffix** in each word. The first one is done for you.

fluff(y)	peaceful	careless
rainy	thoughtful	likeable
blameless	enjoyable	helpful

Write a word with a suffix to match each meaning.

full of hope ____________

without hope ____________

without power ____________

having rain ____________

able to break ____________

full of cheer ____________

Rewrite each sentence, rearranging the words to make each telling sentence, or **statement**, into a **question** and each question into a statement. The first one is done for you.

1. Ellen is getting the gear together.

   Is Ellen getting the gear together?

2. James is packing the car trunk.

   ____

3. Will it be dark when we arrive at the lake?

   ____

4. Joey's job is to put up the tent.

   ____

5. Will we sit around the fire and tell stories?

   ____

Write the value of the quarter. Then, add the value of the dimes, nickels, and pennies.

______ ¢ ______ ¢ ______ ¢ ______ ¢ ______ ¢ ______ ¢

______ ¢ ______ ¢ ______ ¢

Total

Add. **Regroup** as needed.

hundreds	tens	ones	hundreds	tens	ones	hundreds	tens	ones
4	1	8	4	7	1	3	3	4
+ 3	2	3	+ 3	1	9	+ 5	2	8

hundreds	tens	ones	hundreds	tens	ones	hundreds	tens	ones
6	5	9	7	3	6	4	2	6
+ 1	2	7	+ 1	4	5	+ 1	6	5

Read all the sentences. Then, choose the best **adjective** to complete each sentence.

warm	**toasty**	**hot**	**scorching**

1. Let's get inside where it is ____________________.
2. We like to swim on ____________________ days.
3. Would you like a ____________________ cheese sandwich?
4. The ____________________ fire burnt two buildings.

When there are not enough **ones** to subtract from, regroup the **tens**. When there are not enough tens to subtract from, regroup the **hundreds**. **Subtract**. Follow the example.

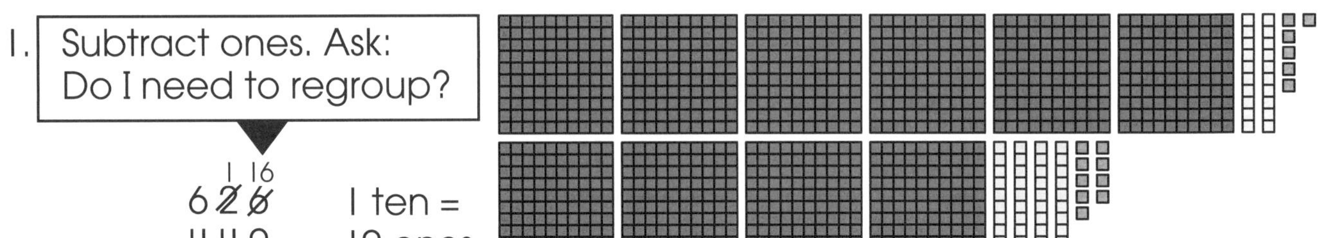

1. Subtract ones. Ask:
Do I need to regroup?
1 16
626
– 449
1 ten =
10 ones

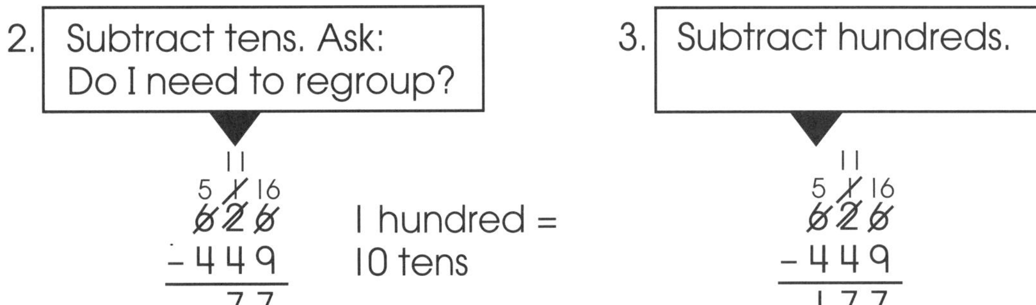

hundreds	tens	ones	hundreds	tens	ones	hundreds	tens	ones
4	3	5	7	4	8	8	4	2
– 3	6	8	– 5	6	9	– 5	9	9

Write the value of the underlined digit. The first one is done for you.

346 300   555 ______   68 ______

268 ______   555 ______   861 ______

190 ______   555 ______   404 ______

Make the words at the end of each line into a **contraction** to complete the sentence.

1. He ____________ know the answer. **did not**

2. ____________ a long way home. **It is**

3. ____________ my house. **Here is**

4. ____________ not going to school today. **We are**

5. ____________ take the bus home tomorrow. **They will**

Leave is a special verb that does not follow the patterns you know. Its **past-tense form** does not end with **ed**. The past tense of **leave** is **left**. Write **leave** or **left** to complete the sentences.

1. Last winter, we ____________ seeds in the bird feeder every day.

2. My mother likes to ____________ food out for the squirrels.

3. When it snows, we ____________ bread for the birds.

4. Yesterday, Mom ____________ popcorn for the animals.

Use a ruler to measure each item to the nearest **centimeter**. Answer the questions.

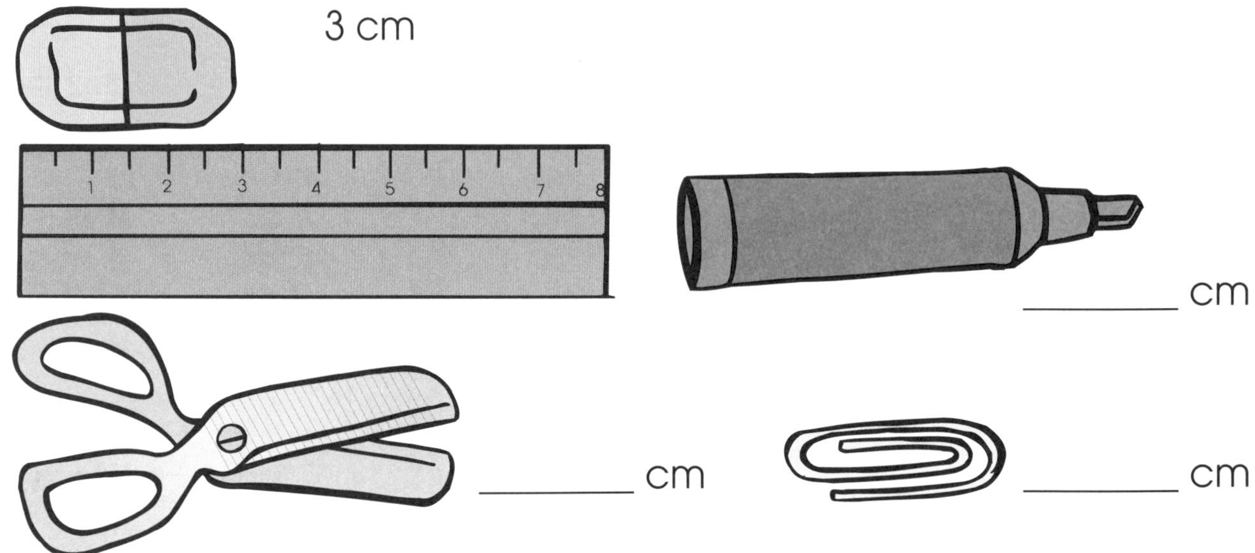

How much shorter is the paper clip than the scissors? ______ cm

How much longer is the marker than the eraser? ______ cm

Write each word that includes a **suffix** beside its meaning. Then, use the numbered letters to find the missing word.

cheerful
safely
speechless
amazement
peaceful
excitement

1. in a safe way ___ ___ ___ ___ ___ ___ (letter 2 is numbered 6)
2. full of cheer ___ ___ ___ ___ ___ ___ ___ ___ (letter 5 is numbered 2)
3. full of peace ___ ___ ___ ___ ___ ___ ___ ___ (letter 2 is numbered 4)
4. state of being amazed ___ ___ ___ ___ ___ ___ ___ ___ ___ (letter 6 is numbered 5)
5. state of being excited ___ ___ ___ ___ ___ ___ ___ ___ ___ ___ (letter 5 is numbered 1)
6. without speech ___ ___ ___ ___ ___ ___ ___ ___ ___ ___ (letter 9 is numbered 3)

You are now on your way to becoming a

___ ___ ___ ___ ___ ___ of suffixes!
5 6 3 1 4 2

Subtract by regrouping. Follow the example.

Step 1: Regroup ones if needed.
Step 2: Subtract ones.
Step 3: Regroup tens if needed.
Step 4: Subtract tens.
Step 5: Subtract hundreds.

hundreds	tens	ones
	5	12
4	~~6~~	~~2~~
− 2	5	3
2	0	9

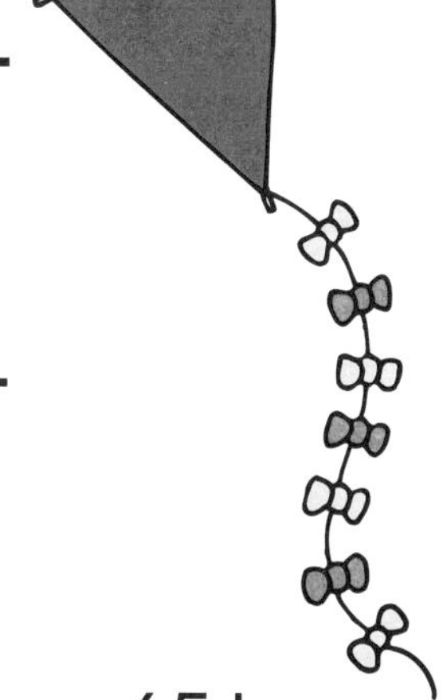

$$\begin{array}{r} 423 \\ -\ 144 \\ \hline \end{array} \qquad \begin{array}{r} 562 \\ -\ 349 \\ \hline \end{array} \qquad \begin{array}{r} 478 \\ -\ 239 \\ \hline \end{array} \qquad \begin{array}{r} 651 \\ -\ 333 \\ \hline \end{array}$$

Find and correct three misspelled words in the letter. Write **commas** inside the boxes to complete the **greeting** and **closing**.

Dear Principal Baylor☐

Pleese come to our class art show on Friday aftur lunch. You will see paintings, drawings, and sculptures. You will be amazd at what we have made. We hope you can come.

Sincerely☐
Room 38

Find the sum of the numbers on the trains. Regroup as needed.

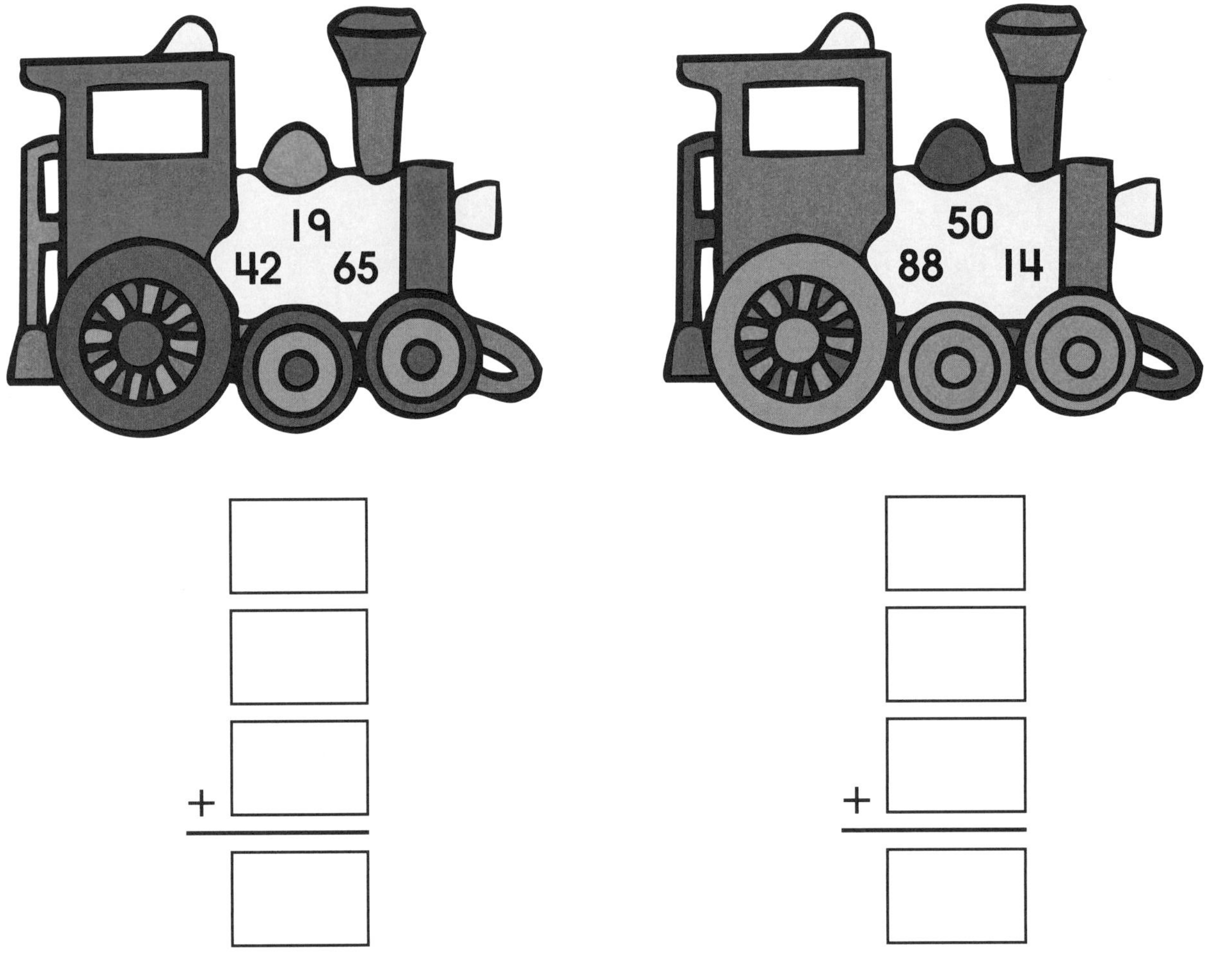

Write the value of the underlined digit. The first one is done for you.

888 800	250 ______	458 ______
221 ______	690 ______	600 ______
69 ______	820 ______	212 ______

Read all the sentences. Then, choose the best **verb** to complete each sentence.

whispered	**stated**	**boasted**	**exclaimed**

1. My uncle ______________ about his new car.

2. During the concert, I ______________ to my sister.

3. Ms. Hu ______________ that the field trip will be on Friday.

4. The kids ______________ when they heard the ice cream truck.

Circle two misspelled words in each sentence. Write the correct spellings on the lines.

1. You hav stired the soup too much.

   ______________ ______________

2. We tryed to be as neet as possible.

   ______________ ______________

3. She cannot sea in the darknes.

   ______________ ______________

4. Wayt for us to joine you!

   ______________ ______________

Connect the dots to make each shape. Not all dots will be used.

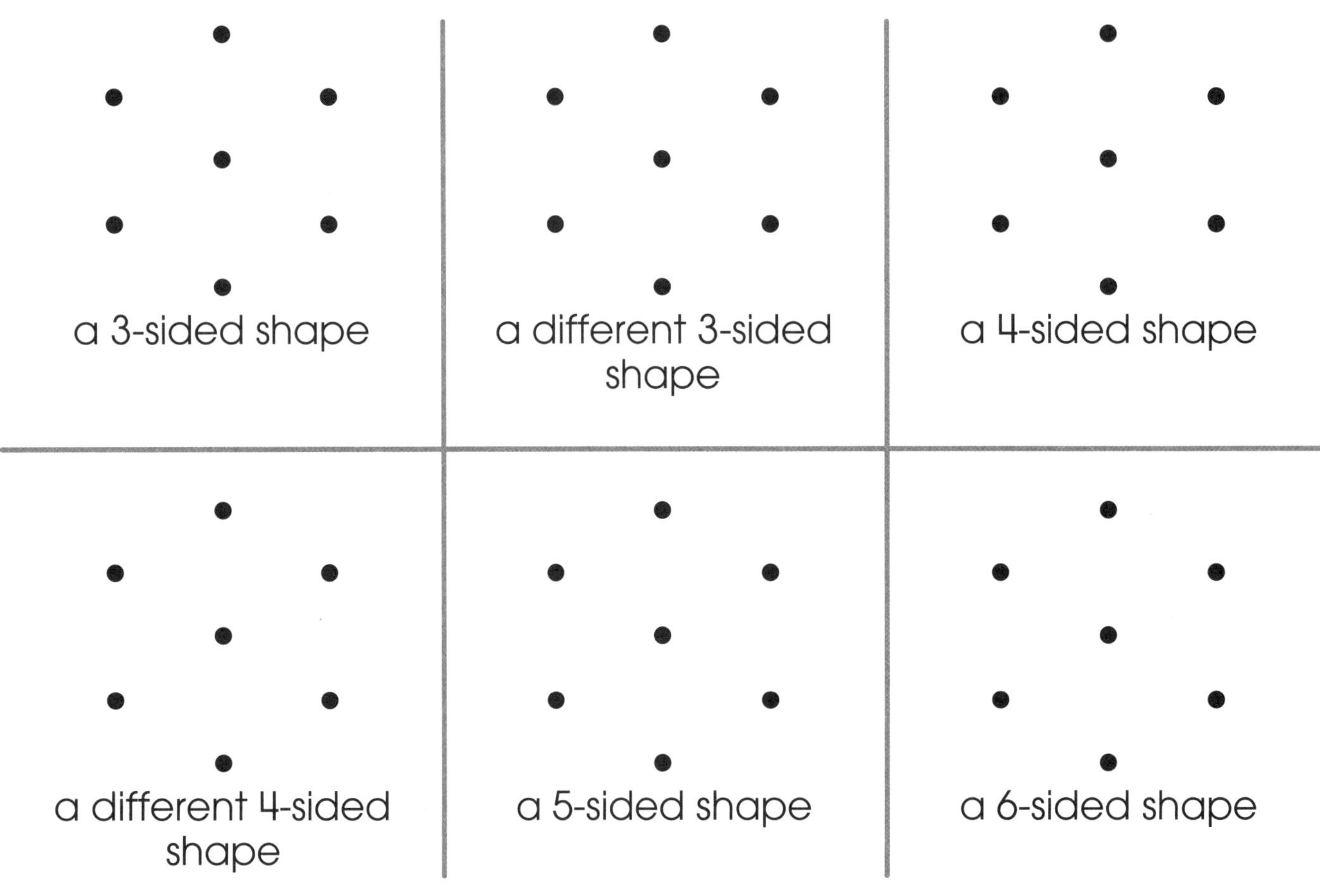

Look at the **bold** verb in the first sentence. Write the correct form of the same present-tense verb to match the **collective noun** in the second sentence.

1. We **cheer** for every batter.

   Our team ________________ loudly.

2. Bruno and Sari **wait** for the play to begin.

   The whole audience ________________ patiently.

3. My sisters **play** hide-and-seek well.

   Our family ________________ together often.

4. The students in this class **have** gym in the afternoon.

   Our class ________________ a great time during gym!

Add by **regrouping**. Follow the example.

Step 1: Add the ones.
Step 2: Add the tens.
Step 3: Add the hundreds.

hundreds	tens	ones
1	1	
3	4	8
+ 4	5	4
8	0	2

$$\begin{array}{r} 348 \\ +\ 214 \\ \hline \end{array} \qquad \begin{array}{r} 172 \\ +\ 418 \\ \hline \end{array} \qquad \begin{array}{r} 575 \\ +\ 329 \\ \hline \end{array} \qquad \begin{array}{r} 623 \\ +\ 268 \\ \hline \end{array}$$

Write a word in each blank to match the **part of speech** shown.

I went for a ____________ (noun). I found a really big ____________ (noun).

It was so ____________ (adjective) that I ____________ (verb) all the

way home. I put it in my ____________ (noun). To my amazement, it

began to ____________ (verb). I ____________ (past-tense verb). I took it to my

____________ (noun). I showed it to all my ____________ (plural noun).

− [ ] [1] [0] + [ ] [1] [0]

What is 10 less than the number? What is 10 more than the number?

_____ , 463, _____ _____ , 16, _____

_____ , 299, _____ _____ , 54, _____

− [1] [0] [0] + [1] [0] [0]

What is 100 less than the number? What is 100 more than the number?

_____ , 290, _____ _____ , 560, _____

_____ , 789, _____ _____ , 103, _____

Some special verbs do not follow the patterns you know. Their **past-tense forms** do not end with **ed**. Write the past-tense form of each verb. The first one is done for you.

Present	Past
hear, hears	heard
draw, draws	
do, does	
give, gives	
sell, sells	

Use the **compound words** to answer the questions.

fireplace	**blueberry**	**classroom**
pigpen	**bookcase**	**beehive**

1. a case for books? ______________________
2. a berry that is blue? ______________________
3. a hive for bees? ______________________
4. a place for fires? ______________________
5. a pen for pigs? ______________________
6. a room for a class? ______________________

Match the amount in each purse to a price tag.

Subtract. Regroup as needed. Draw a line to the kite with the correct answer. Color the kites.

347	144	963	762	287	427
− 218	− 135	− 748	− 553	− 179	− 398

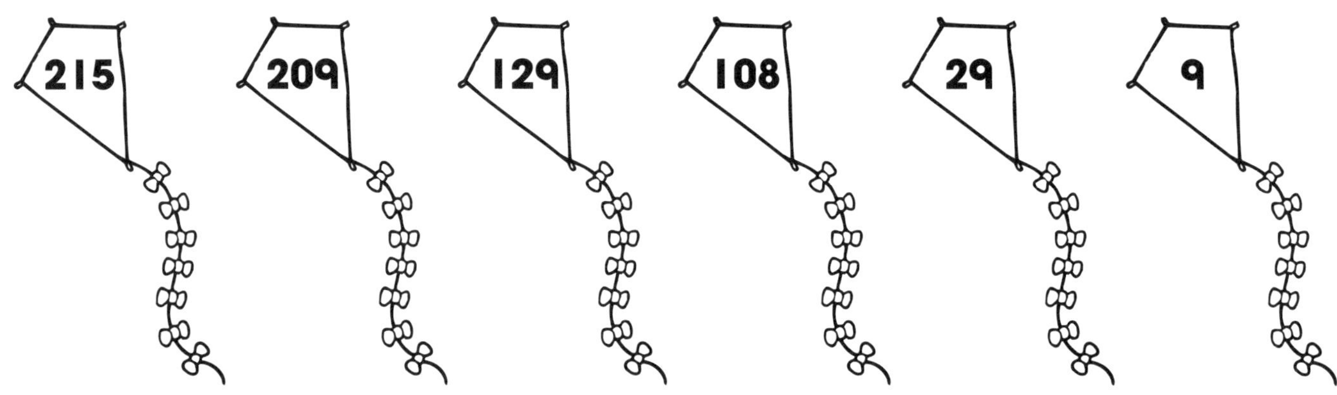

Write each number in **expanded form**. The first one is done for you.

Hundreds	Tens	Ones
4	3	0
400	30	0
430 = 400 + 30 + 0		

1. 547 = 500 + 40 + 7

2. 222 = ________ + ________ + ________

3. 956 = ________ + ________ + ________

4. 563 = ________ + ________ + ________

Read the story. Answer the questions.

Ants are insects. Ants live in many parts of the world and make their homes in soil, sand, wood, and leaves. Most ants live for about 6 to 10 weeks. But the queen ant, who lays the eggs, can live for up to 15 years!

The largest ant is the bulldog ant. This ant can grow to be 5 inches long, and it eats meat! The bulldog ant can be found in Australia.

1. Where do ants make their homes? ______________________

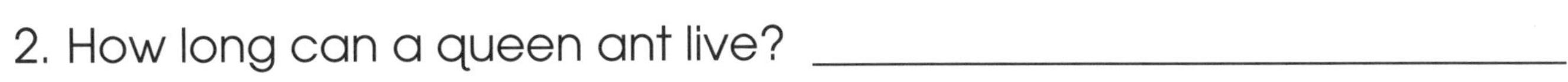

2. How long can a queen ant live? ______________________

____

3. What is the largest ant? ______________________

4. What does it eat? ______________________

Combine **root words** on the eggs with **suffixes** on the baskets. Write the new words on the lines.

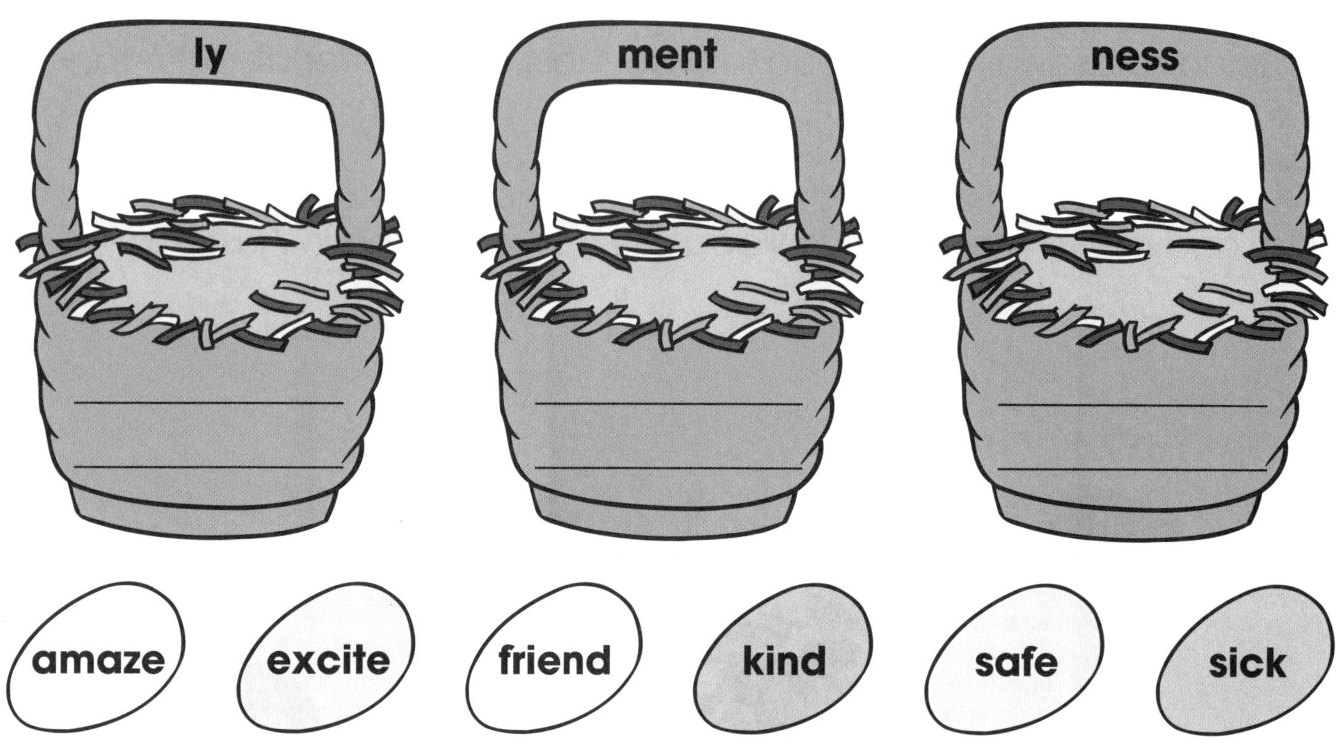

Solve the word problems.

1. The library loaned 56 books in the morning, 82 books in the afternoon, and 99 books in the evening. How many books did the library loan in all that day? ________ books

2. A website had 16 visitors with ages under 12, 49 visitors with ages 13 to 25, and 38 visitors with ages 26 and older. How many visitors did the website have in all? ________ visitors

Use the **bar graph** to answer the questions.

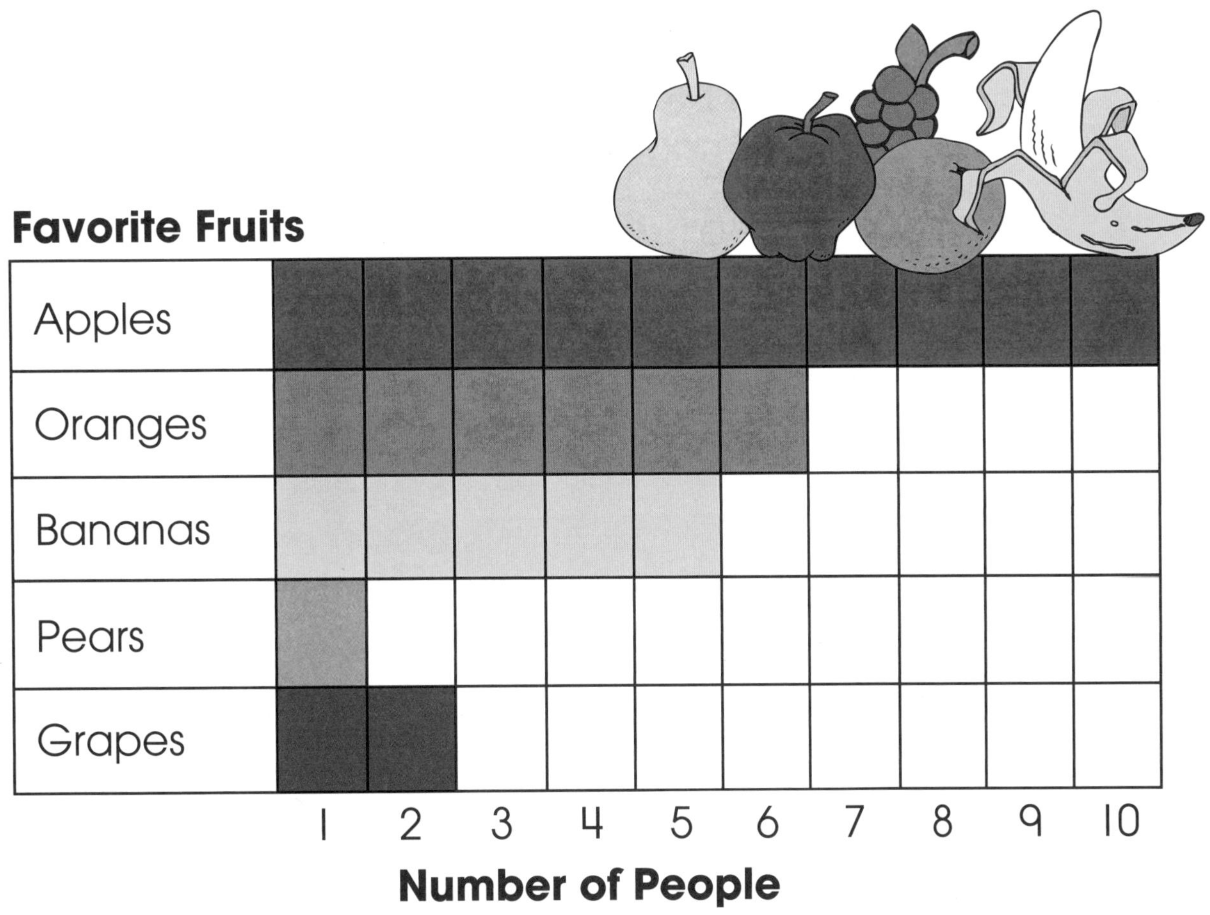

1. Which was the favorite fruit? ______________________

2. Which was the least favorite fruit? ______________________

3. How many more people picked bananas than pears? ____________

4. How many fewer people chose pears than grapes? ____________

5. Which fruit was chosen by 6 people? ______________________

Add by **regrouping**. Follow the example.

Add the ones. Regroup.		Add the tens. Regroup.		Add the hundreds.
1 156 + 267 3	6 + 7 13	1 5 + 6 12	11 156 + 267 23	1 156 + 267 423

162 + 349	273 + 198	655 + 297	783 + 148

Divide the rectangle into eight **columns** and three **rows**.

How many squares are in the rectangle? ________

Divide the rectangle into four columns and two rows.

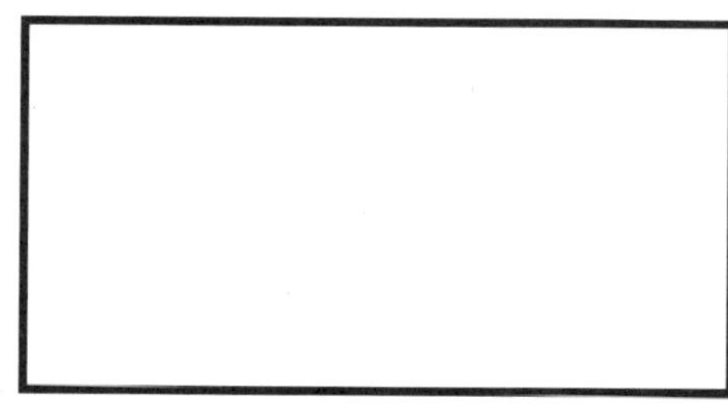

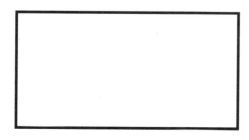

How many squares are in the rectangle? ________

Write a **contraction** that combines the words on each set of balloons.

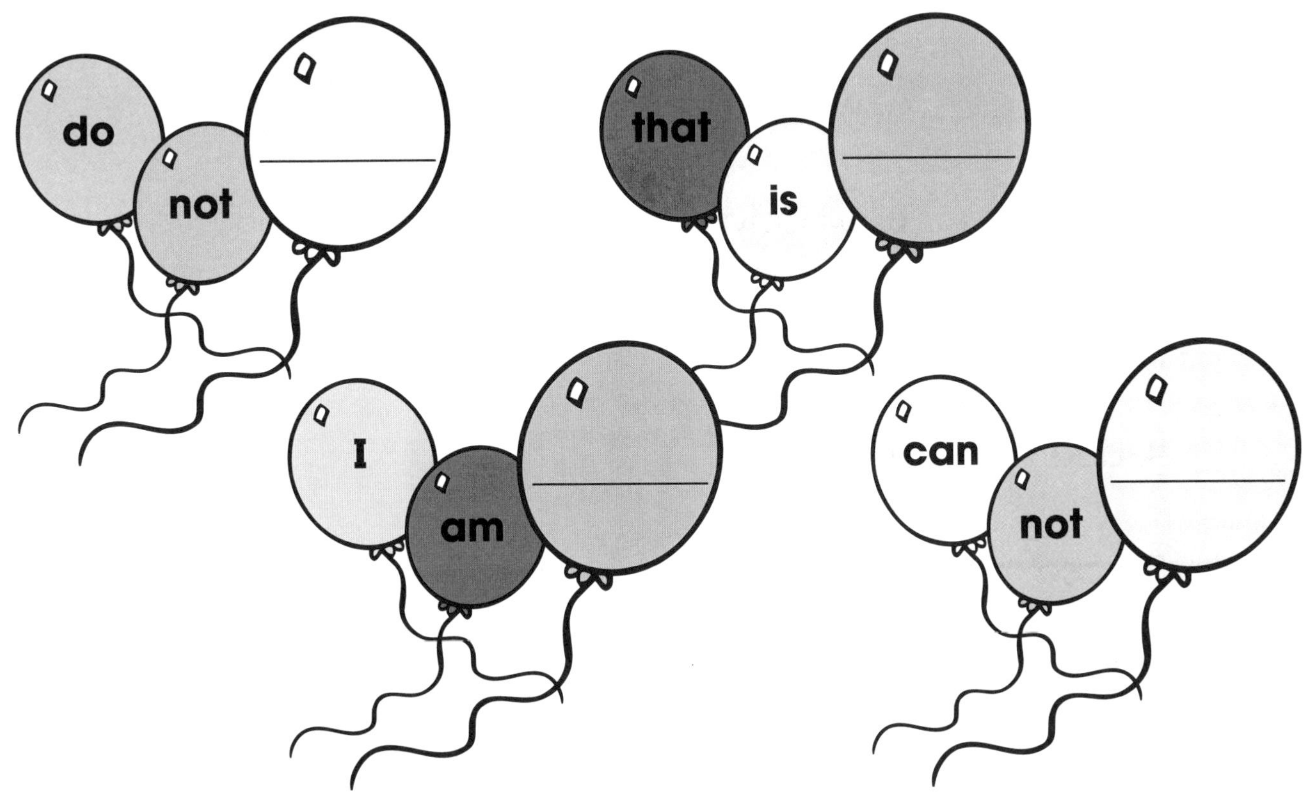

Circle six misspelled words in the story. Write the correct spellings on the lines.

One day, Peter and I were sitting on a bench at the park. A polise woman came and sat in the empty spase beside us. "Have you seen a little dog with thik black fur?" she asked. She was very poolite. "Remember that dog?" I asked Peter. "He was just here!" Peter nodded. He was too shie to say aneething.

________________ ________________

________________ ________________

________________ ________________

Write the letter of the best definition for each **homophone**.

________	1. bare	A. water droplets
________	2. bear	B. a body part used to smell
________	3. dew	C. a large furry animal with a short tail
________	4. due	D. something that is owed
________	5. nose	E. understands; to be certain of something
________	6. knows	F. naked; without any covering

Expand each sentence by adding words to explain why the event might have happened.

She hugged me because ________________________________

____.

We planned to go to the zoo because ________________________

____.

We clapped loudly because ___________________________

____.

Find the sum of the numbers on the trains. Regroup as needed.

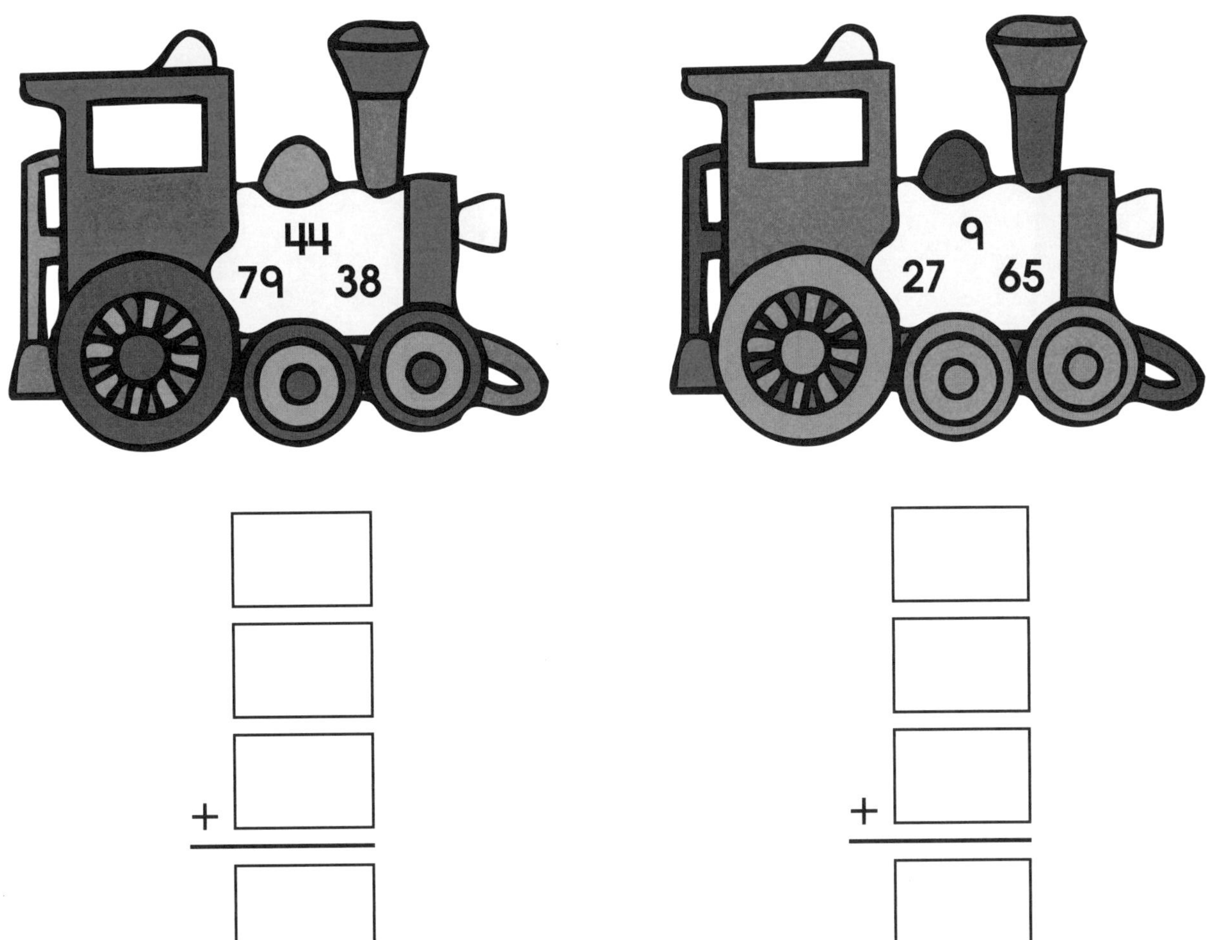

Write each number in **expanded form**. The first one is done for you.

1. **333**

300 + 30 + 3 = 333

2. **509**

_______ + _______ + _______ = 509

3. **826**

_______ + _______ + _______ = 826

4. **740**

_______ + _______ + _______ = 740

Use a ruler to measure each object to the nearest **centimeter**. Answer the question.

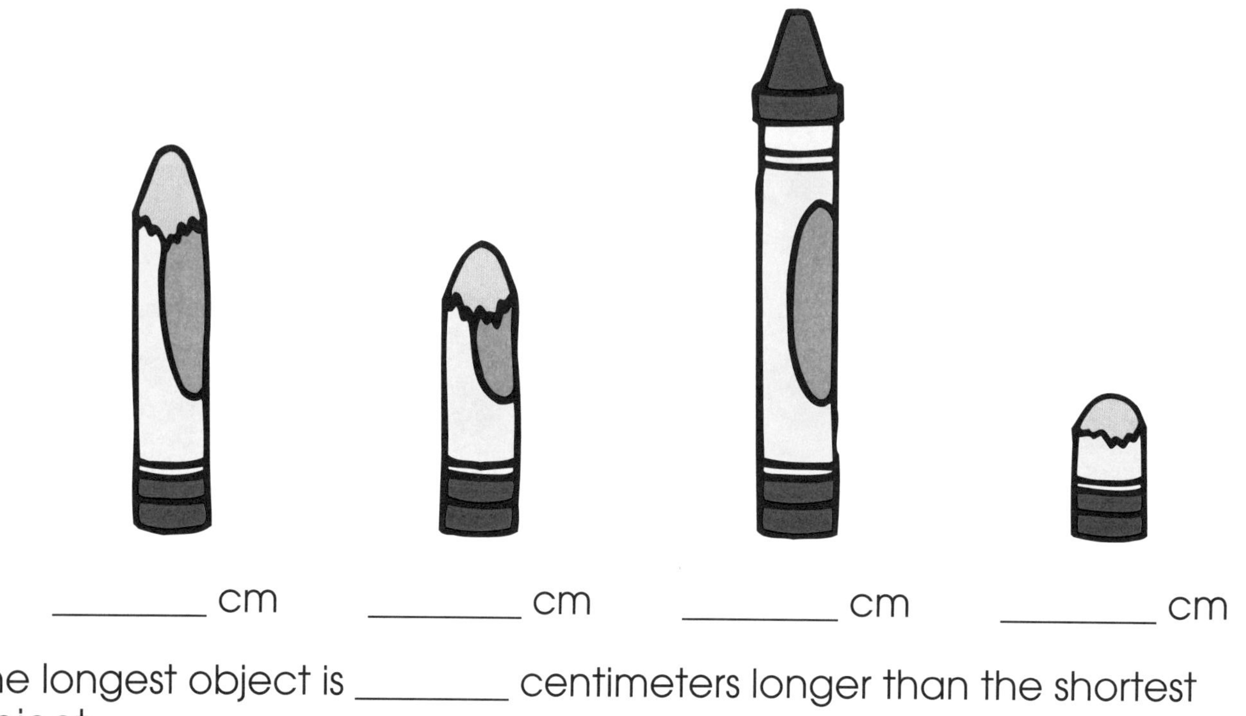

_______ cm _______ cm _______ cm _______ cm

The longest object is _______ centimeters longer than the shortest object.

Find and correct three misspelled words in the letter. Write **commas** inside the boxes to complete the **greeting** and **closing**.

Dear Yumtime Bakery☐

Thank yoo for the tour of your bakery. It was interesting to see how cookies and pies are mayd. My favorite part was watching the cake decorating. The cupcakes you gav us were delicious!

Best Wishes☐
Tori Gonzales

Combine **root words** on the eggs with **suffixes** on the baskets. Write the new words on the lines.

Subtract by **regrouping**. Circle the 9s that appear in the **ones** place.

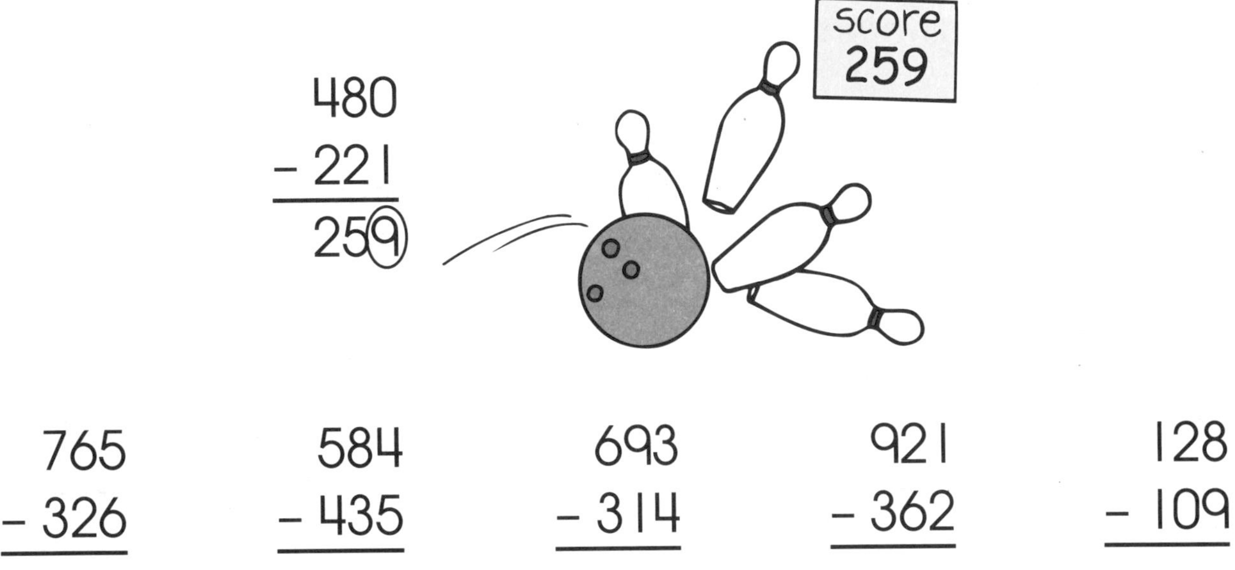

765	584	693	921	128
- 326	- 435	- 314	- 362	- 109

Combine each pair of sentences into one sentence. Choose the important word or words from the second sentence. Then, add them to the first sentence at the arrow.

1. I have a new ↓ skateboard.
   It is purple and black.

____

2. I am writing a ↓ letter to my cousin.
   It is a thank you letter.

____

3. I must study for my ↓ test.
   My test is in science.

____

The words name different **parts of speech**. Use them to label the words in the sentence.

adjective	**verb**	**preposition**	**article**	**noun**

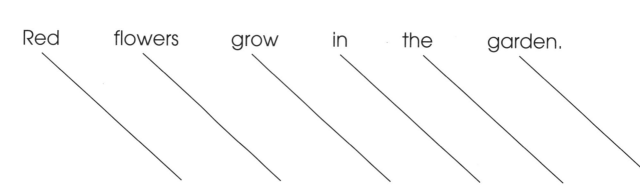

Red flowers grow in the garden.

- [ ] [1] [0]　　+ [ ] [1] [0]

What is 10 less than the number? What is 10 more than the number?

_____, 19, _____　　_____, 722, _____

_____, 68, _____　　_____, 456, _____

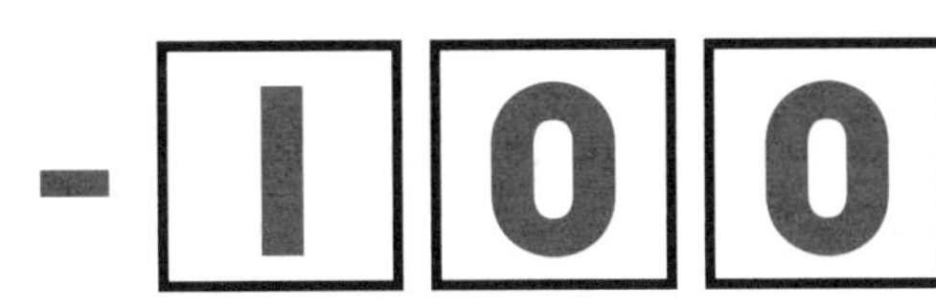

What is 100 less than the number? What is 100 more than the number?

_____, 111, _____　　_____, 658, _____

_____, 433, _____　　_____, 387, _____

Write the numbers that are:

next	**one less**	**one greater**
23, _____, _____	_____, 16	6, _____
674, _____, _____	_____, 247	125, _____
227, _____, _____	_____, 550	499, _____
199, _____, _____	_____, 333	750, _____
329, _____, _____	_____, 862	933, _____

Write a **contraction** that combines the words on each set of balloons.

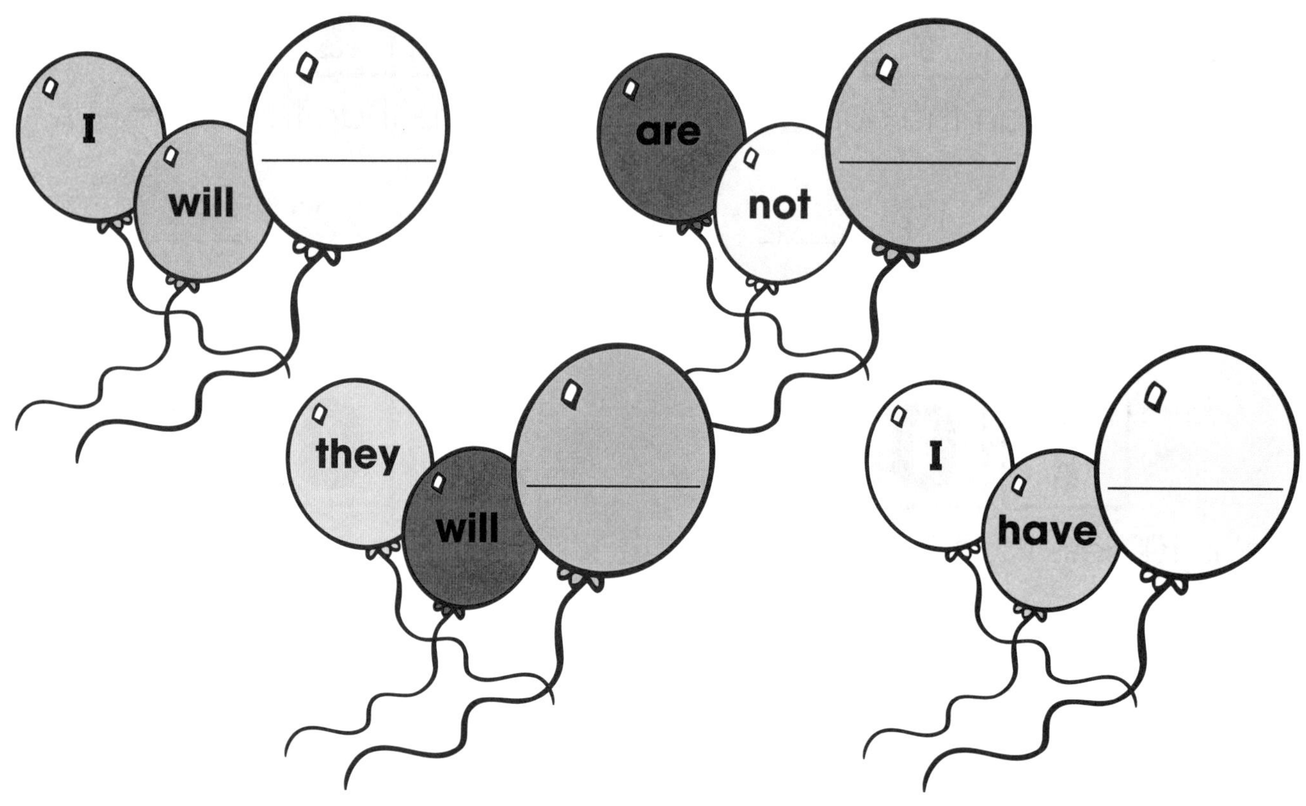

Use the **compound words** to answer the questions.

treetop	dishpan	sunburn
newspaper	broomstick	sailboat

1. a pan for dishes? ______________________
2. a boat to sail? ______________________
3. a paper for news? ______________________
4. a burn from the sun? ______________________
5. the top of a tree? ______________________
6. a stick for a broom? ______________________

Complete each addition square.

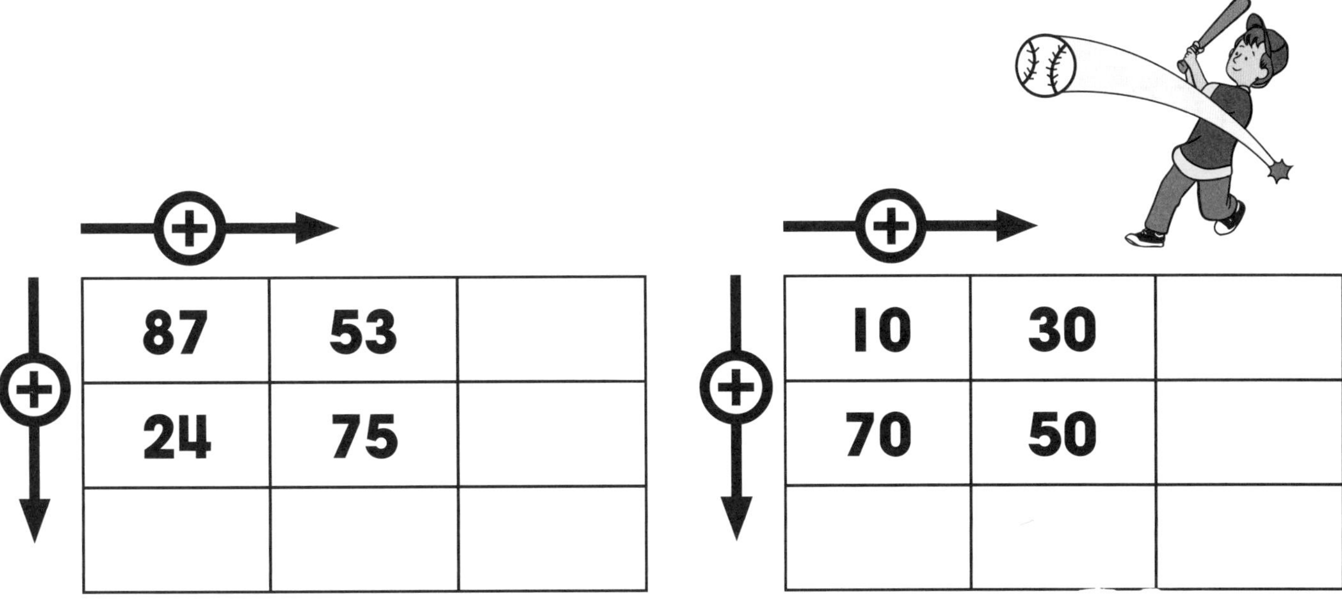

87	53	
24	75	

10	30	
70	50	

Find a die or a square block. Can you count six faces on the cube? Trace the lines that make up the **cube**. Then, copy the shape to draw a cube on your own.

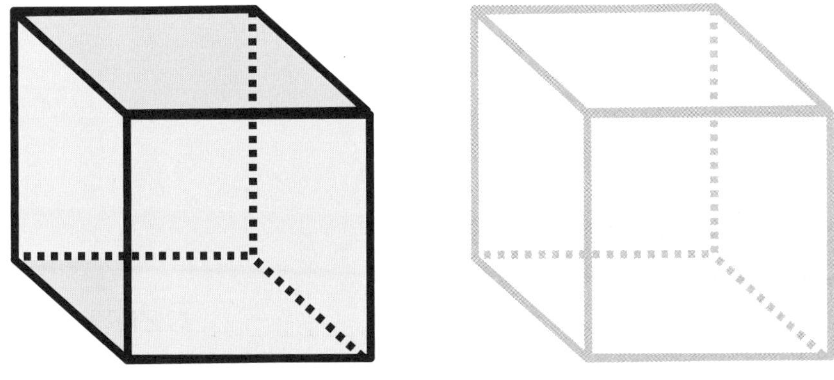

Write each number in **expanded form**. The first one is done for you.

1. **152**

   100 + 50 + 2 = 152

2. **750**

   ______ + ______ + ______ = 750

3. **249**

   ______ + ______ + ______ = 249

4. **900**

   ______ + ______ + ______ = 900

Solve the word problems.

1. A shop sold 62 scoops of vanilla ice cream, 48 scoops of chocolate ice cream, and 39 scoops of banana ice cream. How many scoops did the shop sell in all? ______ scoops

2. Ian bought a clamp for 49¢, wire for 86¢, and a switch for 72¢. How many cents did he spend in all? ______ cents

Read the directions for making clay. Answer the questions.

It is fun to work with clay. Here is what you need to make it:

1 cup salt

2 cups flour

$\frac{3}{4}$ cup water

Mix the salt and flour. Then, add the water. DO NOT eat the clay. It tastes bad. Use your hands to mix and mix. Now, roll it out. What can you make with your clay?

1. Circle the main idea:

   Do not eat clay.

   Mix salt, flour, and water to make clay.

2. Write the steps for making clay.

   a. ______________________________

   b. ______________________________

   c. Mix the clay.

   d. ______________________________

3. Write why you should not eat clay. ______________________________

   ____

Draw the coins you would use to buy each item at the bake sale.

Some special verbs do not follow the patterns you know. Their **past-tense forms** do not end with **ed**. Write the past-tense form of each verb. The first one is done for you.

Present	Past
come, comes	came
fly, flies	
build, builds	
know, knows	
bring, brings	

Subtract. Follow the example. Then, use the code to color the flowers.

```
  647
- 453
  194
```

Steps:

1. Subtract ones.
2. Subtract tens. Five tens cannot be subtracted from 4 tens.
3. Regroup tens by regrouping 6 hundreds (5 hundreds + 10 tens).
4. Add the 10 tens to the four tens.
5. Subtract 5 tens from 14 tens.
6. Subtract the hundreds.

If the answer has:
1 one, color it **red**.
8 ones, color it **pink**.
5 ones, color it **yellow**.

Read each **suffix** and its meaning. Then, write a word you know that uses the suffix. The first one is done for you.

Suffix	**Meaning**	
er	someone who	painter
ful	full of	______
less	without	______
ed	happened in the past	______
ly	like	______

Add. Color the boxes with 5 in the sum to help the dog find its way home.

	658 + 293	768 + 54	29 + 572	317 + 74	259 + 47
189 + 91	495 + 26	194 + 63			
215 + 276	270 + 160	168 + 429			

Write each number in **expanded form**. The first one is done for you.

Hundreds	Tens	Ones
6	2	4
600	20	4
624 = 600 + 20 + 4		

1. 815 = 800 + 10 + 5
2. 549 = ___ + ___ + ___
3. 626 = ___ + ___ + ___
4. 108 = ___ + ___ + ___

Read the sentences. Circle the **nouns**. Draw a box around the **verbs**. Underline the **adjectives**.

1. The children saw a black cloud in the sky.
2. Rain fell from the enormous black cloud.
3. Lightning flashed and thunder crashed.
4. The rain made puddles on the ground.
5. Moving cars splashed water.
6. The children raced into the house.

Use the **picture dictionary** to answer the questions.

baby

A very young child.

band

A group of people who play music.

bank

A place where money is kept.

bark

The sound a dog makes.

berry

A small, juicy fruit.

board

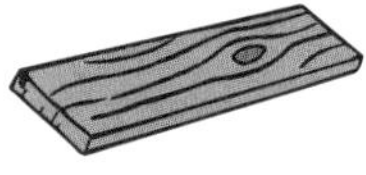

A flat piece of wood.

1. What is a small, juicy fruit? ___________________________
2. What is a group of people who play music? ___________________________
3. What is the name for a very young child? ___________________________
4. What is a flat piece of wood called? ___________________________

Solve the word problems.

1. Mike has 40 cents. Lynette has 23 cents. How much more money does Lynette need to have as much money as Mike? ________¢

   If she had the same amount as Mike, how much money would they have altogether? ________¢

   Does Mike have enough money to buy a ball for 50¢? ________

2. Count to 12. Now, count back 3, up 2, back 8, and up 4. What number do you have now? ________

Subtract to take a ride around the wheel.

Solve mentally. Write the answers quickly.

159	862	624	18	248
− 10	+ 100	− 100	+ 10	− 10
752	98	475	69	861
+ 10	+ 100	− 100	− 10	+ 10

One dollar equals 100 cents. It is written $1.00.

Count the money and write the amounts.

 $\_\_.\_\_\_$

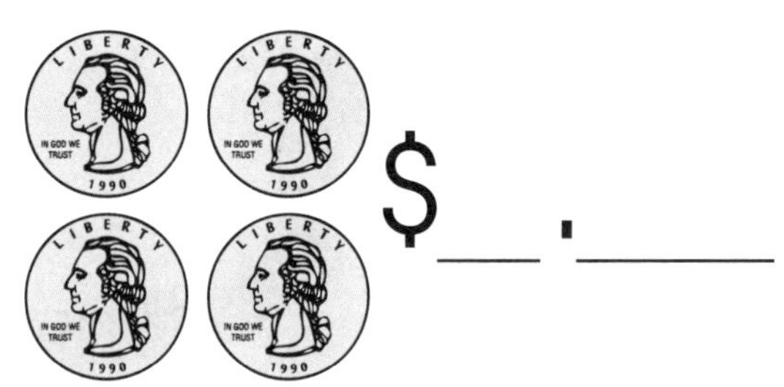 $\_\_.\_\_\_$

 $\_\_.\_\_\_$

 $\_\_.\_\_\_$

Read how to make a pencil holder. Then, follow the instructions.

You can use "junk" to make a pencil holder! First, you need a clean can with one end removed. Make sure there are no sharp edges. Then, you need glue, scissors, and paper. Find colorful paper such as wrapping paper, wallpaper, or construction paper. Cut the paper to fit the can. Glue the paper around the can. Decorate your can with glitter, buttons, and stickers. Then, put your pencils inside!

Write **first**, **second**, **third**, **fourth**, **fifth**, **sixth**, and **seventh** to put the steps in order.

________________ Make sure there are no sharp edges.

________________ Get glue, scissors, and paper.

________________ Cut the paper to fit the can.

________________ Put your pencils in the can!

________________ Glue colorful paper to the can.

________________ Remove one end of a clean can.

________________ Decorate the can with glitter and stickers.

Help the frog hop home. If you can add **ed** or **ing** to a word, color the lily pad **green**.

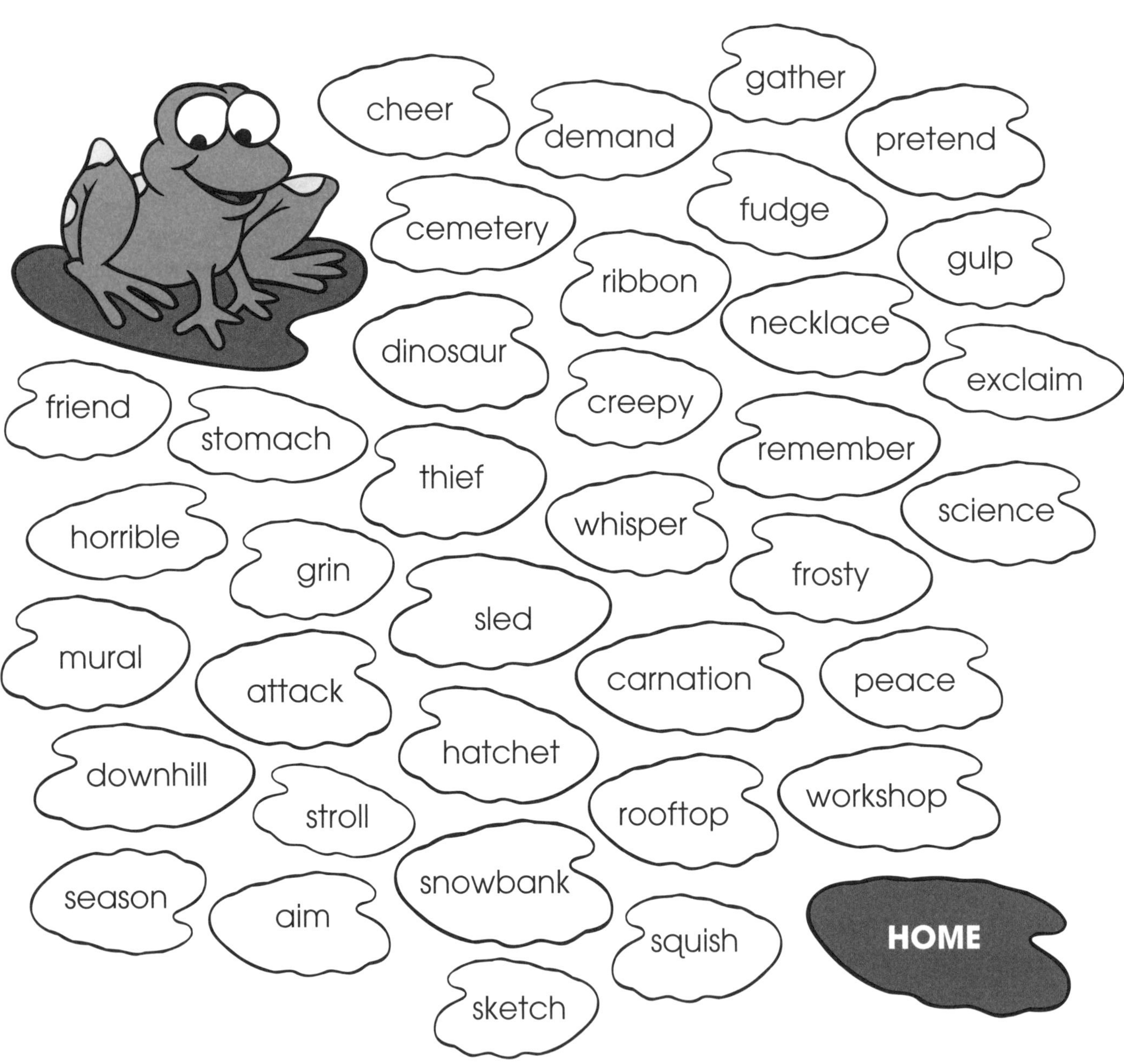

This is certainly a frog of action. All the words it hopped on are...

____________________!

Synonyms are words with similar meanings. Write a synonym for each word on a flowerpot.

afraid	start
fall	hard
scream	kind

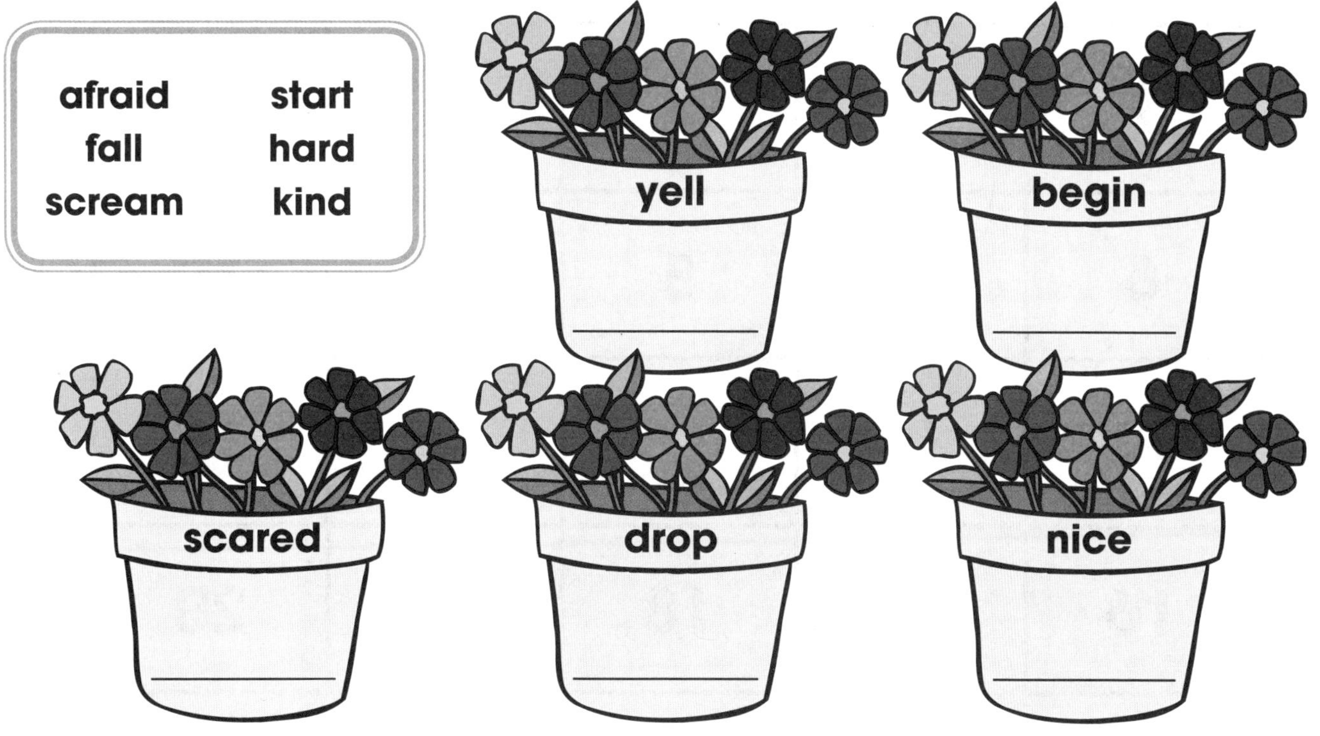

Fill in the chart to show each number in **expanded form**.

Hundreds	Tens	Ones	Number
___ ___ ___	+ 20	+ ___	= 5___4
300	+ 60	+ 6	= ___ ___ ___
___ ___ ___	+ ___ ___	+ ___	= 399
500	+ ___ ___	+ ___	= ___78

Color the boxes with **even** numbers.

1	2	3	4	5
6	7	8	9	10
11	12	13	14	15
16	17	18	19	20

A **quadrilateral** is a shape with four sides. Color the quadrilaterals to match the key.

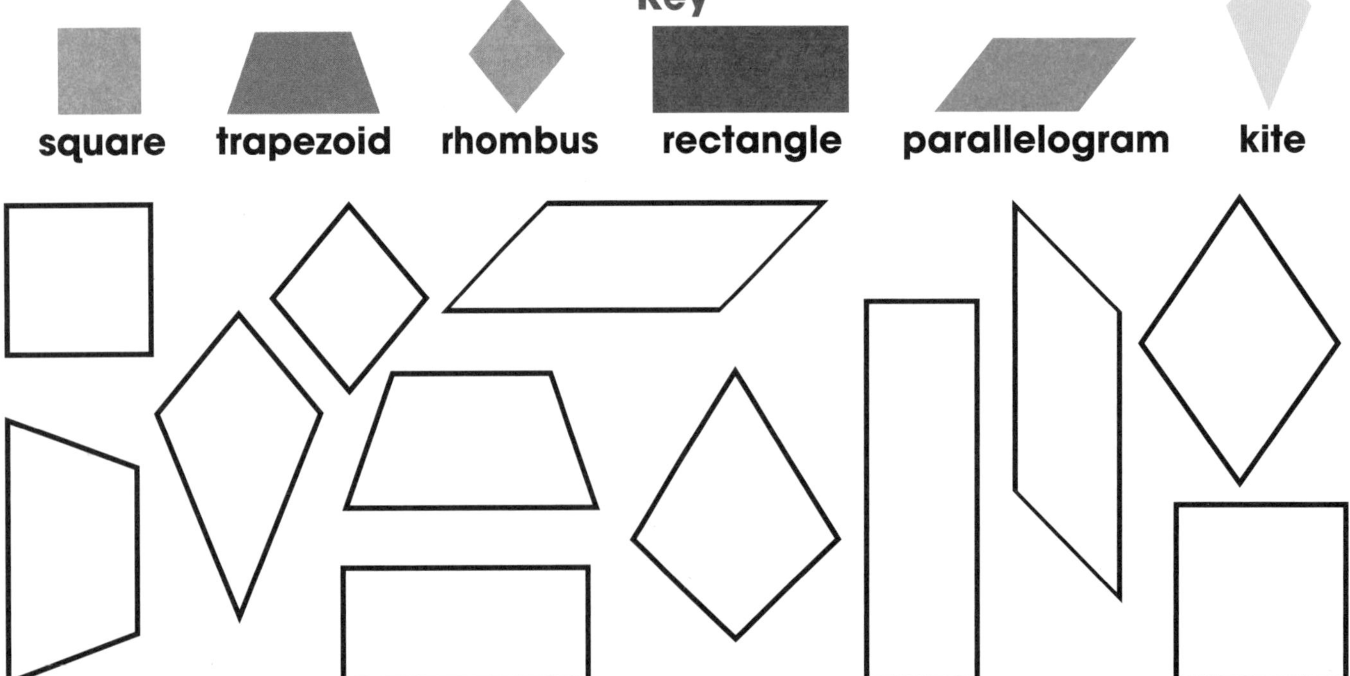

The **subject** of a sentence tells who or what does something. It contains at least one noun. Underline the subject of each sentence. The first one is done for you.

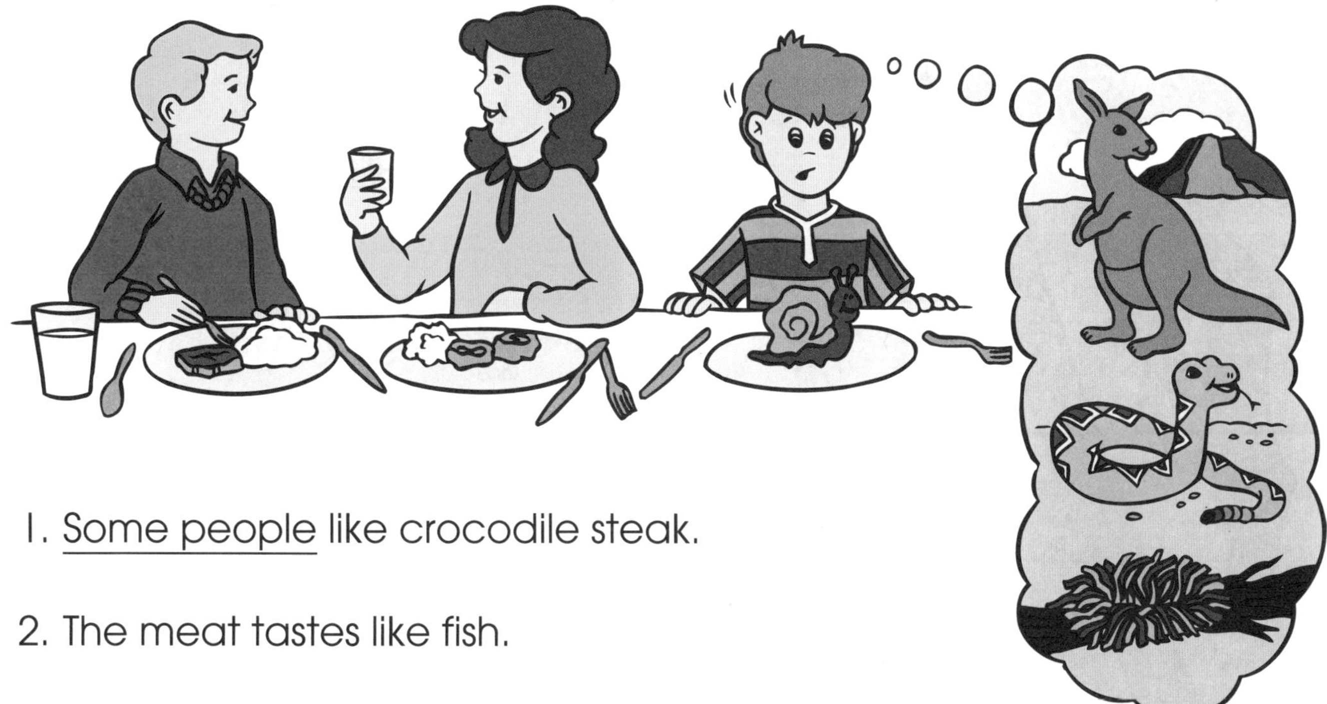

1. <u>Some people</u> like crocodile steak.
2. The meat tastes like fish.
3. Australians eat kangaroo meat.
4. Kangaroo meat tastes like beef.
5. People in the Southwest eat rattlesnake meat.
6. Snails make a delicious treat for some people.
7. Some Africans think roasted termites are tasty.
8. Bird's nest soup is a famous Chinese dish.
9. People in Florida serve alligator meat.
10. Almost everyone treats themselves with ice cream.

Solve the problems to make the windows squeaky clean.

Every **sentence** must have at least two things: a **noun** that tells who or what is doing something and a **verb** that tells what the noun is doing. Add a noun or a verb to make a sentence. Write the sentence on the line with correct capitalization and punctuation.

1. brushes her dog every day

   ____

2. at the beach, we

   ____

3. reads books with me

   ____

4. in the morning, our class

   ____

Circle a misspelled word in each sentence. Write the correct spelling on the line.

1. Which team do you thick will win the game? ____________
2. The dentist filled the cavity in her toth. ____________
3. We will boff ride on the train. ____________
4. A baby kangaroo is about one itch long when it is born. ____________
5. There is an apple for eack person. ____________

Circle the correct **verb** to complete each sentence.

1. Scientists will try to (find, found) the cure.

2. Eric (brings, brought) his lunch to school yesterday.

3. Every day, Latasha (sings, sang) all the way home.

4. Jason (breaks, broke) the vase last night.

5. The ice had (freezes, frozen) in the tray.

Fill in the chart to show each number in **expanded form**.

Hundreds	Tens	Ones	Number
600	+ ___ ___	+ 9	= ___4___
800	+ 0	+ 8	= ___ ___ ___
___ ___ ___	+ 90	+ 0	= 3___ ___
600	+ ___ ___	+ 7	= ___4___

Read each **suffix** and its meaning. Then, write a word you know that uses the suffix. The first one is done for you.

Suffix	**Meaning**	
s	more than one	birds
able	able to do	______
ness	being like	______
ment	act or quality of	______
en	made of	______

Subtract. Color boxes with 3 in the answer to find a path to the cabin.

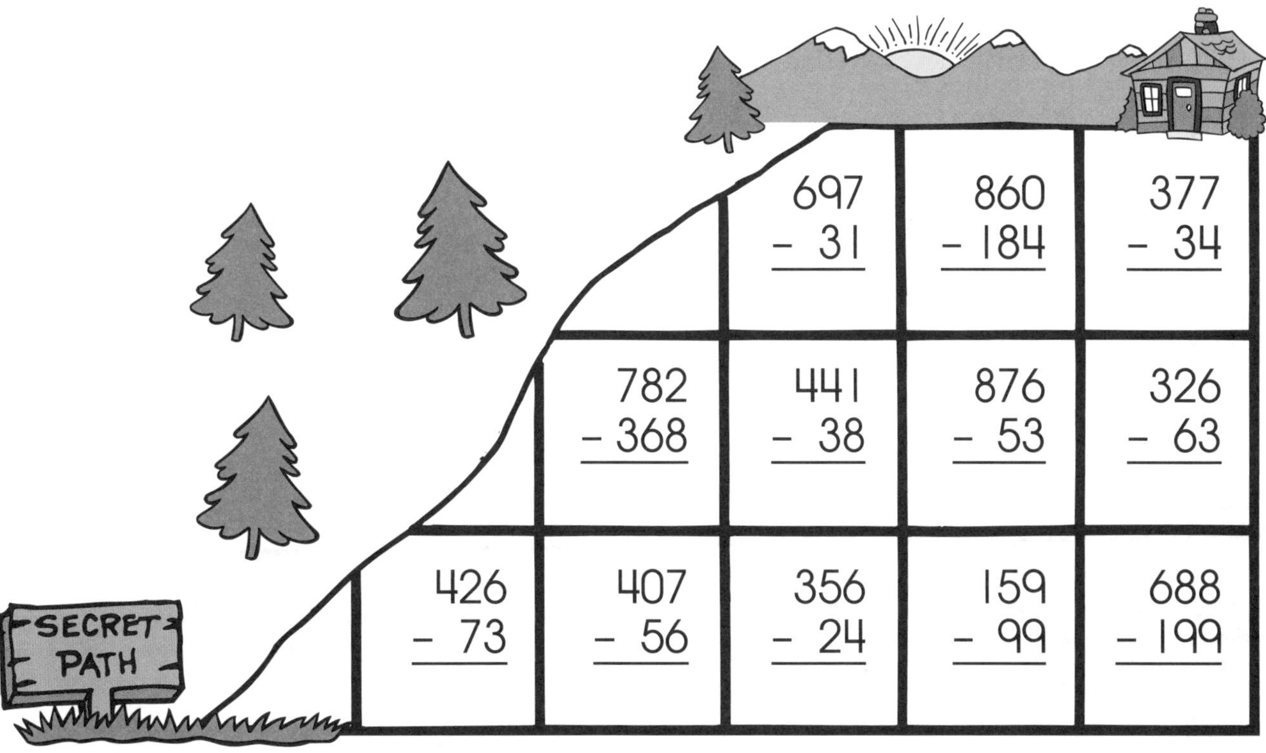

		697 − 31	860 − 184	377 − 34
	782 − 368	441 − 38	876 − 53	326 − 63
426 − 73	407 − 56	356 − 24	159 − 99	688 − 199

Read the **number names**. Write the numbers.

one hundred nineteen ____________

four hundred thirty-four ____________

nine hundred thirty ____________

sixty-six ____________

five hundred twenty-eight ____________

nine ____________

seventy-two ____________

three hundred fifty-seven ____________

One dollar equals 100 cents. It is written $1.00.

Count the money and write the amounts.

$__ . ____

$__ . ____

Use the **picture dictionary** to answer the questions.

safe

A metal box.

sea

A body of water.

seed

The beginning of a plant.

sheep

An animal that has wool.

skate

A shoe with wheels or a blade on it.

snowstorm

A time when much snow falls.

squirrel

A small animal with a bushy tail.

stone

A small rock.

store

A place where items are sold.

1. What kind of animal has wool? ______________________
2. What do you call a shoe with wheels on it? ______________________
3. When a lot of snow falls, what is it called? ______________________
4. What is a small animal with a bushy tail? ______________________
5. What is a place where items are sold? ______________________
6. When a plant starts, what is it called? ______________________

Color the boxes with **odd** numbers.

1	2	3	4	5
6	7	8	9	10
11	12	13	14	15
16	17	18	19	20

Every **sentence** must have at least two things: a **noun** that tells who or what is doing something and a **verb** that tells what the noun is doing. Add a noun or a verb to make a sentence. Write the sentence on the line with correct capitalization and punctuation.

1. the crowd at the beach

____

2. cost too much

____

3. kangaroos and their babies

____

4. was too thick to chew

____

Synonyms are words with similar meanings. Write a synonym for each word on a flowerpot.

hard	tired
dirt	close
put	whisper

Solve the word problems.

1. A clown started the day with 200 balloons. She gave away 128. Some broke. At the end of the day, she had 18 balloons left. How many balloons broke? ________ balloons

2. At a game booth, prizes were given for scoring 500 points in 3 tries. Serena scored 178 points on her first try, 149 points on her second try, and 233 points on her third try. Did Serena win a prize? ________

Insects are easy to tell apart from other animals. Adult insects have three body parts and six legs. The first body part is the **head**. On the head are the mouth, eyes, and antennae. The second body part is the **thorax**. On it are the legs and wings. The third part is the **abdomen**. On it are small openings for breathing.

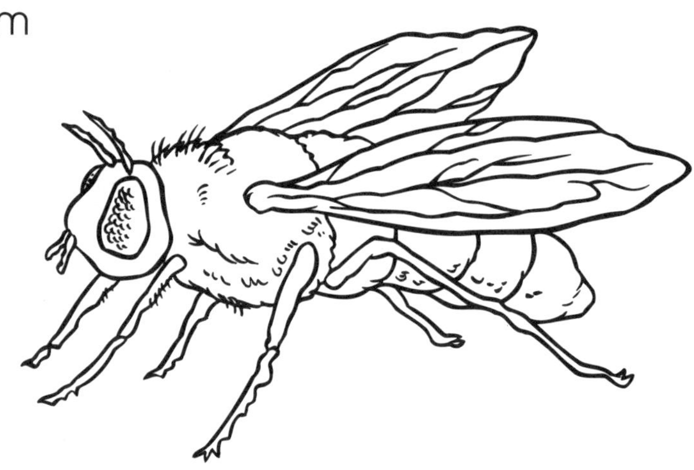

Color the body parts of the insect above.
head — **red**, thorax — **yellow**, abdomen — **blue**

Draw an insect below. Make your insect one-of-a-kind. Be sure it has the correct number of body parts, legs, wings, and antennae. Fill in the information below.

Insect's name: ____________________ Warning: ____________________

Length: ____________________ ____________________

Where found: ____________________ ____________________

Food: ____________________ ____________________

Add the numbers in the corners of each box. Write the sum in the center.

37		74
	______	
53		82

22		13
	______	
31		12

89		44
	______	
35		28

56		72
	______	
43		61

There are ________ rows of 4 mice.

There are ________ columns of 4 mice.

There are ________ mice altogether.

8 + ________ = 16

Complete the addition squares.

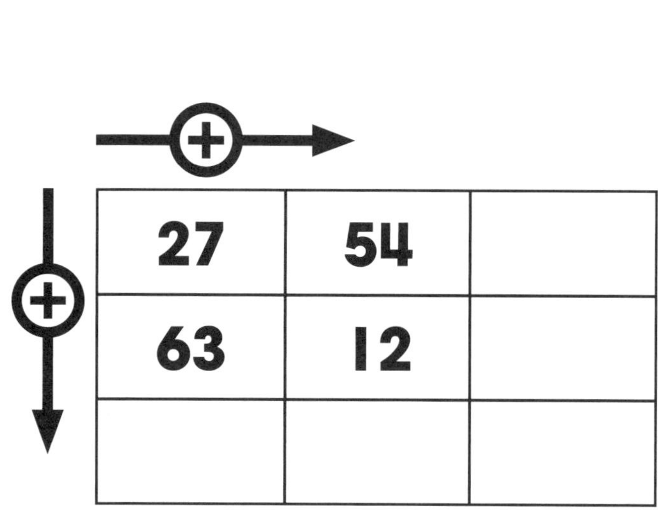

27	54	
63	12	

35	46	
73	94	

Circle a misspelled word in each sentence. Write the correct spelling on the line.

1. Theo had to chanj his clothes after he fell in the mud. ____________
2. What is that furry ting under the table? ____________
3. A star soccer player will teech us how to kick the ball. ____________
4. She wrote a letter to tank her grandmother for the gift. ____________
5. Mom helped the lost cilde find his mother. ____________

The pronouns **I**, **you**, **he**, **she**, **it**, **we**, and **they** are used in the **subject** of a sentence. They tell who or what is doing something. Rewrite the sentences, replacing the underlined words with subject pronouns.

1. Tommy hiked along the trail.

____

2. Jayden and Luis caught up with Tommy.

____

3. Rita met the boys at the trail's end.

____

4. The boys ate their lunches under a tree.

____

Draw or write what comes next in each pattern.

0 2 0 4 0 6 

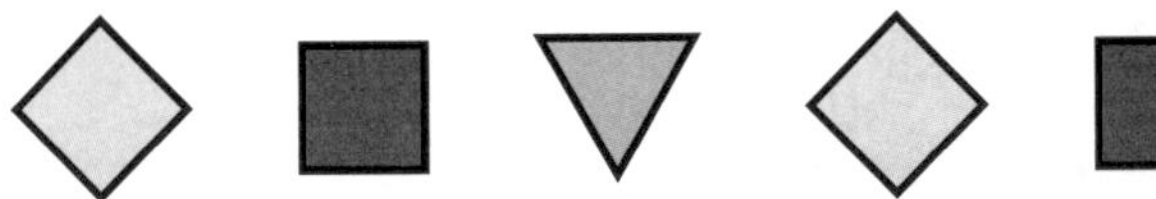  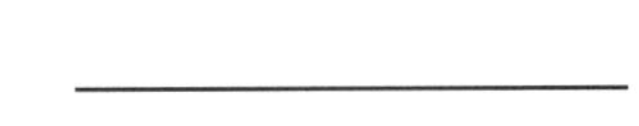

A B C 1 2 3 A ____________

Subtract. Complete the crossword puzzle with your answers.

Across

2. 517 − 228

3. 428 − 249

4. 562 − 274

5. 924 − 348

6. 923 − 346

7. 535 − 248

8. 857 − 389

9. 561 − 247

11. 845 − 599

13. 325 − 186

14. 356 − 168

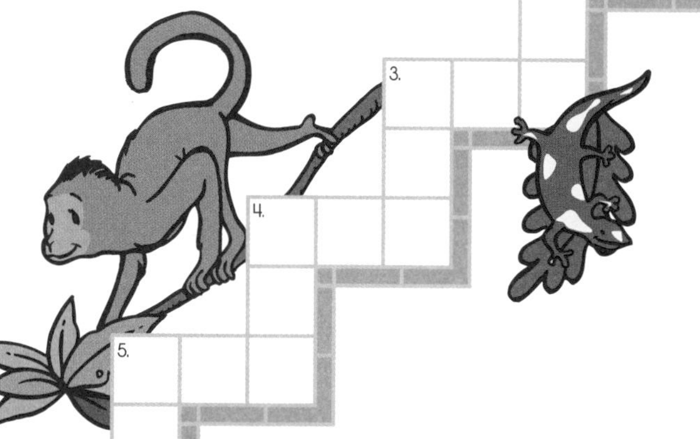

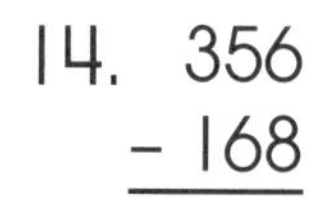

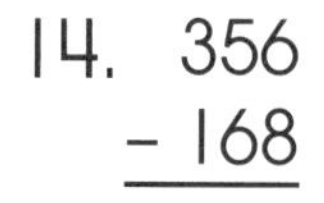

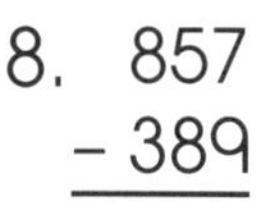

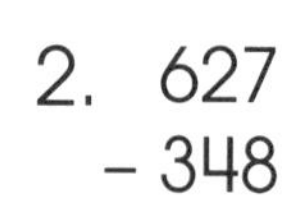

Down

1. 421 − 342

2. 627 − 348

3. 362 − 194

4. 582 − 346

5. 824 − 247

6. 921 − 346

7. 926 − 718

8. 721 − 240

10. 768 − 292

12. 826 − 337

13. 247 − 129

When a sentence has a **compound subject**, two or more subjects are joined by the word **and**. Look at the **bold** subject in each sentence. If the sentence has a compound subject, write **CS**. If it does not, write **No**. The first one is done for you.

No 1. **A predator** is an animal that eats other animals.

________ 2. **Prey** is eaten by predators.

________ 3. **Robins and bluejays** are predators.

________ 4. **Some predators** eat only meat.

________ 5. **Crocodiles and hawks** eat meat only.

________ 6. **Raccoons and foxes** eat both meat and plants.

Combine the subjects of the two sentences to make a compound subject. Write the new sentence on the line.

Snakes are predators. Spiders are predators.

____

Frogs prey on insects. Chameleons prey on insects.

____

Circle the correct **verb** to complete each sentence.

1. Lin (swims, swam) in that pool last summer.
2. Now I (choose, chose) to exercise daily.

3. The teacher (rings, rang) the bell.
4. The boss (speaks, spoke) to us yesterday.
5. She (says, said) it twice already.

Count the money. Write the amount. The first one is done for you.

$3.71

$__.___

$__.___

$__.___

Use the **picture dictionary** to answer the questions.

table

Furniture with legs and a flat top.

tail

A slender part that is on the back of an animal.

teacher

A person who teaches lessons.

ticket

A paper slip or card.

tiger

An animal with stripes.

1. Who is a person who teaches lessons? ____________________
2. What is the name of an animal with stripes? ____________________
3. What is a piece of furniture with legs and a flat top? ____________________
4. What is the definition of a ticket? ____________________

Draw lines to match the numbers and place value descriptions.

Hundreds	**Tens**	**Ones**
8	**5**	**2**

26	zero ones
568	two tens
4	one hundred
107	five hundreds
380	four ones

Combine the words with the **prefix** or **suffix**. Different combinations are possible. You may need to drop final **e** before adding the suffix **er**. Write the new words on the lines.

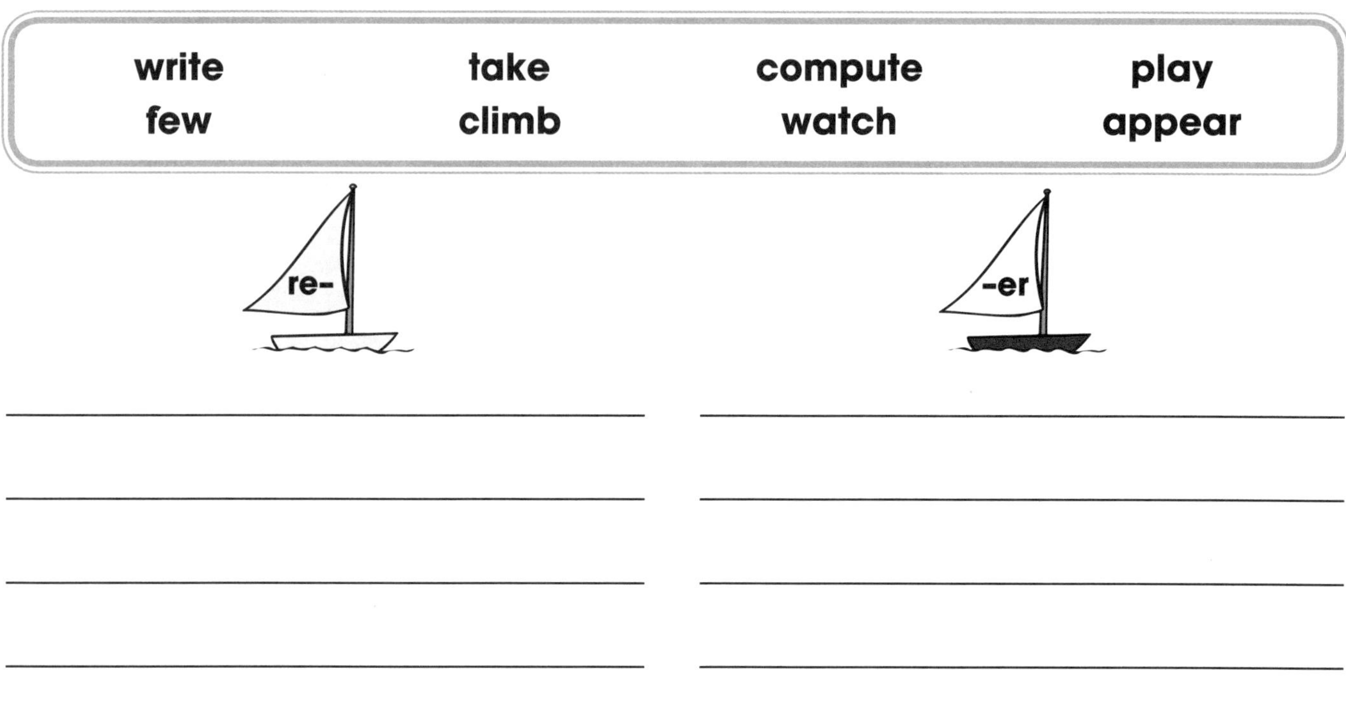

write
take
compute
play
few
climb
watch
appear
re-
-er

Solve the word problems.

1. It took 630 bricks to build the front wall of a house. The back wall took 725 bricks. How many more bricks were needed for the back wall? ________ bricks

2. The side walls of a house have a total of 934 bricks. If the garage has 168 fewer bricks, how many bricks are in the garage? ________ bricks

Read the **number names**. Write the numbers.

four hundred seven ____________

eight hundred ninety ____________

six hundred eighty-four ____________

thirty ____________

six hundred seventy-three ____________

twenty-nine ____________

one hundred sixty ____________

eight hundred eleven ____________

two hundred nine ____________

Rewrite each sentence, capitalizing the **proper nouns**.

1. martin luther king, jr. was born in atlanta, georgia.

   ____

2. In july, we went to canada.

   ____

3. kathy jones moved to utah in january.

   ____

4. My favorite holiday is hanukkah.

   ____

Draw lines to connect the matching **quadrilaterals**.

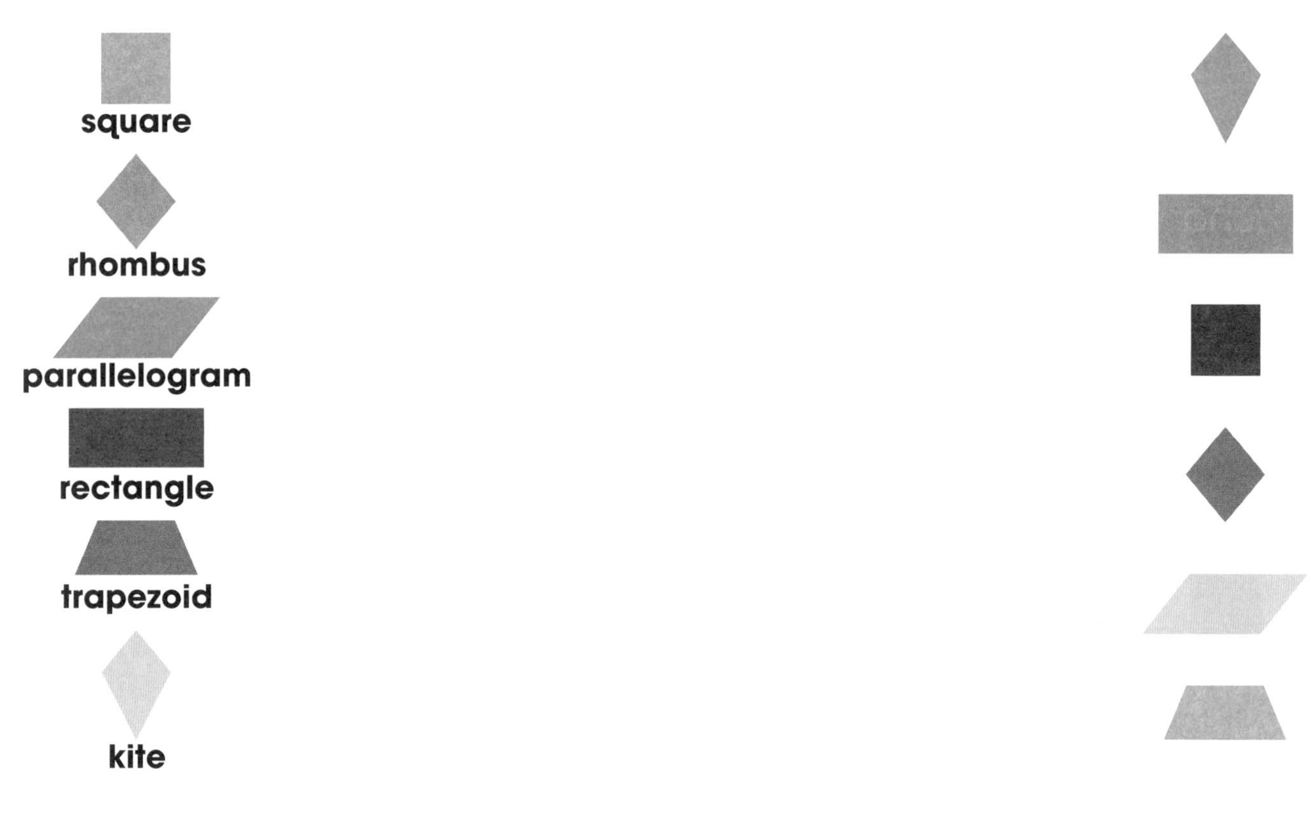

Find a pair of **synonyms** in each sentence. Write the words in the boxes.

That unusual clock is a rare antique.

I am glad you are so happy!

Becky felt unhappy when she heard the sad news.

The **subject** of each sentence is in **bold**. Write the subject pronoun (**he**, **she**, **it**, or **they**) that could replace it.

1. **Mary and David** took a walk in the park. ________
2. **Asya** spent the night at her grandmother's house. ________
3. **The baseball players** lost their game. ________
4. **Mike Van Meter** is a great soccer player. ________
5. **The parrot** can say five different words. ________

Circle the **even** numbers. Write the numbers you circled in the boxes after the equal sign. Then, write two equal addends for each sum. One is done for you.

13, 8, 9, 5, 12, 4, 10, 17, 20, 11, 1, (40)

20 + 20 = [40]   ____ + ____ = [ ]

____ + ____ = [ ]   ____ + ____ = [ ]

____ + ____ = [ ]   ____ + ____ = [ ]

Add. Use the code to find the name of an American president.

248 + 752	642 + 277	386 + 587	184 + 375	578 + 274
653 + 168	453 + 359	761 + 239	393 + 257	199 + 643
721 + 179				

___. ___ ___ ___ ___ ___ ___ ___ ___ ___ ___

900	973	559	821	919	650	852	842	1000	812
N	A	S	I	W	T	H	O	G	N

The **subject** of a sentence tells who or what the sentence is about. Underline the subject of each sentence. The first one is done for you.

1. <u>The Plains Native Americans</u> used almost every part of the buffalo.
2. Their tepees were made of buffalo hides.
3. Clothing was made from the hides of buffalo and deer.
4. They ate the meat of the buffalo.
5. Buffalo stomachs were used as pots for cooking.

6. Bones were used for tools and utensils.
7. The tail was used as a flyswatter.

8. Horns were used as scrapers and cups.
9. Buffalo manure was dried and used for fuel.
10. A kind of glue could be made from the hooves.

Write the word that is a **synonym** for the **bold** word in each sentence.

fix	quickly	biggest	little
autumn	woods	alike	skinniest

1. The deer ran through the **forest**. ____________
2. White mice are very **small** pets. ____________

3. Goldfish move **fast** in the water. ____________
4. The twins look exactly **the same**. ____________

5. Trees lose their leaves in the **fall**. ____________
6. The blue whale is the **largest** animal on Earth. ____________

Circle the **odd** numbers. Write the numbers you circled in the boxes after the equal sign. Then, write two equal addends before + 1 for each sum. One is done for you.

8, 9, 5, 12, 4, 10, 17, 20, 11, 23, (31)

15 + 15 + 1 = 31 ____ + ____ + 1 = ☐

____ + ____ + 1 = ☐ ____ + ____ + 1 = ☐

____ + ____ + 1 = ☐ ____ + ____ + 1 = ☐

Subtract. Color boxes with 9 in the answer to find a path to the picnic basket.

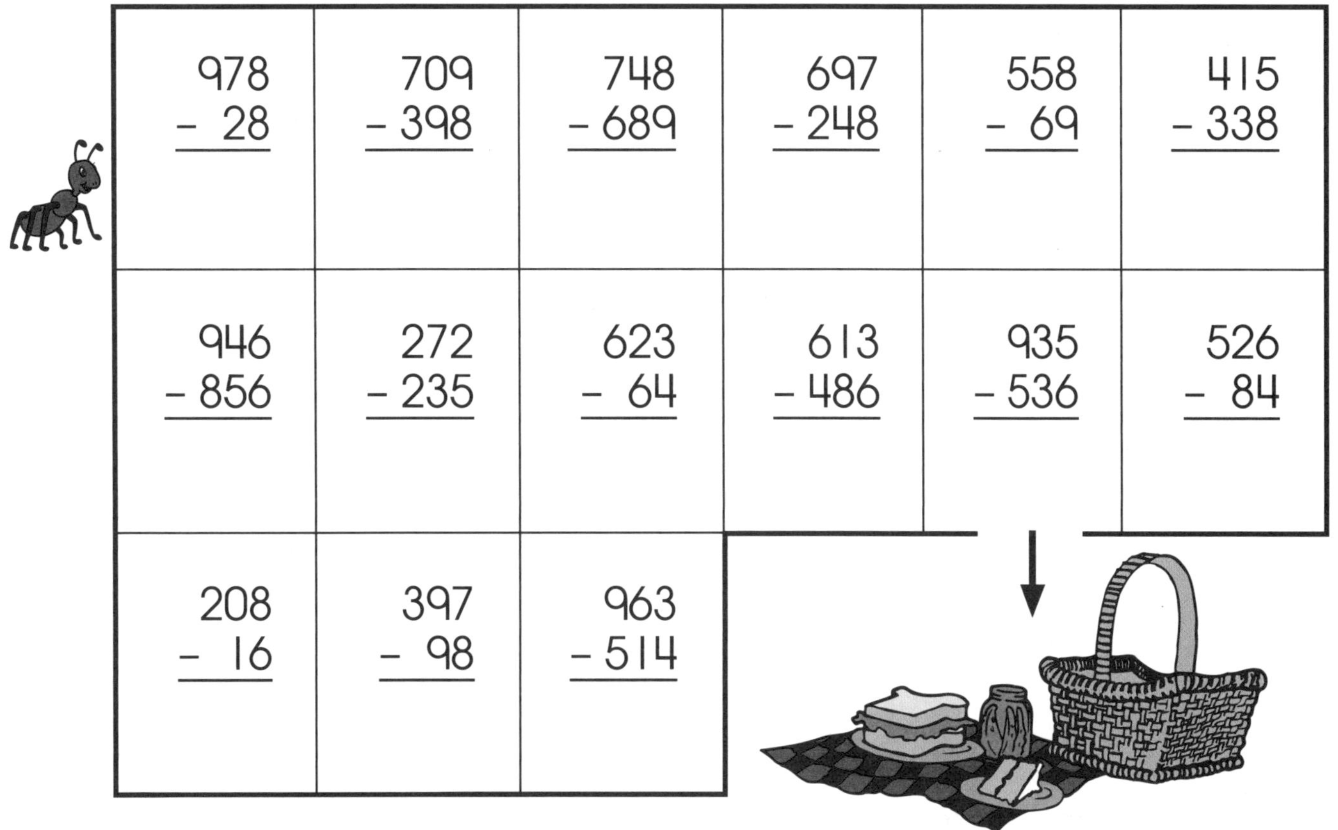

978 − 28	709 − 398	748 − 689	697 − 248	558 − 69	415 − 338
946 − 856	272 − 235	623 − 64	613 − 486	935 − 536	526 − 84
208 − 16	397 − 98	963 − 514			

Circle the **contractions**. Draw a box around the nouns that show **possession**.

can't	children's	she'd	won't
Jon's	woman's	city's	baby's
they've	I'll	he's	teachers'

Solve mentally. Write the answers quickly.

12 − 10	12 + 100	12 + 10	453 − 100	453 + 10
453 − 10	453 + 100	609 + 10	609 − 100	609 + 100

Draw a line from each food item to the amount of money needed to buy it.

$ 1.59

$ .89

$ 1.27

Guide words are the first and last words on a dictionary page. Only words in ABC order between the guide words appear on that page. Look at the guide words. Write the words in ABC order on the page.

far	**fence**	**feed**	**farmer**
feet	**fan**	**family**	**face**

face **fence**

________________ ________________

________________ ________________

________________ ________________

________________ ________________

Rewrite each sentence with a **compound subject**. The first one is done for you.

1. Roses grow in the garden. Tulips grow in the garden.
   Roses and tulips grow in the garden.
2. Apples are fruit. Oranges are fruit. Bananas are fruit.
   ____
3. Bears live in the zoo. Monkeys live in the zoo.
   ____
4. Jackets keep us warm. Sweaters keep us warm.
   ____

Combine the words with the **prefixes** and **suffixes**. Different combinations are possible. You may need to drop final **e** or **y** before adding a suffix. Write the new words on the lines.

happy	**scare**	**usual**	**most**
correct	**like**	**to**	**luck**

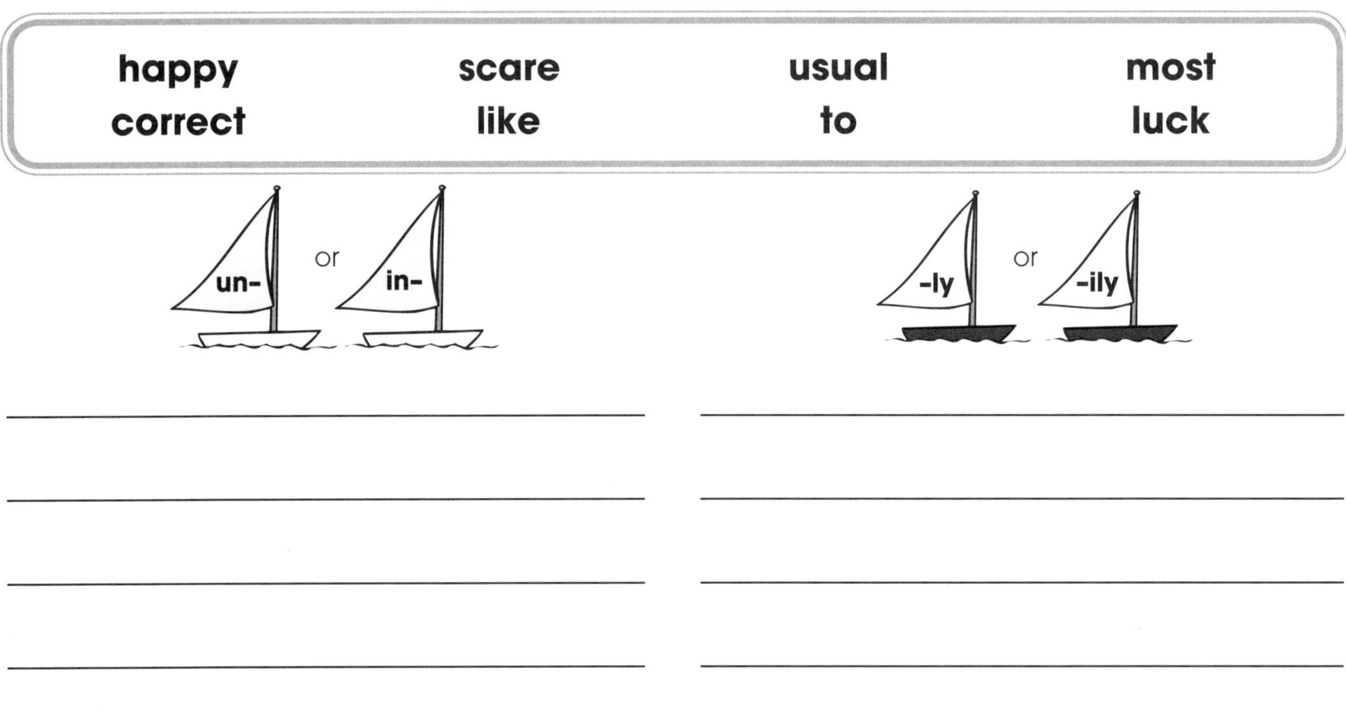

______________________ ______________________

______________________ ______________________

______________________ ______________________

______________________ ______________________

Solve the word problems.

1. A bug crawled 18 inches to a rock, 22 inches over leaves, and 9 inches into the grass. How many inches did it crawl in all? ________ inches

2. It rained 14 centimeters in September, 8 centimeters in October, and 11 centimeters in November. How many more centimeters did it rain in September than in November? ________ centimeters

Circle the **present-tense verb** in each pair.

1. won win
2. feel felt
3. built build
4. tell told
5. eat ate
6. blew blow
7. say said
8. came come
9. grew grow
10. fed feed

There are ________ rows of 5 bees.

There are ________ columns of 4 bees.

There are ________ bees altogether.

10 + ________ = 20

Write the **number names** for each number.

381 ______________________

822 ______________________

601 ______________________

171 ______________________

205 ______________________

296 ______________________

When the letters **le** come at the end of a word, they sometimes have the sound **ul**, as in **raffle**. Draw lines to match the word parts to make words. Write the words on the lines. The first one is done for you.

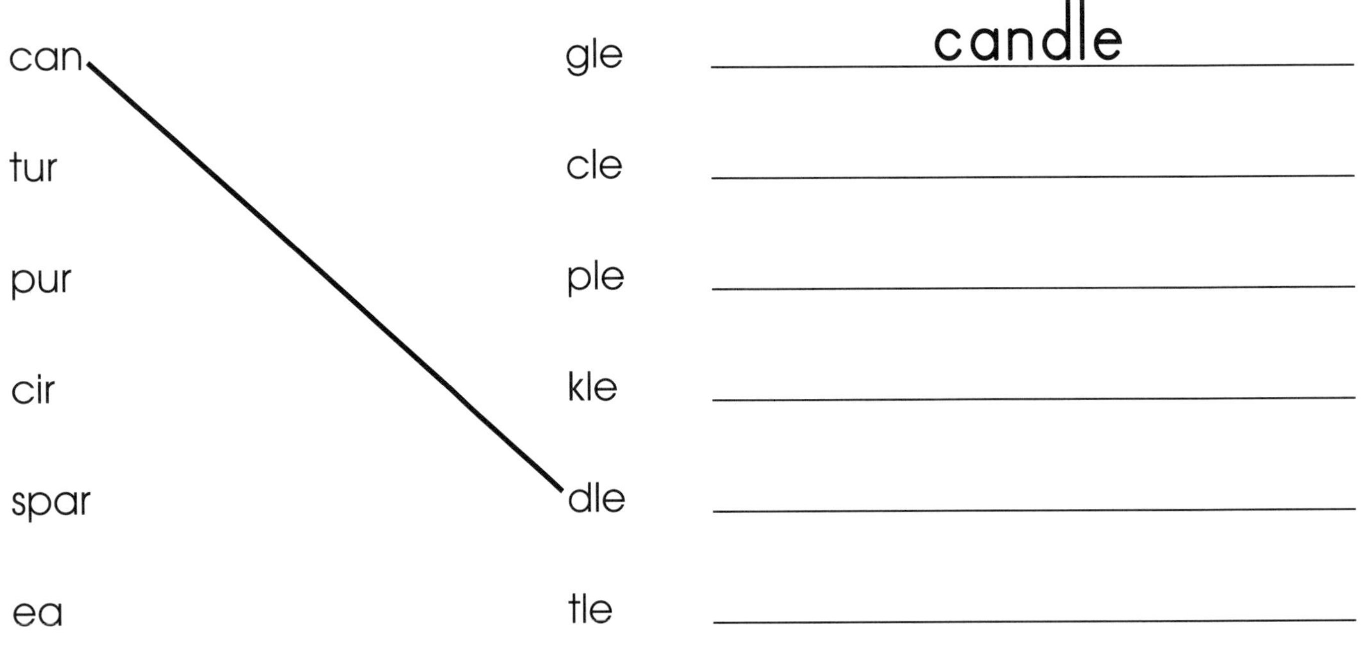

Use **or**, **and**, or **but** to join each pair of sentences into one sentence. Write a **comma** in front of the joining word.

1. Those socks cost a lot. These socks are cheaper.

____

____

2. The kangaroo has a pouch. It lives in Australia.

____

____

3. The zookeeper can start work early. She can stay late.

____

____

Color the **even** numbers **red**. Color the **odd** numbers **blue**.

30	**31**	**32**	**33**	**34**	**35**
36	**37**	**38**	**39**	**40**	**41**
42	**43**	**44**	**45**	**46**	**47**
48	**49**	**50**	**51**	**52**	**53**

Capitalize each **proper noun** and write it under the correct category.

ron polsky	saturday	corning, new york
presidents' day	portland, oregon	harold edwards
blackie	fluffy	april
valentine's day	sunday	october
bozeman, montana	march	molly yoder
tuesday	woofy	arbor day

People's Names

____

____

____

Days

____

____

____

Places

____

____

____

Months

____

____

____

Pet Names

____

____

____

Holidays

____

____

____

Complete the addition squares. Use addition and subtraction to write a number in each space.

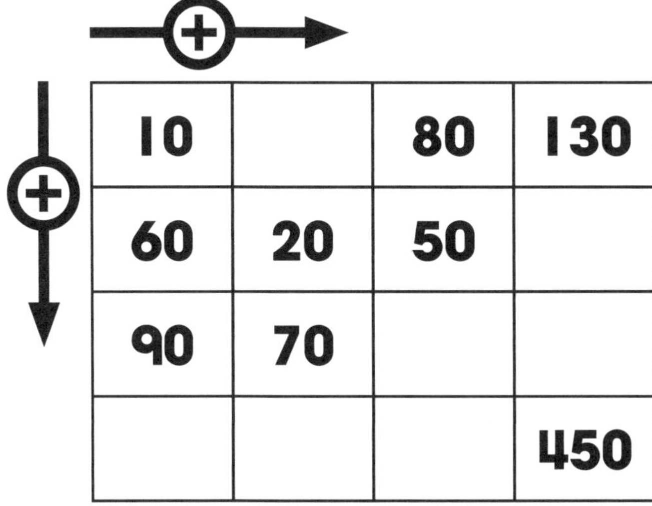

10		80	130
60	20	50	
90	70		
			450

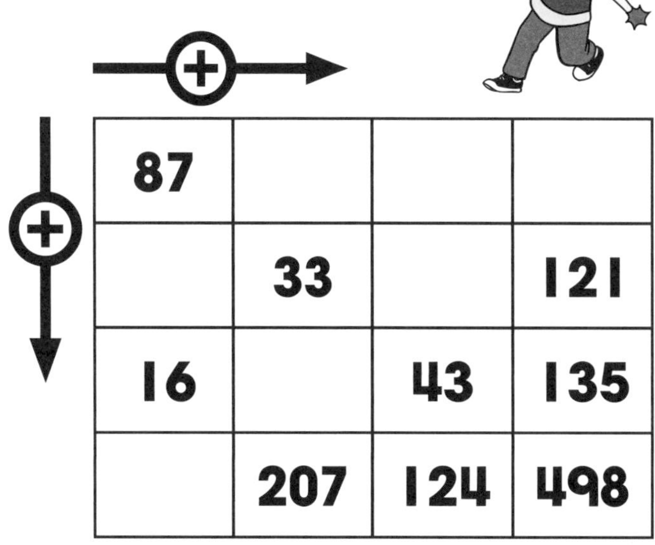

87			
	33		121
16		43	135
	207	124	498

Circle the best estimate for the **length** of each object.

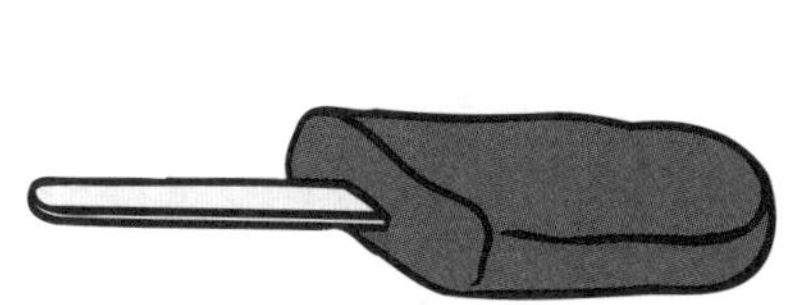

2 centimeters

1 foot

5 inches

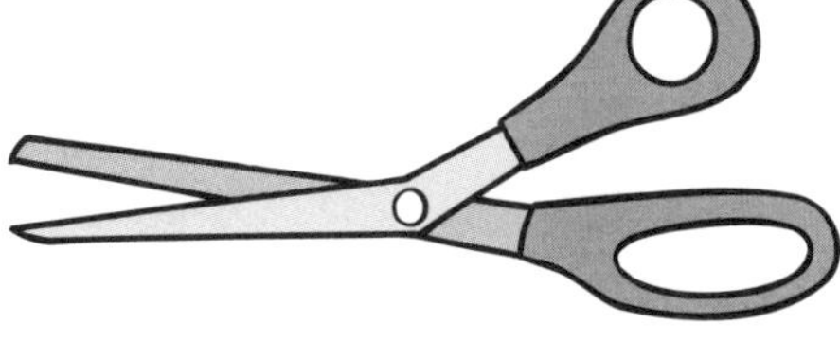

3 feet

15 centimeters

1 inch

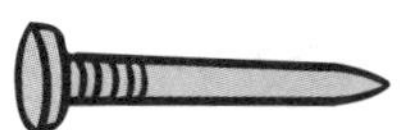

3 centimeters

12 feet

8 inches

Guide words are the first and last words on a dictionary page. Only words in ABC order between the guide words appear on that page. Look at the guide words. Write the words in ABC order on the page.

sieve	sight	sideways	side
sift	sideline	sigh	sidewalk

side **sight**

______________________ ______________________

______________________ ______________________

______________________ ______________________

______________________ ______________________

Draw a line from each food item to the amount of money needed to buy it.

$ 1.09

$.77

$ 1.95

Subtract. Then, **add** to check your answer. The first one is done for you.

43 − 27 = 16 → 16 + 27 = 43	71 − 28 → + ___	52 − 37 → + ___
94 − 18 → + ___	80 − 26 → + ___	64 − 48 → + ___

Circle the **contractions**. Draw a box around the nouns that show **possession**.

Carmen's	aren't	Mrs. Davis's	don't
boys'	they've	she'll	school's
I'm	cat's	it's	Rashaun's

Circle the words on each tree that include the **root word** shown. Cross out words that do not have the root word. Then, choose one word you circled on each tree and write its definition on the lines. Tell how its meaning relates to the meaning of the root word.

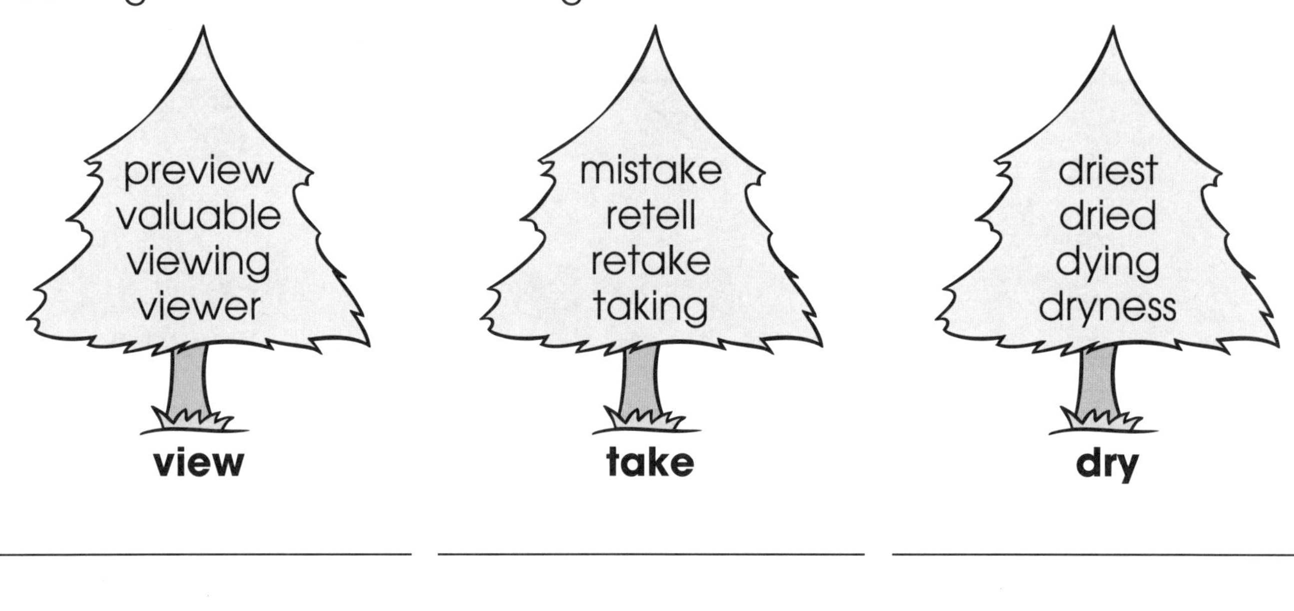

Write the name of each **quadrilateral**.

rhombus	**square**	**kite**
trapezoid	**parallelogram**	**rectangle**

Complete the sentences with **are**, **am**, **is**, or **was**.

1. My sister ______________ a good singer.

2. You ______________ going to the store with me.

3. Wesley ______________ at the movies last week.

4. I ______________ going to the ball game.

5. They ______________ silly.

6. I ______________ glad to help my mother.

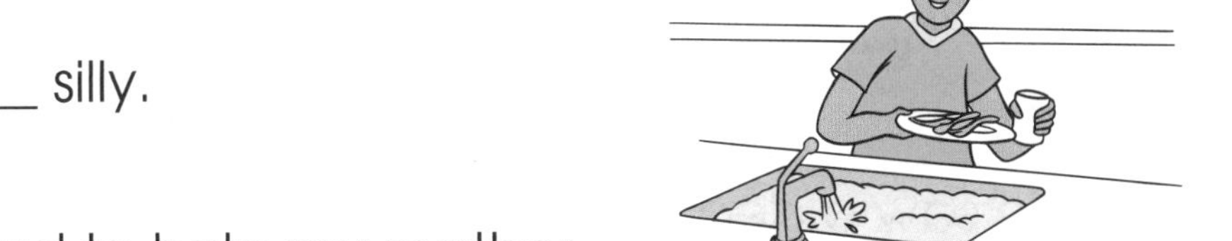

Circle the shape pairs that show equal **halves**.

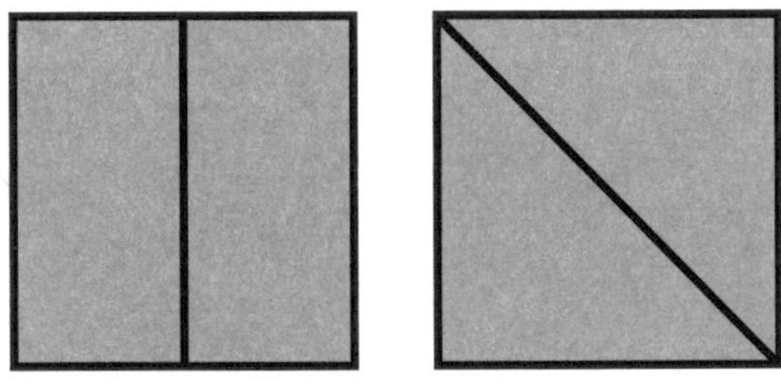

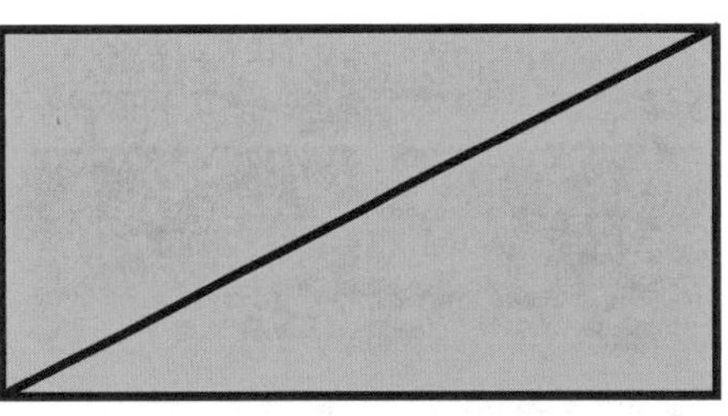

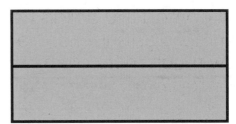

Circle a misspelled word in each sentence. Write the correct spelling on the line.

1. Please meat me at the park. ______________

2. I would like a peace of pie. ______________

3. There were too cookies left. ______________

4. The horse's main needed to be brushed. ______________

5. We saw a dear in the forest.  ______________

Solve the word problems.

1. Over the summer, Jon worked for 126 hours. His uncle Jake worked for 625 hours. How many more hours did Uncle Jake work than Jon? ________ hours

2. Jon earned 360 dollars helping his uncle this summer. Last summer, he earned 285 dollars. How much more did he make this summer than last? $________

Circle the **greater** number in each pair.

596 400	121 112	508 580	492 429

Circle the **smaller** number in each pair.

225 250	950 850	521 621	752 725

Use **if** or **when** to join each pair of sentences into one sentence.

1. The size of the crowd grew. It grew when the game began.

____

____

2. Be careful driving. The fog might be thick.

____

____

3. Pack your suitcases. Do it when you wake up in the morning.

____

____

Antonyms are words with opposite meanings. Help Frog and Toad escape. Color the spaces with antonyms **green**.

Add the numbers in the corners of each box. Write the sum in the center.

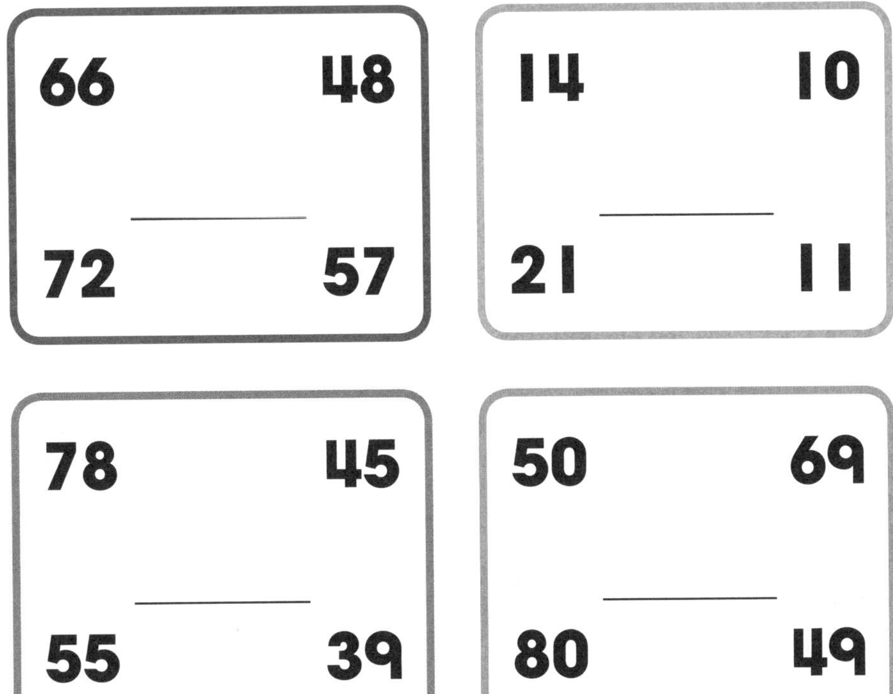

Write the **number names** for each number.

56 ____________________

292 ____________________

742 ____________________

307 ____________________

650 ____________________

18 ____________________

The **predicate** of a sentence tells what the subject is or does. It includes one or more verbs. Underline the predicate in each sentence. The first one is done for you.

1. Sally Ride was an astronaut.
2. She was the first American woman astronaut in space.
3. Sally worked hard for many years to become an astronaut.
4. Sally trained to become a jet pilot.
5. This astronaut practiced using a robot arm.
6. Ms. Ride used the robot arm on two space missions.

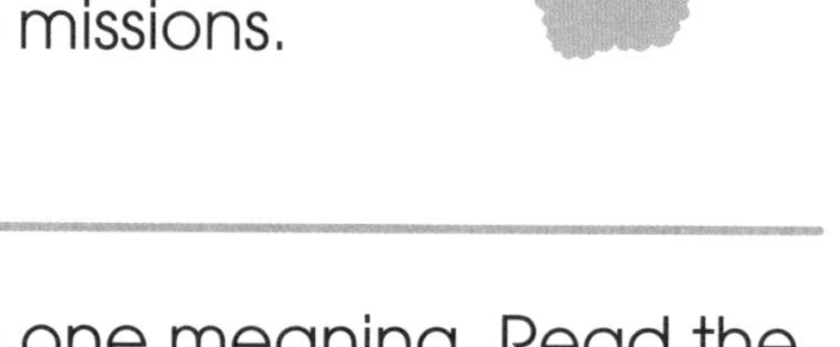

For many words, a **dictionary** gives more than one meaning. Read the meanings of **tag**. Write the number of the correct definition after each sentence.

tag
1. a small strip or tab attached to something else
2. to label
3. to follow closely and constantly
4. a game of chase

1. We will play a game of tag after we study. ______________
2. I will tag this coat with its price. ______________
3. My little brother will tag along with us. ______________
4. My mother already took off the price tag. ______________

Add.

259	187	190	432	27
+ 65	+ 346	+ 180	+ 68	+ 695

295	335	816	389	723
+ 452	+ 268	+ 25	+ 15	+ 199

Use the **line plot** to answer the questions.

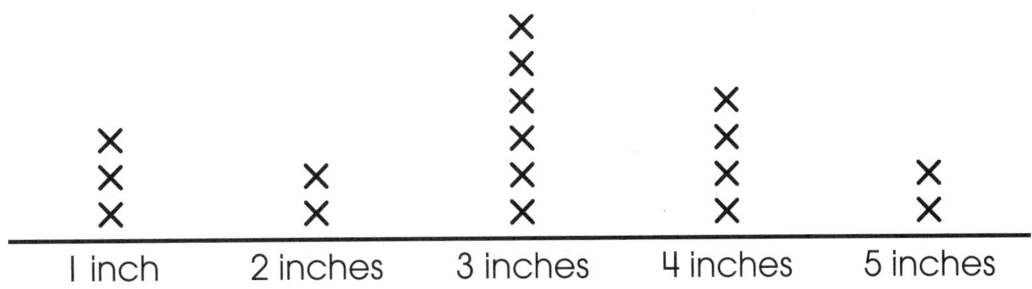

1. How many worms are 2 inches long? ________ worms
2. How many worms are 4 inches long or less? ________ worms
3. How many worms were counted in all? ________ worms

Read the passage. Answer the questions.

Imagine millions of teeny, tiny balloons joined together. That is what your lungs are like. When you breathe, the air goes to your two lungs. One lung is located on each side of your chest. The heart is located between the two lungs. The lungs are soft, spongy, and delicate. That is why there are bones around the lungs. These bones are called the **rib cage**. The rib cage protects the lungs so they can do their job. The lungs bring **oxygen** (ox-i-gin) into the body. They also take waste out of the body. This waste is called **carbon dioxide**. We could not live without our lungs!

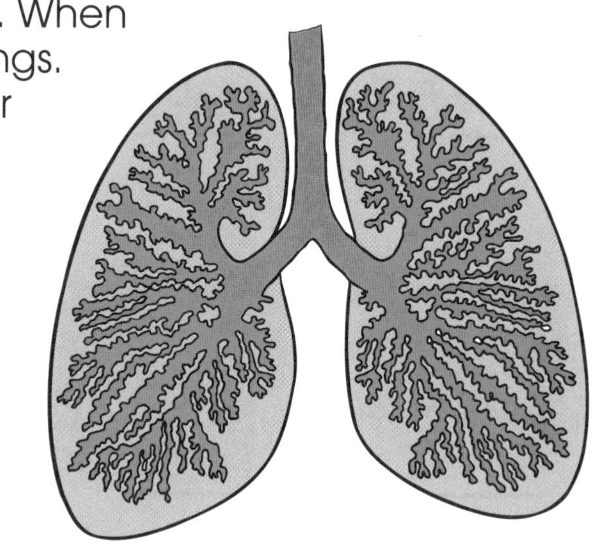

1. What is the name of the bones around your lungs? ____________________

2. What is located between the lungs? ____________________

3. What goes into your lungs when you breathe? ____________________

4. Why are there bones around your lungs? ____________________

Subtract.

932	662	458	538	615
− 62	− 45	− 293	− 157	− 541

842	803	843	658	277
− 26	− 326	− 699	− 74	− 139

Count the money in each box. Write the name of the food that costs that amount.

yogurt . . . **$.95** salad . . . **$1.77** pizza slice . . . **$1.55** sandwich . . . **$2.45**

____

____

____

____

Use the word on the balloon to join the pair of sentences into one sentence.

1. I didn't buy the tickets. They cost too much.

____

____

2. The door opened. The crowd rushed in.

____

____

3. I cut the bread. Everyone had a slice.

____

____

Draw or write what comes next in each pattern.

1 3 5 7 9 11 ____________

      ____________

1 A 2 B 3 C ____________

Write the numbers in order from **least** to **greatest**.

216 532 162 308 ☐ ☐ ☐ ☐

723 415 103 689 ☐ ☐ ☐ ☐

474 447 552 125 ☐ ☐ ☐ ☐

Write the numbers in order from **greatest** to **least**.

829 758 917 719 ☐ ☐ ☐ ☐

617 547 671 218 ☐ ☐ ☐ ☐

760 359 633 395 ☐ ☐ ☐ ☐

Antonyms are words with opposite meanings. Draw lines to match the antonyms.

thaw	**same**
crying	**friend**
enemy	**open**
closed	**freeze**
seek	**hide**
different	**laughing**

The **predicate** of a sentence tells what the subject is or does. It includes one or more verbs. Underline the predicate in each sentence. The first one is done for you.

1. Woodpeckers hunt for insects in the trees.
2. They have strong beaks.
3. They can peck through the bark.
4. The pecking sound can be heard from far away.

Circle the groups of words that can be predicates.

have long tongues	pick up insects
hole in bark	sticky substance
help them climb trees	tree bark

Now, choose the correct predicates from above to finish these sentences.

Woodpeckers ____ .

Their tongues ____ .

Their strong feet ____ .

There are ________ rows of 3 footballs.

There are ________ columns of 5 footballs.

There are ________ footballs altogether.

7 + ________ + 1 = 15

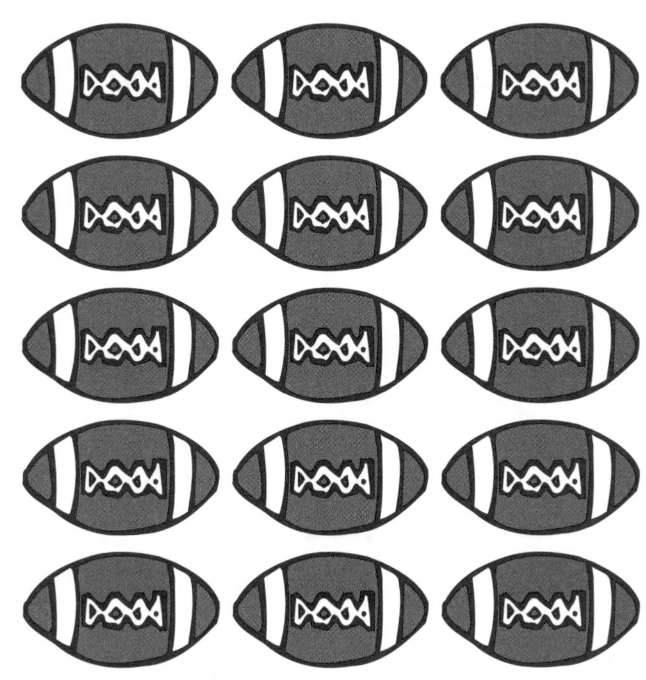

Solve the word problems.

1. There were 762 movie titles listed on the first screen of the online library catalog. On the second screen, there were 238 movie titles listed. How many movie titles were listed in all? ________ movie titles

2. On Saturday, 278 movies were checked out of the library. On Sunday, 192 movies were checked out. How many more movies were checked out on Saturday? ________ movies

Circle the words on each tree that include the **root word** shown. Cross out words that do not have the root word. Then, choose one word you circled on each tree and write its definition on the lines. Tell how its meaning relates to the meaning of the root word.

friend

sure

cover

Circle the best estimate for the **length** of each object.

16 inches
16 centimeters
16 feet

4 feet
4 centimeters
4 inches

3 inches
3 centimeters
3 feet

The pronouns **him**, **her**, **it**, and **them** are **object pronouns**. They are used in the predicate of a sentence. Rewrite each sentence, replacing the underlined words with an object pronoun.

1. Tommy packed <u>sandwiches and apples</u>.

 ____

2. He saw <u>the trail</u>.

 ____

3. Rita met <u>Tommy</u> at the trail's end.

 ____

4. Tommy gave <u>Rita</u> one of his sandwiches.

 ____

5. They ate <u>their lunches</u> under a tree.

 ____

Draw lines to connect the **expanded forms** to the matching **number names**.

60 + 2	one hundred eight
800 + 90 + 8	two hundred thirty
200 + 30	sixty-two
500 + 10 + 4	eight hundred ninety-eight
100 + 0 + 8	five hundred fourteen

Add.

189 + 276	460 + 170	17 + 508	526 + 78	215 + 215
278 + 365	124 + 297	568 + 351	49 + 173	876 + 43

Think of an **antonym** for the **bold** word in each sentence. Use it to complete the sentence.

hairy   **bald**

1. Sometimes my cat is **naughty**, and sometimes she's ______________.
2. The sign said, "**Closed**," but the door was ________________.
3. Is the glass half **empty** or half ________________?
4. I bought **new** shoes, but I like my ________________ ones better.
5. Skating is **easy** for me, but ________________ for my brother.

Rewrite the sentences. Capitalize the first word in each sentence. Capitalize **proper nouns**.

1. we celebrate thanksgiving on the fourth thursday in november.

____

____

2. in june, michelle and mark will go camping every friday.

____

____

3. on mondays in october, I will take piano lessons.

____

____

Write **>** or **<** to **compare** the numbers. Make sure the open "mouth" points to the greater number.

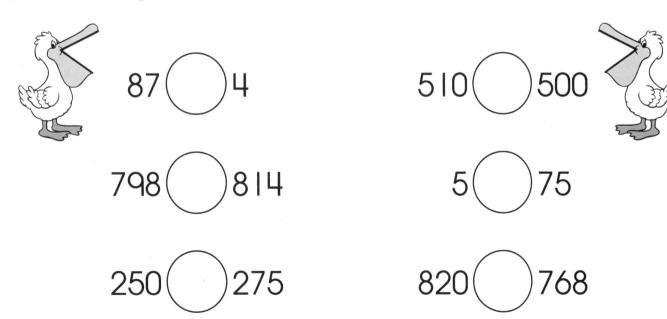

87 ◯ 4

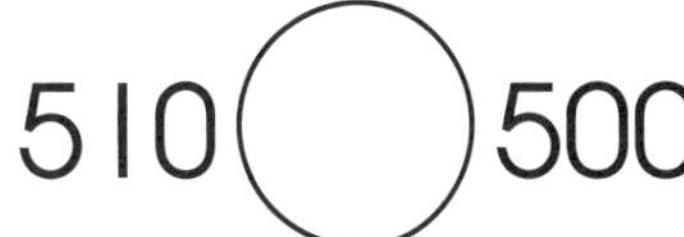

250 ◯ 275

820 ◯ 768

Subtract.

277	722	861	211	932
– 139	– 436	– 174	– 89	– 75

452	522	841	786	263
– 243	– 307	– 523	– 57	– 12

Count the money. Is it enough to buy the item? Circle the answer.

Yes No

Yes No

Yes No

Read the passage. Answer the questions.

For many years, no one knew much about Venus. When people looked through telescopes, they could not see past Venus's clouds. Long ago, people thought the clouds covered living things. Spacecraft radar has shown this is not true. Venus is too hot for life as we know it to exist. The temperature on Venus is about 900 degrees! Remember how hot you were the last time it was 90 degrees? Now imagine it being 10 times hotter. Nothing could exist in that heat. It is also very dry on Venus. For life to exist, water must be present. Because of the heat and dryness, we know there are probably no people, plants, or other life on Venus.

1. What is the temperature on Venus? ______________________

2. This temperature is how many times hotter than a hot day on Earth?

   6 times hotter

   10 times hotter

3. In the past, why did people think life might exist on Venus? ________

   ____

   ____

4. What is a telescope? ______________________

   ____

Circle words with the root word **pay**.

payment	payable	paying	payer
playing	repay	paid	replace

Write the meaning of one word you circled. Explain how it relates to the root word **pay**.

____

____

____

Draw lines to connect the **expanded forms** to the matching **number names**.

700 + 60 + 6	three hundred one
500 + 50 + 5	seven hundred sixty-six
80 + 6	one hundred twenty
300 + 0 + 1	eighty-six
100 + 20	five hundred fifty-five

Solve mentally. Write the answers quickly.

$$\begin{array}{r} 107 \\ -\ 100 \\ \hline \end{array} \quad \begin{array}{r} 107 \\ +\ 10 \\ \hline \end{array} \quad \begin{array}{r} 107 \\ +\ 100 \\ \hline \end{array} \quad \begin{array}{r} 455 \\ +\ 10 \\ \hline \end{array} \quad \begin{array}{r} 455 \\ -\ 100 \\ \hline \end{array}$$

$$\begin{array}{r} 455 \\ -\ 10 \\ \hline \end{array} \quad \begin{array}{r} 455 \\ +\ 100 \\ \hline \end{array} \quad \begin{array}{r} 89 \\ +\ 10 \\ \hline \end{array} \quad \begin{array}{r} 89 \\ -\ 10 \\ \hline \end{array} \quad \begin{array}{r} 89 \\ +\ 100 \\ \hline \end{array}$$

Underline the **predicate** in each sentence. The first one is done for you.

1. Juan <u>looks for rocks everywhere he goes</u>.

2. He has found many interesting rocks in his own backyard.
3. Juan showed me a piece of limestone with fossils in it.
4. Limestone is a kind of sedimentary rock.
5. It is formed underwater from the shells of animals.
6. Juan told me that some rocks come from deep inside Earth.

Read the **dictionary** definitions for **note**. Write the number of the correct meaning after each sentence.

note

1. a short letter or message
2. a written explanation
3. a musical tone
4. to notice

1. Can you sing the high note in this song? ____________
2. I read a book about dinosaurs and took notes. ____________
3. I noted many rhyming words in the poem. ____________
4. Leave a note to tell Mom where we are going. ____________

Solve the word problems.

1. Cody's summer vacation was 94 days long. He spent 68 summer days at his aunt's house. How many summer days were not spent at his aunt's house? ________ days

2. Cody's summer camp cost $275. His sister Faye's camp cost $125. How much did Cody's parents spend to send the two children to camp? $________

Use a ruler to measure each item to the nearest **inch** and **centimeter**.

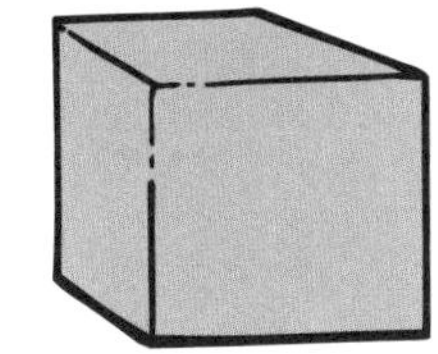

______ in. ______ cm

______ in. ______ cm

______ in. ______ cm

Write the **past-tense form** of each verb.

1. throw ______________________
2. wear ______________________
3. hold ______________________
4. sing ______________________
5. lose ______________________
6. fly ______________________
7. swim ______________________
8. sit ______________________
9. sell ______________________
10. eat ______________________

Use the **line plot** to answer the questions.

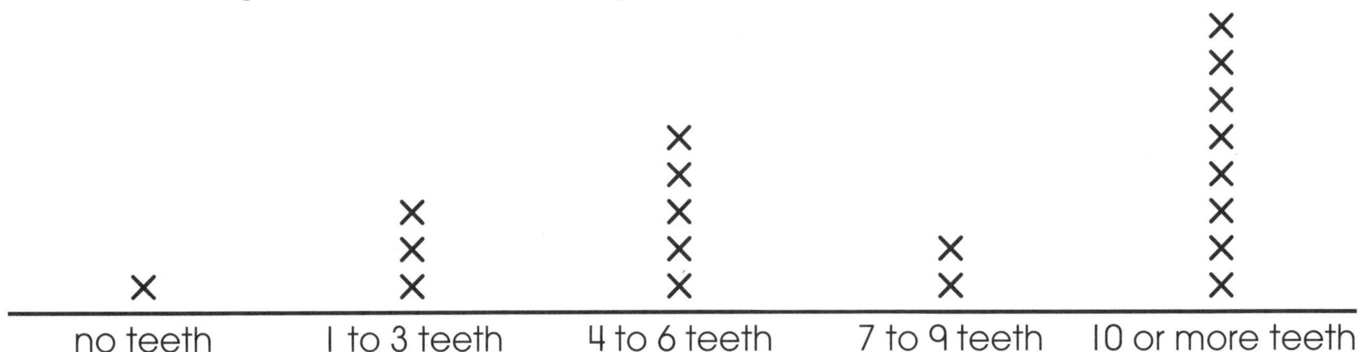

Baby Teeth Lost in Room 126

x = 1 student

1. How many students have lost 4 or more teeth? ________ students
2. How many more students have lost 10 or more teeth than 1 to 3 teeth? ________ students
3. How many students were counted in all? ________ students

Complete the addition squares. Use addition and subtraction to write a number in each space.

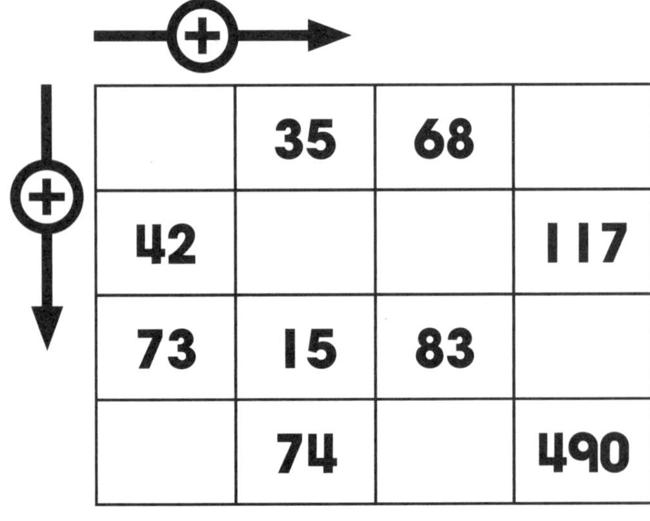

	35	68	
42			117
73	15	83	
	74		490

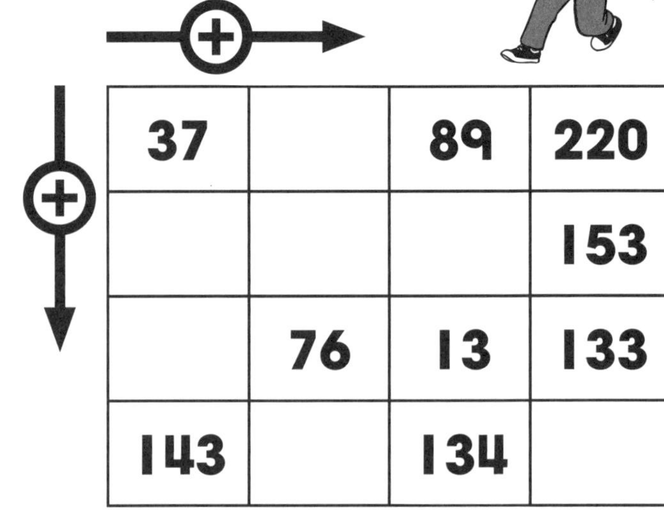

37		89	220
			153
	76	13	133
143		134	

The pronouns **I** and **we** are used in the **subject** of a sentence. The pronouns **me** and **us** are used in the **predicate** of a sentence. Circle the correct pronoun to complete each sentence. Write it in the blank. The first one is done for you.

1. ___I___ am finished with my science project. **(I,) Me**
2. Eric passed the football to ________. **me, I**
3. They ate dinner with ________ last night. **we, us**
4. ________ like spinach better than ice cream. **I, Me**
5. Mom came in the room to tell ________ good night. **me, I**
6. ________ had a pizza party in our backyard. **Us, We**
7. They told ________ the good news. **us, we**
8. Tom and ________ went to the skating rink. **me, I**
9. She is taking ________ with her to the movies. **I, me**
10. Katie and ________ are good friends. **I, me**

Add or **subtract**.

628	135	789	529	862
+ 84	− 54	+ 54	+ 183	− 407

385	516	235	659	422
+ 249	− 48	+ 149	− 39	− 147

Write the **past-tense form** of the verb shown to complete each sentence.

1. I ____________ my library book to my sister. (give)
2. She ____________ for school before I did. (leave)
3. She ____________ the bus at the corner. (catch)
4. My sister ____________ my book on the way to school. (lose)
5. My sister ____________ back to find it. (go)

On each safe, draw dollar bills and coins to show the amount. The first one is done for you.

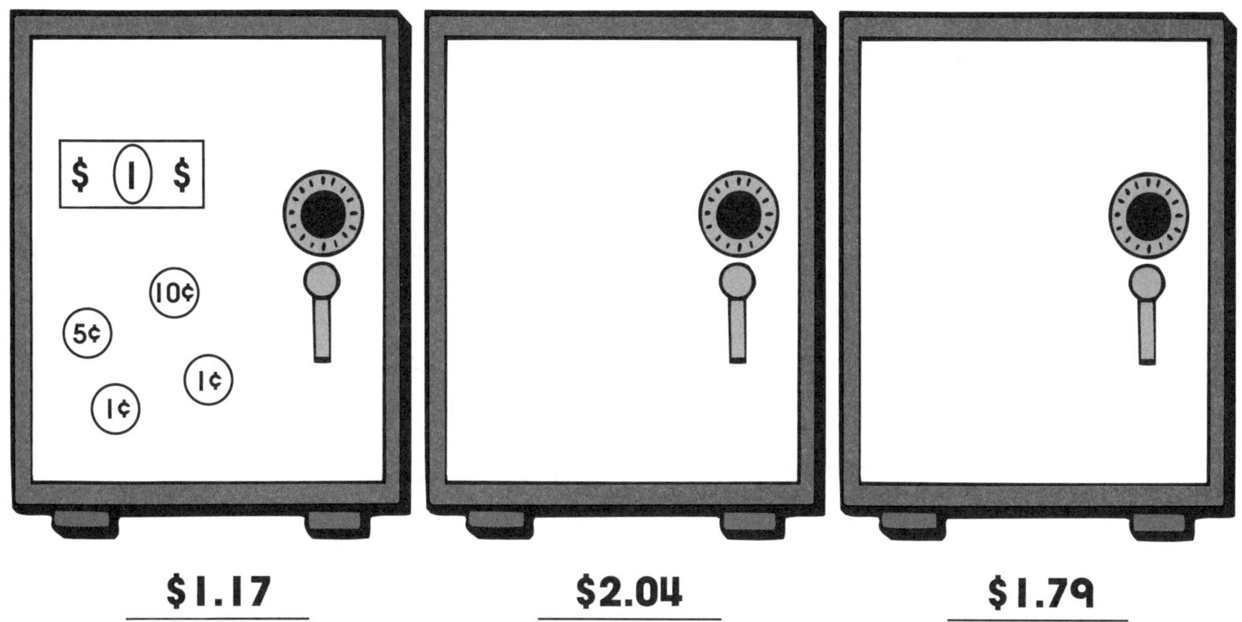

$1.17 **$2.04** **$1.79**

Think of an **antonym** for the **bold** word in each sentence. Use it to complete the sentence.

hot   **cold**

1. The sky is **dark** at night and ____________ during the day.
2. I like a **noisy** house, but my mother likes a ____________ one.
3. My friend says I'm **wrong**, but I say I'm ____________.
4. Jason is a **fast** runner, but Adam is a ____________ runner.
5. We were supposed to be **early**, but we were ____________.

A **sentence** must include a **subject** (with a noun) and a **predicate** (with a verb). Read each group of words. Write **S** in front of each sentence. Write **No** if it is not a sentence.

__________ 1. There are different kinds of chipmunks.

__________ 2. They all have.

__________ 3. They all have stripes to help protect them.

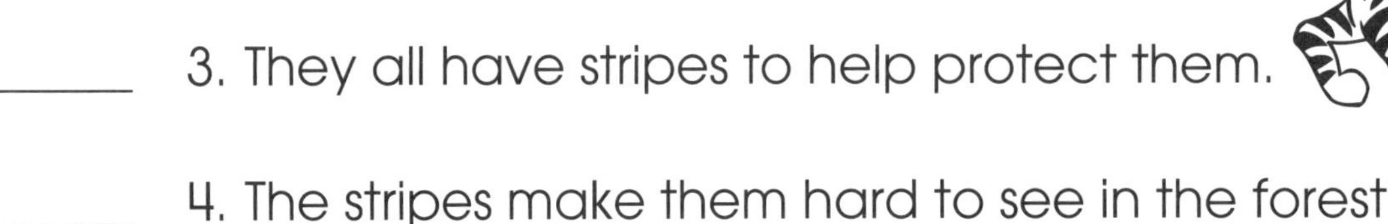

__________ 4. The stripes make them hard to see in the forest.

__________ 5. Zebras and tigers have stripes, too.

__________ 6. Some caterpillars also.

__________ 7. Other animals have spots.

__________ 8. Some dogs have spots.

__________ 9. Beautiful, little fawns.

__________ 10. Their spots help to hide them in the woods.

Write **>** or **<** to **compare** the numbers. Make sure the open "mouth" points to the greater number.

345 ◯ 325

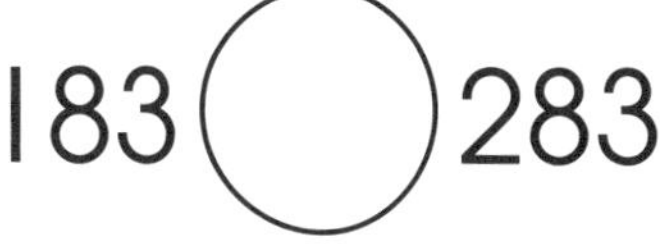

183 ◯ 283

843 ◯ 834

864 ◯ 468

470 ◯ 580

999 ◯ 909

Solve the word problems.

1. The maple tree is 26 feet tall. The oak tree is 48 feet tall. The pine tree is 16 feet tall. How much taller is the oak tree than the pine tree?

________ feet

2. Violet has 36 inches of ribbon. She needs 18 inches to make one friendship bracelet. Does she have enough ribbon to make two bracelets?

____

Circle words with the root word **joy**.

joker	enjoy	unjust	joys
joyful	enjoyment	overjoyed	joking

Write the meaning of one word you circled. Explain how it relates to the root word **joy**.

____

____

____

A **reflexive pronoun** refers back to the subject of a sentence. Reflexive pronouns are compound words made of a pronoun and the word **self**. **Myself**, **himself**, **herself**, **yourself**, and **ourselves** are reflexive pronouns. Circle a reflexive pronoun in each sentence.

1. I looked at myself in the mirror.
2. He reminded himself to be brave.
3. Did you make this meal yourself?
4. We biked to the park by ourselves.
5. Please help yourself to snacks.
6. They grew the plants themselves.

Add or **subtract**.

977 − 918	235 + 149	756 − 32	765 + 70	469 + 123
720 − 153	336 − 187	423 + 538	756 − 295	268 + 61

Complete the chart.

Number	Expanded Form	Number Names
342		three hundred forty-two
		eight hundred ten
426	400 + 20 + 6	
	900 + 10 + 9	

Read the passage. Answer the questions.

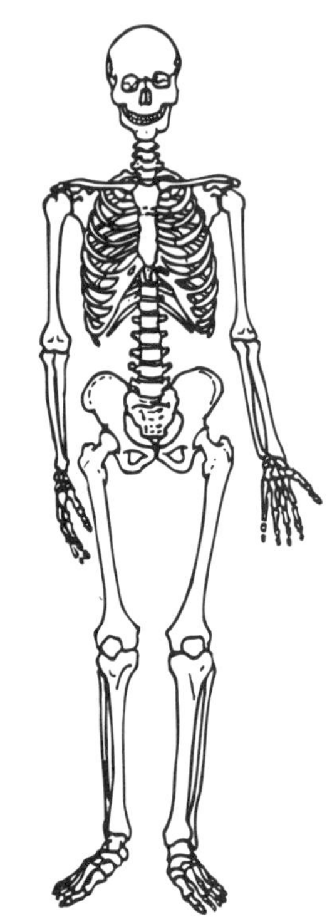

What gives you your shape? Like a house's frame, your body also has a frame. It is called your **skeleton**. Your skeleton is made of more than 200 bones.

Your skeleton helps your body move. It does this by giving your muscles a place to attach. Your skeleton also protects the soft organs inside your body from injury.

Bones have a hard, outer layer made of calcium. Inside each bone is a soft, spongy layer that looks like a honeycomb. The hollow spaces in the honeycomb are filled with marrow. Every minute, millions of blood cells die. But the bone marrow works like a little factory, making new blood cells.

1. What attaches to your skeleton? ___________________________

2. What fills the hollow spaces inside bones? ___________________________

3. How is a skeleton like a house's frame? ___________________________

____

____

4. Write one or more words to finish each sentence.

   Your skeleton gives you your ___________________________ .

   Your skeleton helps your body ___________________________ .

   Your skeleton protects ___________________________ .

Add the numbers in the corners of each box. Write the sum in the center.

98		19
	______	
71		27

31		12
	______	
13		31

47		92
	______	
83		28

15		20
	______	
24		40

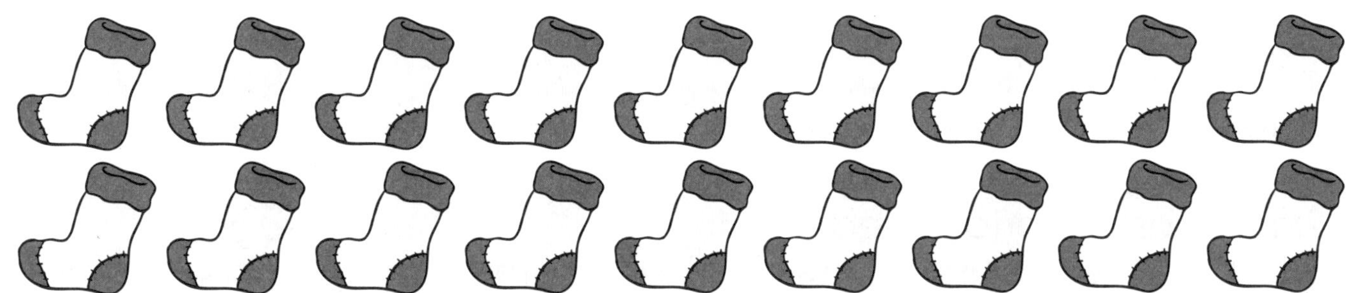

There are ________ rows of 9 socks.

There are ________ columns of 2 socks.

There are ________ socks altogether.

9 + ________ = 18

Use a ruler to measure each item to the nearest **inch** and **centimeter**.

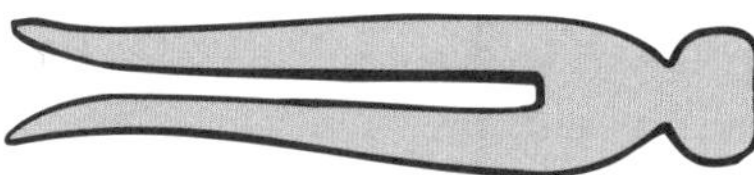

_______ in. _______ cm _______ in.

_______ cm

_______ in. _______ cm

Read the **dictionary** definitions for **key**. Write the number of the correct meaning after each sentence.

key

1. a small piece of metal used to open a lock
2. the most important idea
3. a list that explains symbols on a chart or map
4. a group of related musical notes

1. Check the key to see what brown lines mean on this map. _______
2. Can you play the song in the key of C? _______
3. Hard work is the key to success. _______
4. Don't forget your car keys. _______

Add or **subtract**.

137 + 329	154 − 92	329 − 85	18 + 625	436 − 242
731 − 515	379 + 102	645 + 247	371 + 38	356 − 259

A **compound predicate** has two or more predicates joined by the word **and**. Read each sentence. If it has a compound predicate, write **CP**. If it does not, write **No**. The first one is done for you.

CP 1. Abe Lincoln cut trees and chopped wood.

_______ 2. Abe's family packed up and left Kentucky.

_______ 3. Abe's father built a new home.

_______ 4. Abe's mother became sick and died.

_______ 5. Mr. Lincoln married again.

_______ 6. Abe's new mother loved Abe and his sister and cared for them.

Complete each sentence with an **antonym** for the **bold** word.

1. A **child** is allowed in the museum if he or she is with an ______________.

2. The **huge** crowd of people tried to fit into the ______________ room.

3. The **fussy** baby was soon ______________ and playing in the crib.

4. We'll **freeze** the meat for now, and Dad will ______________ it when we need it.

Now, write your own sentence using one of the antonym pairs.

____

____

Draw or write what comes next in each pattern.

5 10 20 40 80 ______________

      ______________

 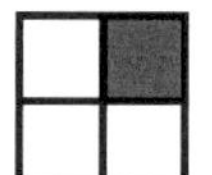 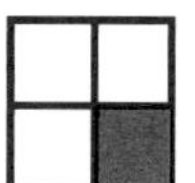 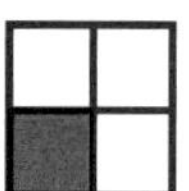  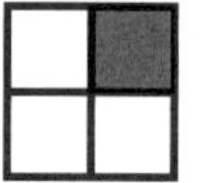 ______________

The pronouns **him**, **her**, **it**, and **them** are used in the predicate of a sentence. They are **object pronouns**. Write the object pronouns that could take the place of the bold words in the sentences.

1. They gave a party for **Teresa**. ______________
2. Everyone in the class was happy for **Tyrone**. ______________
3. The children petted **the giraffe**. ______________
4. Linda put **the kittens** near the warm stove. ______________
5. Give the books to **Herbie**. ______________

Circle the shape pairs that show equal **fourths**.

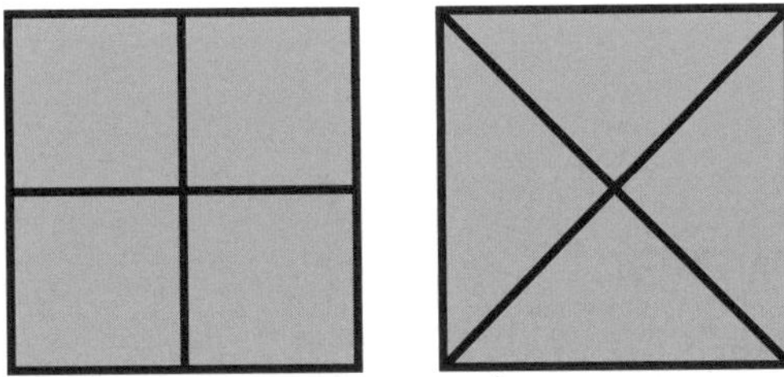

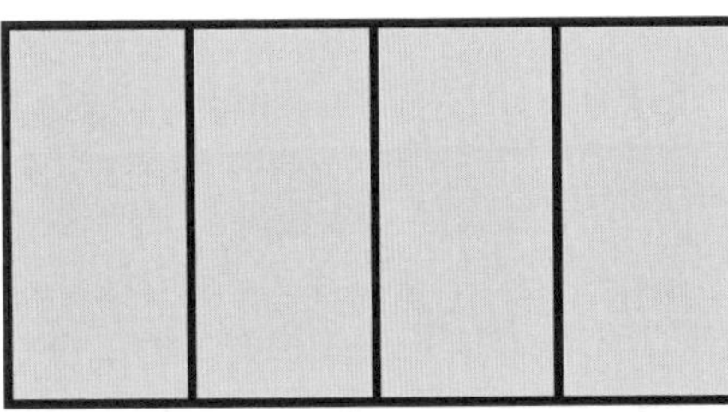

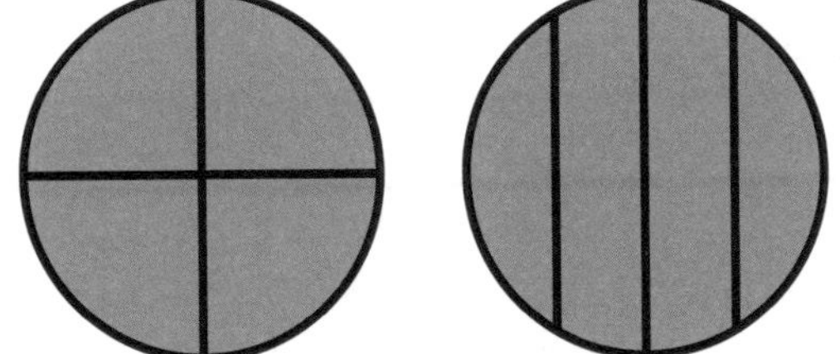

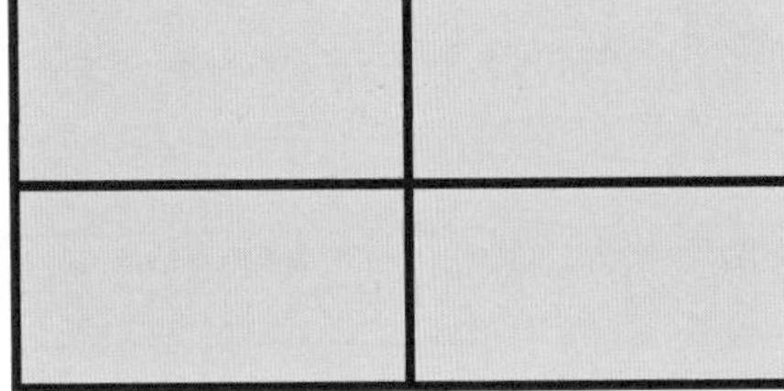

Add or **subtract**.

732 − 61	318 + 19	658 + 293	224 − 137	378 + 295
626 − 352	90 + 350	354 − 97	873 − 32	190 + 85

Make a check mark in front of sentences with correct **verbs**. If the verb is not correct, draw an X on the line. Then, cross out the incorrect verb and write the correct word above.

_________ 1. Seeds travel in many ways.

_________ 2. Sometimes, seeds falls in the water.

_________ 3. Squirrels digs holes to bury seeds.

_________ 4. Cardinals likes to eat sunflower seeds.

_________ 5. The wind scatters seeds, too.

_________ 6. Dogs carries seeds that are stuck in their fur.

Use the word **and** to combine each pair of sentences into one sentence with a **compound predicate**.

1. Dogs can bark loudly. Dogs can do tricks.

   ____

2. The football player caught the ball. The football player ran.

   ____

3. My dad sawed wood. My dad stacked wood.

   ____

4. My teddy bear is soft. My teddy bear likes to be hugged.

   ____

Write **>** or **<** to **compare** the numbers. Make sure the open "mouth" points to the greater number.

259 ◯ 592   199 ◯ 109   76 ◯ 676

860 ◯ 806   462 ◯ 642   505 ◯ 500

58 ◯ 580   450 ◯ 405   198 ◯ 199

Complete the addition squares. Use addition and subtraction to write a number in each space.

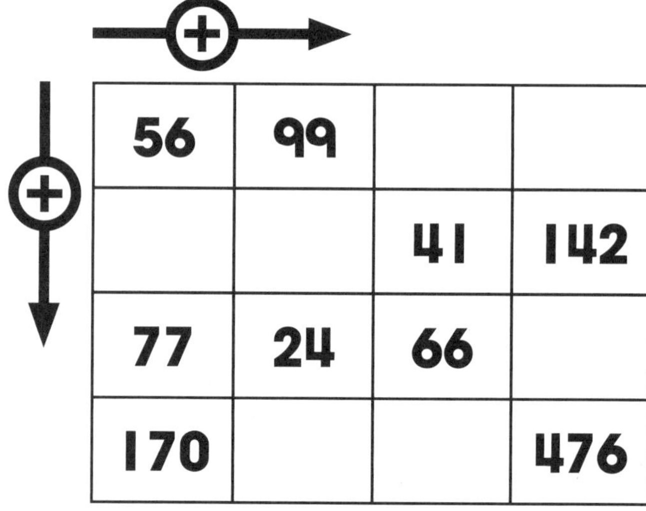

56	99		
		41	142
77	24	66	
170			476

	45	27	
74			208
	39	98	155
156	167		

A **reflexive pronoun** refers back to the subject of a sentence. Reflexive pronouns are compound words made of a pronoun and the word **self**. Circle a reflexive pronoun in each sentence. Draw an arrow to the subject pronoun or noun it refers back to. The first one is done for you.

1. I built a robot by myself.
2. We helped ourselves to fresh fruit.
3. She reminded herself to feed the cat.
4. They planned the trip themselves.
5. The baby entertained herself in the crib.

Circle words with the root word **work**.

worker	rework	working	unworkable
rewrite	overworked	worked	weakness

Write the meaning of one word you circled. Explain how it relates to the root word **work**.

____

____

____

____

Draw dollar bills and coins to show the amount needed to buy each item at the yard sale.

$3.24

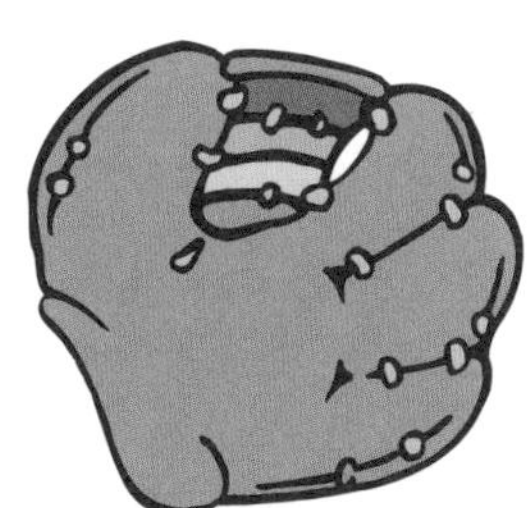

$2.58

$1.35

Use a ruler to measure each item to the nearest **inch** and **centimeter**.

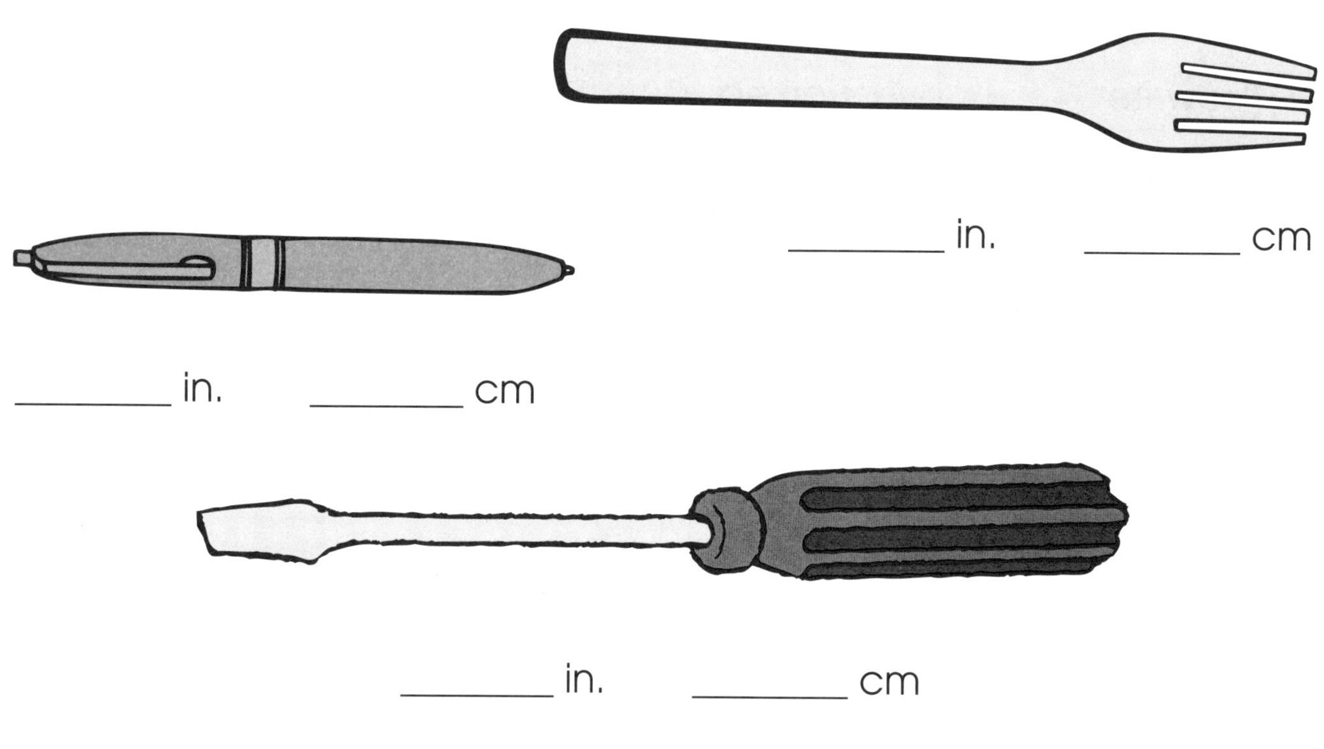

_______ in. _______ cm

_______ in. _______ cm

_______ in. _______ cm

Circle the **contractions**. Draw a box around the nouns that show **possession**.

men's	Marla's	aren't	it's
here's	teachers'	they've	we've
isn't	giraffe's	Grandpa's	students'

Add or **subtract**.

915	152	543	110	728
− 61	+ 268	+ 99	+ 390	− 70

841	612	529	95	539
− 743	− 254	− 486	+ 818	+ 175

Read the **dictionary** definitions for **heart**. Write the number of the correct meaning after each sentence.

heart
1. the organ that pumps blood through the body
2. the main part
3. the part of a person that feels love
4. a shape

1. Color the heart red. ____________
2. I can feel my heart beating. ____________
3. His words come from the heart. ____________
4. This street is in the heart of the city. ____________

Read the recipe. Answer the questions.

Cut the pineapple into chunks. Use a small metal scoop to make balls of the cantaloupe. Slice the pear, bananas, and strawberries. Peel the oranges and divide them into sections. Cut each section into bite-sized pieces. Dip each piece of fruit in lemon juice, then combine them in a large bowl. Cover and chill. Pour fruit dressing of your choice over the chilled fruit, blend well, and serve cold. Makes 4 large servings.

1 fresh pineapple
1 cantaloupe
2 bananas
1 cup strawberries
2 oranges
1 pear
1 cup seedless grapes
lemon juice

1. How many bananas does the recipe require? ______________

2. Which three fruits do you slice? ______________

____

3. Which do you do first? (Check one.)

____ Pour dressing over the fruit.

____ Slice the pear.

____ Serve the fruit salad.

4. Would your fruit salad be as good if you did not cut the pineapple or section the oranges? Why or why not? ______________

____

Complete the chart.

Number	Expanded Form	Number Names
	400 + 20 + 8	
99		
		five hundred eighty-five
647		

Solve the word problems.

1. Marco has a jar full of dimes. A pencil costs 40¢. How many dimes will he use to buy 3 pencils? ________ dimes

2. Cassie's paper airplane will fly 5 feet at a time. How many times will Cassie need to throw her airplane to cross a field that is 30 feet long? ________ times

Try these fun ideas for summer learning.

Basic Skills

- Ask your child to choose a topic such as the beach. Challenge him or her to write as many words as possible that fit the category, such as **sand**, **tide**, **umbrella**, and **starfish**.
- Look for analog clocks in public places. Ask your child to tell the time to the nearest five minutes. Then, let your child check his or her answer by looking at the digital time on your mobile phone.
- Purchase an inexpensive wallet or change purse for your child. Fill it with several dollar bills and a variety of coins. At the store, ask your child to purchase one or more specific items from your shopping list using the money.
- Play "Spelling I Spy" during car trips. Give one letter of the thing you spy, then give another letter, and another, until the object is guessed correctly.

Reading

- Encourage your child to ask questions about a topic of interest, such as trains or gardening. Choose one question and help your child write it on an index card. When you visit the library, help your child use books and other resources to find the answer.

- Read a chapter book aloud. Let your child choose a character to voice. Whenever that character speaks in the story, it is your child's turn to read.
- Have your child set a goal for reading a certain number of books each week or each month during the summer. Create a chart and help your child use it to track progress. Provide a reward when your child reaches the reading goal.
- After reading a book or watching a movie with your child, role-play two of the characters. How would each character respond to different situations?

Writing

- Encourage your child to write a weekly e-mail or newsletter about his or her summer activities and send it to relatives and friends. It could include photos and links.
- Write a list of five unrelated words. Can your child use them to write a story?
- Check out a book of children's dramatic plays from the library. Help your child notice details about how plays are written. Then, encourage your child to write a play version of a favorite story or movie and use it to put on a show with friends.
- Provide poster board and art supplies for your child to use in creating an original board game. It should include a complete set of rules and directions. Play the game together.

Math

- Play with one-dollar bills (hundreds), dimes (tens), and pennies (ones). Use them to represent numbers to 1,000 such as 761, 250, and 468. Ask your child to write each number.
- Encourage your child to do jumping jacks or another physical activity as many times as possible each day and record the number. How soon can your child reach 1,000?
- Print a set of tangrams from the Internet. Encourage your child to use them to create a variety of shapes.
- Use sidewalk chalk and a yardstick to draw a line that is one inch tall, a line that is two inches tall, a line that is three inches tall, etc. Label each line. Encourage your child to find sticks, leaves, and other things to measure against the lines.
- Write numbers **1–20** on squares of masking tape and arrange them in a grid on the floor. Call out addition problems and ask your child to stand on a number to show the sum.

Answer Key

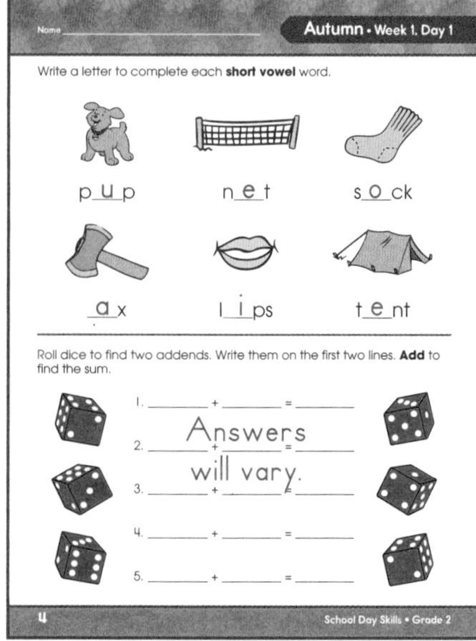
Name __________ **Autumn** • Week 1, Day 1

Write a letter to complete each **short vowel** word.

p u p n e t s o ck

a x l i ps t e nt

Roll dice to find two addends. Write them on the first two lines. **Add** to find the sum.

1. ___ + ___ = ___
2. ___ + ___ = ___
3. ___ + ___ = ___
4. ___ + ___ = ___
5. ___ + ___ = ___

Answers will vary.

4 School Day Skills • Grade 2

Page 4

Name __________ **Autumn** • Week 1, Day 1

A clock face has numbers from 1 to 12. There are 60 minutes in one hour. Fill in the numbers. Count by **ones** on the clock face. Count by **fives** around the clock.

School Day Skills • Grade 2 5

Page 5

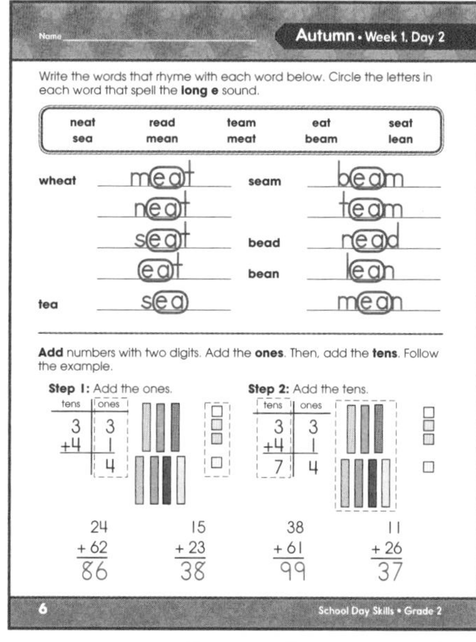
Name __________ **Autumn** • Week 1, Day 2

Write the words that rhyme with each word below. Circle the letters in each word that spell the **long e** sound.

neat	read	team	eat	seat
sea	mean	meat	beam	lean

wheat: meat, neat, seat, eat
tea: sea
seam: beam, team
bead: read
bean: lean, mean

Add numbers with two digits. Add the **ones**. Then, add the **tens**. Follow the example.

Step 1: Add the ones. **Step 2:** Add the tens.

$$33 + 41 = 74$$

24 + 62 = 86 15 + 23 = 38 38 + 61 = 99 11 + 26 = 37

6 School Day Skills • Grade 2

Page 6

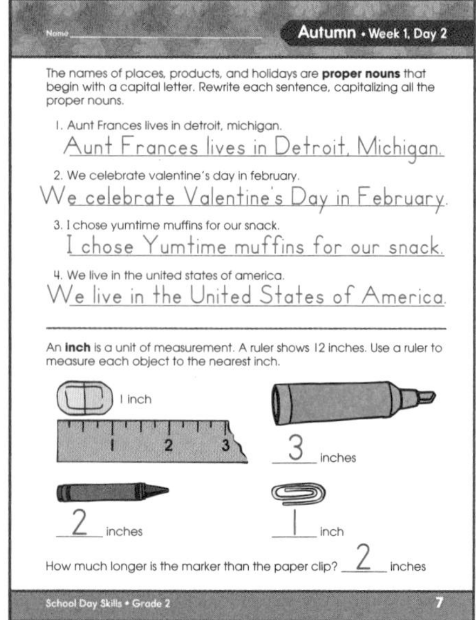
Name __________ **Autumn** • Week 1, Day 2

The names of places, products, and holidays are **proper nouns** that begin with a capital letter. Rewrite each sentence, capitalizing all the proper nouns.

1. Aunt Frances lives in detroit, michigan.
   Aunt Frances lives in Detroit, Michigan.
2. We celebrate valentine's day in february.
   We celebrate Valentine's Day in February.
3. I chose yumtime muffins for our snack.
   I chose Yumtime muffins for our snack.
4. We live in the united states of america.
   We live in the United States of America.

An **inch** is a unit of measurement. A ruler shows 12 inches. Use a ruler to measure each object to the nearest inch.

1 inch 3 inches 2 inches 1 inch

How much longer is the marker than the paper clip? 2 inches

School Day Skills • Grade 2 7

Page 7

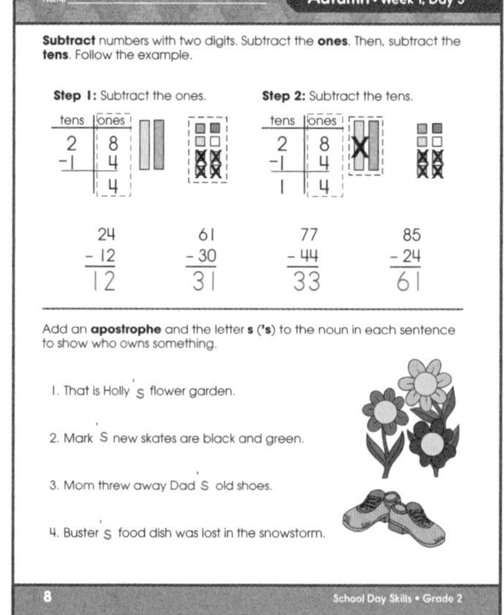
Name __________ **Autumn** • Week 1, Day 3

Subtract numbers with two digits. Subtract the **ones**. Then, subtract the **tens**. Follow the example.

Step 1: Subtract the ones. **Step 2:** Subtract the tens.

$$28 - 14 = 14$$

24 − 12 = 12 61 − 30 = 31 77 − 44 = 33 85 − 24 = 61

Add an **apostrophe** and the letter **s ('s)** to the noun in each sentence to show who owns something.

1. That is Holly's flower garden.
2. Mark's new skates are black and green.
3. Mom threw away Dad's old shoes.
4. Buster's food dish was lost in the snowstorm.

8 School Day Skills • Grade 2

Page 8

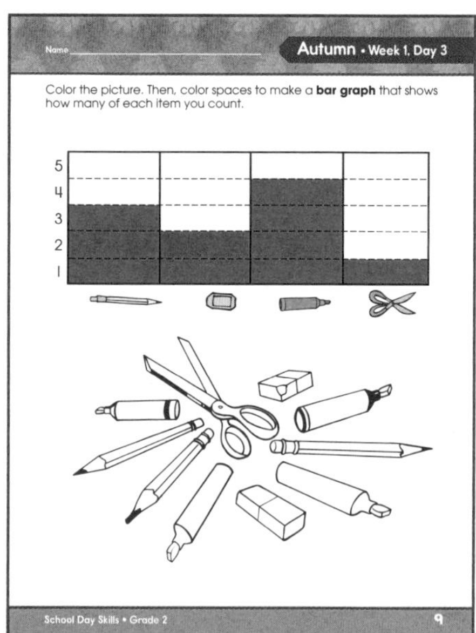
Name __________ **Autumn** • Week 1, Day 3

Color the picture. Then, color spaces to make a **bar graph** that shows how many of each item you count.

School Day Skills • Grade 2 9

Page 9

Answer Key

Name ______ **Autumn** • Week 1, Day 4

Write a letter to complete each **short vowel** word.

h a t f o x p i n

c a ndle p e nny th i mble

An **adverb** is a word that describes a verb. It can tell where, how, or when. Adverbs often end with **ly**. Circle the adverb in each sentence. The first one is done for you.

1. The skateboarder landed (smoothly).
2. Their call was returned (quickly).
3. We (easily) learned the new words.
4. He did the work (perfectly).
5. She lost her purse (somewhere).

10 School Day Skills • Grade 2

Page 10

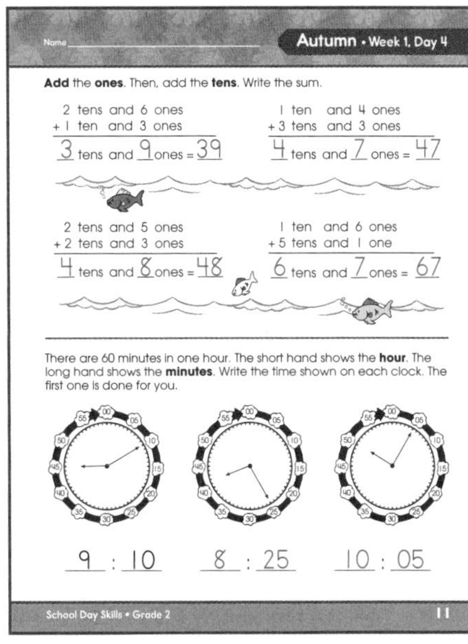

Name ______ **Autumn** • Week 1, Day 4

Add the **ones**. Then, add the **tens**. Write the sum.

2 tens and 6 ones
+ 1 ten and 3 ones
3 tens and 9 ones = 39

1 ten and 4 ones
+ 3 tens and 3 ones
4 tens and 7 ones = 47

2 tens and 5 ones
+ 2 tens and 3 ones
4 tens and 8 ones = 48

1 ten and 6 ones
+ 5 tens and 1 one
6 tens and 7 ones = 67

There are 60 minutes in one hour. The short hand shows the **hour**. The long hand shows the **minutes**. Write the time shown on each clock. The first one is done for you.

9 : 10 8 : 25 10 : 05

School Day Skills • Grade 2 11

Page 11

Name ______ **Autumn** • Week 1, Day 5

Add in one minute or less.

8 + 8 = 16	2 + 3 = 5	7 + 1 = 8	2 + 8 = 10	5 + 7 = 12
9 + 10 = 19	4 + 10 = 14	6 + 0 = 6	9 + 5 = 14	8 + 6 = 14

Adjectives describe nouns. They can tell what kind, how many, or which one. Color each space that has an adjective.

12 School Day Skills • Grade 2

Page 12

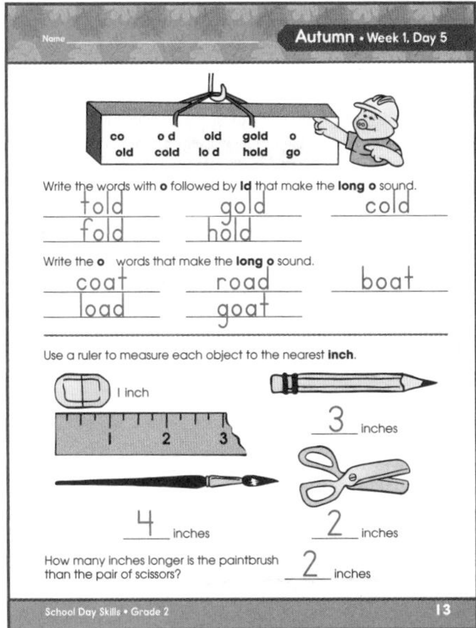

Name ______ **Autumn** • Week 1, Day 5

Write the words with **o** followed by **ld** that make the **long o** sound.

told gold cold
fold hold

Write the **o** _ words that make the **long o** sound.

coat road boat
load goat

Use a ruler to measure each object to the nearest **inch**.

1 inch

3 inches

4 inches

2 inches

How many inches longer is the paintbrush than the pair of scissors? 2 inches

School Day Skills • Grade 2 13

Page 13

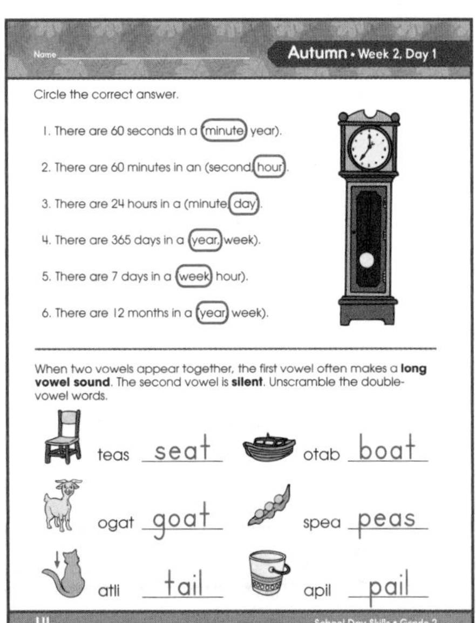

Name ______ **Autumn** • Week 2, Day 1

Circle the correct answer.

1. There are 60 seconds in a (minute) year).
2. There are 60 minutes in an (second, hour).
3. There are 24 hours in a (minute, day).
4. There are 365 days in a (year, week).
5. There are 7 days in a (week, hour).
6. There are 12 months in a (year, week).

When two vowels appear together, the first vowel often makes a **long vowel sound**. The second vowel is **silent**. Unscramble the double-vowel words.

teas seat otab boat

ogat goat spea peas

atli tail apil pail

14 School Day Skills • Grade 2

Page 14

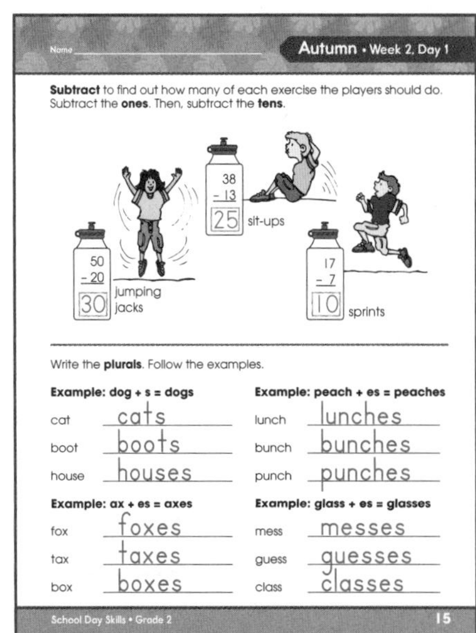

Name ______ **Autumn** • Week 2, Day 1

Subtract to find out how many of each exercise the players should do. Subtract the **ones**. Then, subtract the **tens**.

38 − 13 = 25 sit-ups

50 − 20 = 30 jumping jacks

17 − 7 = 10 sprints

Write the **plurals**. Follow the examples.

Example: dog + s = dogs
cat cats
boot boots
house houses

Example: peach + es = peaches
lunch lunches
bunch bunches
punch punches

Example: ax + es = axes
fox foxes
tax taxes
box boxes

Example: glass + es = glasses
mess messes
guess guesses
class classes

School Day Skills • Grade 2 15

Page 15

Answer Key

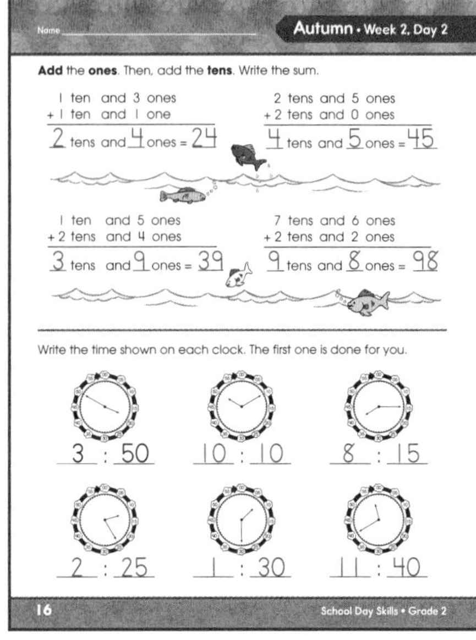
Name

Autumn • Week 2, Day 2

Add the **ones**. Then, add the **tens**. Write the sum.

1 ten and 3 ones
+ 1 ten and 1 one
2 tens and 4 ones = 24

2 tens and 5 ones
+ 2 tens and 0 ones
4 tens and 5 ones = 45

1 ten and 5 ones
+ 2 tens and 4 ones
3 tens and 9 ones = 39

7 tens and 6 ones
+ 2 tens and 2 ones
9 tens and 8 ones = 98

Write the time shown on each clock. The first one is done for you.

3 : 50 10 : 10 8 : 15

2 : 25 1 : 30 11 : 40

16 School Day Skills • Grade 2

Page 16

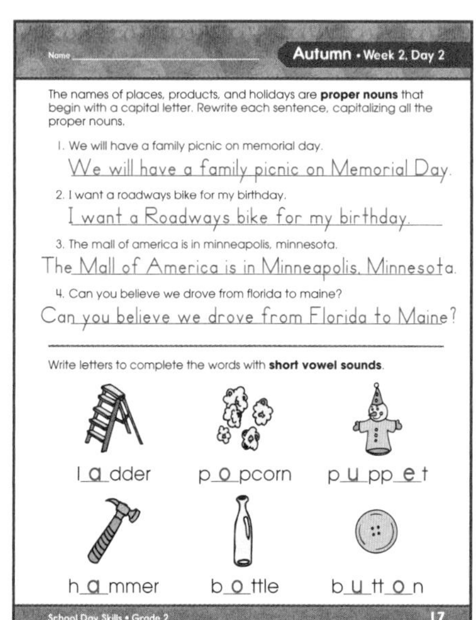
Name

Autumn • Week 2, Day 2

The names of places, products, and holidays are **proper nouns** that begin with a capital letter. Rewrite each sentence, capitalizing all the proper nouns.

1. We will have a family picnic on memorial day.
We will have a family picnic on Memorial Day.
2. I want a roadways bike for my birthday.
I want a Roadways bike for my birthday.
3. The mall of america is in minneapolis, minnesota.
The Mall of America is in Minneapolis, Minnesota.
4. Can you believe we drove from florida to maine?
Can you believe we drove from Florida to Maine?

Write letters to complete the words with **short vowel sounds**.

l a dder p o pcorn p u pp e t

h a mmer b o ttle b u tt o n

School Day Skills • Grade 2 17

Page 17

Name

Autumn • Week 2, Day 3

Find each item. Use a ruler to measure it to the nearest **inch**.

a stack of blocks ______ inches a toy car ______ inches

your foot ______ inches a spoon ______ inches

the length of a book ______ inches a toothbrush ______ inches

Answers will vary.

Which item was shortest? ______

Which item was longest? ______

Add **'s** to the noun in **bold** in the first sentence. Use the new word to complete the second sentence.

1. **Dad** is charging his phone.
Dad's phone is charging.
2. **Isa** has a blue backpack.
Have you seen Isa's blue backpack?
3. **Jake** got a new video game.
Let's play Jake's new video game.
4. **Mrs. Allen** has wilted plants.
We helped water Mrs. Allen's plants.

18 School Day Skills • Grade 2

Page 18

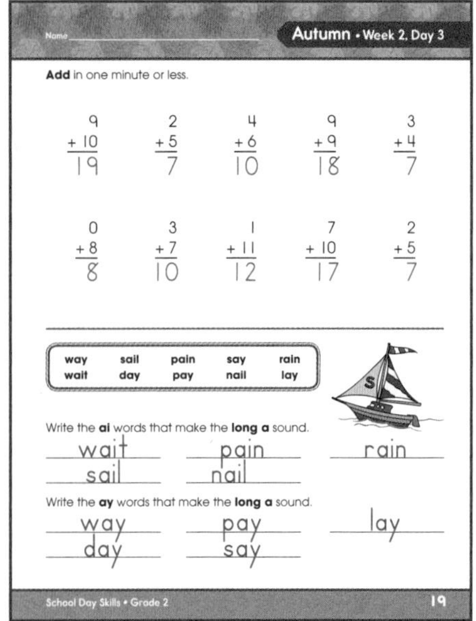
Name

Autumn • Week 2, Day 3

Add in one minute or less.

9 + 10 = 19; 2 + 5 = 7; 4 + 6 = 10; 9 + 9 = 18; 3 + 4 = 7

0 + 8 = 8; 3 + 7 = 10; 1 + 11 = 12; 7 + 10 = 17; 2 + 5 = 7

way sail pain say rain
wait day pay nail lay

Write the **ai** words that make the **long a** sound.
wait pain rain
sail nail

Write the **ay** words that make the **long a** sound.
way pay lay
day say

School Day Skills • Grade 2 19

Page 19

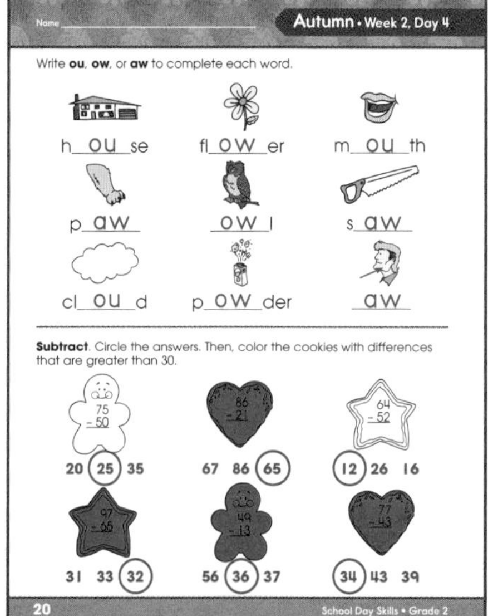
Name

Autumn • Week 2, Day 4

Write **ou**, **ow**, or **aw** to complete each word.

h ou se fl ow er m ou th

p aw ow l s aw

cl ou d p ow der aw

Subtract. Circle the answers. Then, color the cookies with differences that are greater than 30.

75 − 50: 20 (25) 35
86 − 21: 67 86 (65)
64 − 52: (12) 26 16
97 − 65: 31 33 (32)
49 − 13: 56 (36) 37
77 − 43: (34) 43 39

20 School Day Skills • Grade 2

Page 20

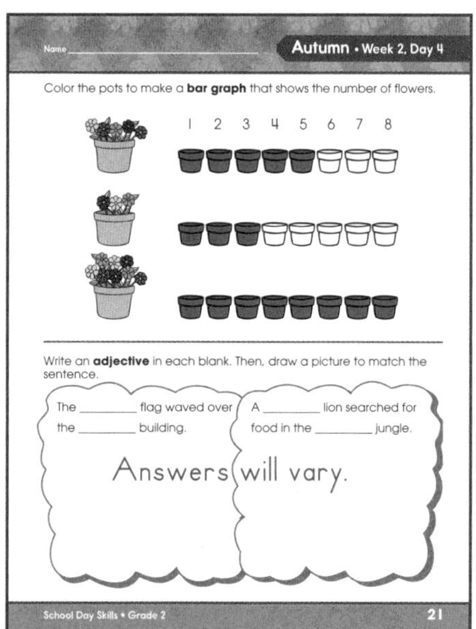
Name

Autumn • Week 2, Day 4

Color the pots to make a **bar graph** that shows the number of flowers.

1 2 3 4 5 6 7 8

Write an **adjective** in each blank. Then, draw a picture to match the sentence.

The ______ flag waved over the ______ building.

A ______ lion searched for food in the ______ jungle.

Answers will vary.

School Day Skills • Grade 2 21

Page 21

Answer Key

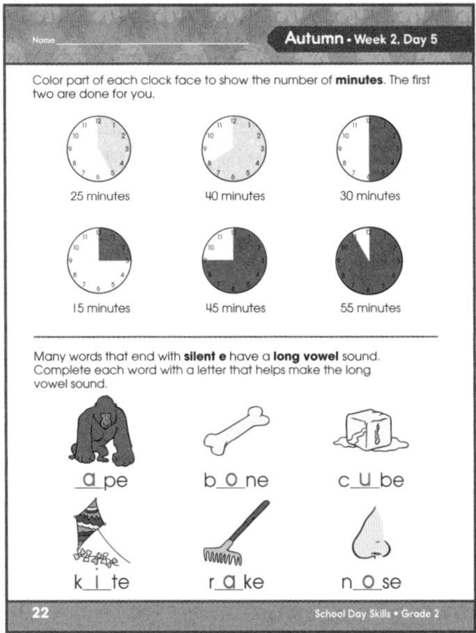

Page 22

Page 23

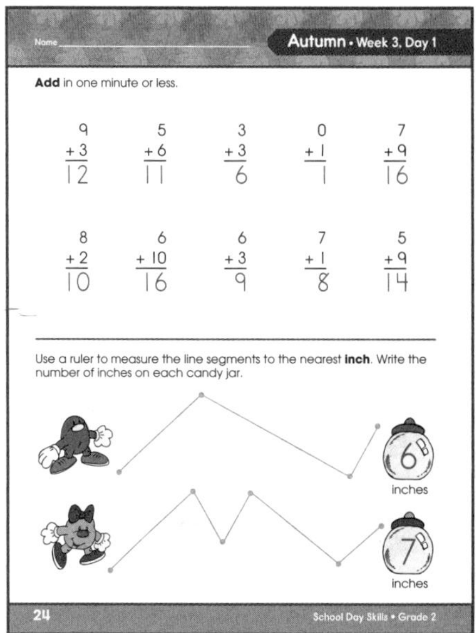

Page 24

Page 25

Page 26

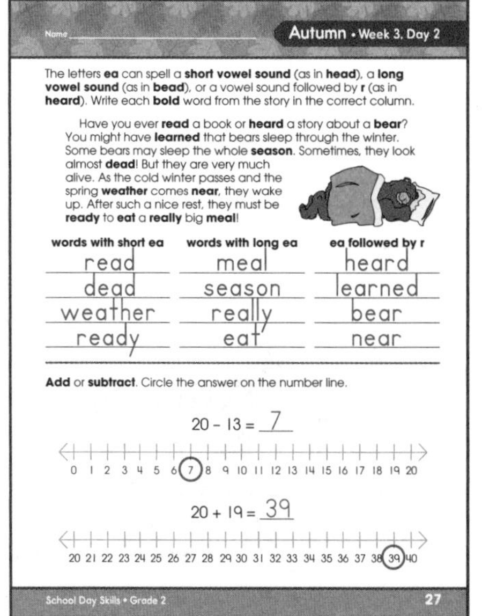

Page 27

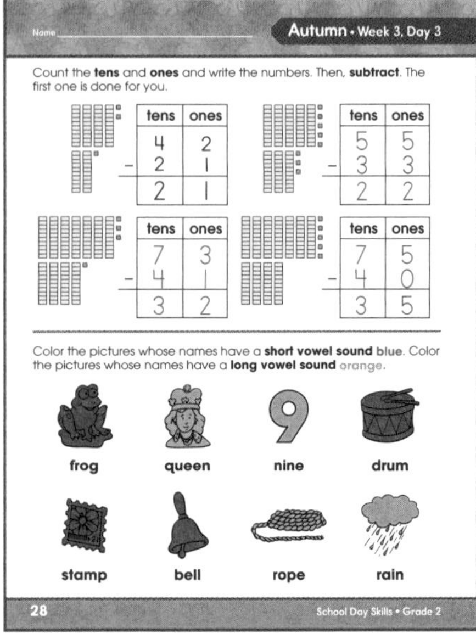
Name ______ **Autumn** • Week 3, Day 3

Count the **tens** and **ones** and write the numbers. Then, **subtract**. The first one is done for you.

	tens	ones
	4	2
−	2	1
	2	1

	tens	ones
	5	5
−	3	3
	2	2

	tens	ones
	7	3
−	4	1
	3	2

	tens	ones
	7	5
−	4	0
	3	5

Color the pictures whose names have a **short vowel sound** blue. Color the pictures whose names have a **long vowel sound** orange.

frog queen nine drum

stamp bell rope rain

28 School Day Skills • Grade 2

Page 28

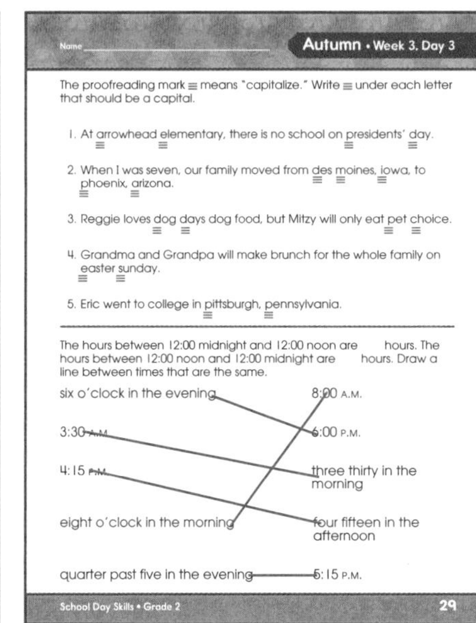
Name ______ **Autumn** • Week 3, Day 3

The proofreading mark ≡ means "capitalize." Write ≡ under each letter that should be a capital.

1. At arrowhead elementary, there is no school on presidents' day.
2. When I was seven, our family moved from des moines, iowa, to phoenix, arizona.
3. Reggie loves dog days dog food, but Mitzy will only eat pet choice.
4. Grandma and Grandpa will make brunch for the whole family on easter sunday.
5. Eric went to college in pittsburgh, pennsylvania.

The hours between 12:00 midnight and 12:00 noon are hours. The hours between 12:00 noon and 12:00 midnight are hours. Draw a line between times that are the same.

six o'clock in the evening — 8:00 A.M.

3:30 A.M. — 6:00 P.M.

4:15 P.M. — three thirty in the morning

eight o'clock in the morning — four fifteen in the afternoon

quarter past five in the evening — 5:15 P.M.

School Day Skills • Grade 2 29

Page 29

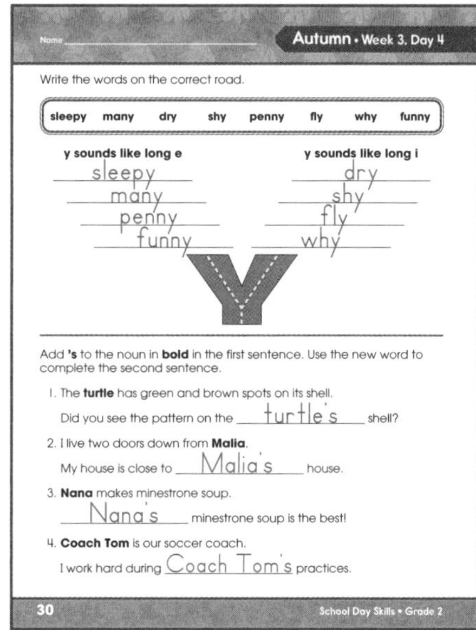
Name ______ **Autumn** • Week 3, Day 4

Write the words on the correct road.

sleepy many dry shy penny fly why funny

y sounds like long e: sleepy, many, penny, funny

y sounds like long i: dry, shy, fly, why

Add **'s** to the noun in **bold** in the first sentence. Use the new word to complete the second sentence.

1. The **turtle** has green and brown spots on its shell.
   Did you see the pattern on the turtle's shell?
2. I live two doors down from **Malia**.
   My house is close to Malia's house.
3. **Nana** makes minestrone soup.
   Nana's minestrone soup is the best!
4. **Coach Tom** is our soccer coach.
   I work hard during Coach Tom's practices.

30 School Day Skills • Grade 2

Page 30

Name ______ **Autumn** • Week 3, Day 4

Add in one minute or less.

9 + 5 = 14	7 + 7 = 14	2 + 10 = 12	5 + 6 = 11	3 + 5 = 8
1 + 4 = 5	9 + 4 = 13	10 + 6 = 16	2 + 2 = 4	4 + 8 = 12

Color: **one half** red		
Color: **one fourth** blue		
Color: **one third** orange		

School Day Skills • Grade 2 31

Page 31

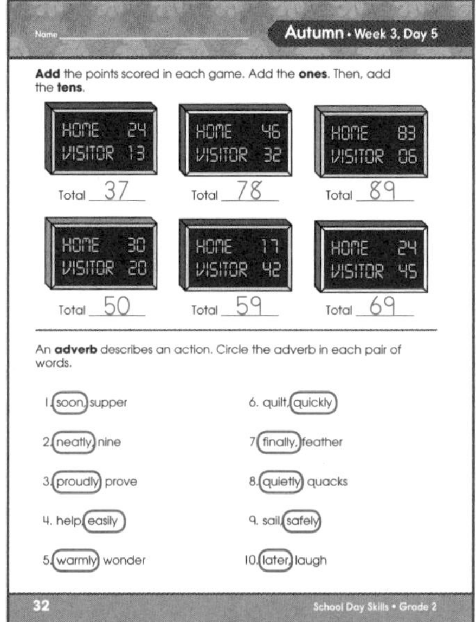
Name ______ **Autumn** • Week 3, Day 5

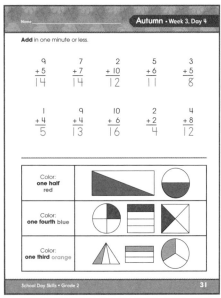

Add the points scored in each game. Add the **ones**. Then, add the **tens**.

HOME 24 VISITOR 13 Total 37

HOME 46 VISITOR 32 Total 78

HOME 83 VISITOR 06 Total 89

HOME 30 VISITOR 20 Total 50

HOME 17 VISITOR 42 Total 59

HOME 24 VISITOR 45 Total 69

An **adverb** describes an action. Circle the adverb in each pair of words.

1. (soon) supper
2. (neatly) nine
3. (proudly) prove
4. help (easily)
5. (warmly) wonder
6. quilt (quickly)
7. (finally) feather
8. (quietly) quacks
9. sail (safely)
10. (later) laugh

32 School Day Skills • Grade 2

Page 32

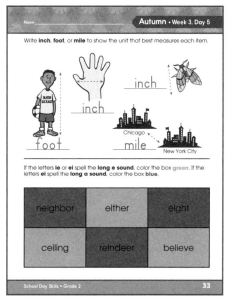

Name ______ **Autumn** • Week 3, Day 5

Write **inch**, **foot**, or **mile** to show the unit that best measures each item.

foot inch inch mile

Chicago New York City

If the letters **ie** or **ei** spell the **long e sound**, color the box green. If the letters **ei** spell the **long a sound**, color the box **blue**.

neighbor	either	eight
ceiling	reindeer	believe

School Day Skills • Grade 2 33

Page 33

Answer Key

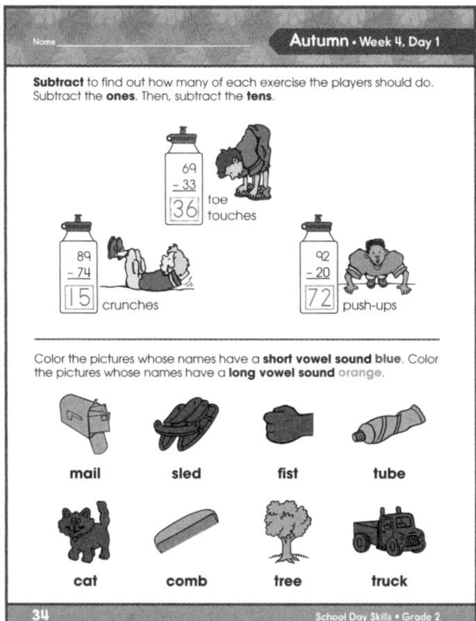

Page 34

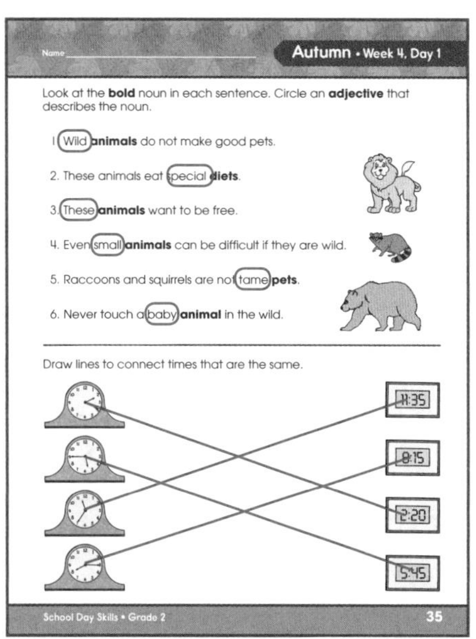

Page 35

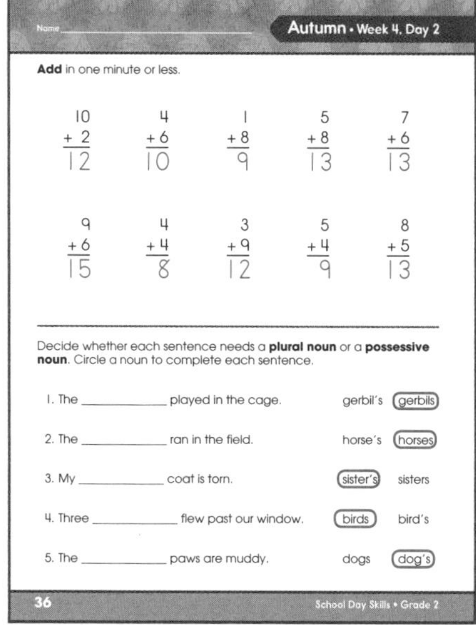

Page 36

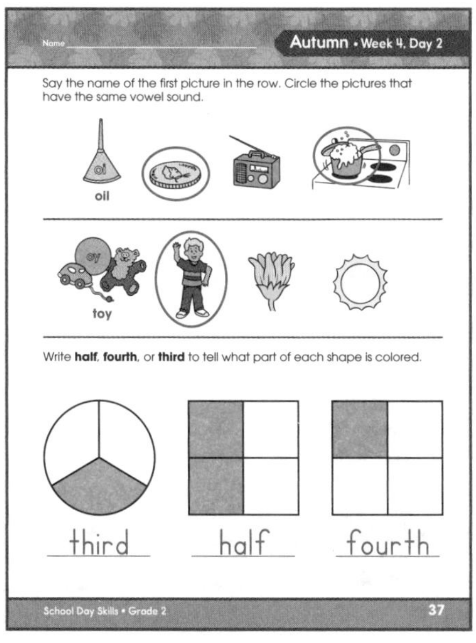

Page 37

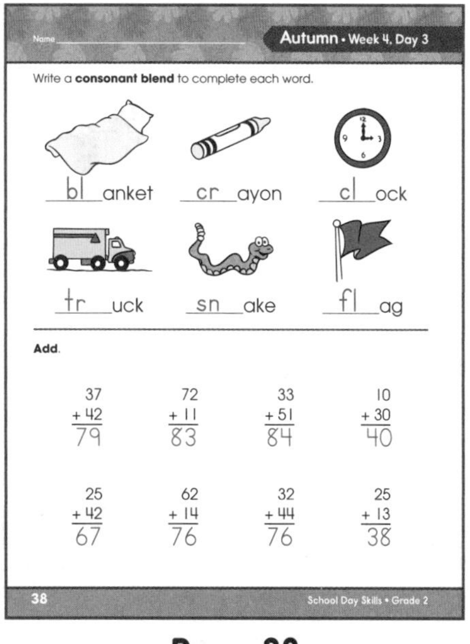

Page 38

Page 39

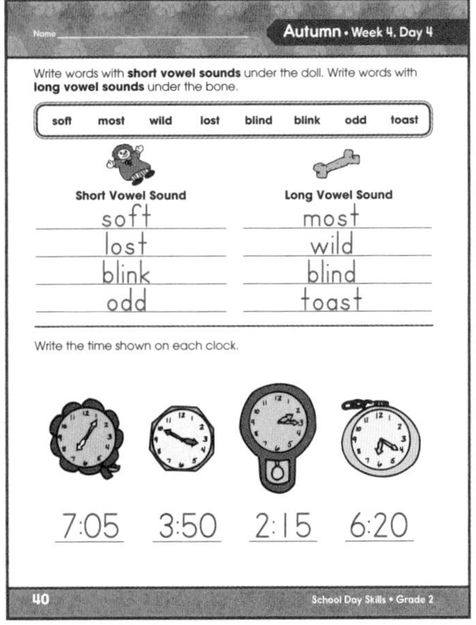

Name ______________ **Autumn** • Week 4, Day 4

Write words with **short vowel sounds** under the doll. Write words with **long vowel sounds** under the bone.

soft most wild lost blind blink odd toast

Short Vowel Sound	Long Vowel Sound
soft	most
lost	wild
blink	blind
odd	toast

Write the time shown on each clock.

7:05 3:50 2:15 6:20

40 School Day Skills • Grade 2

Page 40

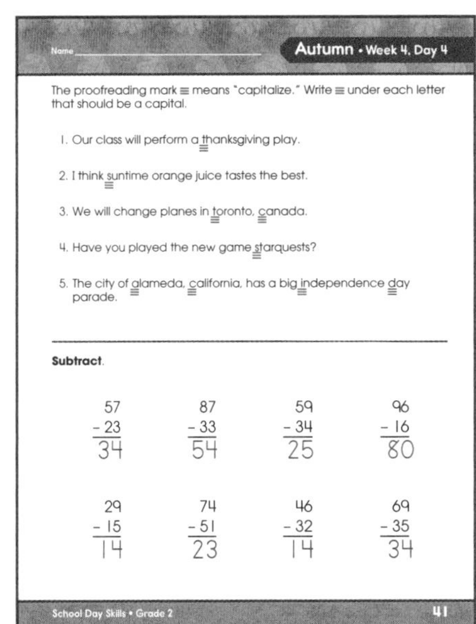

Name ______________ **Autumn** • Week 4, Day 4

The proofreading mark ≡ means "capitalize." Write ≡ under each letter that should be a capital.

1. Our class will perform a thanksgiving play.
2. I think suntime orange juice tastes the best.
3. We will change planes in toronto, canada.
4. Have you played the new game starquests?
5. The city of alameda, california, has a big independence day parade.

Subtract.

57 − 23 = 34	87 − 33 = 54	59 − 34 = 25	96 − 16 = 80
29 − 15 = 14	74 − 51 = 23	46 − 32 = 14	69 − 35 = 34

School Day Skills • Grade 2 41

Page 41

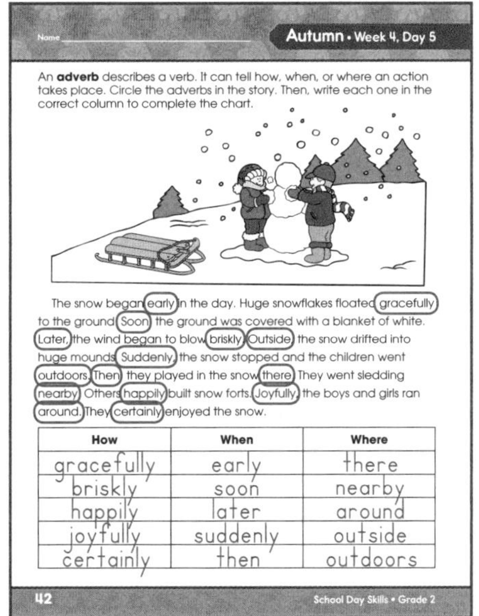

Name ______________ **Autumn** • Week 4, Day 5

An **adverb** describes a verb. It can tell how, when, or where an action takes place. Circle the adverbs in the story. Then, write each one in the correct column to complete the chart.

The snow began early in the day. Huge snowflakes floated gracefully to the ground. Soon the ground was covered with a blanket of white. Later, the wind began to blow briskly. Outside, the snow drifted into huge mounds. Suddenly, the snow stopped and the children went outdoors. Then they played in the snow there. They went sledding nearby. Others happily built snow forts. Joyfully, the boys and girls ran around. They certainly enjoyed the snow.

How	When	Where
gracefully	early	there
briskly	soon	nearby
happily	later	around
joyfully	suddenly	outside
certainly	then	outdoors

42 School Day Skills • Grade 2

Page 42

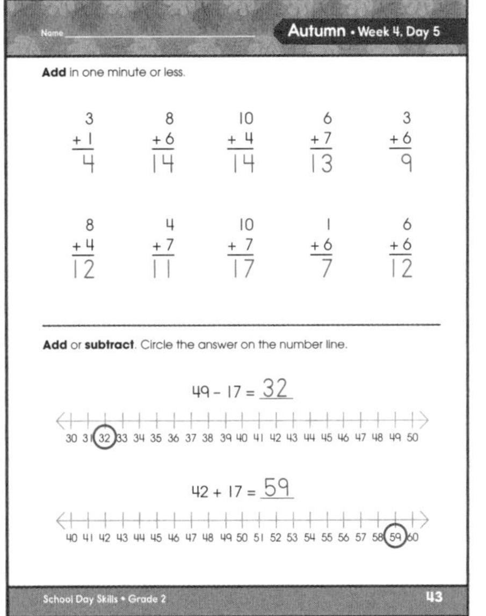

Name ______________ **Autumn** • Week 4, Day 5

Add in one minute or less.

3 + 1 = 4	8 + 6 = 14	10 + 4 = 14	6 + 7 = 13	3 + 6 = 9
8 + 4 = 12	4 + 7 = 11	10 + 7 = 17	1 + 6 = 7	6 + 6 = 12

Add or **subtract**. Circle the answer on the number line.

49 − 17 = 32

30 31 32 33 34 35 36 37 38 39 40 41 42 43 44 45 46 47 48 49 50

42 + 17 = 59

40 41 42 43 44 45 46 47 48 49 50 51 52 53 54 55 56 57 58 59 60

School Day Skills • Grade 2 43

Page 43

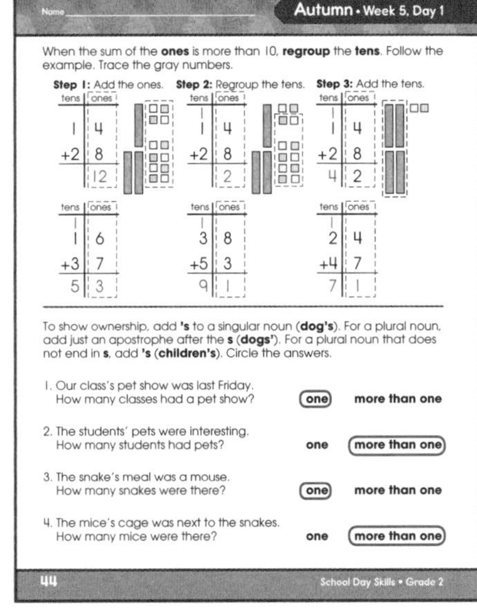

Name ______________ **Autumn** • Week 5, Day 1

When the sum of the **ones** is more than 10, **regroup** the **tens**. Follow the example. Trace the gray numbers.

Step 1: Add the ones. **Step 2:** Regroup the tens. **Step 3:** Add the tens.

tens	ones
1	4
+2	8
4	2

16 + 37 = 53 38 + 53 = 91 24 + 47 = 71

To show ownership, add **'s** to a singular noun (**dog's**). For a plural noun, add just an apostrophe after the **s** (**dogs'**). For a plural noun that does not end in **s**, add **'s** (**children's**). Circle the answers.

1. Our class's pet show was last Friday. How many classes had a pet show? **one** / more than one
2. The students' pets were interesting. How many students had pets? one / **more than one**
3. The snake's meal was a mouse. How many snakes were there? **one** / more than one
4. The mice's cage was next to the snakes. How many mice were there? one / **more than one**

44 School Day Skills • Grade 2

Page 44

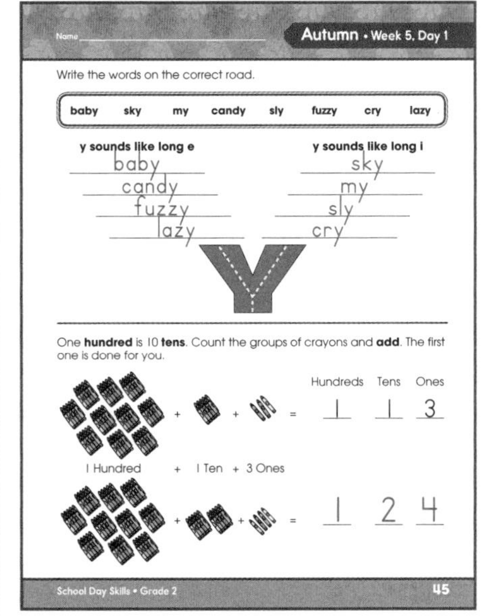

Name ______________ **Autumn** • Week 5, Day 1

Write the words on the correct road.

baby sky my candy sly fuzzy cry lazy

y sounds like long e	y sounds like long i
baby	sky
candy	my
fuzzy	sly
lazy	cry

One **hundred** is 10 **tens**. Count the groups of crayons and **add**. The first one is done for you.

	Hundreds	Tens	Ones
1 Hundred + 1 Ten + 3 Ones =	1	1	3
	1	2	4

School Day Skills • Grade 2 45

Page 45

Answer Key

Page 46

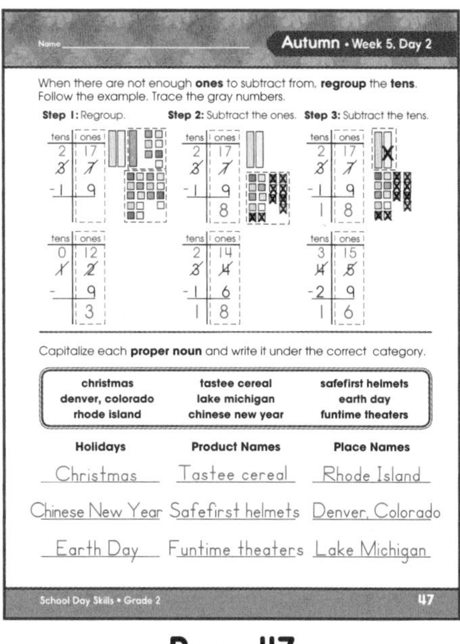

Page 47

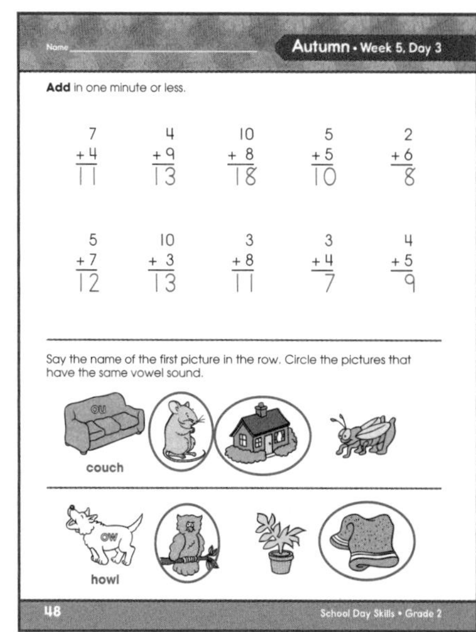

Page 48

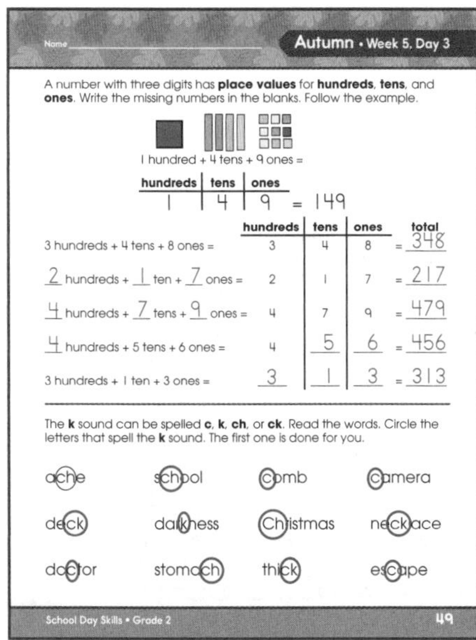

Page 49

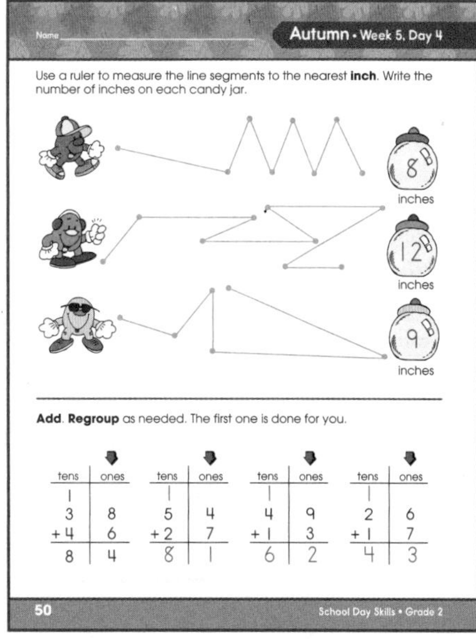

Page 50

Page 51

Answer Key

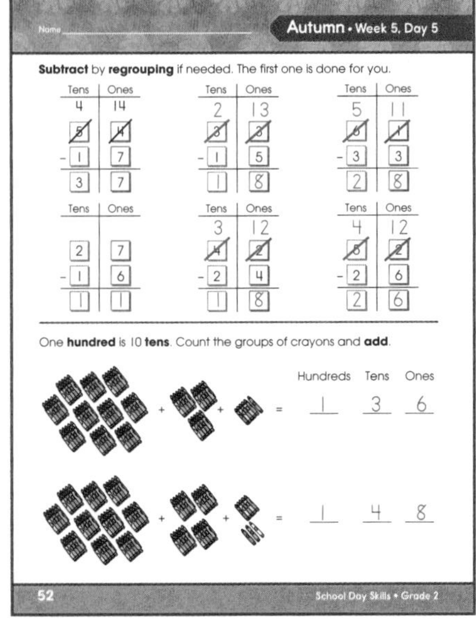

Name ____________ **Autumn** • Week 5, Day 5

Subtract by **regrouping** if needed. The first one is done for you.

Tens	Ones
4	14
~~5~~	~~4~~
- 1	7
3	7

Tens	Ones
2	13
~~3~~	~~3~~
- 1	5
1	8

Tens	Ones
5	11
~~6~~	~~1~~
- 3	3
2	8

Tens	Ones
2	7
- 1	6
1	1

Tens	Ones
3	12
~~4~~	~~2~~
- 2	4
1	8

Tens	Ones
4	12
~~5~~	~~2~~
- 2	6
2	6

One **hundred** is 10 **tens**. Count the groups of crayons and **add**.

Hundreds	Tens	Ones
1	3	6
1	4	8

52 School Day Skills • Grade 2

Page 52

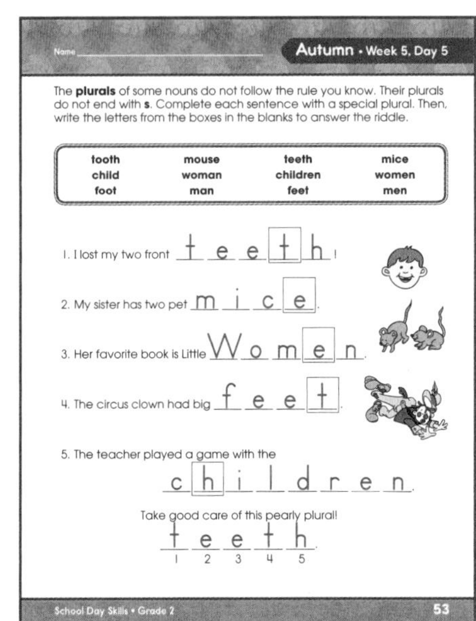

Name ____________ **Autumn** • Week 5, Day 5

The **plurals** of some nouns do not follow the rule you know. Their plurals do not end with **s**. Complete each sentence with a special plural. Then, write the letters from the boxes in the blanks to answer the riddle.

tooth	mouse	teeth	mice
child	woman	children	women
foot	man	feet	men

1. I lost my two front t e e t h!
2. My sister has two pet m i c e.
3. Her favorite book is Little W o m e n.
4. The circus clown had big f e e t.
5. The teacher played a game with the c h i l d r e n.

Take good care of this pearly plural!

t e e t h
1 2 3 4 5

School Day Skills • Grade 2 53

Page 53

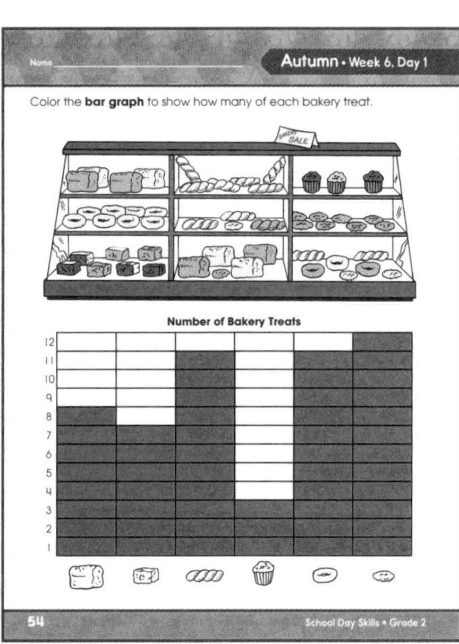

Name ____________ **Autumn** • Week 6, Day 1

Color the **bar graph** to show how many of each bakery treat.

Number of Bakery Treats

54 School Day Skills • Grade 2

Page 54

Name ____________ **Autumn** • Week 6, Day 1

Add in one minute or less.

6 + 9 = 15	8 + 7 = 15	9 + 2 = 11	5 + 3 = 8	10 + 0 = 10
7 + 3 = 10	9 + 8 = 17	2 + 4 = 6	4 + 0 = 4	7 + 8 = 15

Write your own **adverb** to complete each sentence. The first one is done for you.

1. The bees worked busily.
2. The dog barked Answers
3. The baby smiled will vary.
4. She wrote her name ____________.
5. The horse ran ____________.

School Day Skills • Grade 2 55

Page 55

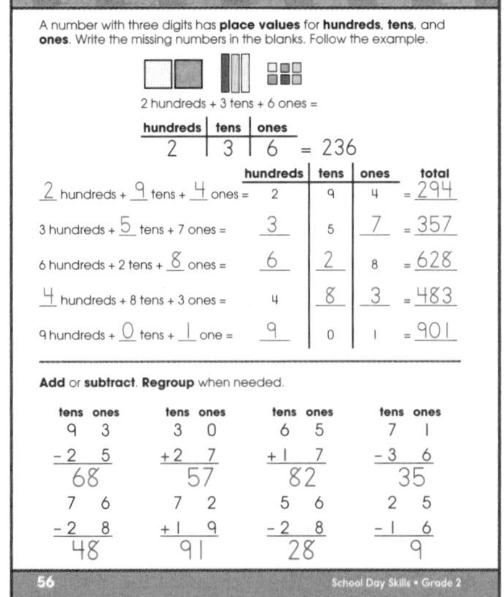

Name ____________ **Autumn** • Week 6, Day 2

A number with three digits has **place values** for **hundreds**, **tens**, and **ones**. Write the missing numbers in the blanks. Follow the example.

2 hundreds + 3 tens + 6 ones =

hundreds	tens	ones	
2	3	6	= 236

	hundreds	tens	ones	total
2 hundreds + 9 tens + 4 ones =	2	9	4	= 294
3 hundreds + 5 tens + 7 ones =	3	5	7	= 357
6 hundreds + 2 tens + 8 ones =	6	2	8	= 628
4 hundreds + 8 tens + 3 ones =	4	8	3	= 483
9 hundreds + 0 tens + 1 one =	9	0	1	= 901

Add or **subtract**. **Regroup** when needed.

93 - 25 = 68	30 + 27 = 57	65 + 17 = 82	71 - 36 = 35
76 - 28 = 48	72 + 19 = 91	56 - 28 = 28	25 - 16 = 9

56 School Day Skills • Grade 2

Page 56

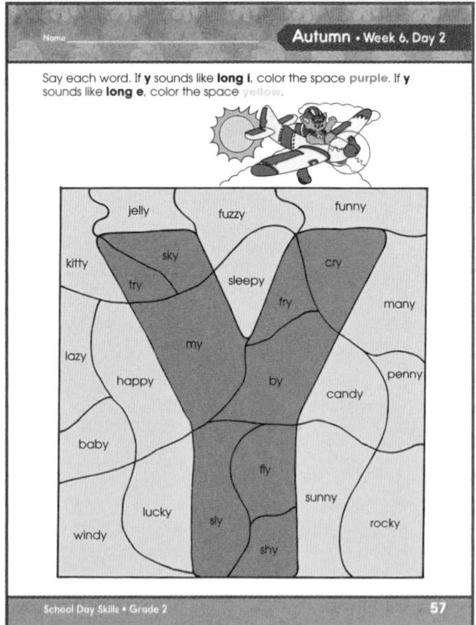

Name ____________ **Autumn** • Week 6, Day 2

Say each word. If **y** sounds like **long i**, color the space purple. If **y** sounds like **long e**, color the space yellow.

School Day Skills • Grade 2 57

Page 57

Answer Key

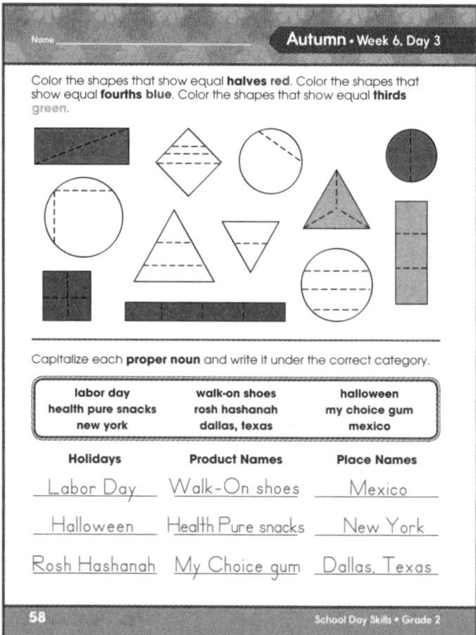

Name ______ **Autumn** • Week 6, Day 3

Color the shapes that show equal **halves red**. Color the shapes that show equal **fourths blue**. Color the shapes that show equal **thirds green**.

Capitalize each **proper noun** and write it under the correct category.

labor day, walk-on shoes, halloween, health pure snacks, rosh hashanah, my choice gum, new york, dallas, texas, mexico

Holidays	Product Names	Place Names
Labor Day	Walk-On shoes	Mexico
Halloween	Health Pure snacks	New York
Rosh Hashanah	My Choice gum	Dallas, Texas

58 School Day Skills • Grade 2

Page 58

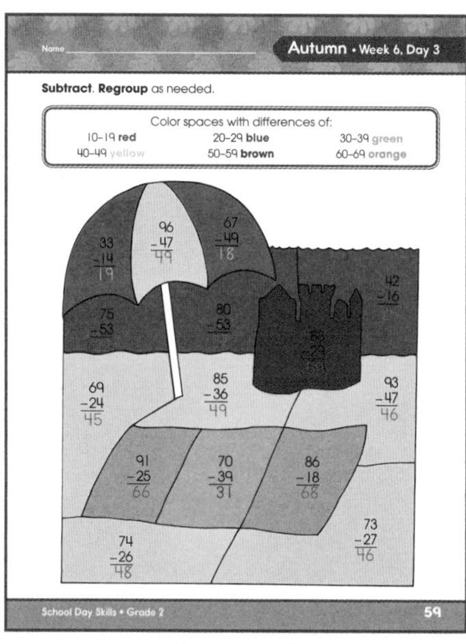

Name ______ **Autumn** • Week 6, Day 3

Subtract. Regroup as needed.

Color spaces with differences of:
10–19 **red** 20–29 **blue** 30–39 green
40–49 yellow 50–59 **brown** 60–69 orange

33 − 14 = 19
96 − 47 = 49
67 − 49 = 18
42 − 16
75 − 53
80 − 53
69 − 24 = 45
85 − 36 = 49
93 − 47 = 46
91 − 25 = 66
70 − 39 = 31
86 − 18 = 68
74 − 26 = 48
73 − 27 = 46

School Day Skills • Grade 2 59

Page 59

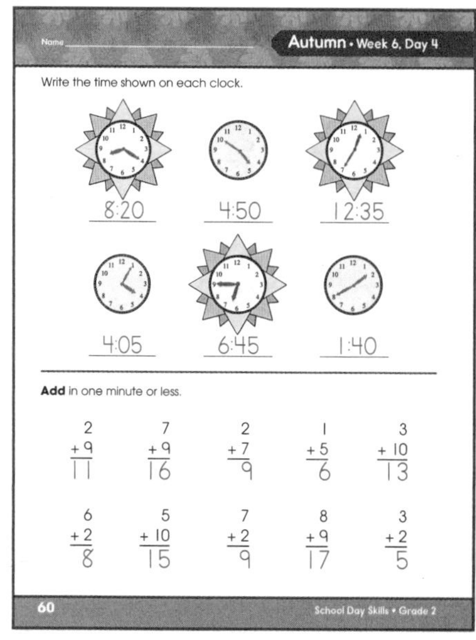

Name ______ **Autumn** • Week 6, Day 4

Write the time shown on each clock.

8:20 4:50 12:35
4:05 6:45 1:40

Add in one minute or less.

2 + 9 = 11
7 + 9 = 16
2 + 7 = 9
1 + 5 = 6
3 + 10 = 13
6 + 2 = 8
5 + 10 = 15
7 + 2 = 9
8 + 9 = 17
3 + 2 = 5

60 School Day Skills • Grade 2

Page 60

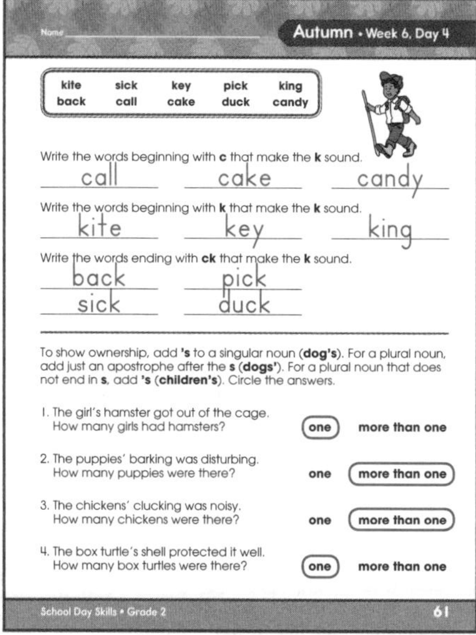

Name ______ **Autumn** • Week 6, Day 4

kite sick key pick king back call cake duck candy

Write the words beginning with **c** that make the **k** sound.
call cake candy

Write the words beginning with **k** that make the **k** sound.
kite key king

Write the words ending with **ck** that make the **k** sound.
back pick
sick duck

To show ownership, add **'s** to a singular noun **(dog's)**. For a plural noun, add just an apostrophe after the **s (dogs')**. For a plural noun that does not end in **s**, add **'s (children's)**. Circle the answers.

1. The girl's hamster got out of the cage. How many girls had hamsters? **(one)** more than one
2. The puppies' barking was disturbing. How many puppies were there? one **(more than one)**
3. The chickens' clucking was noisy. How many chickens were there? one **(more than one)**
4. The box turtle's shell protected it well. How many box turtles were there? **(one)** more than one

School Day Skills • Grade 2 61

Page 61

Name ______ **Autumn** • Week 6, Day 5

Add by **regrouping**. Connect the sums of 83 to make a road for the truck.

17 + 66 = 83
48 + 26 = 74
42 + 19 = 61
28 + 38 = 66
64 + 19 = 83
26 + 57 = 83
58 + 25 = 83
17 + 75 = 92
65 + 29 = 94
37 + 39 = 76
48 + 35 = 83
58 + 37 = 95
65 + 16 = 81
38 + 25 = 63
39 + 59 = 98
59 + 27 = 86
55 + 28 = 83
39 + 44 = 83

62 School Day Skills • Grade 2

Page 62

Name ______ **Autumn** • Week 6, Day 5

Write the words in the correct column.

mice foot children teeth feet mouse child tooth

one	more than one
child	mice
mouse	children
tooth	teeth
foot	feet

Use a ruler to measure each fish to the nearest **inch**.

about 1 inch
about 3 inches
about 3 inches

School Day Skills • Grade 2 63

Page 63

Answer Key

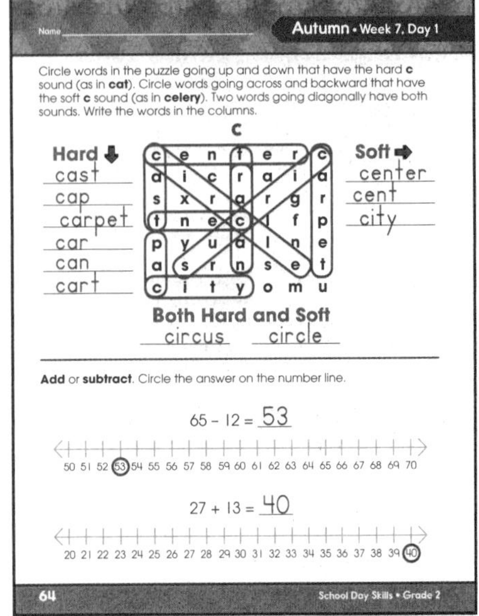

Name ____ **Autumn** • Week 7, Day 1

Circle words in the puzzle going up and down that have the hard **c** sound (as in **cat**). Circle words going across and backward that have the soft **c** sound (as in **celery**). Two words going diagonally have both sounds. Write the words in the columns.

Hard cast, cap, carpet, car, can, cart

Soft center, cent, city

Both Hard and Soft circus, circle

Add or **subtract**. Circle the answer on the number line.

65 – 12 = 53

27 + 13 = 40

64 School Day Skills • Grade 2

Page 64

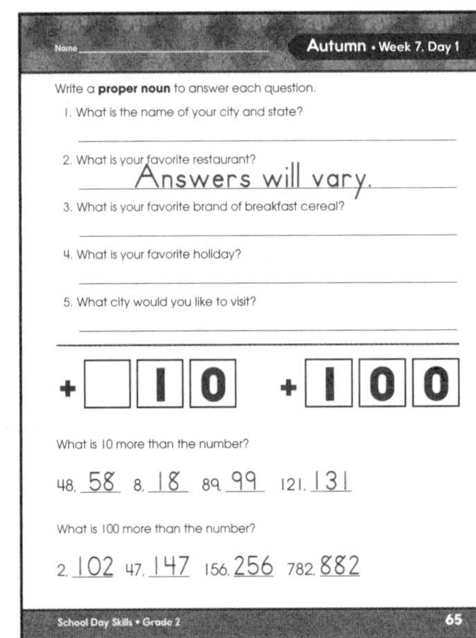

Name ____ **Autumn** • Week 7, Day 1

Write a **proper noun** to answer each question.

1. What is the name of your city and state?
2. What is your favorite restaurant?
3. What is your favorite brand of breakfast cereal?
4. What is your favorite holiday?
5. What city would you like to visit?

Answers will vary.

+ 10 + 100

What is 10 more than the number?

48. 58 8. 18 89. 99 121. 131

What is 100 more than the number?

2. 102 47. 147 156. 256 782. 882

School Day Skills • Grade 2 65

Page 65

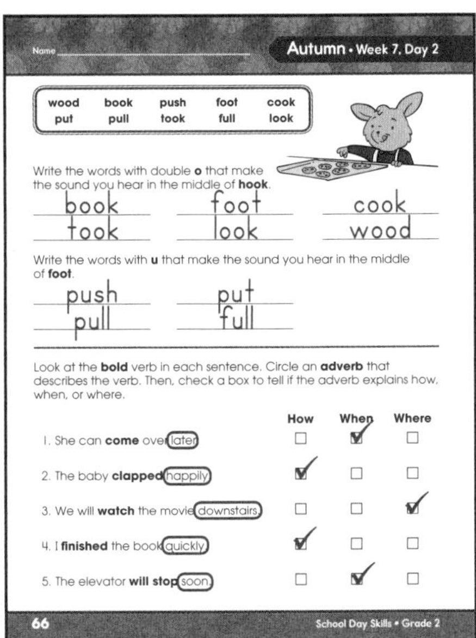

Name ____ **Autumn** • Week 7, Day 2

wood book push foot cook
put pull took full look

Write the words with double **o** that make the sound you hear in the middle of **hook**.

book, foot, cook, took, look, wood

Write the words with **u** that make the sound you hear in the middle of **foot**.

push, put, pull, full

Look at the **bold** verb in each sentence. Circle an **adverb** that describes the verb. Then, check a box to tell if the adverb explains how, when, or where.

	How	When	Where
1. She can **come** over (later).	☐	☑	☐
2. The baby **clapped** (happily).	☑	☐	☐
3. We will **watch** the movie (downstairs).	☐	☐	☑
4. I **finished** the book (quickly).	☑	☐	☐
5. The elevator **will stop** (soon).	☐	☑	☐

66 School Day Skills • Grade 2

Page 66

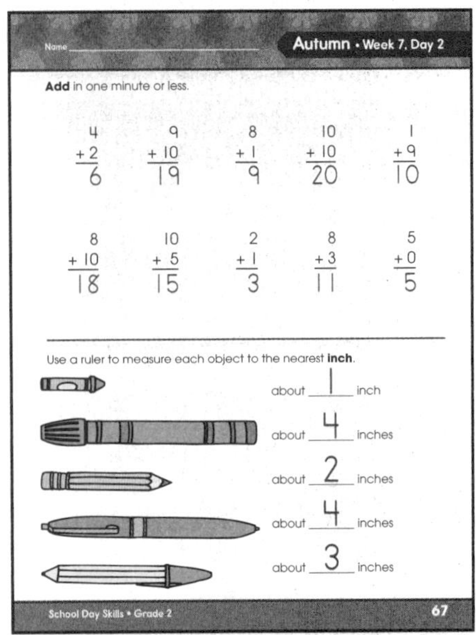

Name ____ **Autumn** • Week 7, Day 2

Add in one minute or less.

4 + 2 = 6; 9 + 10 = 19; 8 + 1 = 9; 10 + 10 = 20; 1 + 9 = 10

8 + 10 = 18; 10 + 5 = 15; 2 + 1 = 3; 8 + 3 = 11; 5 + 0 = 5

Use a ruler to measure each object to the nearest **inch**.

about 1 inch
about 4 inches
about 2 inches
about 4 inches
about 3 inches

School Day Skills • Grade 2 67

Page 67

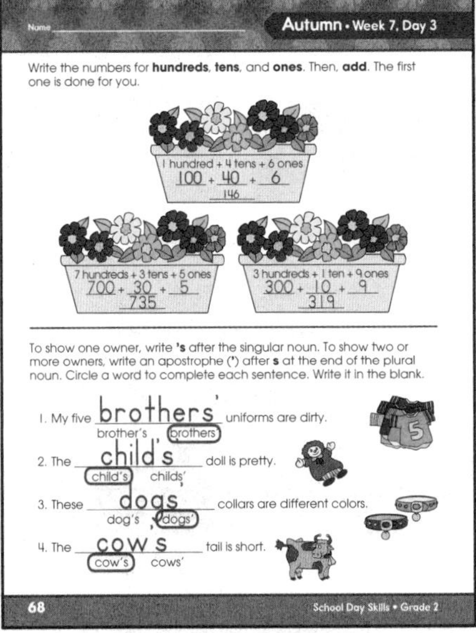

Name ____ **Autumn** • Week 7, Day 3

Write the numbers for **hundreds**, **tens**, and **ones**. Then, **add**. The first one is done for you.

1 hundred + 4 tens + 6 ones: 100 + 40 + 6 = 146

7 hundreds + 3 tens + 5 ones: 700 + 30 + 5 = 735

3 hundreds + 1 ten + 9 ones: 300 + 10 + 9 = 319

To show one owner, write **'s** after the singular noun. To show two or more owners, write an apostrophe (') after **s** at the end of the plural noun. Circle a word to complete each sentence. Write it in the blank.

1. My five brothers' uniforms are dirty. brother's (brothers')
2. The child's doll is pretty. (child's) childs'
3. These dogs' collars are different colors. dog's (dogs')
4. The cow's tail is short. (cow's) cows'

68 School Day Skills • Grade 2

Page 68

Name ____ **Autumn** • Week 7, Day 3

Write **1** or **2** to tell how many syllables each word has. If a word has two syllables, draw a line between the syllables. The first one is done for you.

tim|ber	2	blan|ket	2
brush	1	chair	1
bed|room	2	slip|per	2
street	1	tree	1

Solve the word problems.

1. Maddy rode the bus 26 times in October and 19 times in November. How many times did she ride in all? 45 times

2. Ollie did 21 math problems on Monday and 14 math problems on Tuesday. How many more problems did he do on Monday? 7 problems

School Day Skills • Grade 2 69

Page 69

Answer Key

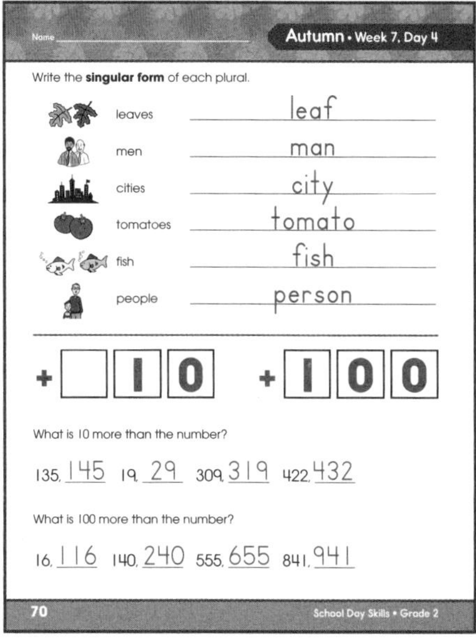
Name ______ **Autumn** • Week 7, Day 4

Write the **singular form** of each plural.

leaves	leaf
men	man
cities	city
tomatoes	tomato
fish	fish
people	person

+ 10 + 100

What is 10 more than the number?

135. 145 19. 29 309. 319 422. 432

What is 100 more than the number?

16. 116 140. 240 555. 655 841. 941

70 School Day Skills • Grade 2

Page 70

Name ______ **Autumn** • Week 7, Day 4

clown	down	how	house	now
our	count	town	about	out

Write the **ou** words that make the vowel sound you hear in **mouse**.

our house about
count out

Write the **ow** words that make the vowel sound you hear in **cow**.

clown down how
now town

Divide the apple into two equal **halves**. Divide the pizza into four equal **fourths**. Divide the cake into three equal **thirds**. Color the pictures.

School Day Skills • Grade 2 71

Page 71

Name ______ **Autumn** • Week 7, Day 5

Write two **adjectives** to describe each noun. Then, write a sentence using all three words.

marshmallows

airplane Answers will vary.

beach

How many **sides** does each shape have? Write the number in the shape.

3	4	4
triangle	square	rectangle
5	6	8
pentagon	hexagon	octagon

72 School Day Skills • Grade 2

Page 72

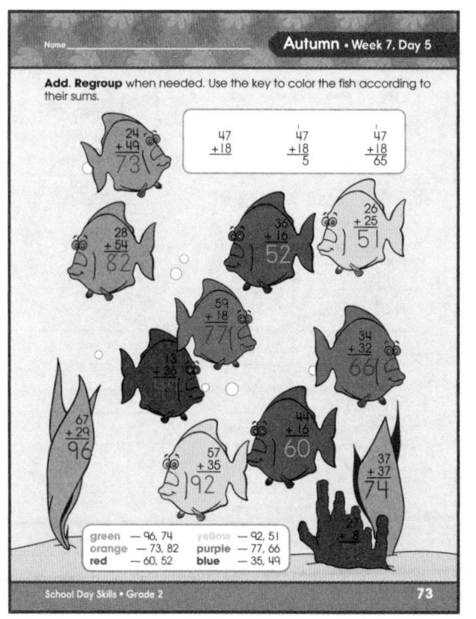
Name ______ **Autumn** • Week 7, Day 5

Add. Regroup when needed. Use the key to color the fish according to their sums.

47 + 18; 47 + 18 = 5; 47 + 18 = 65

24 + 49 = 73
28 + 54 = 82
36 + 16 = 52
26 + 25 = 51
59 + 18 = 77
34 + 32 = 66
67 + 29 = 96
44 + 16 = 60
57 + 35 = 92
37 + 37 = 74

green — 96, 74 yellow — 92, 51
orange — 73, 82 purple — 77, 66
red — 60, 52 blue — 35, 49

School Day Skills • Grade 2 73

Page 73

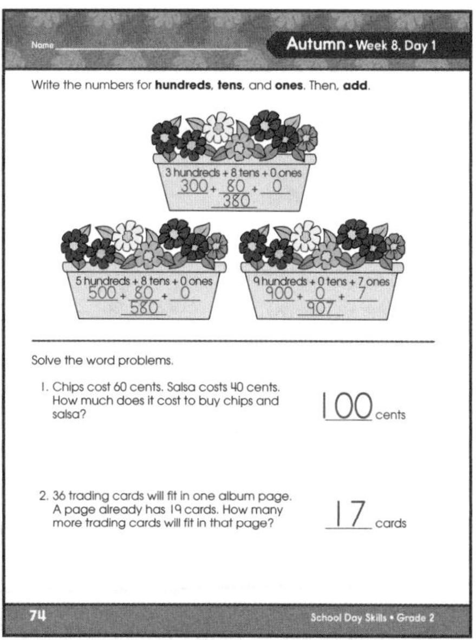
Name ______ **Autumn** • Week 8, Day 1

Write the numbers for **hundreds**, **tens**, and **ones**. Then, **add**.

3 hundreds + 8 tens + 0 ones
300 + 80 + 0 = 380

5 hundreds + 8 tens + 0 ones
500 + 80 + 0 = 580

9 hundreds + 0 tens + 7 ones
900 + 0 + 7 = 907

Solve the word problems.

1. Chips cost 60 cents. Salsa costs 40 cents. How much does it cost to buy chips and salsa? 100 cents
2. 36 trading cards will fit in one album page. A page already has 19 cards. How many more trading cards will fit in that page? 17 cards

74 School Day Skills • Grade 2

Page 74

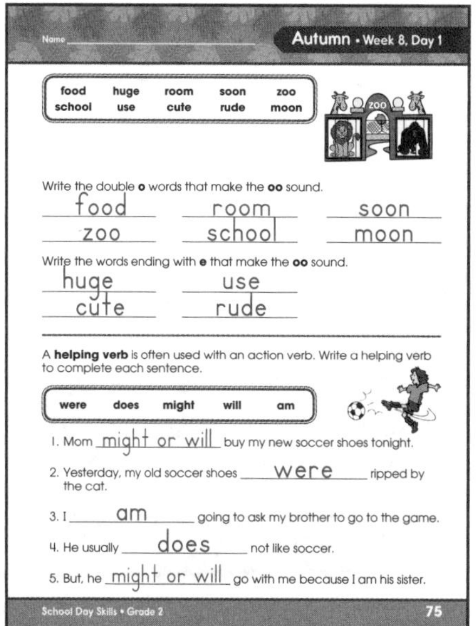
Name ______ **Autumn** • Week 8, Day 1

food	huge	room	soon	zoo
school	use	cute	rude	moon

Write the double **o** words that make the **oo** sound.

food room soon
zoo school moon

Write the words ending with **e** that make the **oo** sound.

huge use
cute rude

A **helping verb** is often used with an action verb. Write a helping verb to complete each sentence.

were	does	might	will	am

1. Mom might or will buy my new soccer shoes tonight.
2. Yesterday, my old soccer shoes were ripped by the cat.
3. I am going to ask my brother to go to the game.
4. He usually does not like soccer.
5. But, he might or will go with me because I am his sister.

School Day Skills • Grade 2 75

Page 75

Answer Key

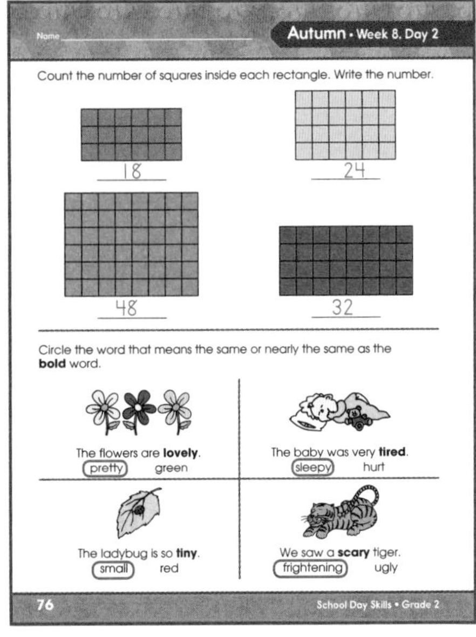

Name ______ **Autumn** • Week 8, Day 2

Count the number of squares inside each rectangle. Write the number.

18 24

48 32

Circle the word that means the same or nearly the same as the **bold** word.

The flowers are **lovely**.
pretty green

The baby was very **tired**.
sleepy hurt

The ladybug is so **tiny**.
small red

We saw a **scary** tiger.
frightening ugly

76 School Day Skills • Grade 2

Page 76

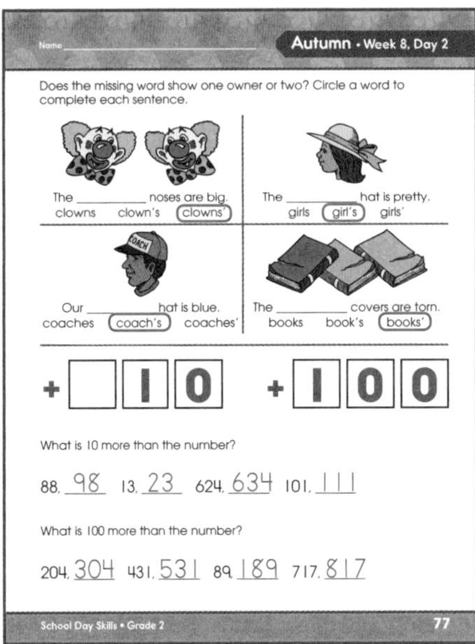

Name ______ **Autumn** • Week 8, Day 2

Does the missing word show one owner or two? Circle a word to complete each sentence.

The ______ noses are big.
clowns clown's clowns'

The ______ hat is pretty.
girls girl's girls'

Our ______ hat is blue.
coaches coach's coaches'

The ______ covers are torn.
books book's books'

+ [ ] [1] [0] + [1] [0] [0]

What is 10 more than the number?

88. 98 13. 23 624. 634 101. 111

What is 100 more than the number?

204. 304 431. 531 89. 189 717. 817

School Day Skills • Grade 2 77

Page 77

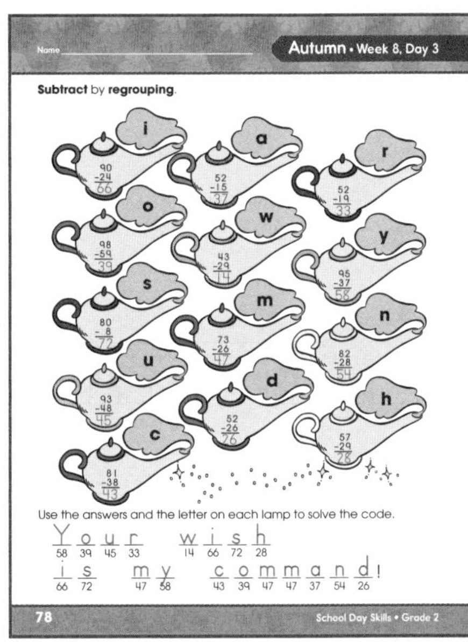

Name ______ **Autumn** • Week 8, Day 3

Subtract by **regrouping**.

i: 90 − 24 = 66
a: 52 − 15 = 37
r: 52 − 19 = 33
o: 98 − 59 = 39
w: 43 − 29 = 14
y: 95 − 37 = 58
s: 80 − 8 = 72
m: 73 − 26 = 47
n: 82 − 28 = 54
u: 93 − 48 = 45
d: 52 − 26 = 26
h: 57 − 29 = 28
c: 81 − 38 = 43

Use the answers and the letter on each lamp to solve the code.

Y o u r (58 39 45 33) w i s h (14 66 72 28)
i s (66 72) m y (47 58) c o m m a n d ! (43 39 47 47 37 54 26)

78 School Day Skills • Grade 2

Page 78

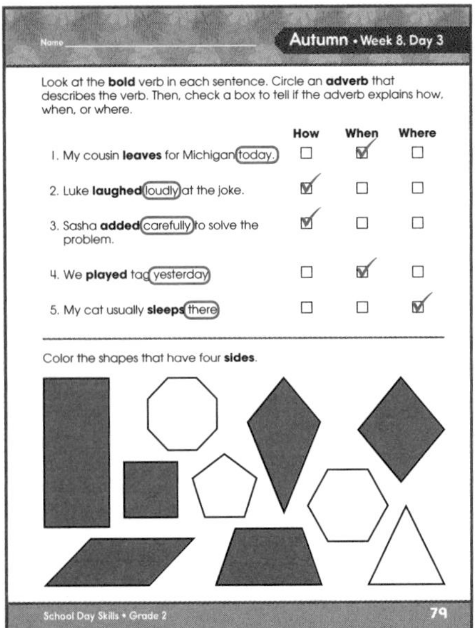

Name ______ **Autumn** • Week 8, Day 3

Look at the **bold** verb in each sentence. Circle an **adverb** that describes the verb. Then, check a box to tell if the adverb explains how, when, or where.

	How	When	Where
1. My cousin **leaves** for Michigan today.	☐	☑	☐
2. Luke **laughed** loudly at the joke.	☑	☐	☐
3. Sasha **added** carefully to solve the problem.	☑	☐	☐
4. We **played** tag yesterday.	☐	☑	☐
5. My cat usually **sleeps** there.	☐	☐	☑

Color the shapes that have four **sides**.

School Day Skills • Grade 2 79

Page 79

Name ______ **Autumn** • Week 8, Day 4

Write the **plural form** for each singular noun.

country — countries
potato — potatoes
deer — deer
wife — wives
half — halves
foot — feet

Solve the word problems.

1. Colby swings 75 times at the playground. She pumps her legs 52 times. For how many swings does she not pump her legs? 23 swings

2. A family on vacation traveled 49 miles in the morning and 46 miles in the afternoon. How many miles did the family travel in all? 95 miles

80 School Day Skills • Grade 2

Page 80

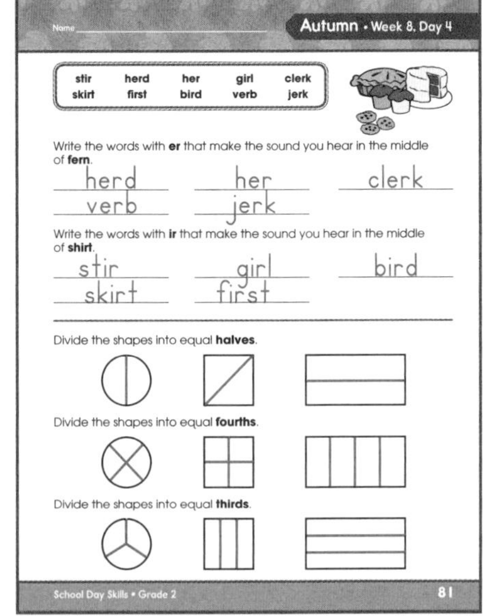

Name ______ **Autumn** • Week 8, Day 4

stir	herd	her	girl	clerk
skirt	first	bird	verb	jerk

Write the words with **er** that make the sound you hear in the middle of **fern**.

herd her clerk
verb jerk

Write the words with **ir** that make the sound you hear in the middle of **shirt**.

stir girl bird
skirt first

Divide the shapes into equal **halves**.

Divide the shapes into equal **fourths**.

Divide the shapes into equal **thirds**.

School Day Skills • Grade 2 81

Page 81

Answer Key

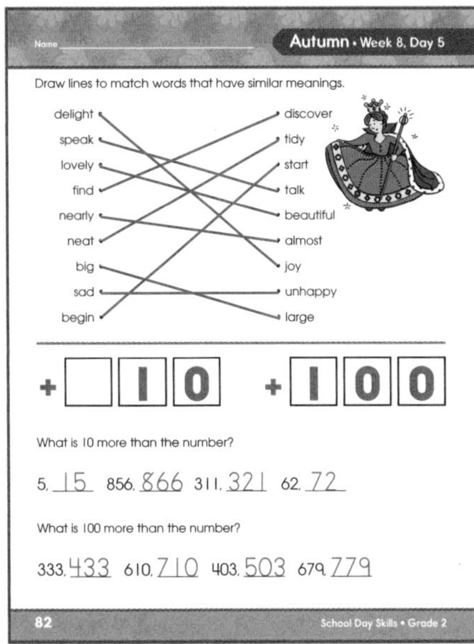
Name
Autumn • Week 8, Day 5

Draw lines to match words that have similar meanings.

delight	discover
speak	tidy
lovely	start
find	talk
nearly	beautiful
neat	almost
big	joy
sad	unhappy
begin	large

+ 10 + 100

What is 10 more than the number?

5. 15 856. 866 311. 321 62. 72

What is 100 more than the number?

333. 433 610. 710 403. 503 679. 779

82 School Day Skills • Grade 2

Page 82

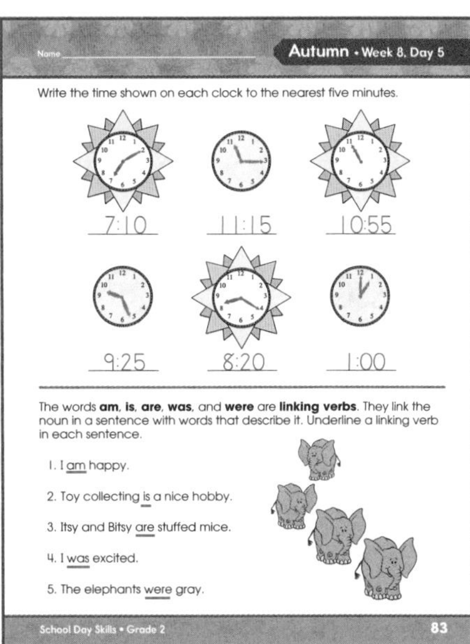
Name
Autumn • Week 8, Day 5

Write the time shown on each clock to the nearest five minutes.

7:10 11:15 10:55

9:25 8:20 1:00

The words **am**, **is**, **are**, **was**, and **were** are **linking verbs**. They link the noun in a sentence with words that describe it. Underline a linking verb in each sentence.

1. I am happy.
2. Toy collecting is a nice hobby.
3. Itsy and Bitsy are stuffed mice.
4. I was excited.
5. The elephants were gray.

School Day Skills • Grade 2 83

Page 83

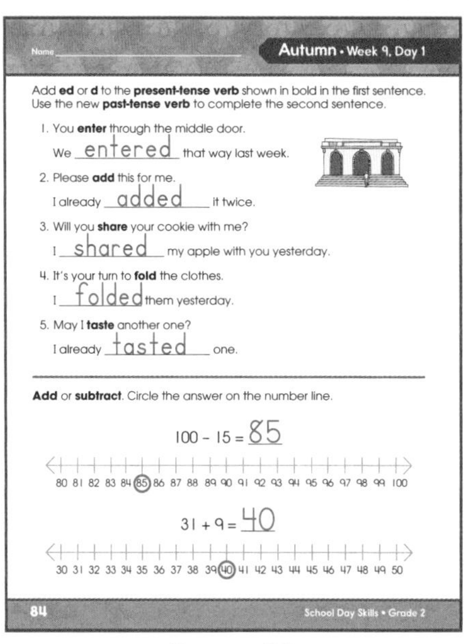
Name
Autumn • Week 9, Day 1

Add **ed** or **d** to the **present-tense verb** shown in bold in the first sentence. Use the new **past-tense verb** to complete the second sentence.

1. You **enter** through the middle door.
   We entered that way last week.
2. Please **add** this for me.
   I already added it twice.
3. Will you **share** your cookie with me?
   I shared my apple with you yesterday.
4. It's your turn to **fold** the clothes.
   I folded them yesterday.
5. May I **taste** another one?
   I already tasted one.

Add or **subtract**. Circle the answer on the number line.

100 – 15 = 85

80 81 82 83 84 85 86 87 88 89 90 91 92 93 94 95 96 97 98 99 100

31 + 9 = 40

30 31 32 33 34 35 36 37 38 39 40 41 42 43 44 45 46 47 48 49 50

84 School Day Skills • Grade 2

Page 84

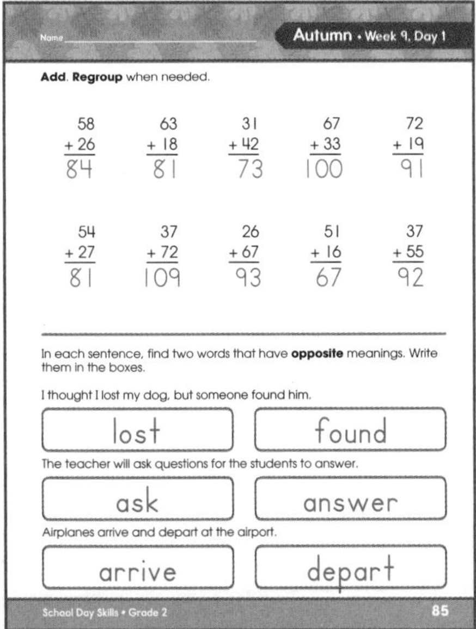
Name
Autumn • Week 9, Day 1

Add. **Regroup** when needed.

58 + 26 = 84 63 + 18 = 81 31 + 42 = 73 67 + 33 = 100 72 + 19 = 91

54 + 27 = 81 37 + 72 = 109 26 + 67 = 93 51 + 16 = 67 37 + 55 = 92

In each sentence, find two words that have **opposite** meanings. Write them in the boxes.

I thought I lost my dog, but someone found him.

lost | found

The teacher will ask questions for the students to answer.

ask | answer

Airplanes arrive and depart at the airport.

arrive | depart

School Day Skills • Grade 2 85

Page 85

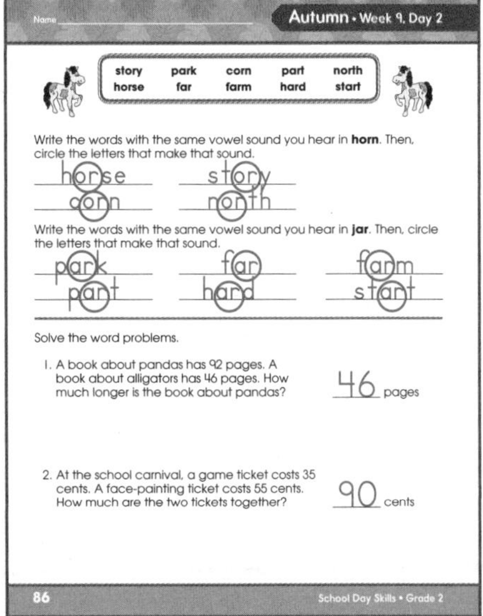
Name
Autumn • Week 9, Day 2

story park corn part north
horse far farm hard start

Write the words with the same vowel sound you hear in **horn**. Then, circle the letters that make that sound.

horse story corn north

Write the words with the same vowel sound you hear in **jar**. Then, circle the letters that make that sound.

park far farm part hard start

Solve the word problems.

1. A book about pandas has 92 pages. A book about alligators has 46 pages. How much longer is the book about pandas? 46 pages
2. At the school carnival, a game ticket costs 35 cents. A face-painting ticket costs 55 cents. How much are the two tickets together? 90 cents

86 School Day Skills • Grade 2

Page 86

Name
Autumn • Week 9, Day 2

Change the **present-tense verb** in the first sentence to a **past-tense verb** to complete the second sentence. Double the consonant at the end of each verb before adding **ed**. The first one is done for you.

1. We skip to school. Yesterday, we skipped the whole way.
2. It's not nice to grab things. When you grabbed my cookie, I felt angry.
3. Did Dad hug you today? Dad hugged me this morning.
4. We plan our vacations every year. Last year, we planned to go to the beach.
5. Is it my turn to stir the pot? You stirred it last time.

Write the name of each shape.

cube triangle rectangle pentagon hexagon

triangle pentagon rectangle

hexagon cube

School Day Skills • Grade 2 87

Page 87

Answer Key

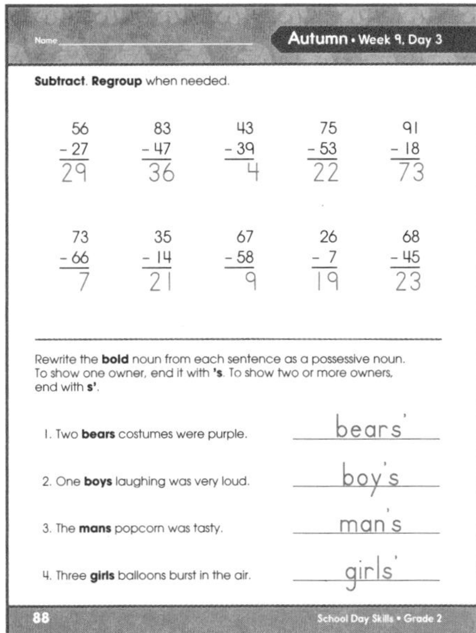
Name ____________ Autumn • Week 9, Day 3

Subtract. Regroup when needed.

56	83	43	75	91
− 27	− 47	− 39	− 53	− 18
29	36	4	22	73

73	35	67	26	68
− 66	− 14	− 58	− 7	− 45
7	21	9	19	23

Rewrite the **bold** noun from each sentence as a possessive noun. To show one owner, end it with **'s**. To show two or more owners, end with **s'**.

1. Two **bears** costumes were purple. bears'
2. One **boys** laughing was very loud. boy's
3. The **mans** popcorn was tasty. man's
4. Three **girls** balloons burst in the air. girls'

88 School Day Skills • Grade 2

Page 88

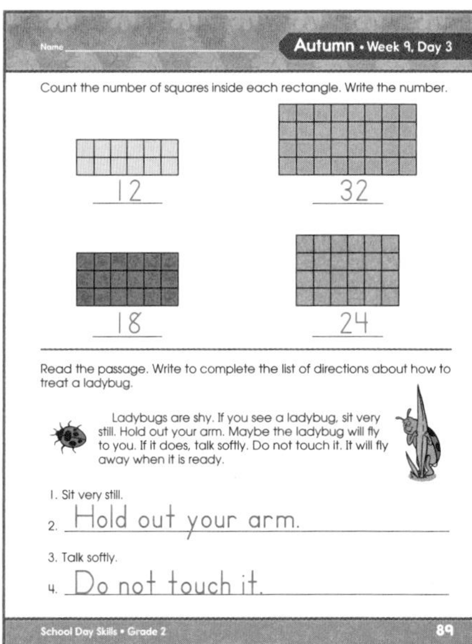
Name ____________ Autumn • Week 9, Day 3

Count the number of squares inside each rectangle. Write the number.

12 32

18 24

Read the passage. Write to complete the list of directions about how to treat a ladybug.

Ladybugs are shy. If you see a ladybug, sit very still. Hold out your arm. Maybe the ladybug will fly to you. If it does, talk softly. Do not touch it. It will fly away when it is ready.

1. Sit very still.
2. Hold out your arm.
3. Talk softly.
4. Do not touch it.

School Day Skills • Grade 2 89

Page 89

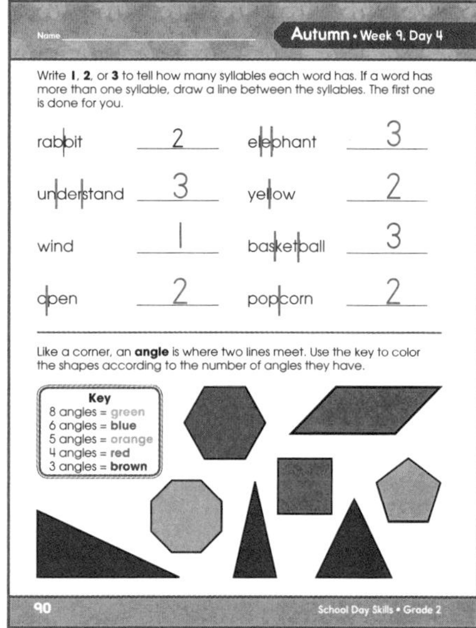
Name ____________ Autumn • Week 9, Day 4

Write **1**, **2**, or **3** to tell how many syllables each word has. If a word has more than one syllable, draw a line between the syllables. The first one is done for you.

rab|bit	2	el|e|phant	3
un|der|stand	3	yel|low	2
wind	1	bas|ket|ball	3
o|pen	2	pop|corn	2

Like a corner, an **angle** is where two lines meet. Use the key to color the shapes according to the number of angles they have.

Key
8 angles = green
6 angles = blue
5 angles = orange
4 angles = red
3 angles = brown

90 School Day Skills • Grade 2

Page 90

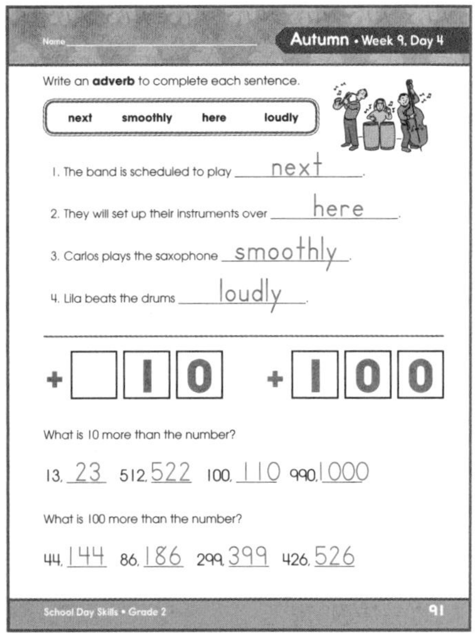
Name ____________ Autumn • Week 9, Day 4

Write an **adverb** to complete each sentence.

next smoothly here loudly

1. The band is scheduled to play next.
2. They will set up their instruments over here.
3. Carlos plays the saxophone smoothly.
4. Lila beats the drums loudly.

+ 10 + 100

What is 10 more than the number?

13. 23 512. 522 100. 110 990. 1,000

What is 100 more than the number?

44. 144 86. 186 299. 399 426. 526

School Day Skills • Grade 2 91

Page 91

Name ____________ Autumn • Week 9, Day 5

Write each number. The first one is done for you.

1 hundred, 3 tens, 2 ones = 132

1 hundred, 4 tens, 7 ones = 147

3 hundreds, 3 tens, 9 ones = 339

5 hundreds, 1 ten, 1 one = 511

Form the **past tense** of most verbs by adding **ed**. Sometimes, you only need to add **d**. Other times, you need to double the final consonant before adding **ed**. Write the past tense of each verb.

stir	stirred	smile	smiled
search	searched	load	loaded
clap	clapped	decide	decided
dance	danced	plan	planned

92 School Day Skills • Grade 2

Page 92

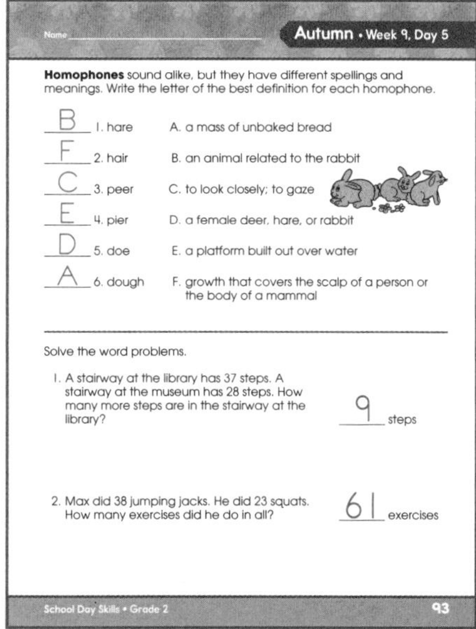
Name ____________ Autumn • Week 9, Day 5

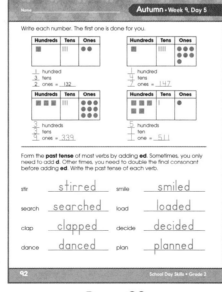

Homophones sound alike, but they have different spellings and meanings. Write the letter of the best definition for each homophone.

B 1. hare — A. a mass of unbaked bread
F 2. hair — B. an animal related to the rabbit
C 3. peer — C. to look closely; to gaze
E 4. pier — D. a female deer, hare, or rabbit
D 5. doe — E. a platform built out over water
A 6. dough — F. growth that covers the scalp of a person or the body of a mammal

Solve the word problems.

1. A stairway at the library has 37 steps. A stairway at the museum has 28 steps. How many more steps are in the stairway at the library? 9 steps
2. Max did 38 jumping jacks. He did 23 squats. How many exercises did he do in all? 61 exercises

School Day Skills • Grade 2 93

Page 93

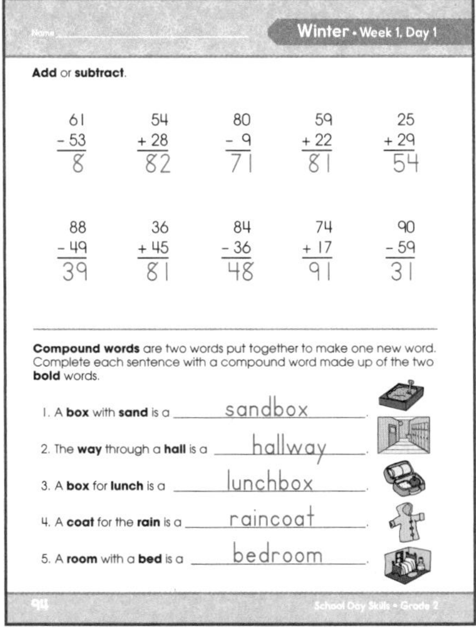
Name ______ **Winter** • Week 1, Day 1

Add or **subtract**.

61 − 53 = 8 | 54 + 28 = 82 | 80 − 9 = 71 | 59 + 22 = 81 | 25 + 29 = 54

88 − 49 = 39 | 36 + 45 = 81 | 84 − 36 = 48 | 74 + 17 = 91 | 90 − 59 = 31

Compound words are two words put together to make one new word. Complete each sentence with a compound word made up of the two **bold** words.

1. A **box** with **sand** is a sandbox.
2. The **way** through a **hall** is a hallway.
3. A **box** for **lunch** is a lunchbox.
4. A **coat** for the **rain** is a raincoat.
5. A **room** with a **bed** is a bedroom.

94 School Day Skills • Grade 2

Page 94

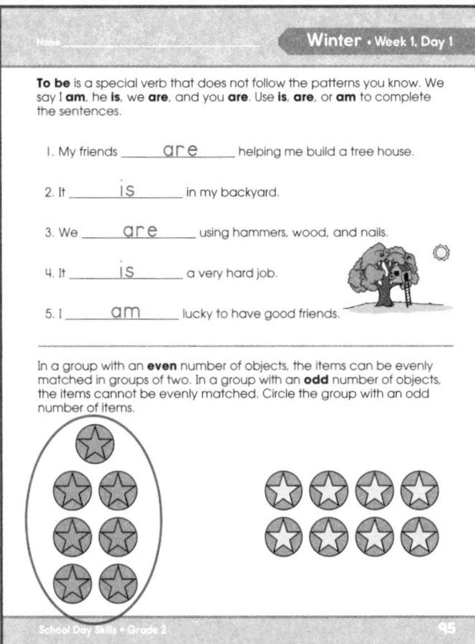
Name ______ **Winter** • Week 1, Day 1

To be is a special verb that does not follow the patterns you know. We say I **am**, he **is**, we **are**, and you **are**. Use **is**, **are**, or **am** to complete the sentences.

1. My friends are helping me build a tree house.
2. It is in my backyard.
3. We are using hammers, wood, and nails.
4. It is a very hard job.
5. I am lucky to have good friends.

In a group with an **even** number of objects, the items can be evenly matched in groups of two. In a group with an **odd** number of objects, the items cannot be evenly matched. Circle the group with an odd number of items.

School Day Skills • Grade 2 95

Page 95

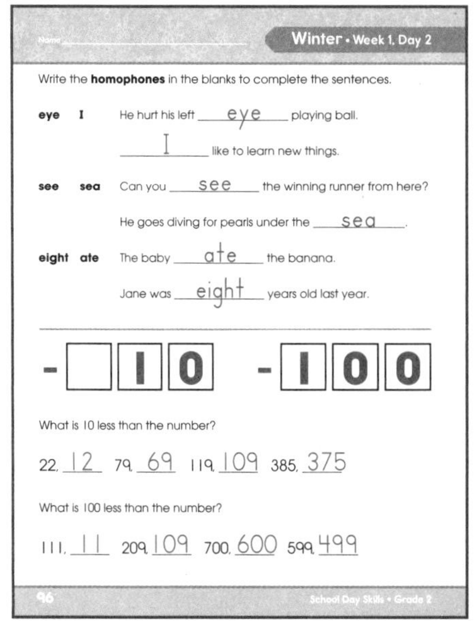
Name ______ **Winter** • Week 1, Day 2

Write the **homophones** in the blanks to complete the sentences.

eye I — He hurt his left eye playing ball. / I like to learn new things.

see sea — Can you see the winning runner from here? / He goes diving for pearls under the sea.

eight ate — The baby ate the banana. / Jane was eight years old last year.

−10 −100

What is 10 less than the number?

22, 12 79, 69 119, 109 385, 375

What is 100 less than the number?

111, 11 209, 109 700, 600 599, 499

96 School Day Skills • Grade 2

Page 96

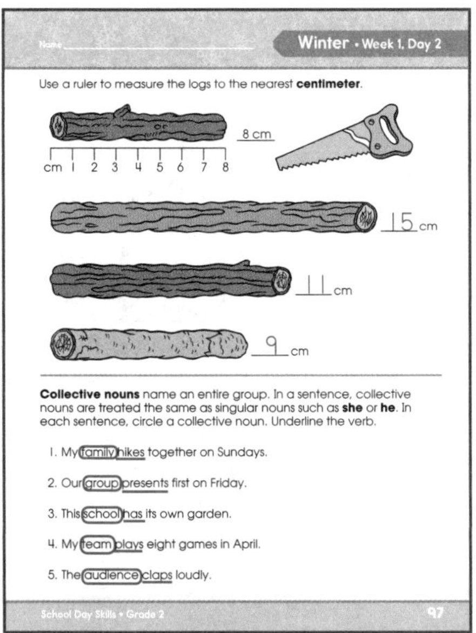
Name ______ **Winter** • Week 1, Day 2

Use a ruler to measure the logs to the nearest **centimeter**.

8 cm

15 cm

11 cm

9 cm

Collective nouns name an entire group. In a sentence, collective nouns are treated the same as singular nouns such as **she** or **he**. In each sentence, circle a collective noun. Underline the verb.

1. My family hikes together on Sundays.
2. Our group presents first on Friday.
3. This school has its own garden.
4. My team plays eight games in April.
5. The audience claps loudly.

School Day Skills • Grade 2 97

Page 97

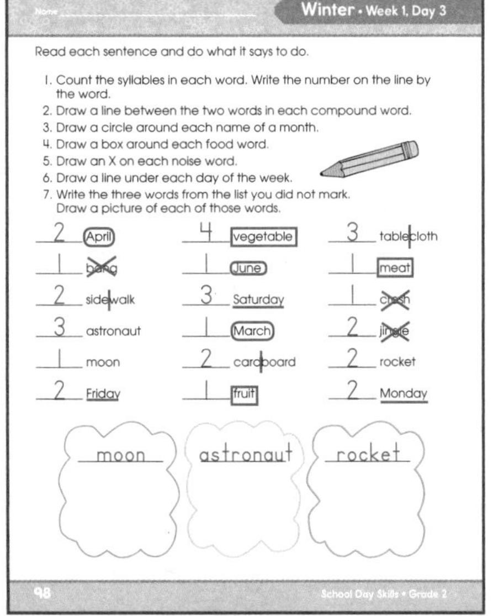
Name ______ **Winter** • Week 1, Day 3

Read each sentence and do what it says to do.

1. Count the syllables in each word. Write the number on the line by the word.
2. Draw a line between the two words in each compound word.
3. Draw a circle around each name of a month.
4. Draw a box around each food word.
5. Draw an X on each noise word.
6. Draw a line under each day of the week.
7. Write the three words from the list you did not mark. Draw a picture of each of those words.

2 April | 4 vegetable | 3 tablecloth
1 bang | 1 June | 1 meat
2 sidewalk | 3 Saturday | 1 crash
3 astronaut | 1 March | 2 jingle
1 moon | 2 cardboard | 2 rocket
2 Friday | 1 fruit | 2 Monday

moon | astronaut | rocket

98 School Day Skills • Grade 2

Page 98

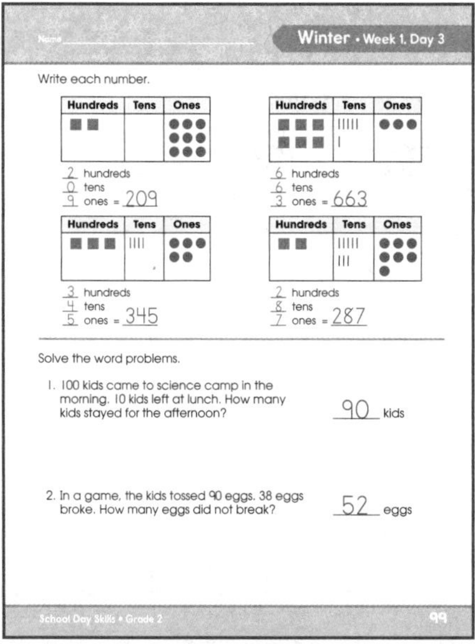
Name ______ **Winter** • Week 1, Day 3

Write each number.

2 hundreds 0 tens 9 ones = 209

6 hundreds 6 tens 3 ones = 663

3 hundreds 4 tens 5 ones = 345

2 hundreds 8 tens 7 ones = 287

Solve the word problems.

1. 100 kids came to science camp in the morning. 10 kids left at lunch. How many kids stayed for the afternoon? 90 kids
2. In a game, the kids tossed 90 eggs. 38 eggs broke. How many eggs did not break? 52 eggs

School Day Skills • Grade 2 99

Page 99

Answer Key

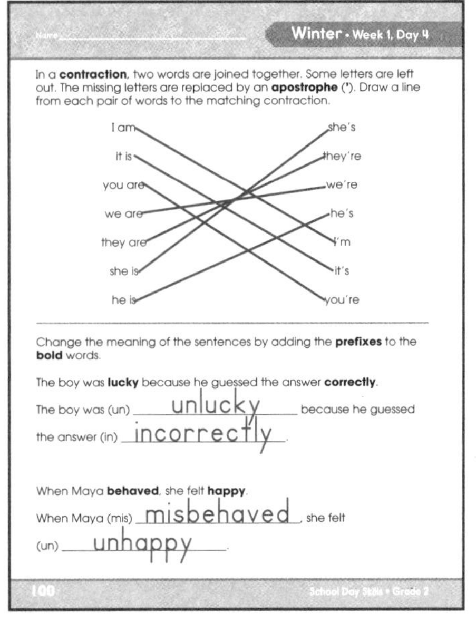

Name ___ **Winter** • Week 1, Day 4

In a **contraction**, two words are joined together. Some letters are left out. The missing letters are replaced by an **apostrophe** ('). Draw a line from each pair of words to the matching contraction.

I am	she's
it is	they're
you are	we're
we are	he's
they are	I'm
she is	it's
he is	you're

Change the meaning of the sentences by adding the **prefixes** to the **bold** words.

The boy was **lucky** because he guessed the answer **correctly**.

The boy was (un) unlucky because he guessed the answer (in) incorrectly.

When Maya **behaved**, she felt **happy**.

When Maya (mis) misbehaved, she felt (un) unhappy.

100 School Day Skills • Grade 2

Page 100

Name ___ **Winter** • Week 1, Day 4

Connect the dots to make each shape. Not all dots will be used.

a rectangle | a triangle | a different triangle

Shapes will vary.

a four-sided shape | a six-sided shape | a different four-sided shape

Add or **subtract**.

54 + 28 = 82	90 − 42 = 48	55 − 22 = 33	63 − 33 = 30	59 + 25 = 84
71 − 52 = 19	48 + 38 = 86	24 + 67 = 91	17 + 18 = 35	53 − 44 = 9

School Day Skills • Grade 2 101

Page 101

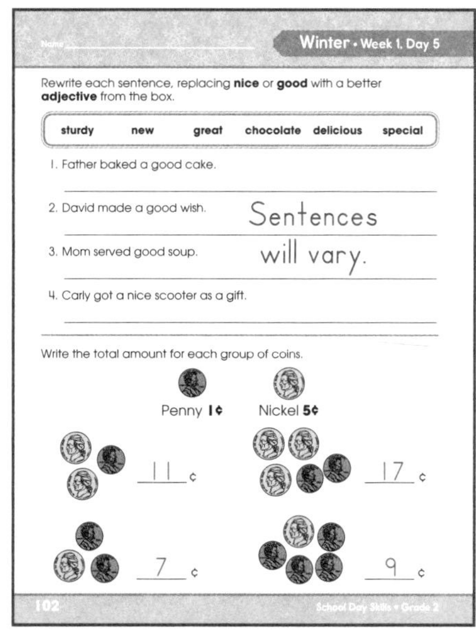

Name ___ **Winter** • Week 1, Day 5

Rewrite each sentence, replacing **nice** or **good** with a better **adjective** from the box.

sturdy new great chocolate delicious special

1. Father baked a good cake.
2. David made a good wish. Sentences
3. Mom served good soup. will vary.
4. Carly got a nice scooter as a gift.

Write the total amount for each group of coins.

Penny **1¢** Nickel **5¢**

11 ¢ 17 ¢

7 ¢ 9 ¢

102 School Day Skills • Grade 2

Page 102

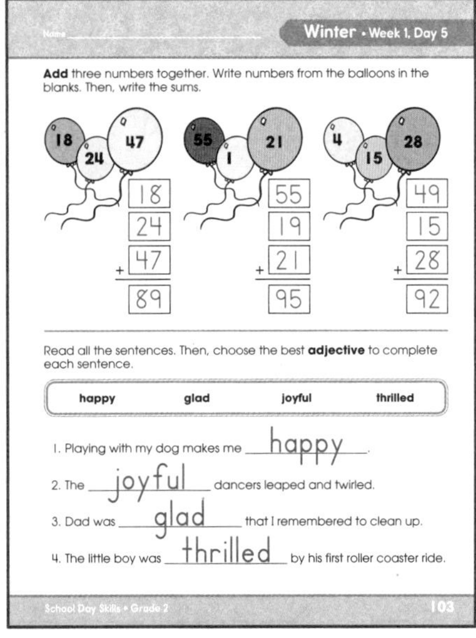

Name ___ **Winter** • Week 1, Day 5

Add three numbers together. Write numbers from the balloons in the blanks. Then, write the sums.

18, 24, 47 → 18 + 24 + 47 = 89

55, 1, 21 → 55 + 19 + 21 = 95

4, 15, 28 → 49 + 15 + 28 = 92

Read all the sentences. Then, choose the best **adjective** to complete each sentence.

happy glad joyful thrilled

1. Playing with my dog makes me happy.
2. The joyful dancers leaped and twirled.
3. Dad was glad that I remembered to clean up.
4. The little boy was thrilled by his first roller coaster ride.

School Day Skills • Grade 2 103

Page 103

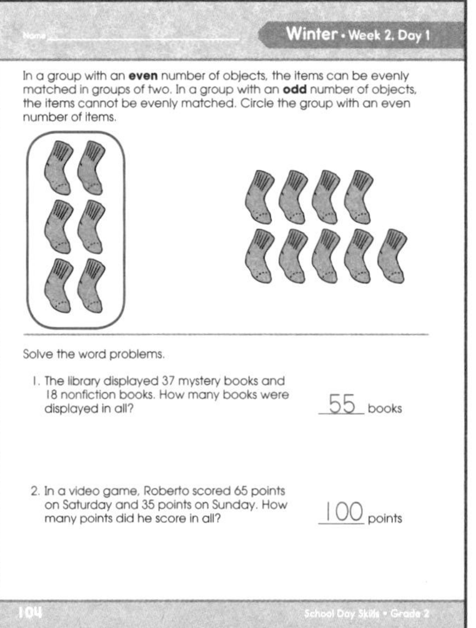

Name ___ **Winter** • Week 2, Day 1

In a group with an **even** number of objects, the items can be evenly matched in groups of two. In a group with an **odd** number of objects, the items cannot be evenly matched. Circle the group with an even number of items.

Solve the word problems.

1. The library displayed 37 mystery books and 18 nonfiction books. How many books were displayed in all? 55 books
2. In a video game, Roberto scored 65 points on Saturday and 35 points on Sunday. How many points did he score in all? 100 points

104 School Day Skills • Grade 2

Page 104

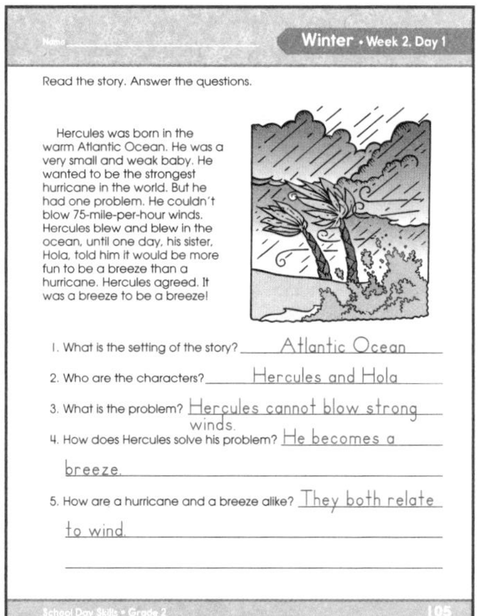

Name ___ **Winter** • Week 2, Day 1

Read the story. Answer the questions.

Hercules was born in the warm Atlantic Ocean. He was a very small and weak baby. He wanted to be the strongest hurricane in the world. But he had one problem. He couldn't blow 75-mile-per-hour winds. Hercules blew and blew in the ocean, until one day, his sister, Hola, told him it would be more fun to be a breeze than a hurricane. Hercules agreed. It was a breeze to be a breeze!

1. What is the setting of the story? Atlantic Ocean
2. Who are the characters? Hercules and Hola
3. What is the problem? Hercules cannot blow strong winds.
4. How does Hercules solve his problem? He becomes a breeze.
5. How are a hurricane and a breeze alike? They both relate to wind.

School Day Skills • Grade 2 105

Page 105

Answer Key

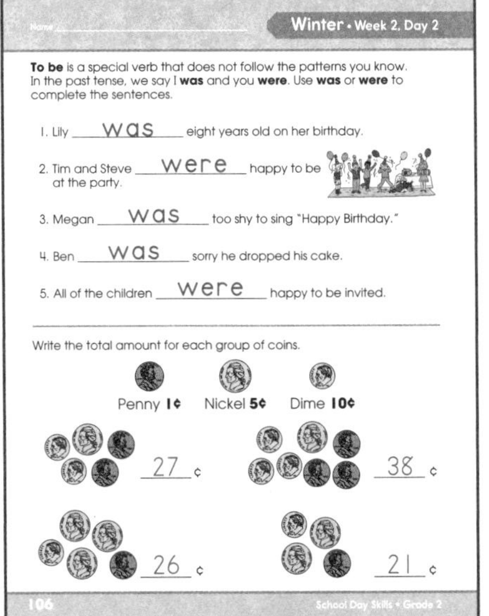

Name ______ **Winter** • Week 2, Day 2

To be is a special verb that does not follow the patterns you know. In the past tense, we say I **was** and you **were**. Use **was** or **were** to complete the sentences.

1. Lily __was__ eight years old on her birthday.
2. Tim and Steve __were__ happy to be at the party.
3. Megan __was__ too shy to sing "Happy Birthday."
4. Ben __was__ sorry he dropped his cake.
5. All of the children __were__ happy to be invited.

Write the total amount for each group of coins.

Penny **1¢** Nickel **5¢** Dime **10¢**

__27__ ¢ __38__ ¢

__26__ ¢ __21__ ¢

106 School Day Skills • Grade 2

Page 106

Name ______ **Winter** • Week 2, Day 2

Add or **subtract**.

52 − 37 = 15	45 − 24 = 21	45 + 36 = 81	74 − 30 = 44	82 − 43 = 39
59 + 15 = 74	18 + 52 = 70	76 − 26 = 50	48 + 46 = 94	35 + 25 = 60

Underline the **compound word** in each sentence. On the line, write the two smaller words that make up the compound word.

1. A firetruck came to help put out the fire. __fire truck__
2. I will be nine years old on my next birthday. __birth day__
3. We built a treehouse last summer. __tree house__
4. Dad put a scarecrow in his garden. __scare crow__
5. It is fun to make footprints in the snow. __foot prints__

School Day Skills • Grade 2 107

Page 107

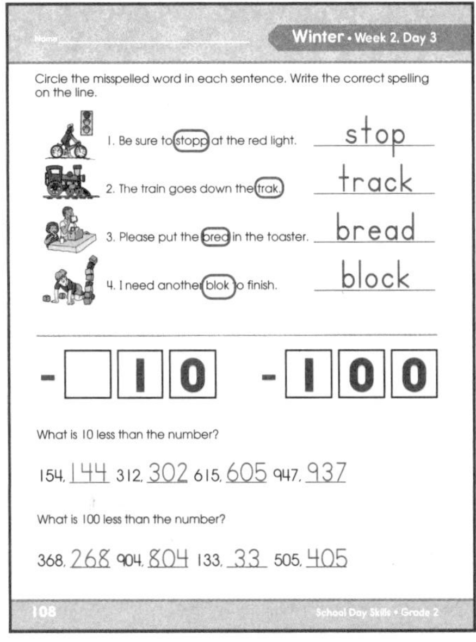

Name ______ **Winter** • Week 2, Day 3

Circle the misspelled word in each sentence. Write the correct spelling on the line.

1. Be sure to stopp at the red light. __stop__
2. The train goes down the trak. __track__
3. Please put the bred in the toaster. __bread__
4. I need another blok to finish. __block__

- ☐ 1 0   - 1 0 0

What is 10 less than the number?

154. __144__ 312. __302__ 615. __605__ 947. __937__

What is 100 less than the number?

368. __268__ 904. __804__ 133. __33__ 505. __405__

108 School Day Skills • Grade 2

Page 108

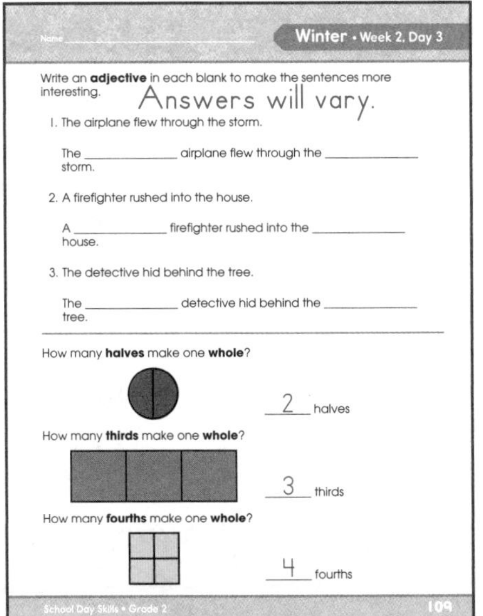

Name ______ **Winter** • Week 2, Day 3

Write an **adjective** in each blank to make the sentences more interesting. Answers will vary.

1. The airplane flew through the storm.

   The ______ airplane flew through the ______ storm.
2. A firefighter rushed into the house.

   A ______ firefighter rushed into the ______ house.
3. The detective hid behind the tree.

   The ______ detective hid behind the ______ tree.

How many **halves** make one **whole**? __2__ halves

How many **thirds** make one **whole**? __3__ thirds

How many **fourths** make one **whole**? __4__ fourths

School Day Skills • Grade 2 109

Page 109

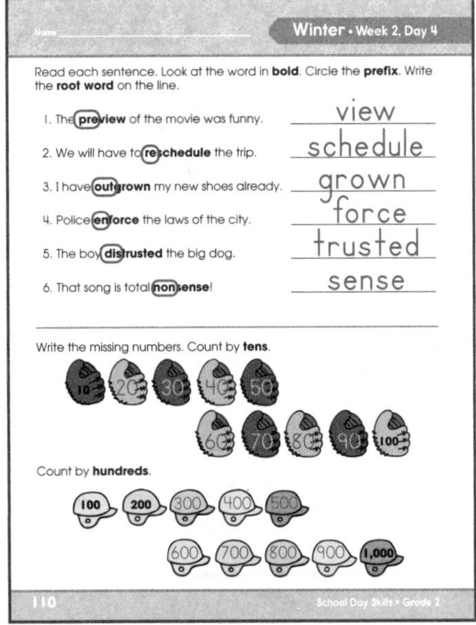

Name ______ **Winter** • Week 2, Day 4

Read each sentence. Look at the word in **bold**. Circle the **prefix**. Write the **root word** on the line.

1. The **preview** of the movie was funny. __view__
2. We will have to **reschedule** the trip. __schedule__
3. I have **outgrown** my new shoes already. __grown__
4. Police **enforce** the laws of the city. __force__
5. The boy **distrusted** the big dog. __trusted__
6. That song is total **nonsense**! __sense__

Write the missing numbers. Count by **tens**.

10, 20, 30, 40, 50, 60, 70, 80, 90, 100

Count by **hundreds**.

100, 200, 300, 400, 500, 600, 700, 800, 900, 1,000

110 School Day Skills • Grade 2

Page 110

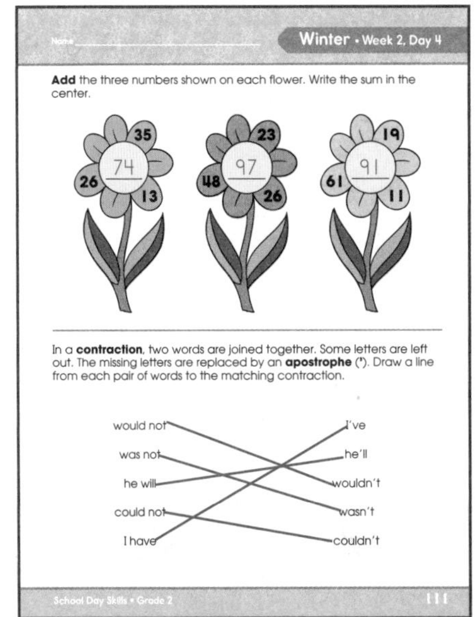

Name ______ **Winter** • Week 2, Day 4

Add the three numbers shown on each flower. Write the sum in the center.

35, 26, 13: __74__ 23, 48, 26: __97__ 19, 61, 11: __91__

In a **contraction**, two words are joined together. Some letters are left out. The missing letters are replaced by an **apostrophe** ('). Draw a line from each pair of words to the matching contraction.

would not — wouldn't
was not — wasn't
he will — he'll
could not — couldn't
I have — I've

School Day Skills • Grade 2 111

Page 111

Answer Key

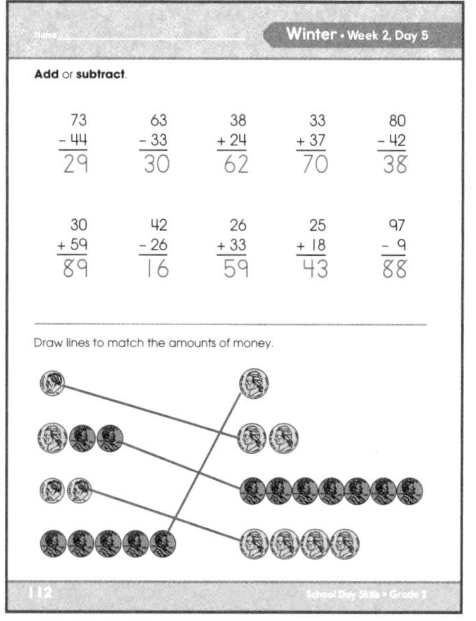

Page 112

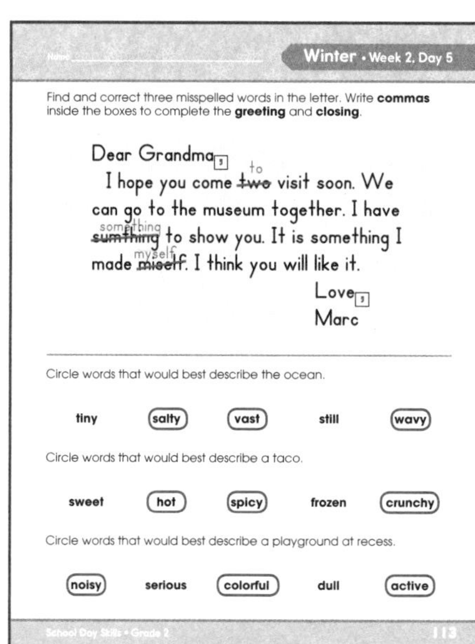

Page 113

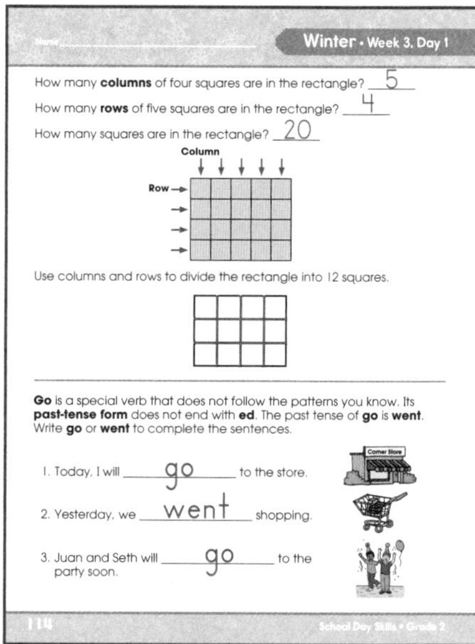

Page 114

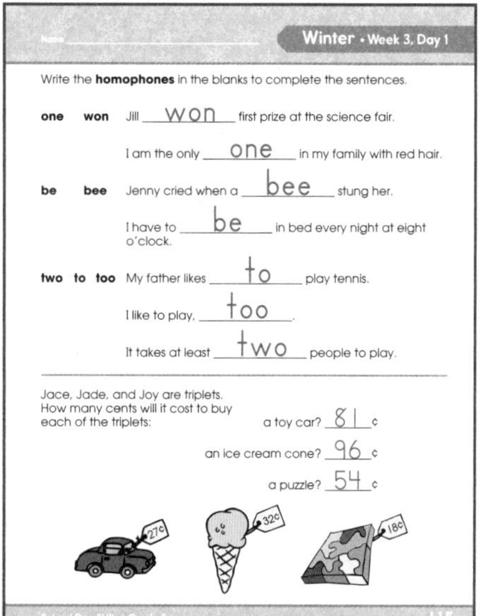

Page 115

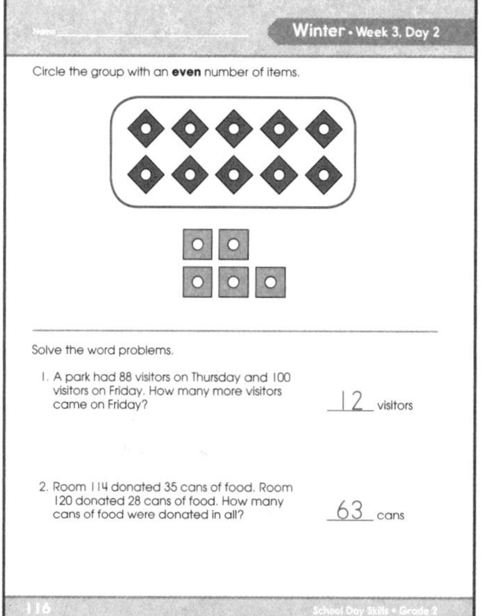

Page 116

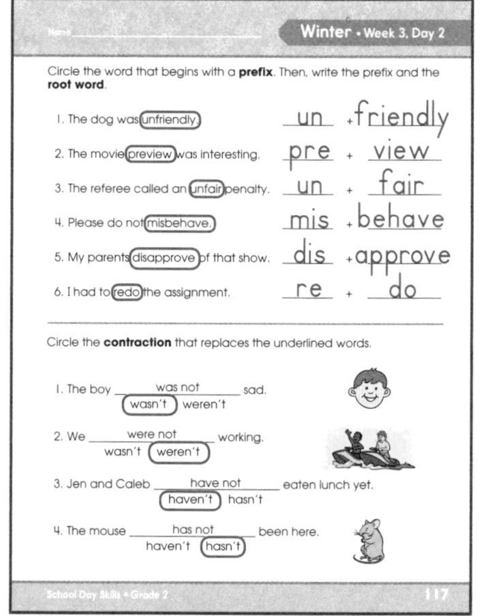

Page 117

Answer Key

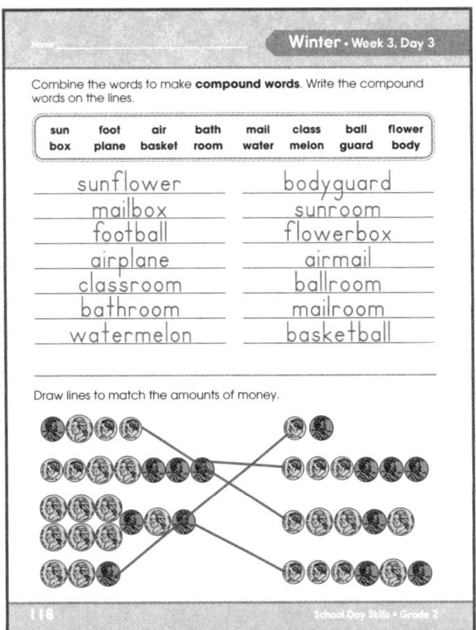

Page 118

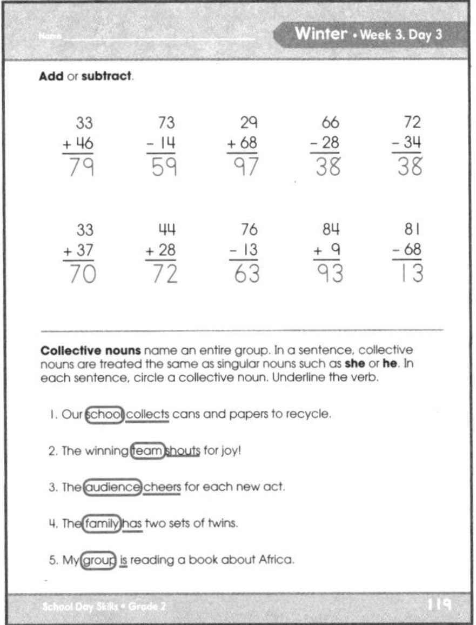

Page 119

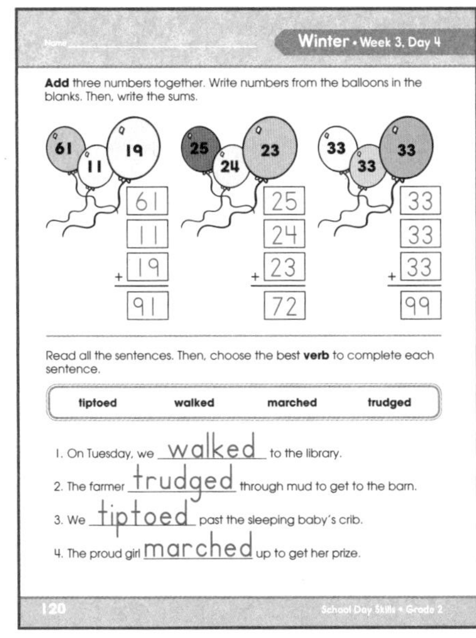

Page 120

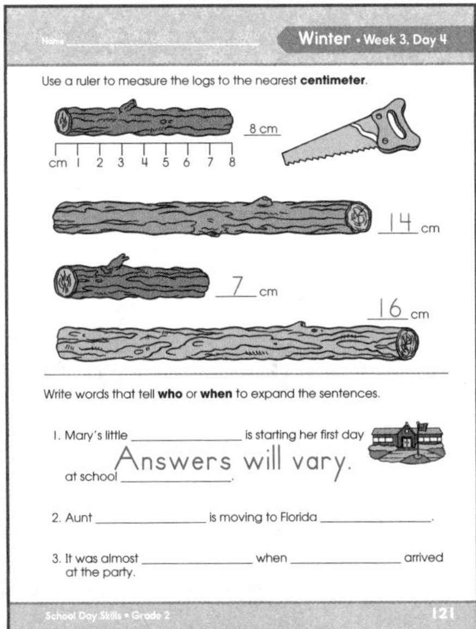

Page 121

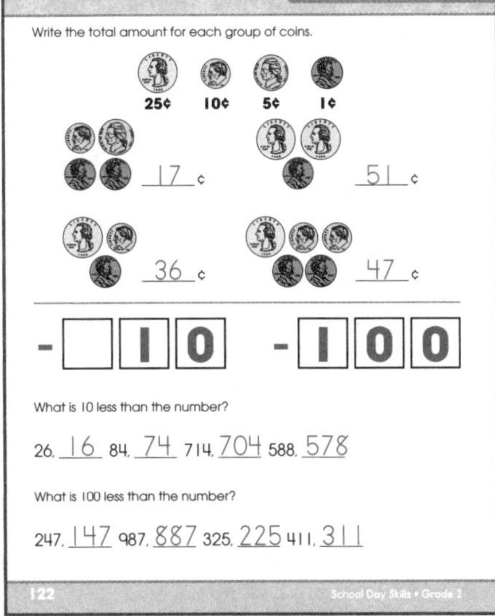

Page 122

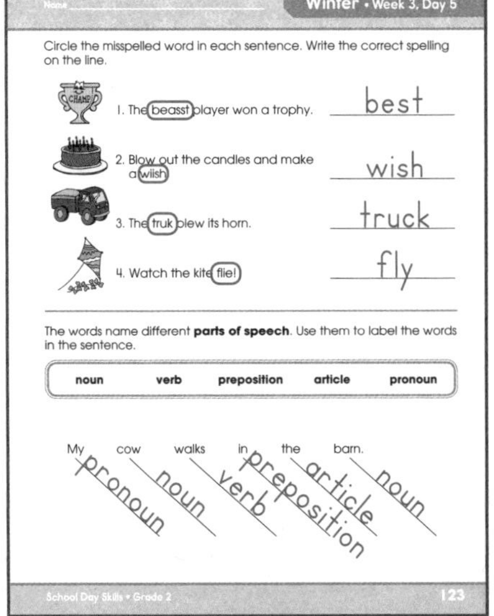

Page 123

Answer Key

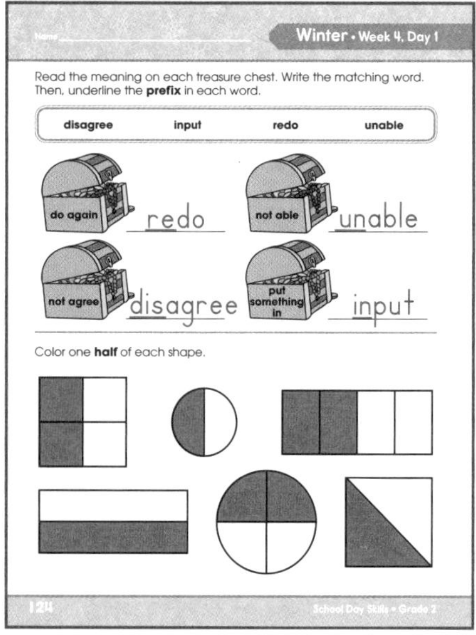

Name ______ **Winter** • Week 4, Day 1

Read the meaning on each treasure chest. Write the matching word. Then, underline the **prefix** in each word.

disagree input redo unable

do again: redo

not able: unable

not agree: disagree

put something in: input

Color one **half** of each shape.

124 School Day Skills • Grade 2

Page 124

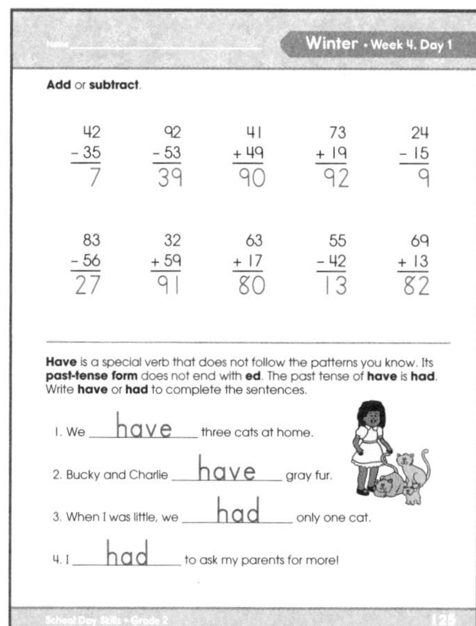

Name ______ **Winter** • Week 4, Day 1

Add or **subtract**.

42 − 35 = 7	92 − 53 = 39	41 + 49 = 90	73 + 19 = 92	24 − 15 = 9
83 − 56 = 27	32 + 59 = 91	63 + 17 = 80	55 − 42 = 13	69 + 13 = 82

Have is a special verb that does not follow the patterns you know. Its **past-tense form** does not end with **ed**. The past tense of **have** is **had**. Write **have** or **had** to complete the sentences.

1. We have three cats at home.
2. Bucky and Charlie have gray fur.
3. When I was little, we had only one cat.
4. I had to ask my parents for more!

School Day Skills • Grade 2 125

Page 125

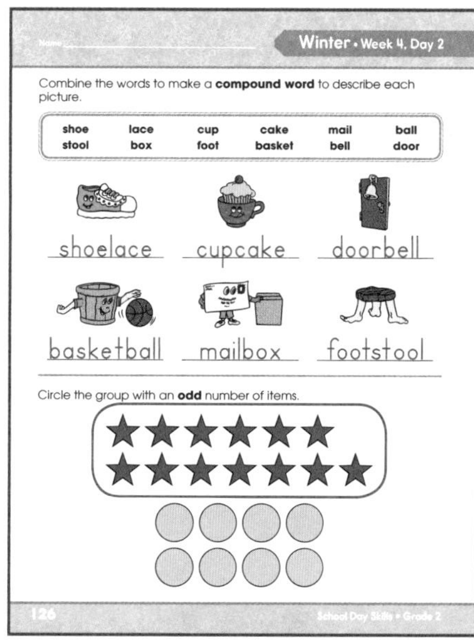

Name ______ **Winter** • Week 4, Day 2

Combine the words to make a **compound word** to describe each picture.

shoe	lace	cup	cake	mail	ball
stool	box	foot	basket	bell	door

shoelace cupcake doorbell

basketball mailbox footstool

Circle the group with an **odd** number of items.

126 School Day Skills • Grade 2

Page 126

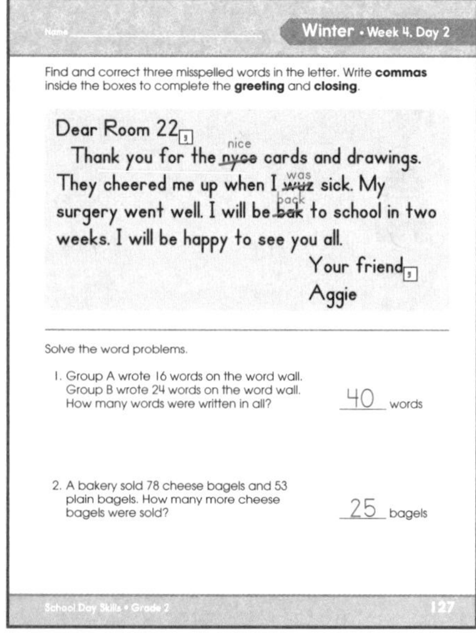

Name ______ **Winter** • Week 4, Day 2

Find and correct three misspelled words in the letter. Write **commas** inside the boxes to complete the **greeting** and **closing**.

Dear Room 22,
Thank you for the ~~nyce~~ nice cards and drawings. They cheered me up when I ~~wuz~~ was sick. My surgery went well. I will be ~~bak~~ back to school in two weeks. I will be happy to see you all.
Your friend,
Aggie

Solve the word problems.

1. Group A wrote 16 words on the word wall. Group B wrote 24 words on the word wall. How many words were written in all? 40 words
2. A bakery sold 78 cheese bagels and 53 plain bagels. How many more cheese bagels were sold? 25 bagels

School Day Skills • Grade 2 127

Page 127

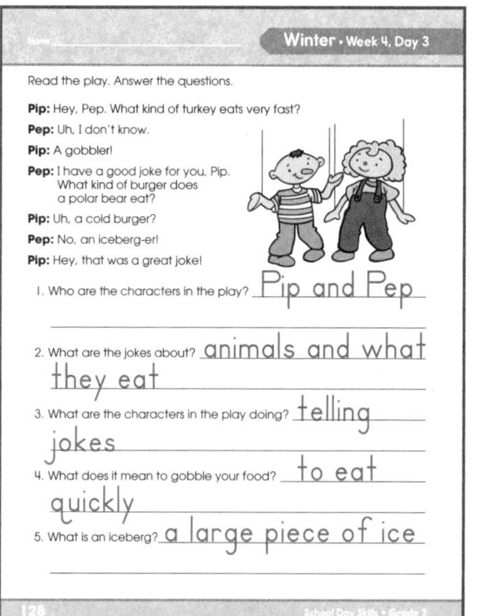

Name ______ **Winter** • Week 4, Day 3

Read the play. Answer the questions.

Pip: Hey, Pep. What kind of turkey eats very fast?
Pep: Uh, I don't know.
Pip: A gobbler!
Pep: I have a good joke for you, Pip. What kind of burger does a polar bear eat?
Pip: Uh, a cold burger?
Pep: No, an iceberg-er!
Pip: Hey, that was a great joke!

1. Who are the characters in the play? Pip and Pep
2. What are the jokes about? animals and what they eat
3. What are the characters in the play doing? telling jokes
4. What does it mean to gobble your food? to eat quickly
5. What is an iceberg? a large piece of ice

128 School Day Skills • Grade 2

Page 128

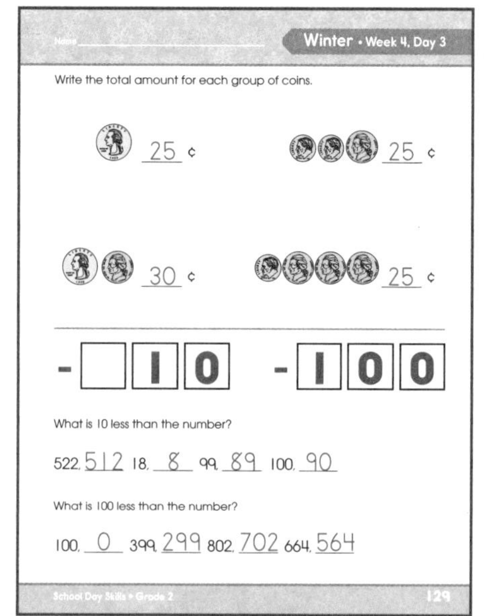

Name ______ **Winter** • Week 4, Day 3

Write the total amount for each group of coins.

25 ¢ 25 ¢

30 ¢ 25 ¢

−10 −100

What is 10 less than the number?

522, 512 18, 8 99, 89 100, 90

What is 100 less than the number?

100, 0 399, 299 802, 702 664, 564

School Day Skills • Grade 2 129

Page 129

Answer Key

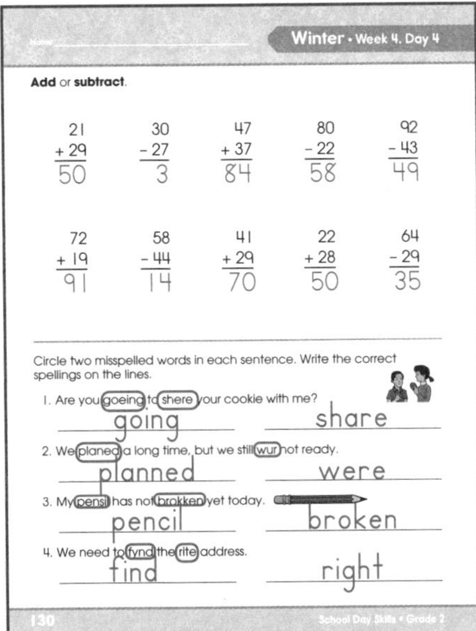

Name ______________ **Winter** • Week 4, Day 4

Add or **subtract**.

21	30	47	80	92
+ 29	− 27	+ 37	− 22	− 43
50	3	84	58	49

72	58	41	22	64
+ 19	− 44	+ 29	+ 28	− 29
91	14	70	50	35

Circle two misspelled words in each sentence. Write the correct spellings on the lines.

1. Are you goeing to shere your cookie with me? going share
2. We planed a long time, but we still wur not ready. planned were
3. My pensil has not brokken yet today. pencil broken
4. We need to fynd the rite address. find right

130 School Day Skills • Grade 2

Page 130

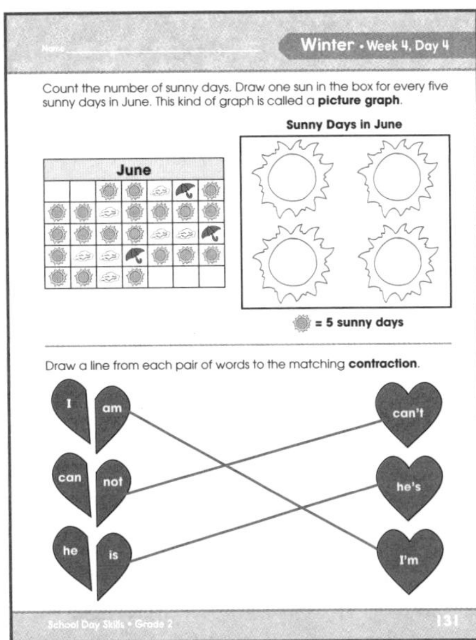

Name ______________ **Winter** • Week 4, Day 4

Count the number of sunny days. Draw one sun in the box for every five sunny days in June. This kind of graph is called a **picture graph**.

Draw a line from each pair of words to the matching **contraction**.

School Day Skills • Grade 2 131

Page 131

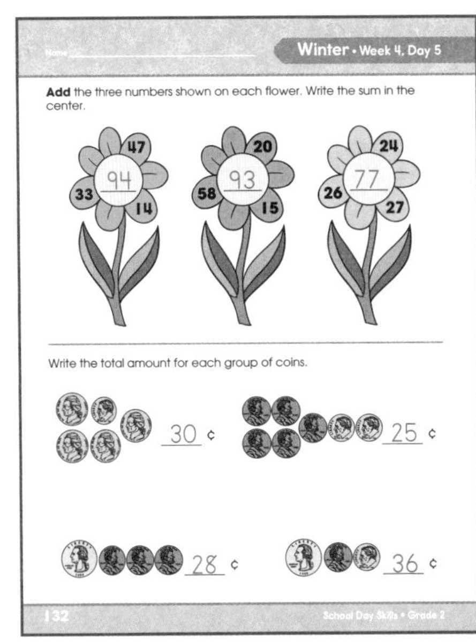

Name ______________ **Winter** • Week 4, Day 5

Add the three numbers shown on each flower. Write the sum in the center.

Write the total amount for each group of coins.

30 ¢ 25 ¢

28 ¢ 36 ¢

132 School Day Skills • Grade 2

Page 132

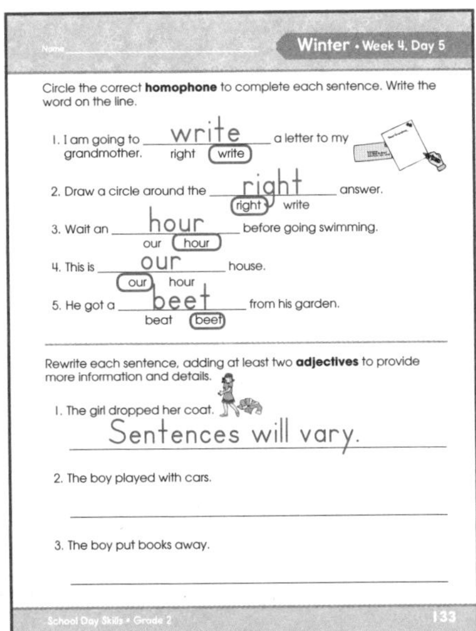

Name ______________ **Winter** • Week 4, Day 5

Circle the correct **homophone** to complete each sentence. Write the word on the line.

1. I am going to write a letter to my grandmother. right (write)
2. Draw a circle around the right answer. (right) write
3. Wait an hour before going swimming. our (hour)
4. This is our house. (our) hour
5. He got a beet from his garden. beat (beet)

Rewrite each sentence, adding at least two **adjectives** to provide more information and details.

1. The girl dropped her coat.
   Sentences will vary.
2. The boy played with cars.
3. The boy put books away.

School Day Skills • Grade 2 133

Page 133

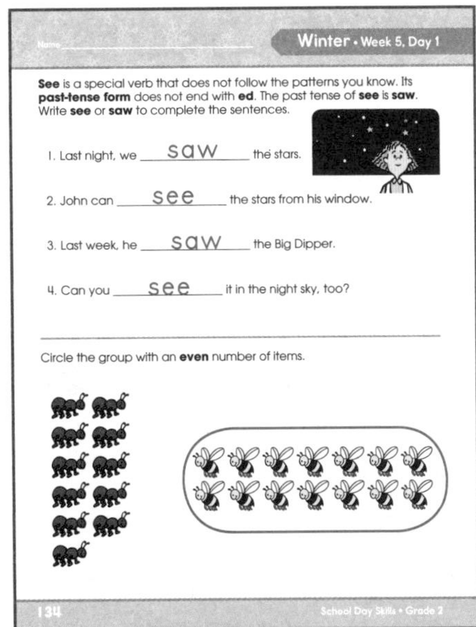

Name ______________ **Winter** • Week 5, Day 1

See is a special verb that does not follow the patterns you know. Its **past-tense form** does not end with **ed**. The past tense of **see** is **saw**. Write **see** or **saw** to complete the sentences.

1. Last night, we saw the stars.
2. John can see the stars from his window.
3. Last week, he saw the Big Dipper.
4. Can you see it in the night sky, too?

Circle the group with an **even** number of items.

134 School Day Skills • Grade 2

Page 134

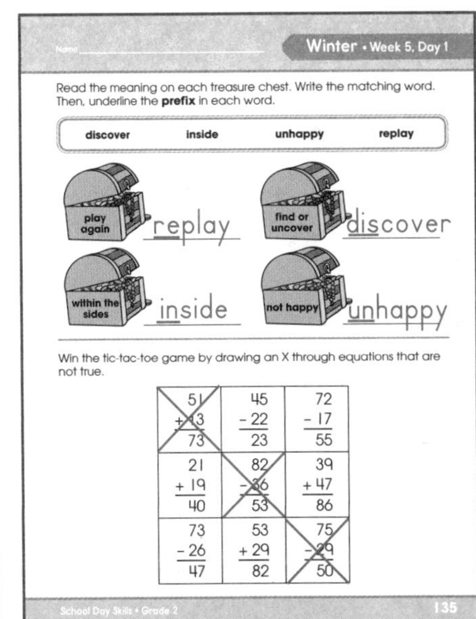

Name ______________ **Winter** • Week 5, Day 1

Read the meaning on each treasure chest. Write the matching word. Then, underline the **prefix** in each word.

discover inside unhappy replay

replay discover inside unhappy

Win the tic-tac-toe game by drawing an X through equations that are not true.

51 + 13 = 73 (X)	45 − 22 = 23	72 − 17 = 55
21 + 19 = 40	82 − 36 = 53 (X)	39 + 47 = 86
73 − 26 = 47	53 + 29 = 82	75 − 29 = 50 (X)

School Day Skills • Grade 2 135

Page 135

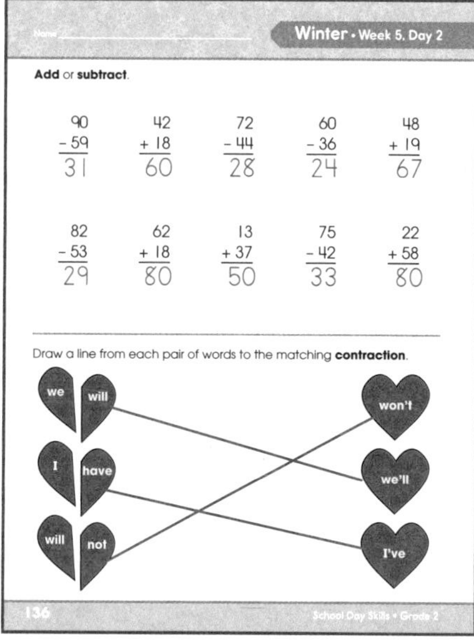

Page 136

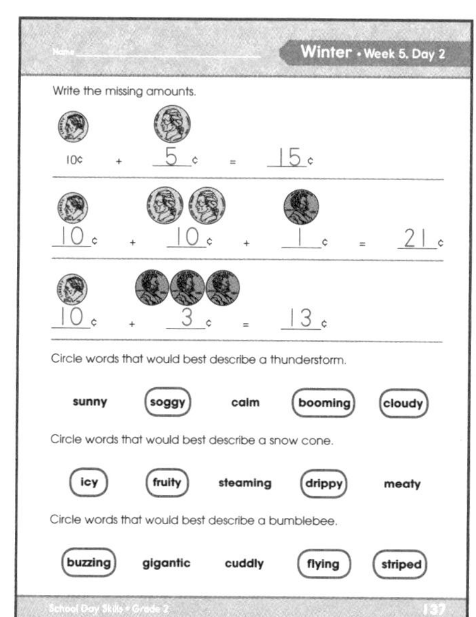

Page 137

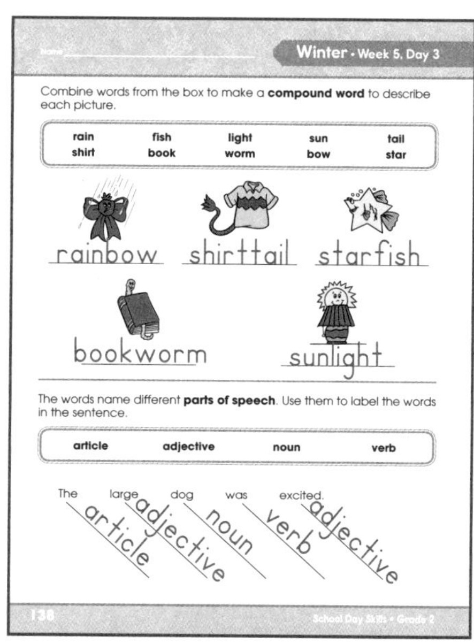

Page 138

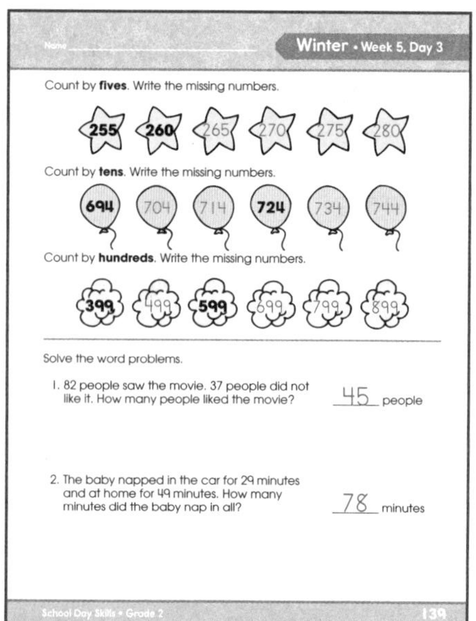

Page 139

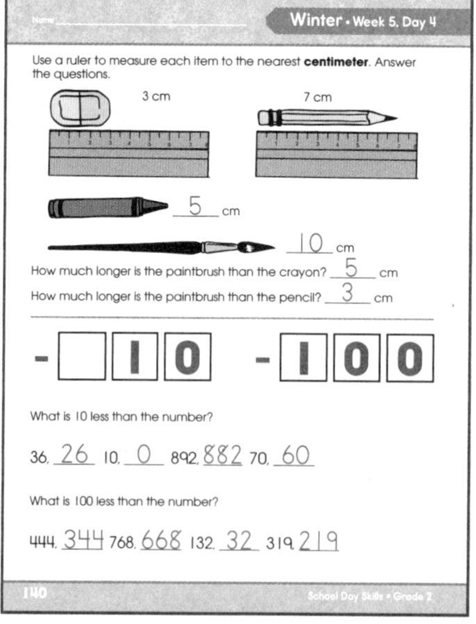

Page 140

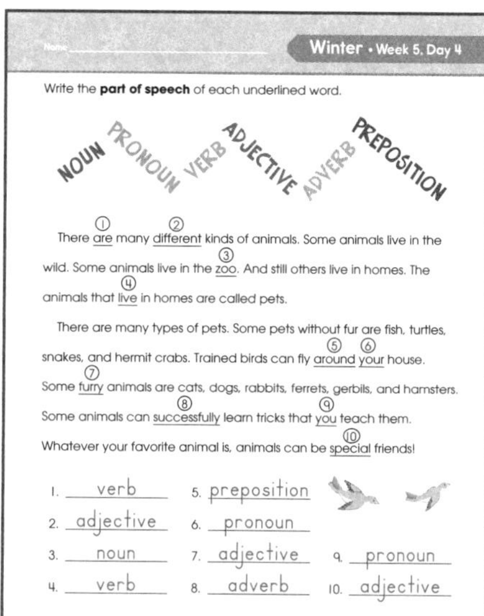

Page 141

Answer Key

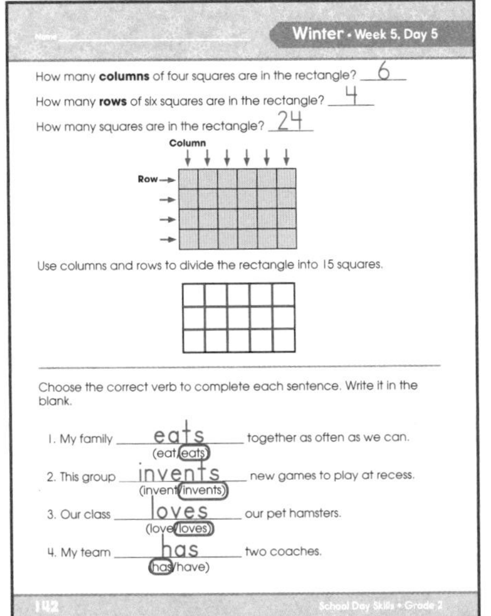

Winter • Week 5, Day 5

How many **columns** of four squares are in the rectangle? 6

How many **rows** of six squares are in the rectangle? 4

How many squares are in the rectangle? 24

Use columns and rows to divide the rectangle into 15 squares.

Choose the correct verb to complete each sentence. Write it in the blank.

1. My family eats together as often as we can. (eat/eats)
2. This group invents new games to play at recess. (invent/invents)
3. Our class loves our pet hamsters. (love/loves)
4. My team has two coaches. (has/have)

142 School Day Skills • Grade 2

Page 142

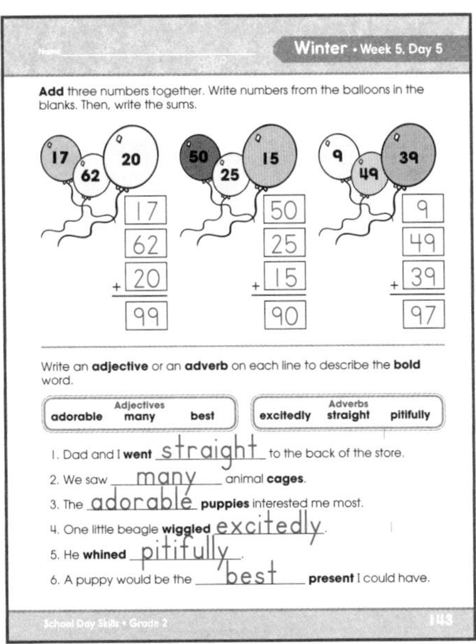

Winter • Week 5, Day 5

Add three numbers together. Write numbers from the balloons in the blanks. Then, write the sums.

17	50	9
62	25	49
+ 20	+ 15	+ 39
99	90	97

Write an **adjective** or an **adverb** on each line to describe the **bold** word.

Adjectives: adorable, many, best

Adverbs: excitedly, straight, pitifully

1. Dad and I **went** straight to the back of the store.
2. We saw many animal **cages**.
3. The adorable **puppies** interested me most.
4. One little beagle **wiggled** excitedly.
5. He **whined** pitifully.
6. A puppy would be the best **present** I could have.

School Day Skills • Grade 2 143

Page 143

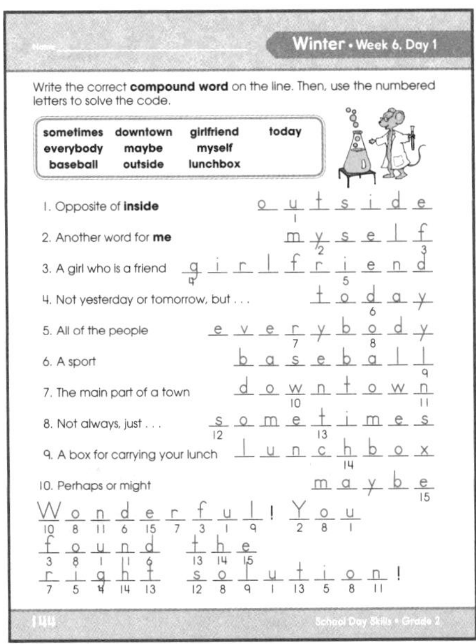

Winter • Week 6, Day 1

Write the correct **compound word** on the line. Then, use the numbered letters to solve the code.

sometimes, downtown, girlfriend, today, everybody, maybe, myself, baseball, outside, lunchbox

1. Opposite of **inside** — outside
2. Another word for **me** — myself
3. A girl who is a friend — girlfriend
4. Not yesterday or tomorrow, but . . . — today
5. All of the people — everybody
6. A sport — baseball
7. The main part of a town — downtown
8. Not always, just . . . — sometimes
9. A box for carrying your lunch — lunchbox
10. Perhaps or might — maybe

Wonderful! You found the right solution!

144 School Day Skills • Grade 2

Page 144

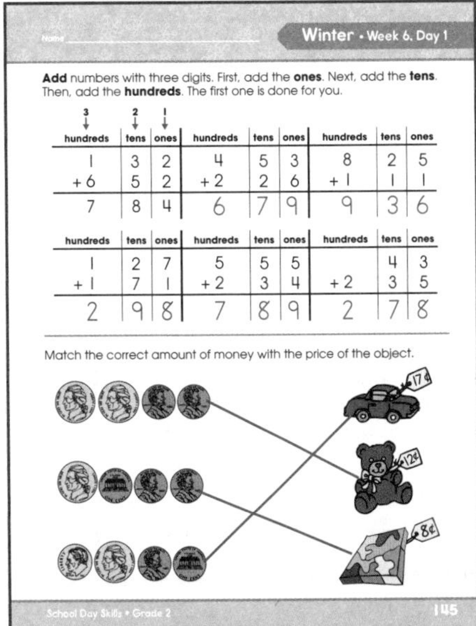

Winter • Week 6, Day 1

Add numbers with three digits. First, add the **ones**. Next, add the **tens**. Then, add the **hundreds**. The first one is done for you.

hundreds	tens	ones	hundreds	tens	ones	hundreds	tens	ones
1	3	2	4	5	3	8	2	5
+ 6	5	2	+ 2	2	6	+ 1	1	1
7	8	4	6	7	9	9	3	6

hundreds	tens	ones	hundreds	tens	ones	hundreds	tens	ones
1	2	7	5	5	5		4	3
+ 1	7	1	+ 2	3	4	+ 2	3	5
2	9	8	7	8	9	2	7	8

Match the correct amount of money with the price of the object.

School Day Skills • Grade 2 145

Page 145

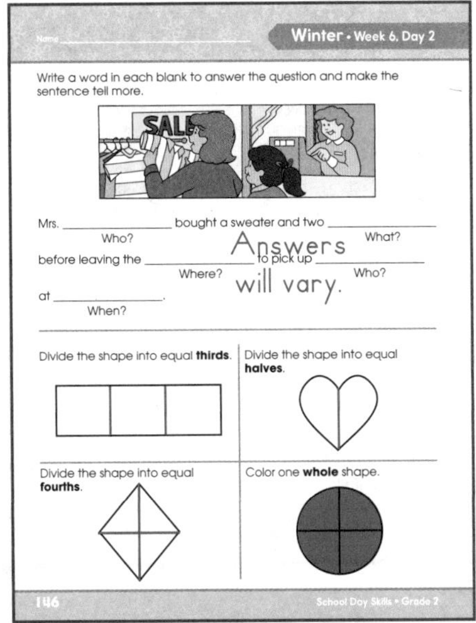

Winter • Week 6, Day 2

Write a word in each blank to answer the question and make the sentence tell more.

Mrs. ______ (Who?) bought a sweater and two ______ (What?) before leaving the ______ (Where?) to pick up ______ (Who?) at ______ (When?).

Answers will vary.

Divide the shape into equal **thirds**.

Divide the shape into equal **halves**.

Divide the shape into equal **fourths**.

Color one **whole** shape.

146 School Day Skills • Grade 2

Page 146

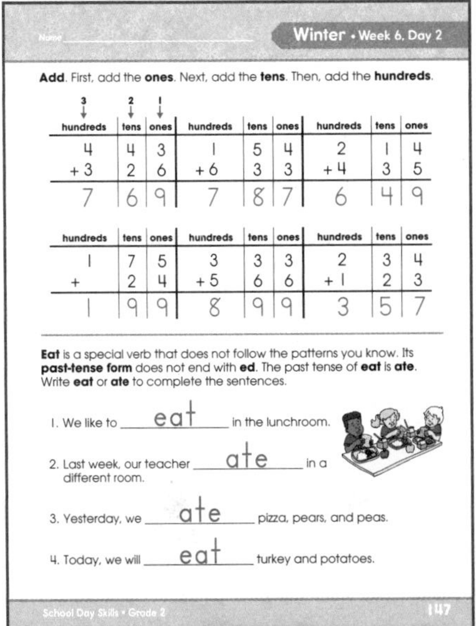

Winter • Week 6, Day 2

Add. First, add the **ones**. Next, add the **tens**. Then, add the **hundreds**.

hundreds	tens	ones	hundreds	tens	ones	hundreds	tens	ones
4	4	3	1	5	4	2	1	4
+ 3	2	6	+ 6	3	3	+ 4	3	5
7	6	9	7	8	7	6	4	9

hundreds	tens	ones	hundreds	tens	ones	hundreds	tens	ones
1	7	5	3	3	3	2	3	4
+	2	4	+ 5	6	6	+ 1	2	3
1	9	9	8	9	9	3	5	7

Eat is a special verb that does not follow the patterns you know. Its **past-tense form** does not end with **ed**. The past tense of **eat** is **ate**. Write **eat** or **ate** to complete the sentences.

1. We like to eat in the lunchroom.
2. Last week, our teacher ate in a different room.
3. Yesterday, we ate pizza, pears, and peas.
4. Today, we will eat turkey and potatoes.

School Day Skills • Grade 2 147

Page 147

Answer Key

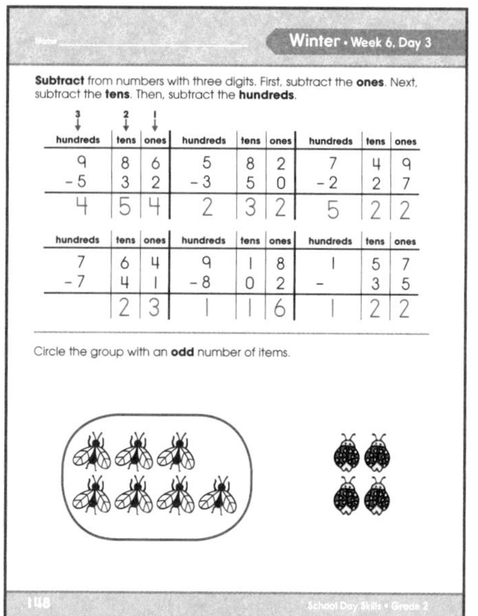
Name ____________ Winter • Week 6, Day 3

Subtract from numbers with three digits. First, subtract the **ones**. Next, subtract the **tens**. Then, subtract the **hundreds**.

hundreds	tens	ones	hundreds	tens	ones	hundreds	tens	ones
9	8	6	5	8	2	7	4	9
−5	3	2	−3	5	0	−2	2	7
4	5	4	2	3	2	5	2	2

hundreds	tens	ones	hundreds	tens	ones	hundreds	tens	ones
7	6	4	9	1	8	1	5	7
−7	4	1	−8	0	2	−	3	5
	2	3	1	1	6	1	2	2

Circle the group with an **odd** number of items.

148 School Day Skills • Grade 2

Page 148

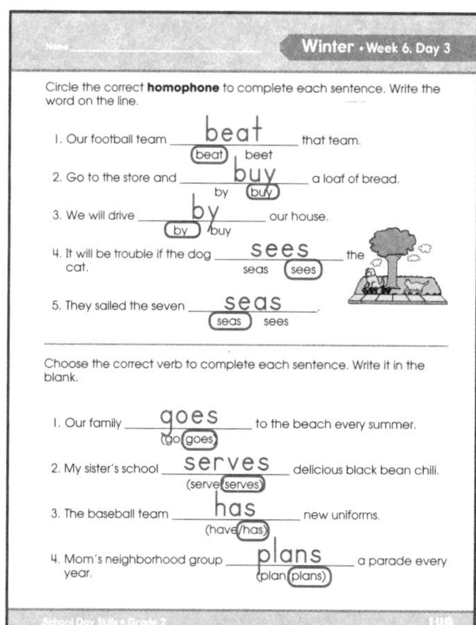
Name ____________ Winter • Week 6, Day 3

Circle the correct **homophone** to complete each sentence. Write the word on the line.

1. Our football team beat that team. (beat) beet
2. Go to the store and buy a loaf of bread. by (buy)
3. We will drive by our house. (by) buy
4. It will be trouble if the dog sees the cat. seas (sees)
5. They sailed the seven seas. (seas) sees

Choose the correct verb to complete each sentence. Write it in the blank.

1. Our family goes to the beach every summer. (go/goes)
2. My sister's school serves delicious black bean chili. (serve/serves)
3. The baseball team has new uniforms. (have/has)
4. Mom's neighborhood group plans a parade every year. (plan/plans)

School Day Skills • Grade 2 149

Page 149

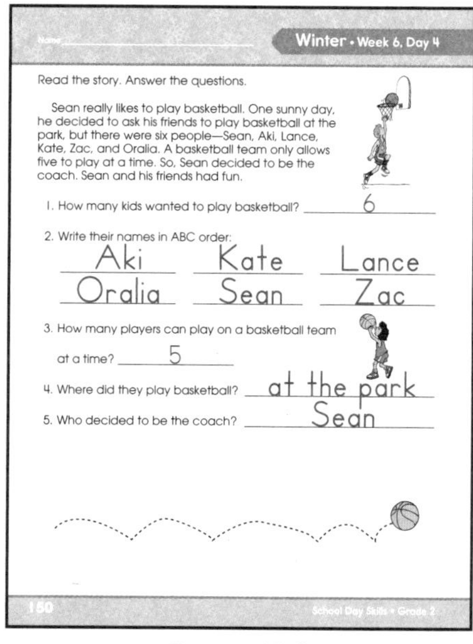
Name ____________ Winter • Week 6, Day 4

Read the story. Answer the questions.

Sean really likes to play basketball. One sunny day, he decided to ask his friends to play basketball at the park, but there were six people—Sean, Aki, Lance, Kate, Zac, and Oralia. A basketball team only allows five to play at a time. So, Sean decided to be the coach. Sean and his friends had fun.

1. How many kids wanted to play basketball? 6
2. Write their names in ABC order: Aki, Kate, Lance, Oralia, Sean, Zac
3. How many players can play on a basketball team at a time? 5
4. Where did they play basketball? at the park
5. Who decided to be the coach? Sean

150 School Day Skills • Grade 2

Page 150

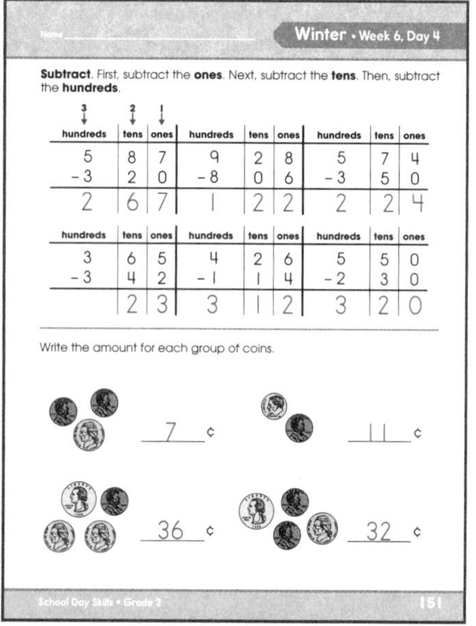
Name ____________ Winter • Week 6, Day 4

Subtract. First, subtract the **ones**. Next, subtract the **tens**. Then, subtract the **hundreds**.

hundreds	tens	ones	hundreds	tens	ones	hundreds	tens	ones
5	8	7	9	2	8	5	7	4
−3	2	0	−8	0	6	−3	5	0
2	6	7	1	2	2	2	2	4

hundreds	tens	ones	hundreds	tens	ones	hundreds	tens	ones
3	6	5	4	2	6	5	5	0
−3	4	2	−1	1	4	−2	3	0
	2	3	3	1	2	3	2	0

Write the amount for each group of coins.

7 ¢ 11 ¢

36 ¢ 32 ¢

School Day Skills • Grade 2 151

Page 151

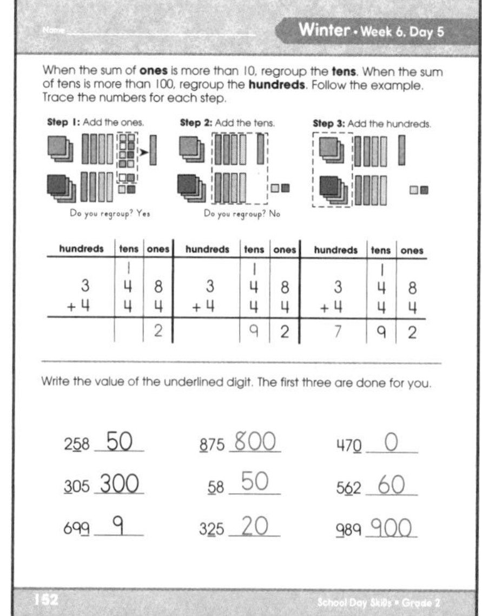
Name ____________ Winter • Week 6, Day 5

When the sum of **ones** is more than 10, regroup the **tens**. When the sum of tens is more than 100, regroup the **hundreds**. Follow the example. Trace the numbers for each step.

Step 1: Add the ones. Do you regroup? Yes

Step 2: Add the tens. Do you regroup? No

Step 3: Add the hundreds.

hundreds	tens	ones	hundreds	tens	ones	hundreds	tens	ones
	1			1			1	
3	4	8	3	4	8	3	4	8
+4	4	4	+4	4	4	+4	4	4
		2		9	2	7	9	2

Write the value of the underlined digit. The first three are done for you.

258 50 875 800 470 0

305 300 58 50 562 60

699 9 325 20 989 900

152 School Day Skills • Grade 2

Page 152

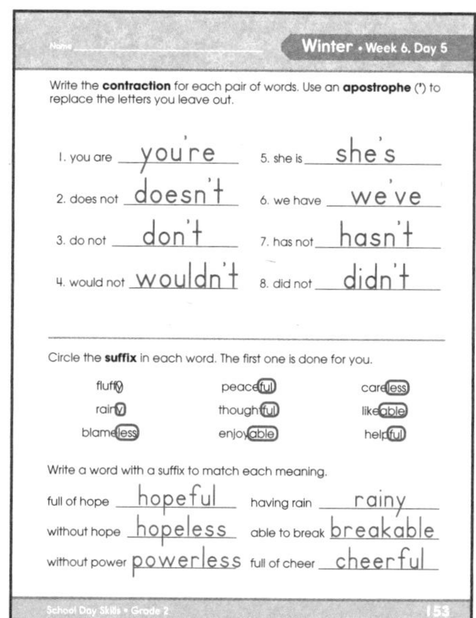
Name ____________ Winter • Week 6, Day 5

Write the **contraction** for each pair of words. Use an **apostrophe** (') to replace the letters you leave out.

1. you are you're
2. does not doesn't
3. do not don't
4. would not wouldn't
5. she is she's
6. we have we've
7. has not hasn't
8. did not didn't

Circle the **suffix** in each word. The first one is done for you.

fluffy peaceful careless

rainy thoughtful likeable

blameless enjoyable helpful

Write a word with a suffix to match each meaning.

full of hope hopeful having rain rainy

without hope hopeless able to break breakable

without power powerless full of cheer cheerful

School Day Skills • Grade 2 153

Page 153

Answer Key

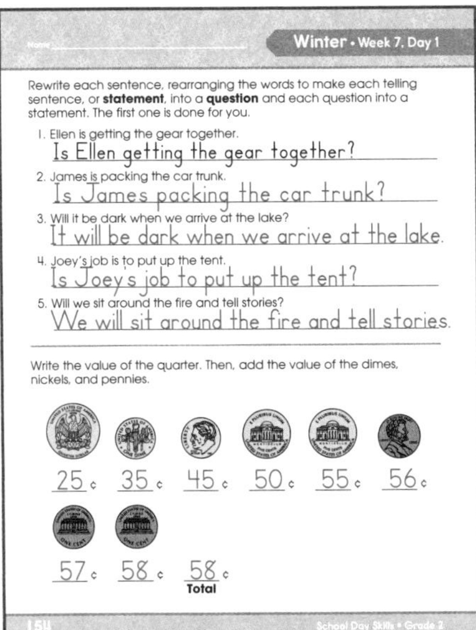

Name ________ Winter • Week 7, Day 1

Rewrite each sentence, rearranging the words to make each telling sentence, or **statement**, into a **question** and each question into a statement. The first one is done for you.

1. Ellen is getting the gear together.
   Is Ellen getting the gear together?
2. James is packing the car trunk.
   Is James packing the car trunk?
3. Will it be dark when we arrive at the lake?
   It will be dark when we arrive at the lake.
4. Joey's job is to put up the tent.
   Is Joey's job to put up the tent?
5. Will we sit around the fire and tell stories?
   We will sit around the fire and tell stories.

Write the value of the quarter. Then, add the value of the dimes, nickels, and pennies.

25¢ 35¢ 45¢ 50¢ 55¢ 56¢

57¢ 58¢ 58¢ Total

154 School Day Skills • Grade 2

Page 154

Name ________ Winter • Week 7, Day 1

Add. Regroup as needed.

hundreds	tens	ones	hundreds	tens	ones	hundreds	tens	ones
4	1	8	4	7	1	3	3	4
+ 3	2	3	+ 3	1	9	+ 5	2	8
7	4	1	7	9	0	8	6	2

hundreds	tens	ones	hundreds	tens	ones	hundreds	tens	ones
6	5	9	7	3	6	4	2	6
+ 1	2	7	+ 1	4	5	+ 1	6	5
7	8	6	8	8	1	5	9	1

Read all the sentences. Then, choose the best **adjective** to complete each sentence.

warm toasty hot scorching

1. Let's get inside where it is warm.
2. We like to swim on hot days.
3. Would you like a toasty cheese sandwich?
4. The scorching fire burnt two buildings.

School Day Skills • Grade 2 155

Page 155

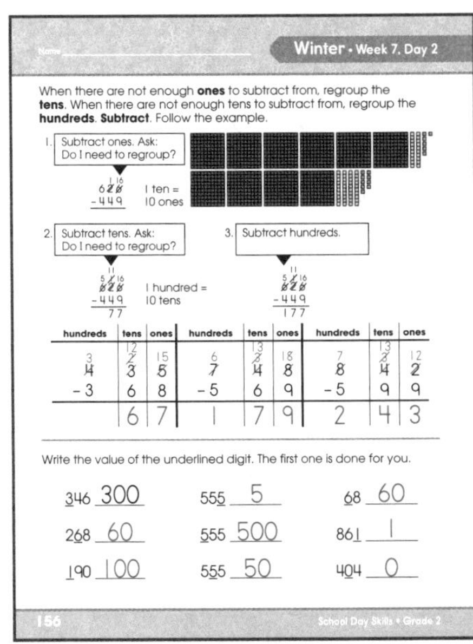

Name ________ Winter • Week 7, Day 2

When there are not enough **ones** to subtract from, regroup the **tens**. When there are not enough tens to subtract from, regroup the **hundreds**. **Subtract**. Follow the example.

1. Subtract ones. Ask: Do I need to regroup?
   $626 - 449$; 1 ten = 10 ones
2. Subtract tens. Ask: Do I need to regroup?
   $626 - 449 = 77$; 1 hundred = 10 tens
3. Subtract hundreds.
   $626 - 449 = 177$

hundreds	tens	ones	hundreds	tens	ones	hundreds	tens	ones
4	3	5	7	4	8	8	4	2
- 3	6	8	- 5	6	9	- 5	9	9
	6	7	1	7	9	2	4	3

Write the value of the underlined digit. The first one is done for you.

346 300 555 5 68 60

268 60 555 500 861 1

190 100 555 50 404 0

156 School Day Skills • Grade 2

Page 156

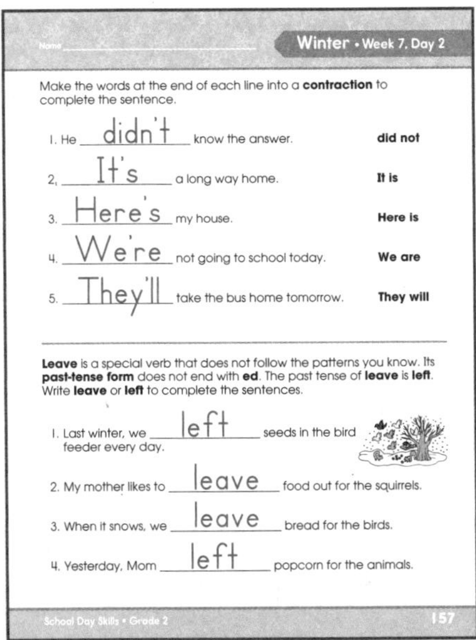

Name ________ Winter • Week 7, Day 2

Make the words at the end of each line into a **contraction** to complete the sentence.

1. He didn't know the answer. **did not**
2. It's a long way home. **It is**
3. Here's my house. **Here is**
4. We're not going to school today. **We are**
5. They'll take the bus home tomorrow. **They will**

Leave is a special verb that does not follow the patterns you know. Its **past-tense form** does not end with **ed**. The past tense of **leave** is **left**. Write **leave** or **left** to complete the sentences.

1. Last winter, we left seeds in the bird feeder every day.
2. My mother likes to leave food out for the squirrels.
3. When it snows, we leave bread for the birds.
4. Yesterday, Mom left popcorn for the animals.

School Day Skills • Grade 2 157

Page 157

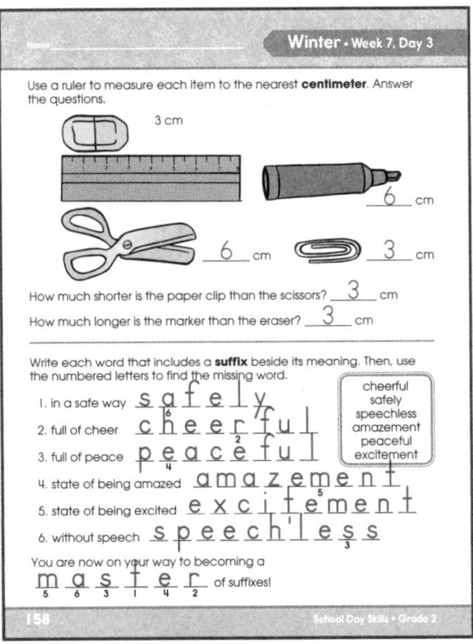

Name ________ Winter • Week 7, Day 3

Use a ruler to measure each item to the nearest **centimeter**. Answer the questions.

3 cm

6 cm

6 cm 3 cm

How much shorter is the paper clip than the scissors? 3 cm

How much longer is the marker than the eraser? 3 cm

Write each word that includes a **suffix** beside its meaning. Then, use the numbered letters to find the missing word.

cheerful, safely, speechless, amazement, peaceful, excitement

1. in a safe way safely
2. full of cheer cheerful
3. full of peace peaceful
4. state of being amazed amazement
5. state of being excited excitement
6. without speech speechless

You are now on your way to becoming a master of suffixes!

158 School Day Skills • Grade 2

Page 158

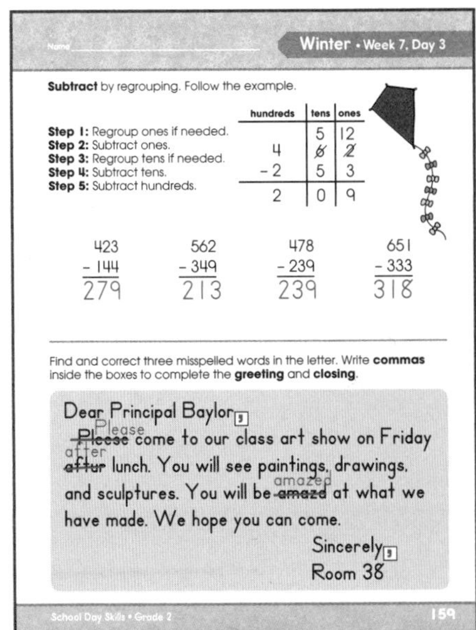

Name ________ Winter • Week 7, Day 3

Subtract by regrouping. Follow the example.

Step 1: Regroup ones if needed.
Step 2: Subtract ones.
Step 3: Regroup tens if needed.
Step 4: Subtract tens.
Step 5: Subtract hundreds.

hundreds	tens	ones
4	5	12
- 2	5	3
2	0	9

$423 - 144 = 279$ $562 - 349 = 213$ $478 - 239 = 239$ $651 - 333 = 318$

Find and correct three misspelled words in the letter. Write **commas** inside the boxes to complete the **greeting** and **closing**.

Dear Principal Baylor,
Please come to our class art show on Friday after lunch. You will see paintings, drawings, and sculptures. You will be amazed at what we have made. We hope you can come.
Sincerely,
Room 38

School Day Skills • Grade 2 159

Page 159

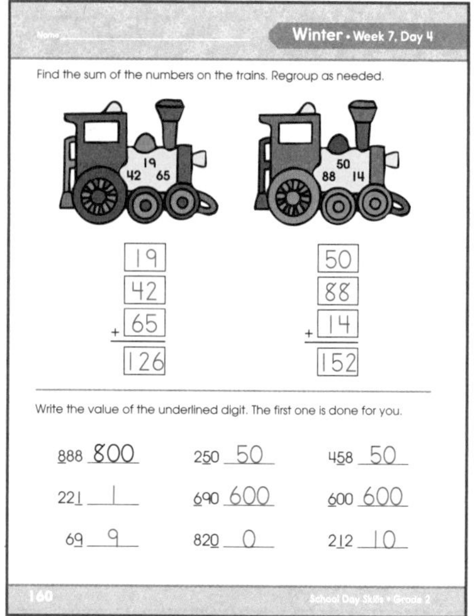
Winter • Week 7, Day 4

Find the sum of the numbers on the trains. Regroup as needed.

19 + 42 + 65 = 126

50 + 88 + 14 = 152

Write the value of the underlined digit. The first one is done for you.

888 800 | 250 50 | 458 50
221 1 | 690 600 | 600 600
69 9 | 820 0 | 212 10

160 School Day Skills • Grade 2

Page 160

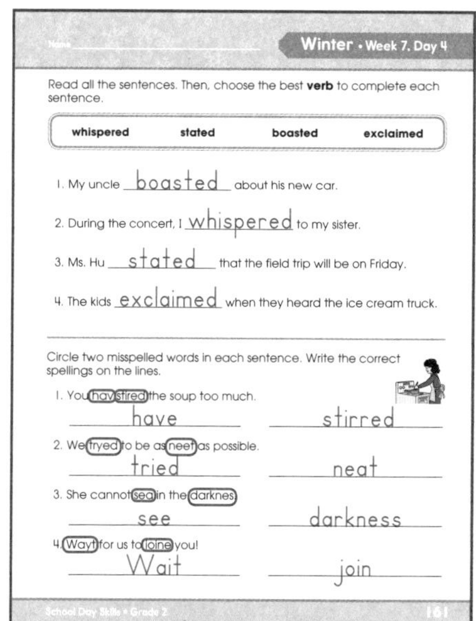
Winter • Week 7, Day 4

Read all the sentences. Then, choose the best **verb** to complete each sentence.

whispered stated boasted exclaimed

1. My uncle boasted about his new car.
2. During the concert, I whispered to my sister.
3. Ms. Hu stated that the field trip will be on Friday.
4. The kids exclaimed when they heard the ice cream truck.

Circle two misspelled words in each sentence. Write the correct spellings on the lines.

1. You hav stired the soup too much. — have, stirred
2. We tryed to be as neet as possible. — tried, neat
3. She cannot sea in the darknes. — see, darkness
4. Wayt for us to joine you! — Wait, join

School Day Skills • Grade 2 161

Page 161

Winter • Week 7, Day 5

Connect the dots to make each shape. Not all dots will be used.

a 3-sided shape | a different 3-sided shape | a 4-sided shape
a different 4-sided shape | a 5-sided shape | a 6-sided shape

Shapes will vary.

Look at the **bold** verb in the first sentence. Write the correct form of the same present-tense verb to match the **collective noun** in the second sentence.

1. We **cheer** for every batter. Our team cheers loudly.
2. Bruno and Sari **wait** for the play to begin. The whole audience waits patiently.
3. My sisters **play** hide-and-seek well. Our family plays together often.
4. The students in this class **have** gym in the afternoon. Our class has a great time during gym!

162 School Day Skills • Grade 2

Page 162

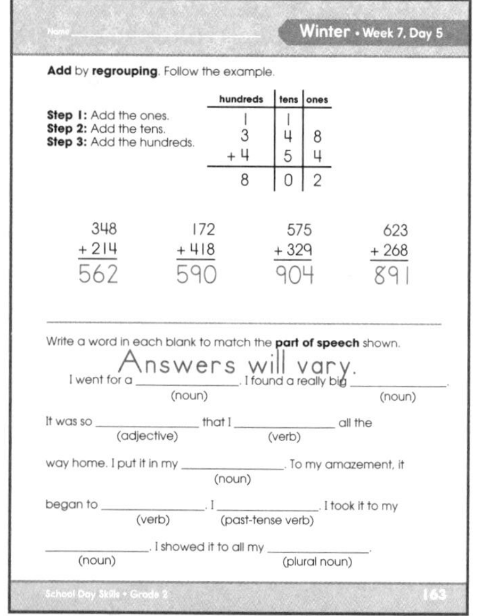
Winter • Week 7, Day 5

Add by **regrouping**. Follow the example.

Step 1: Add the ones.
Step 2: Add the tens.
Step 3: Add the hundreds.

348 + 214 = 562
172 + 418 = 590
575 + 329 = 904
623 + 268 = 891

Write a word in each blank to match the **part of speech** shown.

Answers will vary.

I went for a ____ (noun). I found a really big ____ (noun). It was so ____ (adjective) that I ____ (verb) all the way home. I put it in my ____ (noun). To my amazement, it began to ____ (verb). I ____ (past-tense verb). I took it to my ____ (noun). I showed it to all my ____ (plural noun).

School Day Skills • Grade 2 163

Page 163

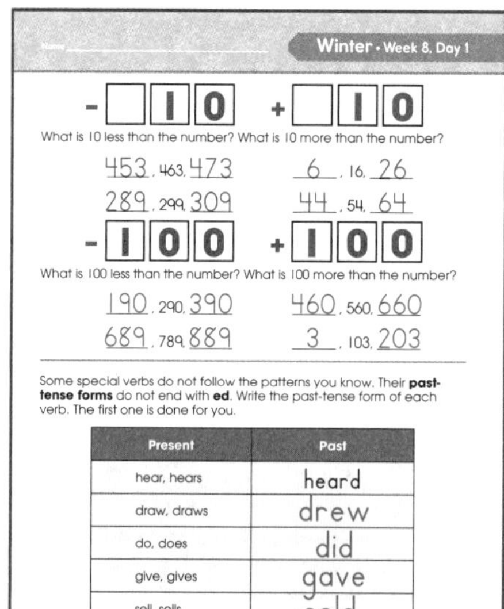
Winter • Week 8, Day 1

What is 10 less than the number? What is 10 more than the number?

453, 463, 473 | 6, 16, 26
289, 299, 309 | 44, 54, 64

What is 100 less than the number? What is 100 more than the number?

190, 290, 390 | 460, 560, 660
689, 789, 889 | 3, 103, 203

Some special verbs do not follow the patterns you know. Their **past-tense forms** do not end with **ed**. Write the past-tense form of each verb. The first one is done for you.

Present	Past
hear, hears	heard
draw, draws	drew
do, does	did
give, gives	gave
sell, sells	sold

164 School Day Skills • Grade 2

Page 164

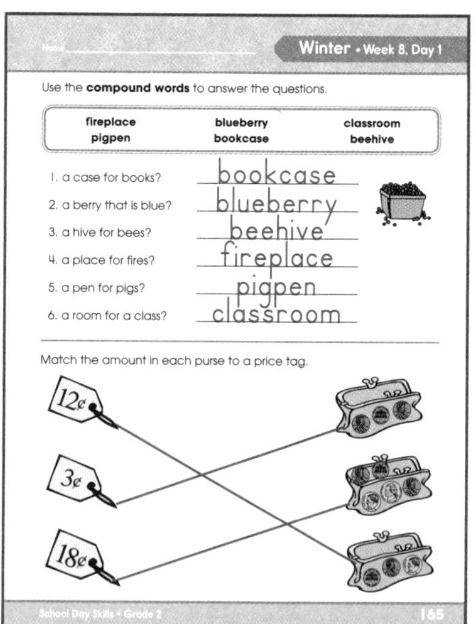
Winter • Week 8, Day 1

Use the **compound words** to answer the questions.

fireplace blueberry classroom pigpen bookcase beehive

1. a case for books? bookcase
2. a berry that is blue? blueberry
3. a hive for bees? beehive
4. a place for fires? fireplace
5. a pen for pigs? pigpen
6. a room for a class? classroom

Match the amount in each purse to a price tag.

12¢ 3¢ 18¢

School Day Skills • Grade 2 165

Page 165

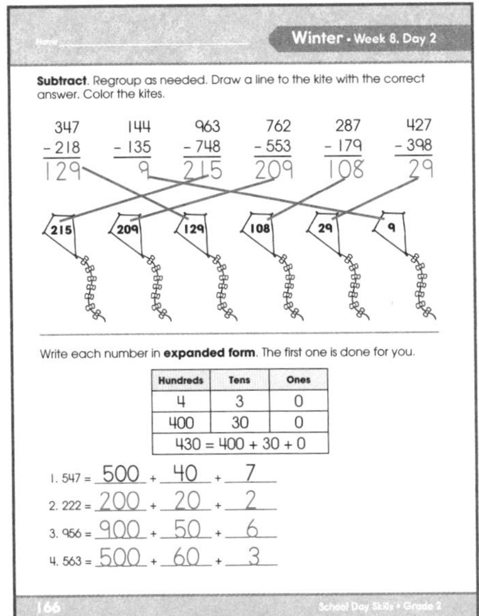
Name ______ Winter • Week 8, Day 2

Subtract. Regroup as needed. Draw a line to the kite with the correct answer. Color the kites.

347	144	963	762	287	427
− 218	− 135	− 748	− 553	− 179	− 398
129	9	215	209	108	29

215 209 129 108 29 9

Write each number in **expanded form**. The first one is done for you.

Hundreds	Tens	Ones
4	3	0
400	30	0
430 = 400 + 30 + 0		

1. 547 = 500 + 40 + 7
2. 222 = 200 + 20 + 2
3. 956 = 900 + 50 + 6
4. 563 = 500 + 60 + 3

166 School Day Skills • Grade 2

Page 166

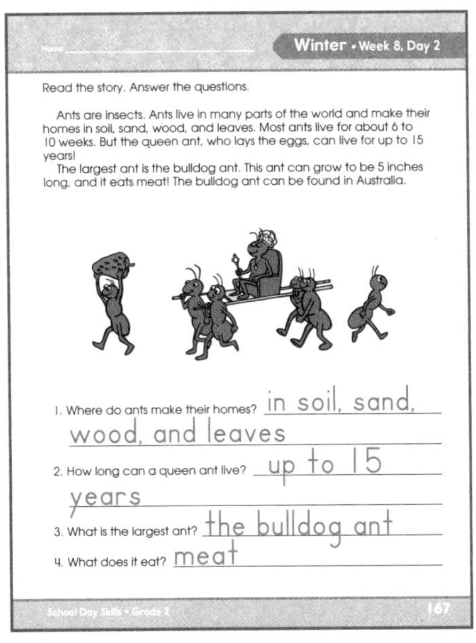
Name ______ Winter • Week 8, Day 2

Read the story. Answer the questions.

Ants are insects. Ants live in many parts of the world and make their homes in soil, sand, wood, and leaves. Most ants live for about 6 to 10 weeks. But the queen ant, who lays the eggs, can live for up to 15 years!

The largest ant is the bulldog ant. This ant can grow to be 5 inches long, and it eats meat! The bulldog ant can be found in Australia.

1. Where do ants make their homes? in soil, sand, wood, and leaves
2. How long can a queen ant live? up to 15 years
3. What is the largest ant? the bulldog ant
4. What does it eat? meat

School Day Skills • Grade 2 167

Page 167

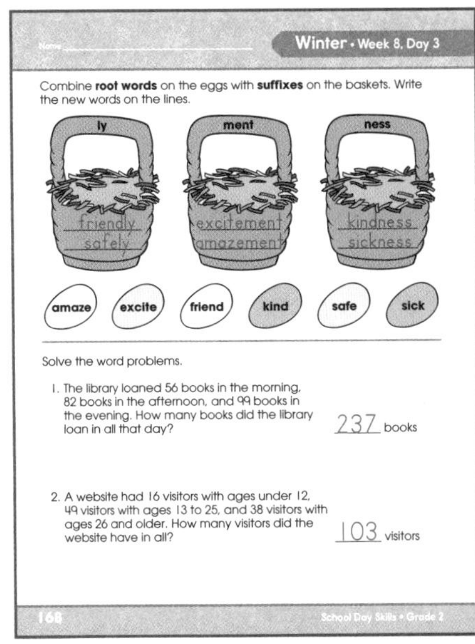
Name ______ Winter • Week 8, Day 3

Combine **root words** on the eggs with **suffixes** on the baskets. Write the new words on the lines.

ly: friendly, safely
ment: excitement, amazement
ness: kindness, sickness

amaze excite friend kind safe sick

Solve the word problems.

1. The library loaned 56 books in the morning, 82 books in the afternoon, and 99 books in the evening. How many books did the library loan in all that day? 237 books
2. A website had 16 visitors with ages under 12, 49 visitors with ages 13 to 25, and 38 visitors with ages 26 and older. How many visitors did the website have in all? 103 visitors

168 School Day Skills • Grade 2

Page 168

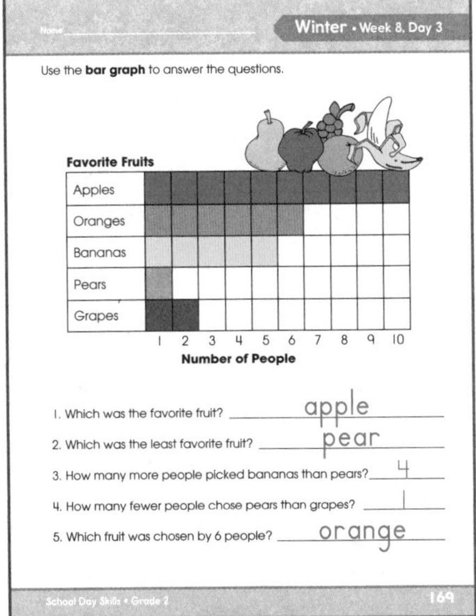
Name ______ Winter • Week 8, Day 3

Use the **bar graph** to answer the questions.

Favorite Fruits

Apples, Oranges, Bananas, Pears, Grapes

1 2 3 4 5 6 7 8 9 10

Number of People

1. Which was the favorite fruit? apple
2. Which was the least favorite fruit? pear
3. How many more people picked bananas than pears? 4
4. How many fewer people chose pears than grapes? 1
5. Which fruit was chosen by 6 people? orange

School Day Skills • Grade 2 169

Page 169

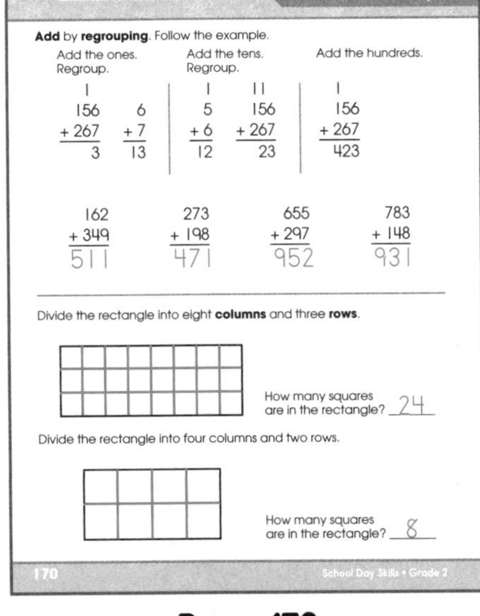
Name ______ Winter • Week 8, Day 4

Add by **regrouping**. Follow the example.

Add the ones. Regroup. 156 + 267 = 3; 6 + 7 = 13

Add the tens. Regroup. 5 + 6 = 12; 156 + 267 = 23

Add the hundreds. 156 + 267 = 423

162	273	655	783
+ 349	+ 198	+ 297	+ 148
511	471	952	931

Divide the rectangle into eight **columns** and three **rows**.

How many squares are in the rectangle? 24

Divide the rectangle into four columns and two rows.

How many squares are in the rectangle? 8

170 School Day Skills • Grade 2

Page 170

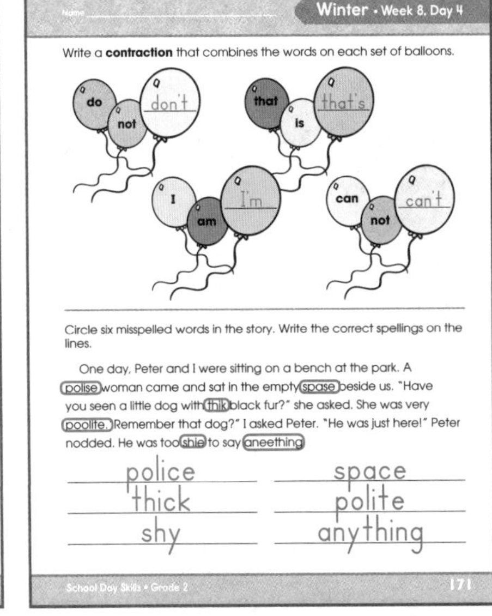
Name ______ Winter • Week 8, Day 4

Write a **contraction** that combines the words on each set of balloons.

do not: don't
that is: that's
I am: I'm
can not: can't

Circle six misspelled words in the story. Write the correct spellings on the lines.

One day, Peter and I were sitting on a bench at the park. A polise woman came and sat in the empty spase beside us. "Have you seen a little dog with thik black fur?" she asked. She was very poolite. "Remember that dog?" I asked Peter. "He was just here!" Peter nodded. He was too shie to say aneething.

police, space, thick, polite, shy, anything

School Day Skills • Grade 2 171

Page 171

Answer Key

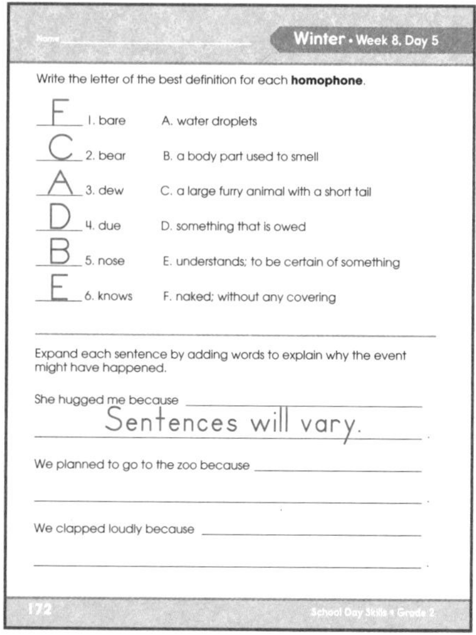

Name ______ Winter • Week 8, Day 5

Write the letter of the best definition for each **homophone**.

F 1. bare — A. water droplets
C 2. bear — B. a body part used to smell
A 3. dew — C. a large furry animal with a short tail
D 4. due — D. something that is owed
B 5. nose — E. understands; to be certain of something
E 6. knows — F. naked; without any covering

Expand each sentence by adding words to explain why the event might have happened.

She hugged me because ______
Sentences will vary.

We planned to go to the zoo because ______

We clapped loudly because ______

172 School Day Skills • Grade 2

Page 172

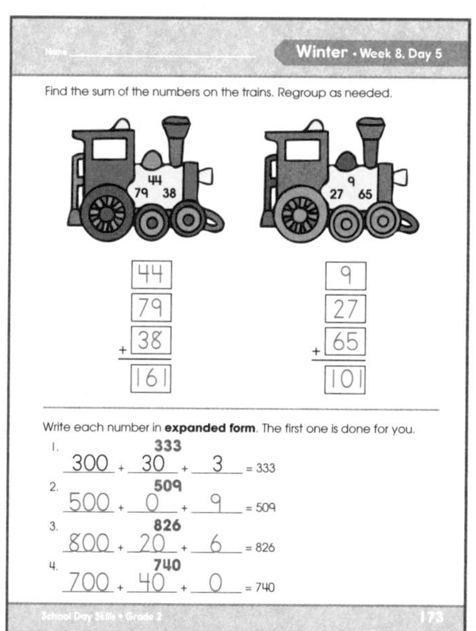

Name ______ Winter • Week 8, Day 5

Find the sum of the numbers on the trains. Regroup as needed.

44 + 79 + 38 = 161

9 + 27 + 65 = 101

Write each number in **expanded form**. The first one is done for you.

1. 333: 300 + 30 + 3 = 333
2. 509: 500 + 0 + 9 = 509
3. 826: 800 + 20 + 6 = 826
4. 740: 700 + 40 + 0 = 740

School Day Skills • Grade 2 173

Page 173

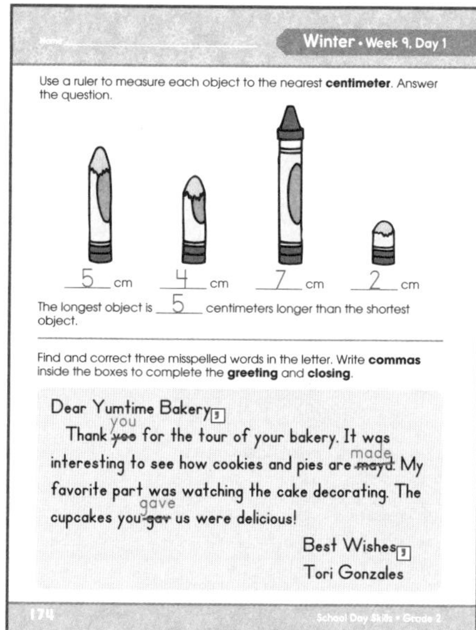

Name ______ Winter • Week 9, Day 1

Use a ruler to measure each object to the nearest **centimeter**. Answer the question.

5 cm 4 cm 7 cm 2 cm

The longest object is 5 centimeters longer than the shortest object.

Find and correct three misspelled words in the letter. Write **commas** inside the boxes to complete the **greeting** and **closing**.

Dear Yumtime Bakery,
Thank ~~yoo~~ you for the tour of your bakery. It was interesting to see how cookies and pies are ~~mayd~~ made. My favorite part was watching the cake decorating. The cupcakes you ~~gav~~ gave us were delicious!
Best Wishes,
Tori Gonzales

174 School Day Skills • Grade 2

Page 174

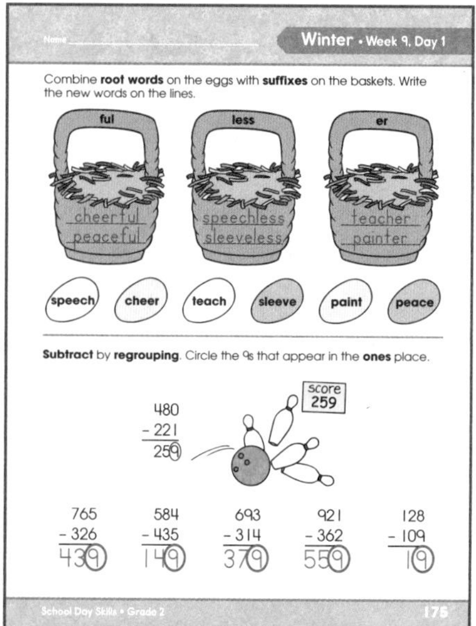

Name ______ Winter • Week 9, Day 1

Combine **root words** on the eggs with **suffixes** on the baskets. Write the new words on the lines.

ful: cheerful, peaceful
less: speechless, sleeveless
er: teacher, painter

speech cheer teach sleeve paint peace

Subtract by **regrouping**. Circle the 9s that appear in the **ones** place.

480 − 221 = 259 (Score 259)

765 − 326 = 439
584 − 435 = 149
693 − 314 = 379
921 − 362 = 559
128 − 109 = 19

School Day Skills • Grade 2 175

Page 175

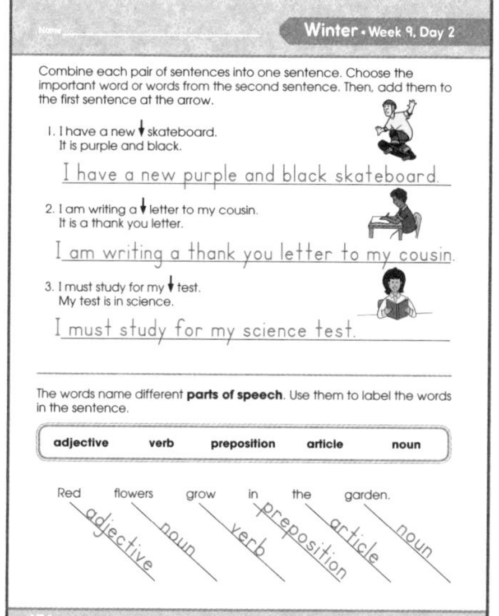

Name ______ Winter • Week 9, Day 2

Combine each pair of sentences into one sentence. Choose the important word or words from the second sentence. Then, add them to the first sentence at the arrow.

1. I have a new ↓ skateboard. It is purple and black.
I have a new purple and black skateboard.
2. I am writing a ↓ letter to my cousin. It is a thank you letter.
I am writing a thank you letter to my cousin.
3. I must study for my ↓ test. My test is in science.
I must study for my science test.

The words name different **parts of speech**. Use them to label the words in the sentence.

adjective verb preposition article noun

Red flowers grow in the garden.
Red — adjective; flowers — noun; grow — verb; in — preposition; the — article; garden — noun

176 School Day Skills • Grade 2

Page 176

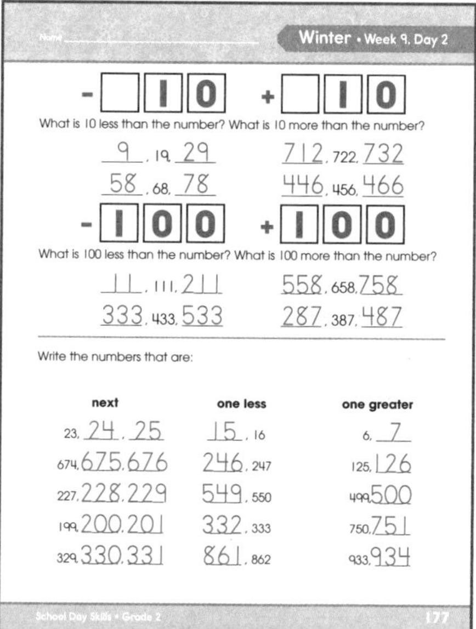

Name ______ Winter • Week 9, Day 2

−10 +10

What is 10 less than the number? What is 10 more than the number?

9, 19, 29 — 712, 722, 732
58, 68, 78 — 446, 456, 466

−100 +100

What is 100 less than the number? What is 100 more than the number?

11, 111, 211 — 558, 658, 758
333, 433, 533 — 287, 387, 487

Write the numbers that are:

next	one less	one greater
23, 24, 25	15, 16	6, 7
674, 675, 676	246, 247	125, 126
227, 228, 229	549, 550	499, 500
199, 200, 201	332, 333	750, 751
329, 330, 331	861, 862	933, 934

School Day Skills • Grade 2 177

Page 177

Answer Key

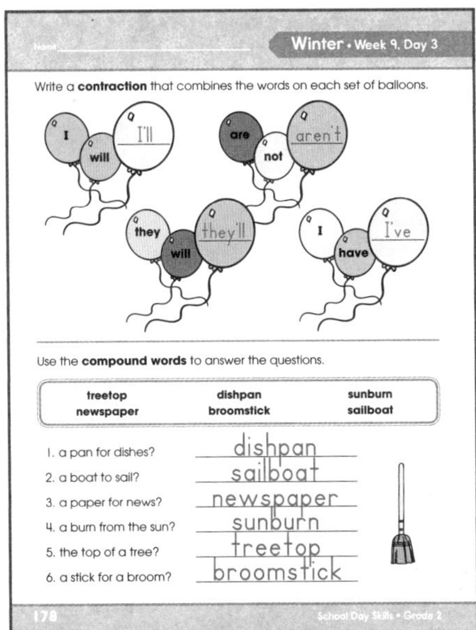

Winter • Week 9, Day 3

Write a **contraction** that combines the words on each set of balloons.

I will — I'll
are not — aren't
they will — they'll
I have — I've

Use the **compound words** to answer the questions.

treetop	dishpan	sunburn
newspaper	broomstick	sailboat

1. a pan for dishes? dishpan
2. a boat to sail? sailboat
3. a paper for news? newspaper
4. a burn from the sun? sunburn
5. the top of a tree? treetop
6. a stick for a broom? broomstick

178 School Day Skills • Grade 2

Page 178

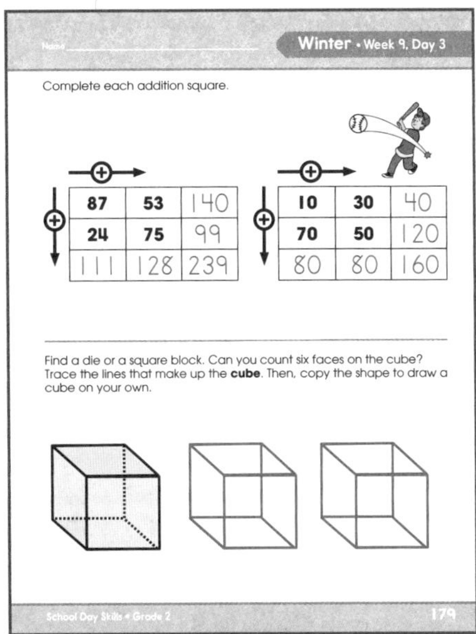

Winter • Week 9, Day 3

Complete each addition square.

87	53	140
24	75	99
111	128	239

10	30	40
70	50	120
80	80	160

Find a die or a square block. Can you count six faces on the cube? Trace the lines that make up the **cube**. Then, copy the shape to draw a cube on your own.

School Day Skills • Grade 2 179

Page 179

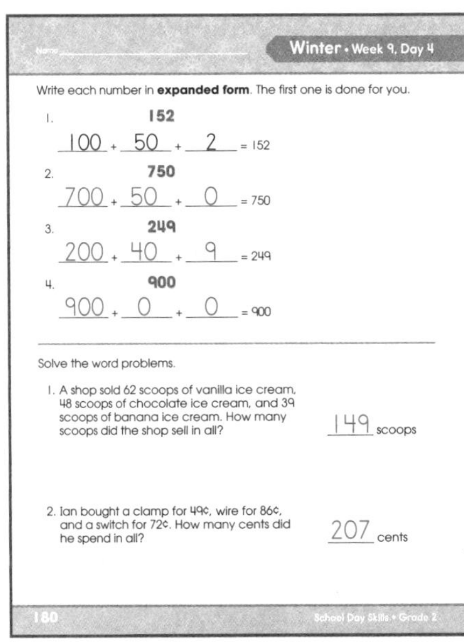

Winter • Week 9, Day 4

Write each number in **expanded form**. The first one is done for you.

1. 152: 100 + 50 + 2 = 152
2. 750: 700 + 50 + 0 = 750
3. 249: 200 + 40 + 9 = 249
4. 900: 900 + 0 + 0 = 900

Solve the word problems.

1. A shop sold 62 scoops of vanilla ice cream, 48 scoops of chocolate ice cream, and 39 scoops of banana ice cream. How many scoops did the shop sell in all? 149 scoops
2. Ian bought a clamp for 49¢, wire for 86¢, and a switch for 72¢. How many cents did he spend in all? 207 cents

180 School Day Skills • Grade 2

Page 180

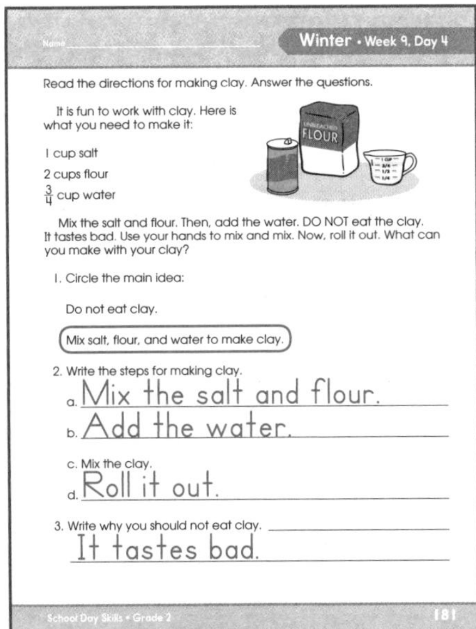

Winter • Week 9, Day 4

Read the directions for making clay. Answer the questions.

It is fun to work with clay. Here is what you need to make it:

1 cup salt
2 cups flour
$\frac{3}{4}$ cup water

Mix the salt and flour. Then, add the water. DO NOT eat the clay. It tastes bad. Use your hands to mix and mix. Now, roll it out. What can you make with your clay?

1. Circle the main idea:

Do not eat clay.

Mix salt, flour, and water to make clay.

2. Write the steps for making clay.

a. Mix the salt and flour.
b. Add the water.
c. Mix the clay.
d. Roll it out.

3. Write why you should not eat clay. It tastes bad.

School Day Skills • Grade 2 181

Page 181

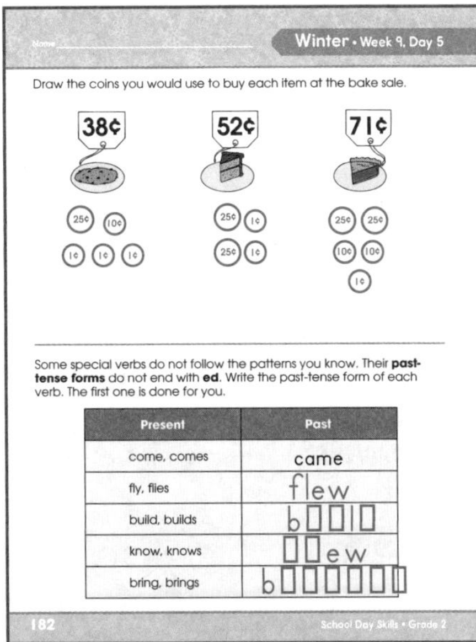

Winter • Week 9, Day 5

Draw the coins you would use to buy each item at the bake sale.

38¢ — 25¢, 10¢, 1¢, 1¢, 1¢
52¢ — 25¢, 1¢, 25¢, 1¢
71¢ — 25¢, 25¢, 10¢, 10¢, 1¢

Some special verbs do not follow the patterns you know. Their **past-tense forms** do not end with **ed**. Write the past-tense form of each verb. The first one is done for you.

Present	Past
come, comes	came
fly, flies	flew
build, builds	built
know, knows	knew
bring, brings	brought

182 School Day Skills • Grade 2

Page 182

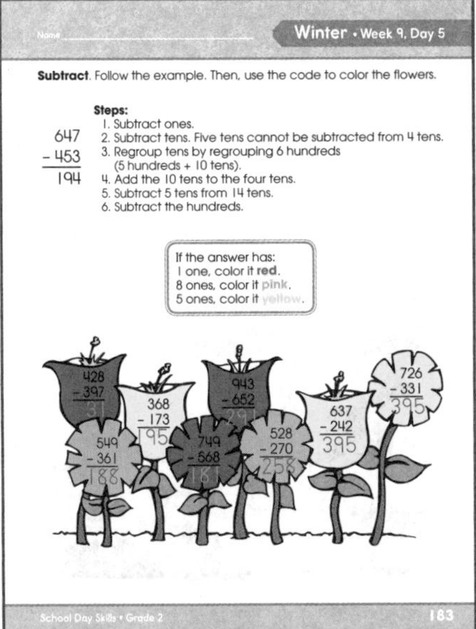

Winter • Week 9, Day 5

Subtract. Follow the example. Then, use the code to color the flowers.

647
− 453
194

Steps:
1. Subtract ones.
2. Subtract tens. Five tens cannot be subtracted from 4 tens.
3. Regroup tens by regrouping 6 hundreds (5 hundreds + 10 tens).
4. Add the 10 tens to the four tens.
5. Subtract 5 tens from 14 tens.
6. Subtract the hundreds.

If the answer has:
1 one, color it red.
8 ones, color it pink.
5 ones, color it yellow.

428 − 397 = 31; 368 − 173 = 195; 943 − 652 = 291; 549 − 361 = 188; 749 − 568 = 181; 528 − 270 = 258; 637 − 242 = 395; 726 − 331 = 395

School Day Skills • Grade 2 183

Page 183

Answer Key

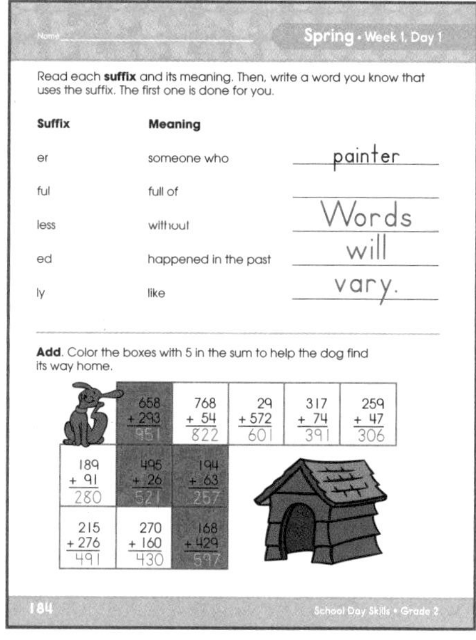
Name ____ Spring • Week 1, Day 1

Read each **suffix** and its meaning. Then, write a word you know that uses the suffix. The first one is done for you.

Suffix	Meaning	
er	someone who	painter
ful	full of	
less	without	Words
ed	happened in the past	will
ly	like	vary.

Add. Color the boxes with 5 in the sum to help the dog find its way home.

	658 + 293 = 951	768 + 54 = 822	29 + 572 = 601	317 + 74 = 391	259 + 47 = 306
189 + 91 = 280	495 + 26 = 521	194 + 63 = 257			
215 + 276 = 491	270 + 160 = 430	168 + 429 = 597			

184 School Day Skills • Grade 2

Page 184

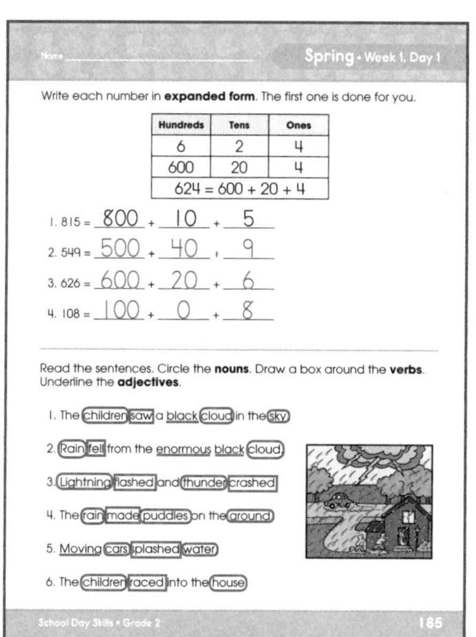
Name ____ Spring • Week 1, Day 1

Write each number in **expanded form**. The first one is done for you.

Hundreds	Tens	Ones
6	2	4
600	20	4
624 = 600 + 20 + 4		

1. 815 = 800 + 10 + 5
2. 549 = 500 + 40 + 9
3. 626 = 600 + 20 + 6
4. 108 = 100 + 0 + 8

Read the sentences. Circle the **nouns**. Draw a box around the **verbs**. Underline the **adjectives**.

1. The children saw a black cloud in the sky.
2. Rain fell from the enormous black cloud.
3. Lightning flashed and thunder crashed.
4. The rain made puddles on the ground.
5. Moving cars splashed water.
6. The children raced into the house.

School Day Skills • Grade 2 185

Page 185

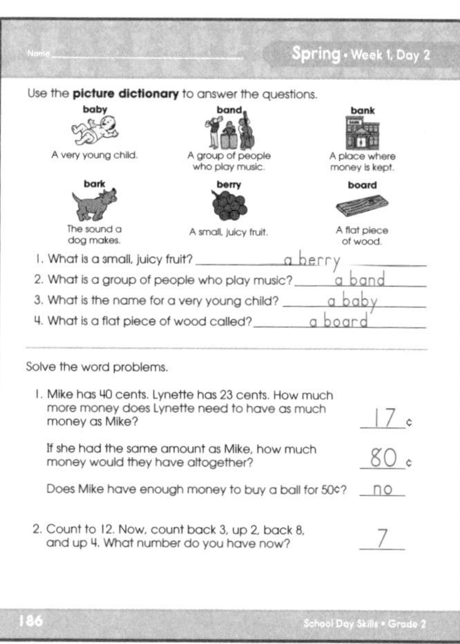
Name ____ Spring • Week 1, Day 2

Use the **picture dictionary** to answer the questions.

1. What is a small, juicy fruit? a berry
2. What is a group of people who play music? a band
3. What is the name for a very young child? a baby
4. What is a flat piece of wood called? a board

Solve the word problems.

1. Mike has 40 cents. Lynette has 23 cents. How much more money does Lynette need to have as much money as Mike? 17 ¢

   If she had the same amount as Mike, how much money would they have altogether? 80 ¢

   Does Mike have enough money to buy a ball for 50¢? no

2. Count to 12. Now, count back 3, up 2, back 8, and up 4. What number do you have now? 7

186 School Day Skills • Grade 2

Page 186

Name ____ Spring • Week 1, Day 2

Subtract to take a ride around the wheel.

School Day Skills • Grade 2 187

Page 187

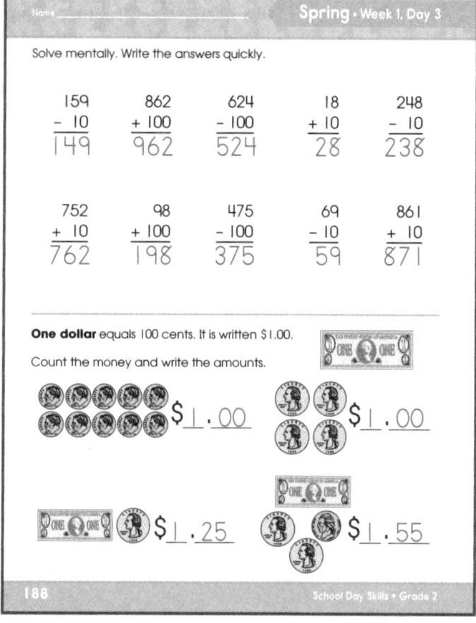
Name ____ Spring • Week 1, Day 3

Solve mentally. Write the answers quickly.

159 − 10 = 149	862 + 100 = 962	624 − 100 = 524	18 + 10 = 28	248 − 10 = 238
752 + 10 = 762	98 + 100 = 198	475 − 100 = 375	69 − 10 = 59	861 + 10 = 871

One dollar equals 100 cents. It is written $1.00.

Count the money and write the amounts.

$1.00 $1.00

$1.25 $1.55

188 School Day Skills • Grade 2

Page 188

Name ____ Spring • Week 1, Day 3

Read how to make a pencil holder. Then, follow the instructions.

You can use "junk" to make a pencil holder! First, you need a clean can with one end removed. Make sure there are no sharp edges. Then, you need glue, scissors, and paper. Find colorful paper such as wrapping paper, wallpaper, or construction paper. Cut the paper to fit the can. Glue the paper around the can. Decorate your can with glitter, buttons, and stickers. Then, put your pencils inside!

Write **first**, **second**, **third**, **fourth**, **fifth**, **sixth**, and **seventh** to put the steps in order.

- second — Make sure there are no sharp edges.
- third — Get glue, scissors, and paper.
- fourth — Cut the paper to fit the can.
- seventh — Put your pencils in the can!
- fifth — Glue colorful paper to the can.
- first — Remove one end of a clean can.
- sixth — Decorate the can with glitter and stickers.

School Day Skills • Grade 2 189

Page 189

Answer Key

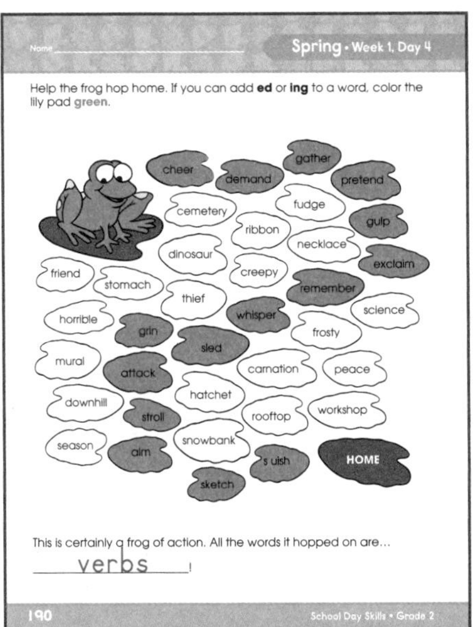

Name ______ **Spring** • Week 1, Day 4

Help the frog hop home. If you can add **ed** or **ing** to a word, color the lily pad green.

This is certainly a frog of action. All the words it hopped on are... verbs!

190 School Day Skills • Grade 2

Page 190

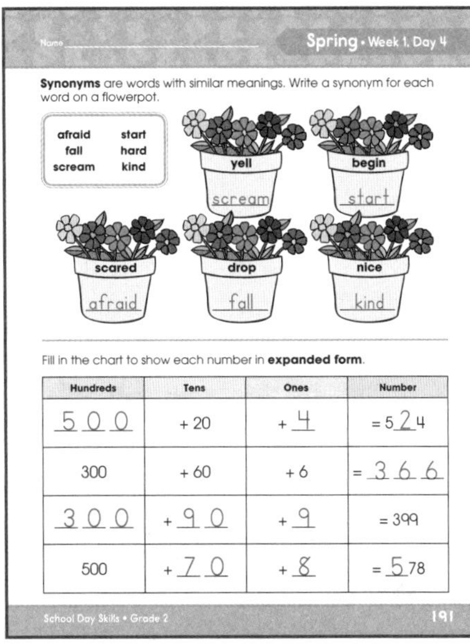

Name ______ **Spring** • Week 1, Day 4

Synonyms are words with similar meanings. Write a synonym for each word on a flowerpot.

Fill in the chart to show each number in **expanded form**.

Hundreds	Tens	Ones	Number
500	+ 20	+ 4	= 524
300	+ 60	+ 6	= 366
300	+ 90	+ 9	= 399
500	+ 70	+ 8	= 578

School Day Skills • Grade 2 191

Page 191

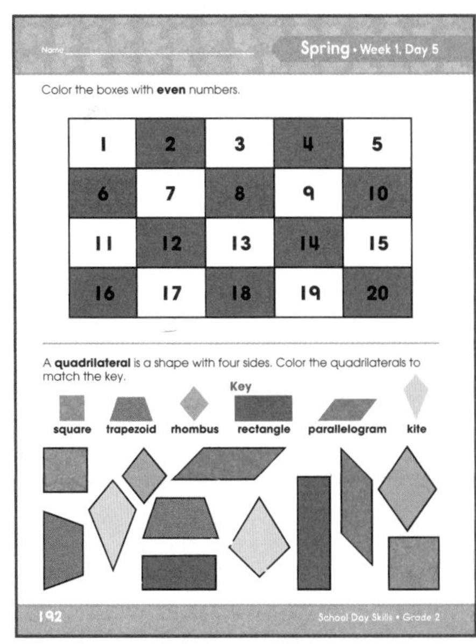

Name ______ **Spring** • Week 1, Day 5

Color the boxes with **even** numbers.

1	2	3	4	5
6	7	8	9	10
11	12	13	14	15
16	17	18	19	20

A **quadrilateral** is a shape with four sides. Color the quadrilaterals to match the key.

192 School Day Skills • Grade 2

Page 192

Name ______ **Spring** • Week 1, Day 5

The **subject** of a sentence tells who or what does something. It contains at least one noun. Underline the subject of each sentence. The first one is done for you.

1. Some people like crocodile steak.
2. The meat tastes like fish.
3. Australians eat kangaroo meat.
4. Kangaroo meat tastes like beef.
5. People in the Southwest eat rattlesnake meat.
6. Snails make a delicious treat for some people.
7. Some Africans think roasted termites are tasty.
8. Bird's nest soup is a famous Chinese dish.
9. People in Florida serve alligator meat.
10. Almost everyone treats themselves with ice cream.

School Day Skills • Grade 2 193

Page 193

Name ______ **Spring** • Week 2, Day 1

Solve the problems to make the windows squeaky clean.

194 School Day Skills • Grade 2

Page 194

Name ______ **Spring** • Week 2, Day 1

Every **sentence** must have at least two things: a **noun** that tells who or what is doing something and a **verb** that tells what the noun is doing. Add a noun or a verb to make a sentence. Write the sentence on the line with correct capitalization and punctuation.

1. brushes her dog every day
2. at the beach, we
3. reads books with me
4. in the morning, our class

Answers will vary.

Circle a misspelled word in each sentence. Write the correct spelling on the line.

1. Which team do you thick will win the game? think
2. The dentist filled the cavity in her toth. tooth
3. We will boft ride on the train. both
4. A baby kangaroo is about one itch long when it is born. inch
5. There is an apple for eack person. each

School Day Skills • Grade 2 195

Page 195

Answer Key

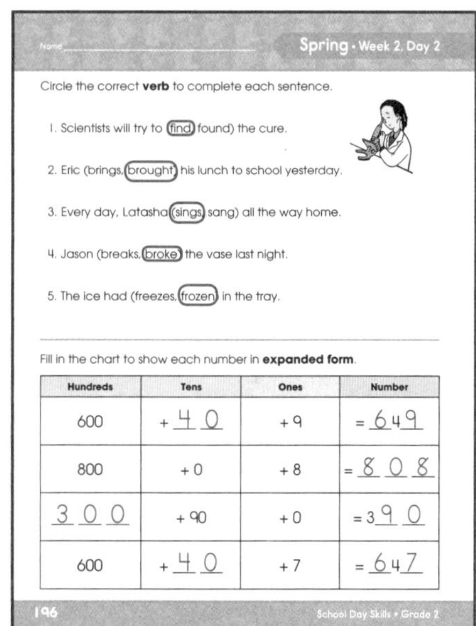

Name ______________ Spring • Week 2, Day 2

Circle the correct **verb** to complete each sentence.

1. Scientists will try to (find, found) the cure.
2. Eric (brings, brought) his lunch to school yesterday.
3. Every day, Latasha (sings, sang) all the way home.
4. Jason (breaks, broke) the vase last night.
5. The ice had (freezes, frozen) in the tray.

Fill in the chart to show each number in **expanded form**.

Hundreds	Tens	Ones	Number
600	+ 40	+ 9	= 649
800	+ 0	+ 8	= 808
300	+ 90	+ 0	= 390
600	+ 40	+ 7	= 647

196 School Day Skills • Grade 2

Page 196

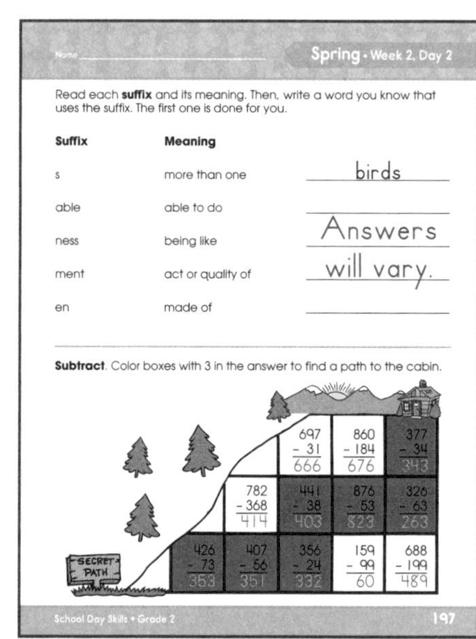

Name ______________ Spring • Week 2, Day 2

Read each **suffix** and its meaning. Then, write a word you know that uses the suffix. The first one is done for you.

Suffix	Meaning	
s	more than one	birds
able	able to do	
ness	being like	Answers
ment	act or quality of	will vary.
en	made of	

Subtract. Color boxes with 3 in the answer to find a path to the cabin.

		697 − 31 = 666	860 − 184 = 676	377 − 34 = 343
	782 − 368 = 414	441 − 38 = 403	876 − 53 = 823	326 − 63 = 263
426 − 73 = 353	407 − 56 = 351	356 − 24 = 332	159 − 99 = 60	688 − 199 = 489

School Day Skills • Grade 2 197

Page 197

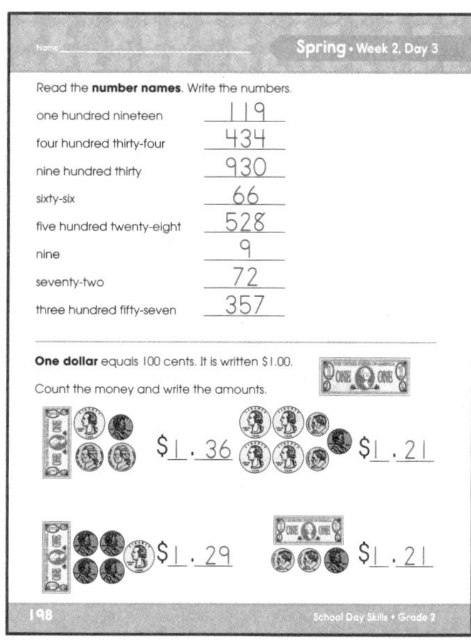

Name ______________ Spring • Week 2, Day 3

Read the **number names**. Write the numbers.

one hundred nineteen	119
four hundred thirty-four	434
nine hundred thirty	930
sixty-six	66
five hundred twenty-eight	528
nine	9
seventy-two	72
three hundred fifty-seven	357

One dollar equals 100 cents. It is written $1.00.

Count the money and write the amounts.

$1.36 $1.21

$1.29 $1.21

198 School Day Skills • Grade 2

Page 198

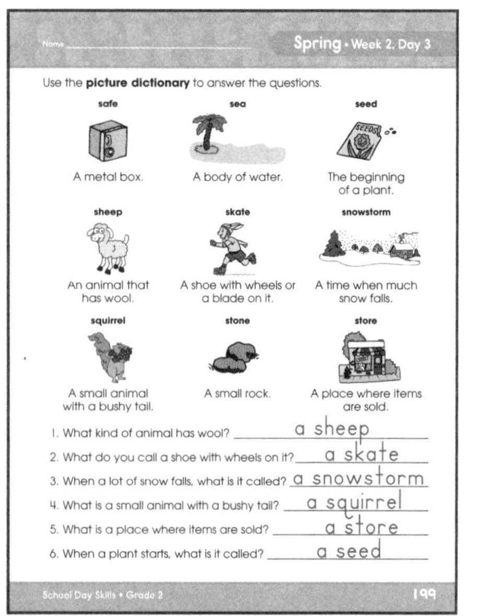

Name ______________ Spring • Week 2, Day 3

Use the **picture dictionary** to answer the questions.

safe — A metal box.
sea — A body of water.
seed — The beginning of a plant.
sheep — An animal that has wool.
skate — A shoe with wheels or a blade on it.
snowstorm — A time when much snow falls.
squirrel — A small animal with a bushy tail.
stone — A small rock.
store — A place where items are sold.

1. What kind of animal has wool? a sheep
2. What do you call a shoe with wheels on it? a skate
3. When a lot of snow falls, what is it called? a snowstorm
4. What is a small animal with a bushy tail? a squirrel
5. What is a place where items are sold? a store
6. When a plant starts, what is it called? a seed

School Day Skills • Grade 2 199

Page 199

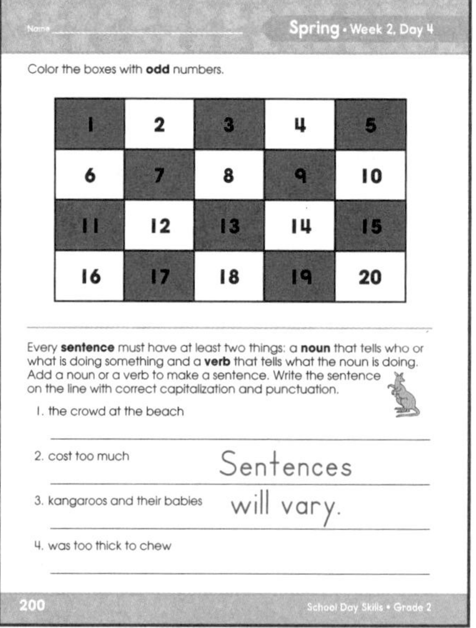

Name ______________ Spring • Week 2, Day 4

Color the boxes with **odd** numbers.

1	2	3	4	5
6	7	8	9	10
11	12	13	14	15
16	17	18	19	20

Every **sentence** must have at least two things: a **noun** that tells who or what is doing something and a **verb** that tells what the noun is doing. Add a noun or a verb to make a sentence. Write the sentence on the line with correct capitalization and punctuation.

1. the crowd at the beach
2. cost too much
3. kangaroos and their babies
4. was too thick to chew

Sentences will vary.

200 School Day Skills • Grade 2

Page 200

Name ______________ Spring • Week 2, Day 4

Synonyms are words with similar meanings. Write a synonym for each word on a flowerpot.

hard, tired, dirt, close, put, whisper

sleepy — tired
soil — dirt
near — close
place — put
difficult — hard

Solve the word problems.

1. A clown started the day with 200 balloons. She gave away 128. Some broke. At the end of the day, she had 18 balloons left. How many balloons broke? 54 balloons
2. At a game booth, prizes were given for scoring 500 points in 3 tries. Serena scored 178 points on her first try, 149 points on her second try, and 233 points on her third try. Did Serena win a prize? yes

School Day Skills • Grade 2 201

Page 201

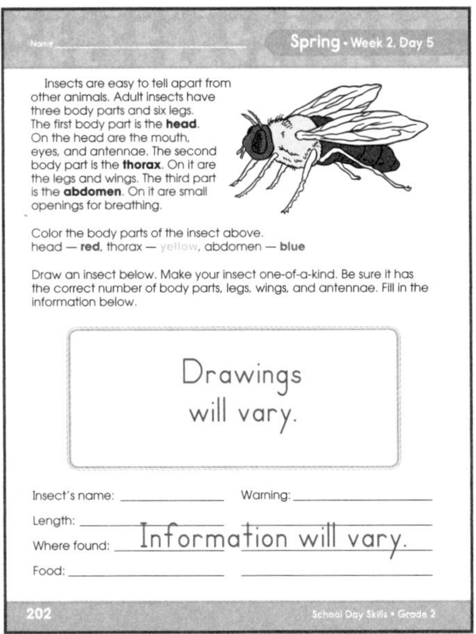
Name ______ **Spring • Week 2, Day 5**

Insects are easy to tell apart from other animals. Adult insects have three body parts and six legs. The first body part is the **head**. On the head are the mouth, eyes, and antennae. The second body part is the **thorax**. On it are the legs and wings. The third part is the **abdomen**. On it are small openings for breathing.

Color the body parts of the insect above.
head — **red**, thorax — yellow, abdomen — **blue**

Draw an insect below. Make your insect one-of-a-kind. Be sure it has the correct number of body parts, legs, wings, and antennae. Fill in the information below.

Drawings will vary.

Insect's name: ______ Warning: ______
Length: ______
Where found: Information will vary.
Food: ______

202 School Day Skills • Grade 2

Page 202

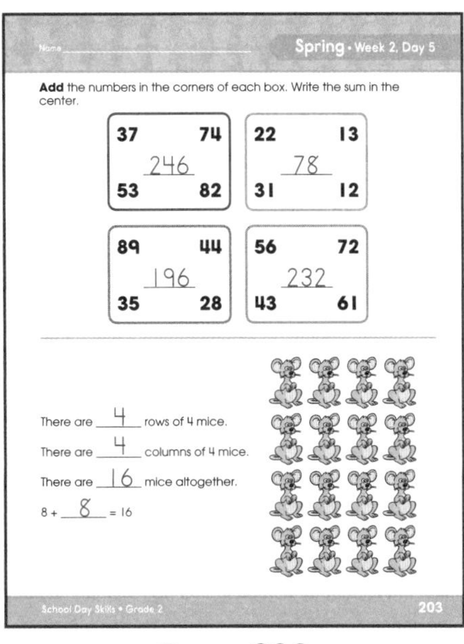
Name ______ **Spring • Week 2, Day 5**

Add the numbers in the corners of each box. Write the sum in the center.

37		74
	246	
53		82

22		13
	78	
31		12

89		44
	196	
35		28

56		72
	232	
43		61

There are 4 rows of 4 mice.
There are 4 columns of 4 mice.
There are 16 mice altogether.
8 + 8 = 16

School Day Skills • Grade 2 203

Page 203

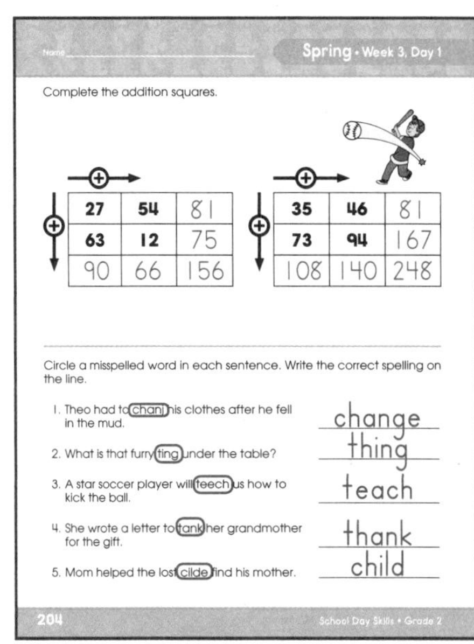
Name ______ **Spring • Week 3, Day 1**

Complete the addition squares.

27	54	81
63	12	75
90	66	156

35	46	81
73	94	167
108	140	248

Circle a misspelled word in each sentence. Write the correct spelling on the line.

1. Theo had to chanj his clothes after he fell in the mud. change
2. What is that furry ting under the table? thing
3. A star soccer player will teech us how to kick the ball. teach
4. She wrote a letter to tank her grandmother for the gift. thank
5. Mom helped the lost cilde find his mother. child

204 School Day Skills • Grade 2

Page 204

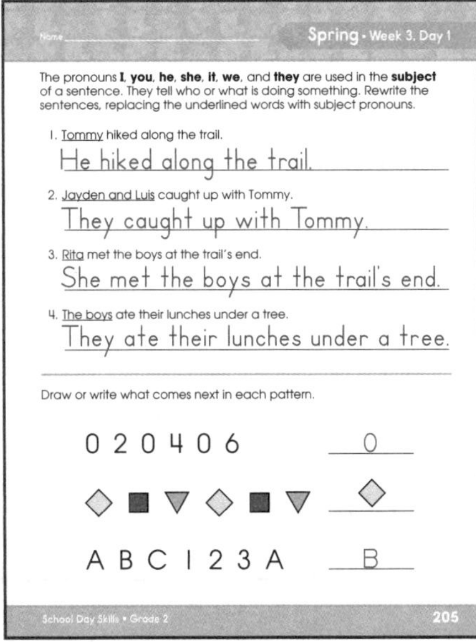
Name ______ **Spring • Week 3, Day 1**

The pronouns **I**, **you**, **he**, **she**, **it**, **we**, and **they** are used in the **subject** of a sentence. They tell who or what is doing something. Rewrite the sentences, replacing the underlined words with subject pronouns.

1. Tommy hiked along the trail.
He hiked along the trail.
2. Jayden and Luis caught up with Tommy.
They caught up with Tommy.
3. Rita met the boys at the trail's end.
She met the boys at the trail's end.
4. The boys ate their lunches under a tree.
They ate their lunches under a tree.

Draw or write what comes next in each pattern.

0 2 0 4 0 6 — 0
◇ ■ ▽ ◇ ■ ▽ — ◇
A B C 1 2 3 A — B

School Day Skills • Grade 2 205

Page 205

Name ______ **Spring • Week 3, Day 2**

Subtract. Complete the crossword puzzle with your answers.

Across
2. 517 − 228
3. 428 − 249
4. 562 − 274
5. 924 − 348
6. 923 − 346
7. 535 − 248
8. 857 − 389
9. 561 − 247
11. 845 − 599
13. 325 − 186
14. 356 − 168

Down
1. 421 − 342
2. 627 − 348
3. 362 − 194
4. 582 − 346
5. 824 − 247
6. 921 − 346
7. 926 − 718
8. 721 − 240
10. 768 − 292
12. 826 − 337
13. 247 − 129

206 School Day Skills • Grade 2

Page 206

Name ______ **Spring • Week 3, Day 2**

When a sentence has a **compound subject**, two or more subjects are joined by the word **and**. Look at the **bold** subject in each sentence. If the sentence has a compound subject, write **CS**. If it does not, write **No**. The first one is done for you.

No 1. **A predator** is an animal that eats other animals.
No 2. **Prey** is eaten by predators.
CS 3. **Robins and bluejays** are predators.
No 4. **Some predators** eat only meat.
CS 5. **Crocodiles and hawks** eat meat only.
CS 6. **Raccoons and foxes** eat both meat and plants.

Combine the subjects of the two sentences to make a compound subject. Write the new sentence on the line.

Snakes are predators. Spiders are predators.
Snakes and spiders are predators.

Frogs prey on insects. Chameleons prey on insects.
Frogs and chameleons prey on insects.

School Day Skills • Grade 2 207

Page 207

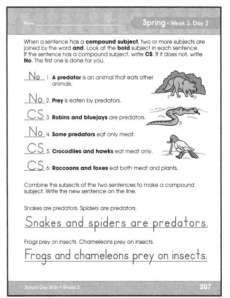

Answer Key

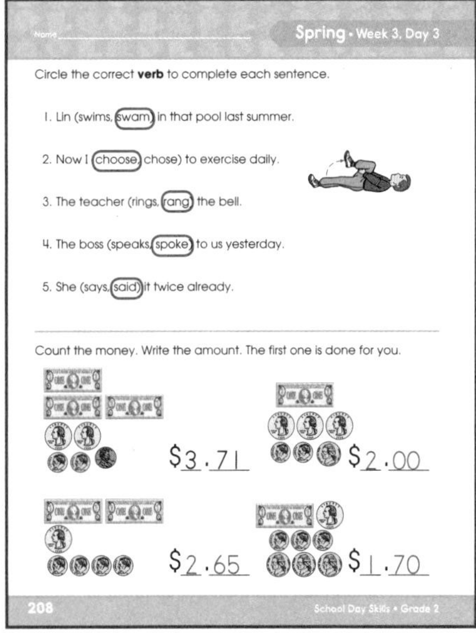
Name ______ Spring • Week 3, Day 3

Circle the correct **verb** to complete each sentence.

1. Lin (swims, swam) in that pool last summer.
2. Now I (choose, chose) to exercise daily.
3. The teacher (rings, rang) the bell.
4. The boss (speaks, spoke) to us yesterday.
5. She (says, said) it twice already.

Count the money. Write the amount. The first one is done for you.

$3.71 $2.00

$2.65 $1.70

208 School Day Skills • Grade 2

Page 208

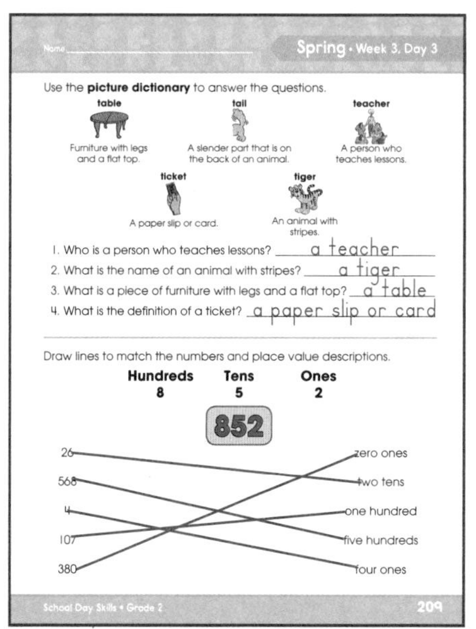
Name ______ Spring • Week 3, Day 3

Use the **picture dictionary** to answer the questions.

table — Furniture with legs and a flat top.
tail — A slender part that is on the back of an animal.
teacher — A person who teaches lessons.
ticket — A paper slip or card.
tiger — An animal with stripes.

1. Who is a person who teaches lessons? a teacher
2. What is the name of an animal with stripes? a tiger
3. What is a piece of furniture with legs and a flat top? a table
4. What is the definition of a ticket? a paper slip or card

Draw lines to match the numbers and place value descriptions.

Hundreds	Tens	Ones
8	5	2

852

26 — zero ones
568 — two tens
4 — one hundred
107 — five hundreds
380 — four ones

School Day Skills • Grade 2 209

Page 209

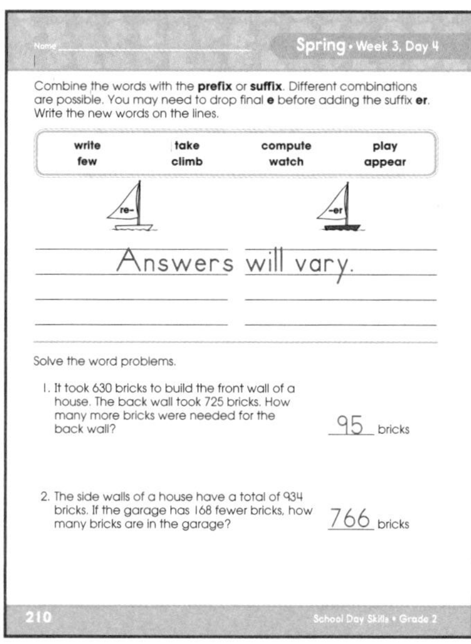
Name ______ Spring • Week 4, Day 4

Combine the words with the **prefix** or **suffix**. Different combinations are possible. You may need to drop final **e** before adding the suffix **er**. Write the new words on the lines.

write take compute play
few climb watch appear

re- -er

Answers will vary.

Solve the word problems.

1. It took 630 bricks to build the front wall of a house. The back wall took 725 bricks. How many more bricks were needed for the back wall? 95 bricks
2. The side walls of a house have a total of 934 bricks. If the garage has 168 fewer bricks, how many bricks are in the garage? 766 bricks

210 School Day Skills • Grade 2

Page 210

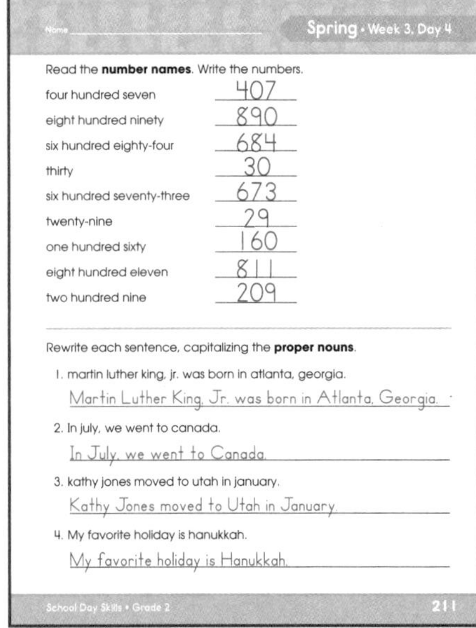
Name ______ Spring • Week 3, Day 4

Read the **number names**. Write the numbers.

four hundred seven	407
eight hundred ninety	890
six hundred eighty-four	684
thirty	30
six hundred seventy-three	673
twenty-nine	29
one hundred sixty	160
eight hundred eleven	811
two hundred nine	209

Rewrite each sentence, capitalizing the **proper nouns**.

1. martin luther king, jr. was born in atlanta, georgia.
Martin Luther King, Jr. was born in Atlanta, Georgia.
2. In july, we went to canada.
In July, we went to Canada.
3. kathy jones moved to utah in january.
Kathy Jones moved to Utah in January.
4. My favorite holiday is hanukkah.
My favorite holiday is Hanukkah.

School Day Skills • Grade 2 211

Page 211

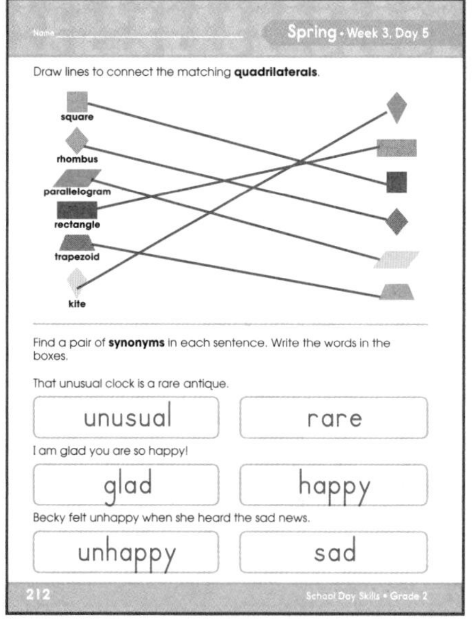
Name ______ Spring • Week 3, Day 5

Draw lines to connect the matching **quadrilaterals**.

square
rhombus
parallelogram
rectangle
trapezoid
kite

Find a pair of **synonyms** in each sentence. Write the words in the boxes.

That unusual clock is a rare antique.
unusual rare

I am glad you are so happy!
glad happy

Becky felt unhappy when she heard the sad news.
unhappy sad

212 School Day Skills • Grade 2

Page 212

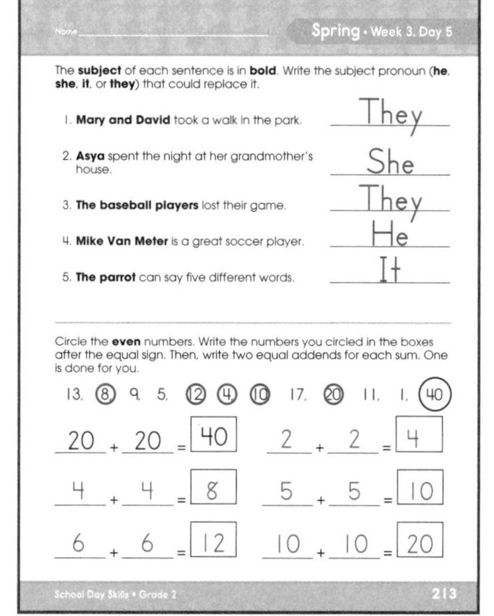
Name ______ Spring • Week 3, Day 5

The **subject** of each sentence is in **bold**. Write the subject pronoun (**he**, **she**, **it**, or **they**) that could replace it.

1. **Mary and David** took a walk in the park. They
2. **Asya** spent the night at her grandmother's house. She
3. **The baseball players** lost their game. They
4. **Mike Van Meter** is a great soccer player. He
5. **The parrot** can say five different words. It

Circle the **even** numbers. Write the numbers you circled in the boxes after the equal sign. Then, write two equal addends for each sum. One is done for you.

13, 8, 9, 5, 12, 4, 10, 17, 20, 11, 1, 40

20 + 20 = 40 2 + 2 = 4

4 + 4 = 8 5 + 5 = 10

6 + 6 = 12 10 + 10 = 20

School Day Skills • Grade 2 213

Page 213

Answer Key

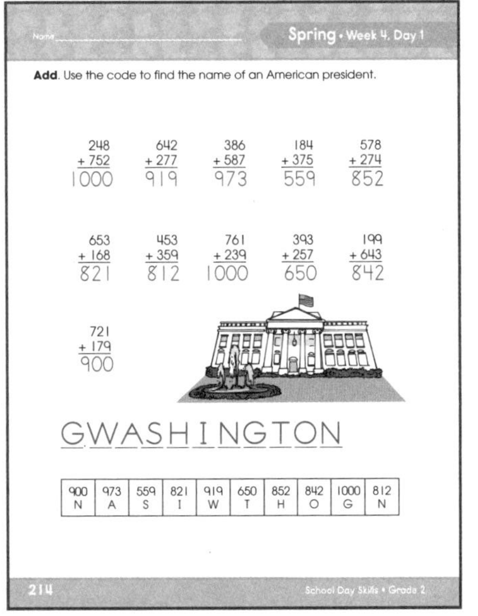

Name ________ **Spring** • Week 4, Day 1

Add. Use the code to find the name of an American president.

248 + 752 = 1000	642 + 277 = 919	386 + 587 = 973	184 + 375 = 559	578 + 274 = 852
653 + 168 = 821	453 + 359 = 812	761 + 239 = 1000	393 + 257 = 650	199 + 643 = 842
721 + 179 = 900				

G W A S H I N G T O N

900	973	559	821	919	650	852	842	1000	812
N	A	S	I	W	T	H	O	G	N

214 School Day Skills • Grade 2

Page 214

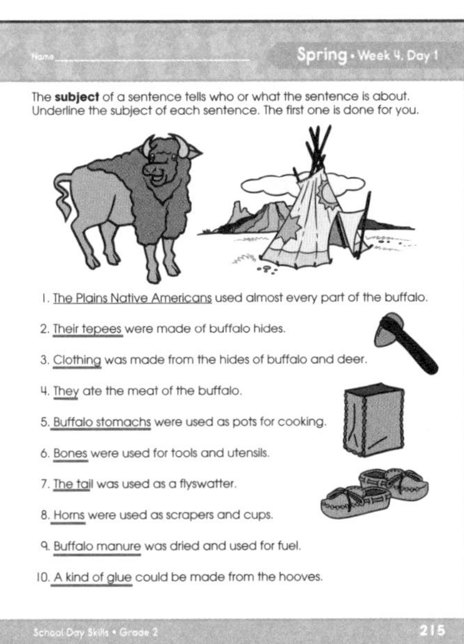

Name ________ **Spring** • Week 4, Day 1

The **subject** of a sentence tells who or what the sentence is about. Underline the subject of each sentence. The first one is done for you.

1. The Plains Native Americans used almost every part of the buffalo.
2. Their tepees were made of buffalo hides.
3. Clothing was made from the hides of buffalo and deer.
4. They ate the meat of the buffalo.
5. Buffalo stomachs were used as pots for cooking.
6. Bones were used for tools and utensils.
7. The tail was used as a flyswatter.
8. Horns were used as scrapers and cups.
9. Buffalo manure was dried and used for fuel.
10. A kind of glue could be made from the hooves.

School Day Skills • Grade 2 215

Page 215

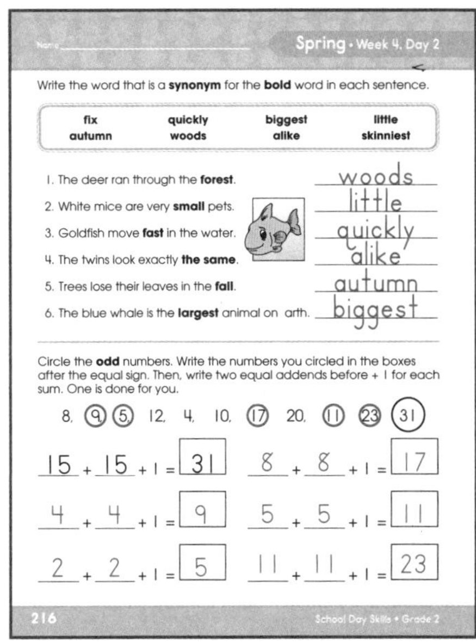

Name ________ **Spring** • Week 4, Day 2

Write the word that is a **synonym** for the **bold** word in each sentence.

fix	quickly	biggest	little
autumn	woods	alike	skinniest

1. The deer ran through the **forest**. woods
2. White mice are very **small** pets. little
3. Goldfish move **fast** in the water. quickly
4. The twins look exactly **the same**. alike
5. Trees lose their leaves in the **fall**. autumn
6. The blue whale is the **largest** animal on arth. biggest

Circle the **odd** numbers. Write the numbers you circled in the boxes after the equal sign. Then, write two equal addends before + 1 for each sum. One is done for you.

8. (9) (5) 12. 4. 10. (17) 20. (11) (23) (31)

15 + 15 + 1 = 31   8 + 8 + 1 = 17

4 + 4 + 1 = 9   5 + 5 + 1 = 11

2 + 2 + 1 = 5   11 + 11 + 1 = 23

216 School Day Skills • Grade 2

Page 216

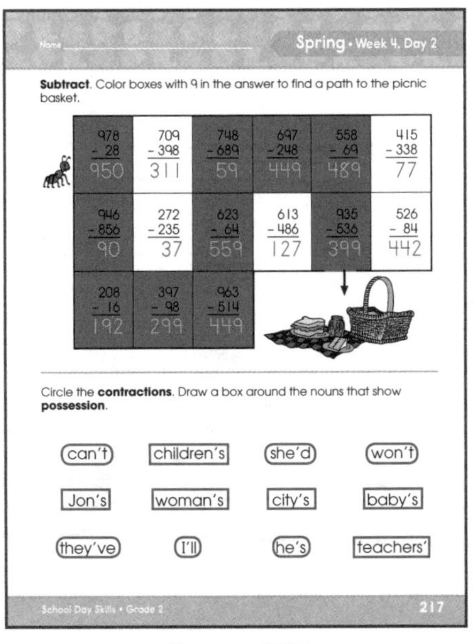

Name ________ **Spring** • Week 4, Day 2

Subtract. Color boxes with 9 in the answer to find a path to the picnic basket.

978 − 28 = 950	709 − 398 = 311	748 − 689 = 59	697 − 248 = 449	558 − 69 = 489	415 − 338 = 77
946 − 856 = 90	272 − 235 = 37	623 − 64 = 559	613 − 486 = 127	935 − 536 = 399	526 − 84 = 442
208 − 16 = 192	397 − 98 = 299	963 − 514 = 449			

Circle the **contractions**. Draw a box around the nouns that show **possession**.

(can't) [children's] (she'd) (won't)

[Jon's] [woman's] [city's] [baby's]

(they've) (I'll) (he's) [teachers']

School Day Skills • Grade 2 217

Page 217

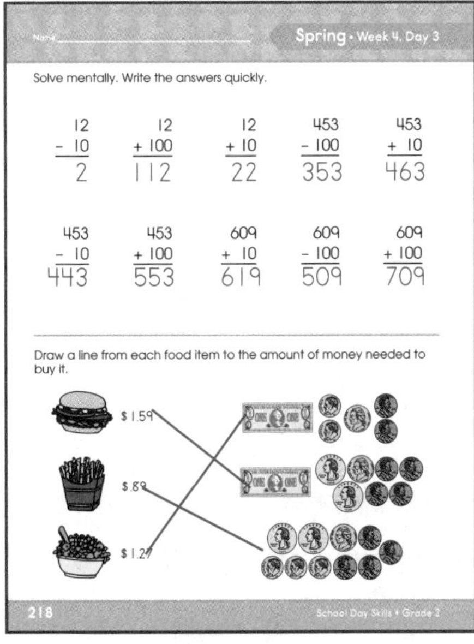

Name ________ **Spring** • Week 4, Day 3

Solve mentally. Write the answers quickly.

12 − 10 = 2	12 + 100 = 112	12 + 10 = 22	453 − 100 = 353	453 + 10 = 463
453 − 10 = 443	453 + 100 = 553	609 + 10 = 619	609 − 100 = 509	609 + 100 = 709

Draw a line from each food item to the amount of money needed to buy it.

$1.59 $.89 $1.27

218 School Day Skills • Grade 2

Page 218

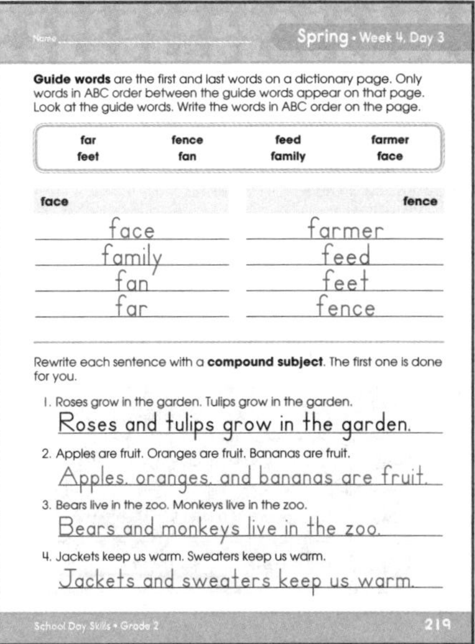

Name ________ **Spring** • Week 4, Day 3

Guide words are the first and last words on a dictionary page. Only words in ABC order between the guide words appear on that page. Look at the guide words. Write the words in ABC order on the page.

far	fence	feed	farmer
feet	fan	family	face

face ... **fence**

face, family, fan, far, farmer, feed, feet, fence

Rewrite each sentence with a **compound subject**. The first one is done for you.

1. Roses grow in the garden. Tulips grow in the garden.
   Roses and tulips grow in the garden.
2. Apples are fruit. Oranges are fruit. Bananas are fruit.
   Apples, oranges, and bananas are fruit.
3. Bears live in the zoo. Monkeys live in the zoo.
   Bears and monkeys live in the zoo.
4. Jackets keep us warm. Sweaters keep us warm.
   Jackets and sweaters keep us warm.

School Day Skills • Grade 2 219

Page 219

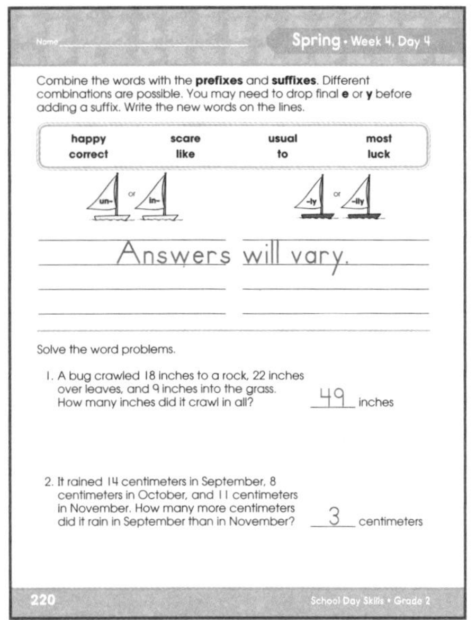
Name ______ Spring • Week 4, Day 4

Combine the words with the **prefixes** and **suffixes**. Different combinations are possible. You may need to drop final **e** or **y** before adding a suffix. Write the new words on the lines.

happy	scare	usual	most
correct	like	to	luck

un- or in-   -ly or -ily

Answers will vary.

Solve the word problems.

1. A bug crawled 18 inches to a rock, 22 inches over leaves, and 9 inches into the grass. How many inches did it crawl in all? 49 inches
2. It rained 14 centimeters in September, 8 centimeters in October, and 11 centimeters in November. How many more centimeters did it rain in September than in November? 3 centimeters

220 School Day Skills • Grade 2

Page 220

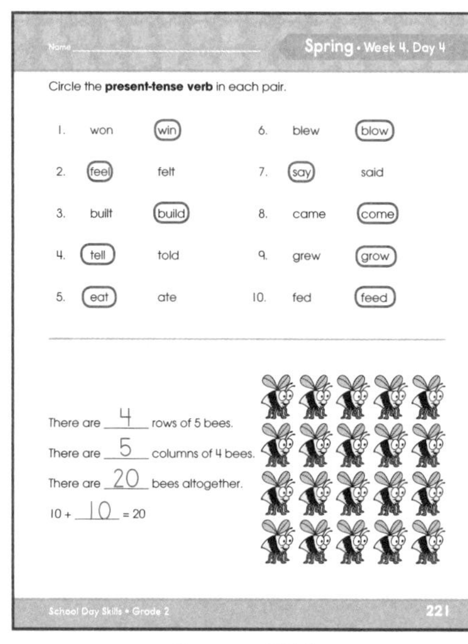
Name ______ Spring • Week 4, Day 4

Circle the **present-tense verb** in each pair.

1. won (win)
2. (feel) felt
3. built (build)
4. (tell) told
5. (eat) ate
6. blew (blow)
7. (say) said
8. came (come)
9. grew (grow)
10. fed (feed)

There are 4 rows of 5 bees.
There are 5 columns of 4 bees.
There are 20 bees altogether.
10 + 10 = 20

School Day Skills • Grade 2 221

Page 221

Name ______ Spring • Week 4, Day 5

Write the **number names** for each number.

381 three hundred eighty-one
822 eight hundred twenty-two
601 six hundred one
171 one hundred seventy-one
205 two hundred five
296 two hundred ninety-six

When the letters **le** come at the end of a word, they sometimes have the sound **ul**, as in **raffle**. Draw lines to match the word parts to make words. Write the words on the lines. The first one is done for you.

can — gle — candle
tur — cle — turtle
pur — ple — purple
cir — kle — circle
spar — dle — sparkle
ea — tle — eagle

222 School Day Skills • Grade 2

Page 222

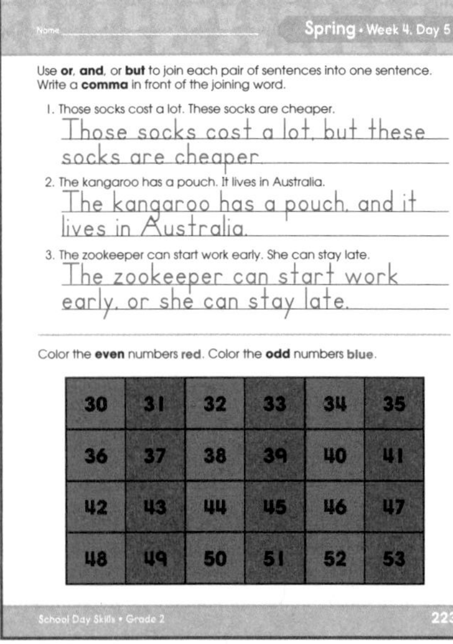
Name ______ Spring • Week 4, Day 5

Use **or**, **and**, or **but** to join each pair of sentences into one sentence. Write a **comma** in front of the joining word.

1. Those socks cost a lot. These socks are cheaper.
   Those socks cost a lot, but these socks are cheaper.
2. The kangaroo has a pouch. It lives in Australia.
   The kangaroo has a pouch, and it lives in Australia.
3. The zookeeper can start work early. She can stay late.
   The zookeeper can start work early, or she can stay late.

Color the **even** numbers **red**. Color the **odd** numbers **blue**.

30	31	32	33	34	35
36	37	38	39	40	41
42	43	44	45	46	47
48	49	50	51	52	53

School Day Skills • Grade 2 223

Page 223

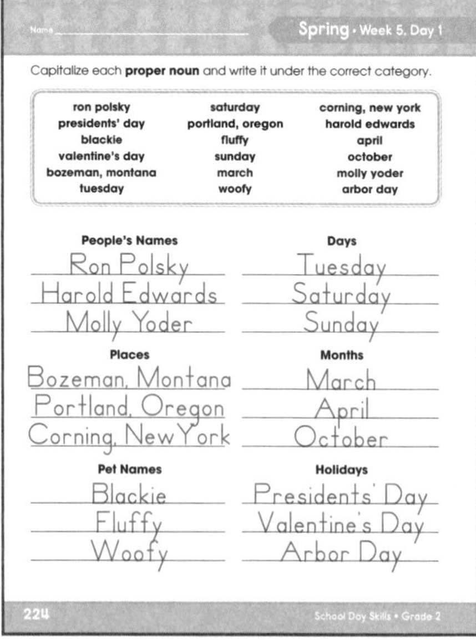
Name ______ Spring • Week 5, Day 1

Capitalize each **proper noun** and write it under the correct category.

ron polsky	saturday	corning, new york
presidents' day	portland, oregon	harold edwards
blackie	fluffy	april
valentine's day	sunday	october
bozeman, montana	march	molly yoder
tuesday	woofy	arbor day

People's Names: Ron Polsky, Harold Edwards, Molly Yoder
Days: Tuesday, Saturday, Sunday
Places: Bozeman, Montana; Portland, Oregon; Corning, New York
Months: March, April, October
Pet Names: Blackie, Fluffy, Woofy
Holidays: Presidents' Day, Valentine's Day, Arbor Day

224 School Day Skills • Grade 2

Page 224

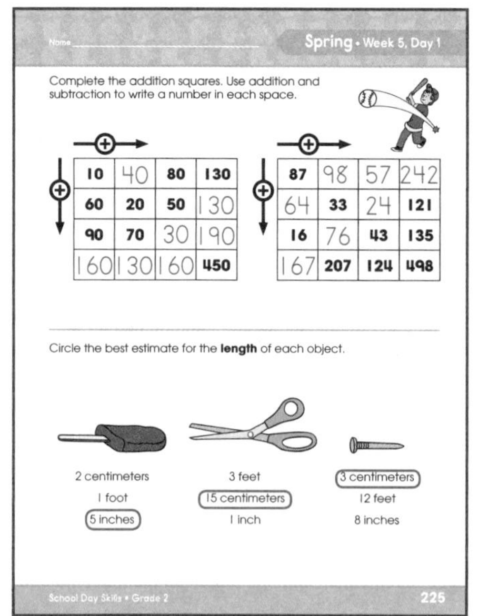
Name ______ Spring • Week 5, Day 1

Complete the addition squares. Use addition and subtraction to write a number in each space.

10	40	80	130
60	20	50	130
90	70	30	190
160	130	160	450

87	98	57	242
64	33	24	121
16	76	43	135
167	207	124	498

Circle the best estimate for the **length** of each object.

2 centimeters, 1 foot, (5 inches)
3 feet, (15 centimeters), 1 inch
(3 centimeters), 12 feet, 8 inches

School Day Skills • Grade 2 225

Page 225

Answer Key

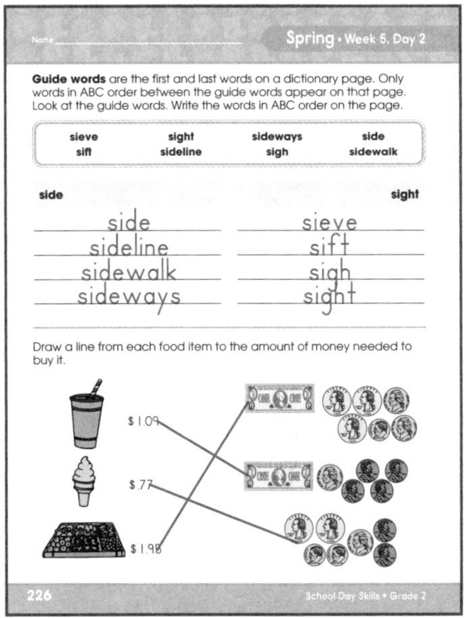

Page 226

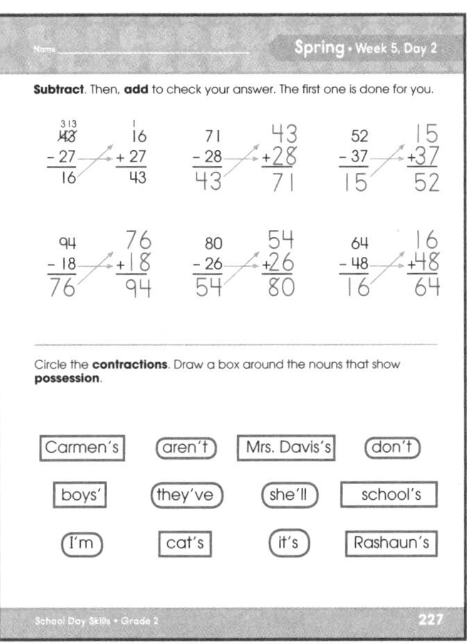

Page 227

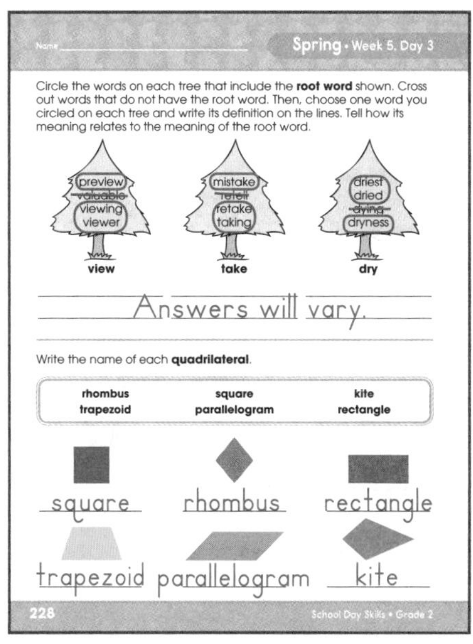

Page 228

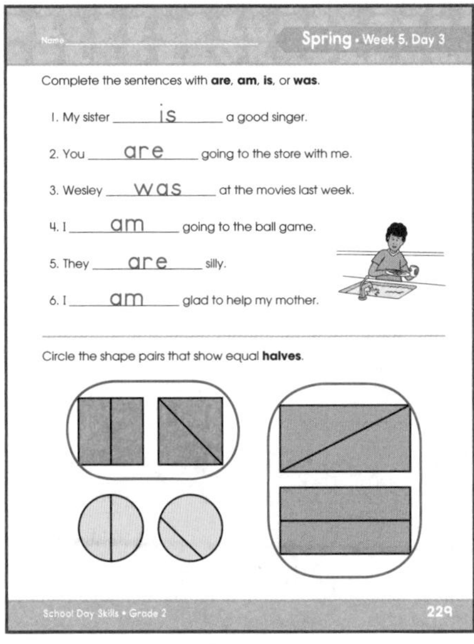

Page 229

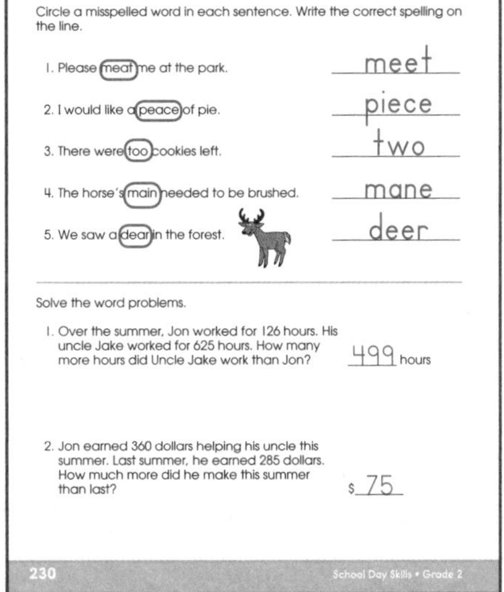

Page 230

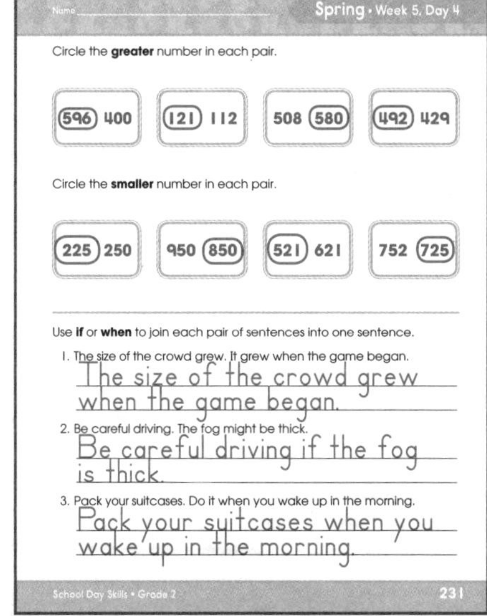

Page 231

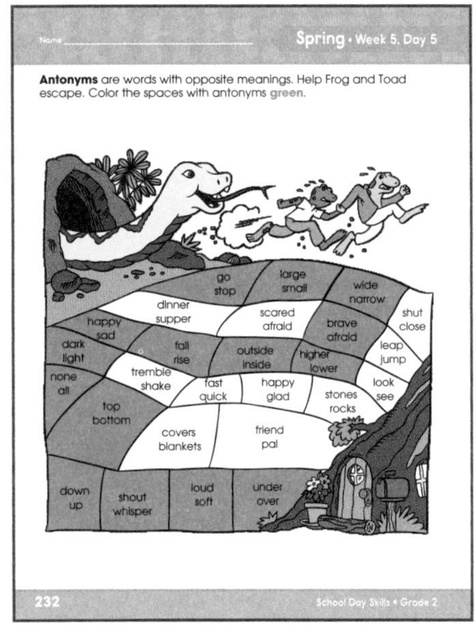
Name ______ Spring • Week 5, Day 5

Antonyms are words with opposite meanings. Help Frog and Toad escape. Color the spaces with antonyms **green**.

232 School Day Skills • Grade 2

Page 232

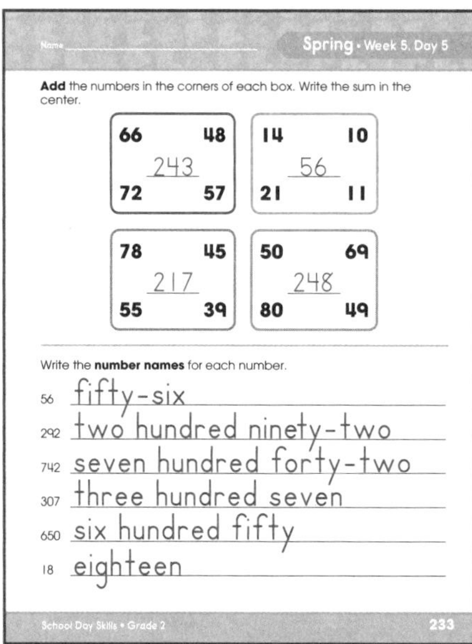
Name ______ Spring • Week 5, Day 5

Add the numbers in the corners of each box. Write the sum in the center.

66		48
	243	
72		57

14		10
	56	
21		11

78		45
	217	
55		39

50		69
	248	
80		49

Write the **number names** for each number.

56 fifty-six
292 two hundred ninety-two
742 seven hundred forty-two
307 three hundred seven
650 six hundred fifty
18 eighteen

School Day Skills • Grade 2 233

Page 233

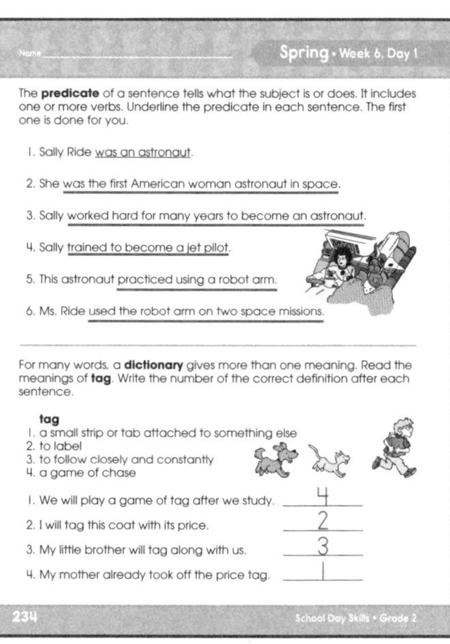
Name ______ Spring • Week 6, Day 1

The **predicate** of a sentence tells what the subject is or does. It includes one or more verbs. Underline the predicate in each sentence. The first one is done for you.

1. Sally Ride was an astronaut.
2. She was the first American woman astronaut in space.
3. Sally worked hard for many years to become an astronaut.
4. Sally trained to become a jet pilot.
5. This astronaut practiced using a robot arm.
6. Ms. Ride used the robot arm on two space missions.

For many words, a **dictionary** gives more than one meaning. Read the meanings of **tag**. Write the number of the correct definition after each sentence.

tag
1. a small strip or tab attached to something else
2. to label
3. to follow closely and constantly
4. a game of chase

1. We will play a game of tag after we study. 4
2. I will tag this coat with its price. 2
3. My little brother will tag along with us. 3
4. My mother already took off the price tag. 1

234 School Day Skills • Grade 2

Page 234

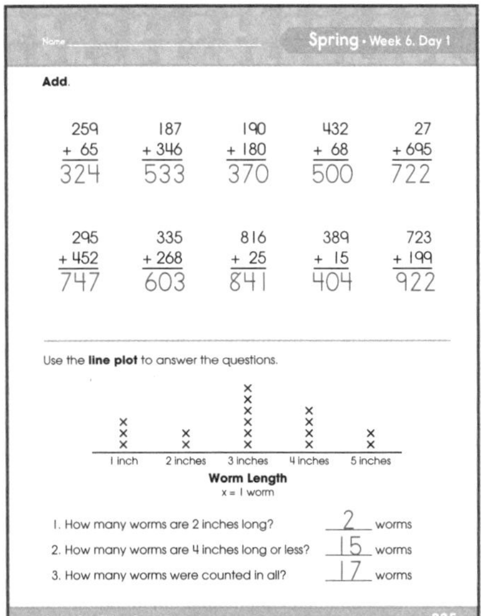
Name ______ Spring • Week 6, Day 1

Add.

259 + 65	187 + 346	190 + 180	432 + 68	27 + 695
324	533	370	500	722
295 + 452	335 + 268	816 + 25	389 + 15	723 + 199
747	603	841	404	922

Use the **line plot** to answer the questions.

1. How many worms are 2 inches long? 2 worms
2. How many worms are 4 inches long or less? 15 worms
3. How many worms were counted in all? 17 worms

School Day Skills • Grade 2 235

Page 235

Name ______ Spring • Week 6, Day 2

Read the passage. Answer the questions.

Imagine millions of teeny, tiny balloons joined together. That is what your lungs are like. When you breathe, the air goes to your two lungs. One lung is located on each side of your chest. The heart is located between the two lungs. The lungs are soft, spongy, and delicate. That is why there are bones around the lungs. These bones are called the **rib cage**. The rib cage protects the lungs so they can do their job. The lungs bring **oxygen** (ox-i-gin) into the body. They also take waste out of the body. This waste is called **carbon dioxide**. We could not live without our lungs!

1. What is the name of the bones around your lungs? the rib cage
2. What is located between the lungs? the heart
3. What goes into your lungs when you breathe? air
4. Why are there bones around your lungs? to protect them

236 School Day Skills • Grade 2

Page 236

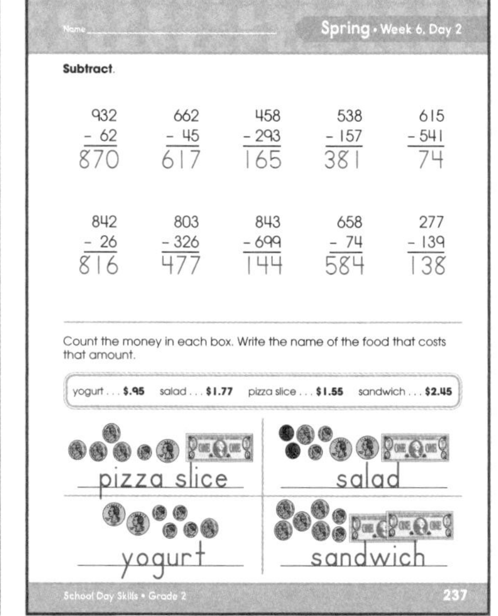
Name ______ Spring • Week 6, Day 2

Subtract.

932 − 62	662 − 45	458 − 293	538 − 157	615 − 541
870	617	165	381	74
842 − 26	803 − 326	843 − 699	658 − 74	277 − 139
816	477	144	584	138

Count the money in each box. Write the name of the food that costs that amount.

yogurt . . . $.95 salad . . . $1.77 pizza slice . . . $1.55 sandwich . . . $2.45

pizza slice
salad
yogurt
sandwich

School Day Skills • Grade 2 237

Page 237

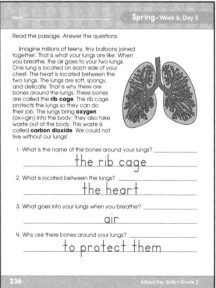

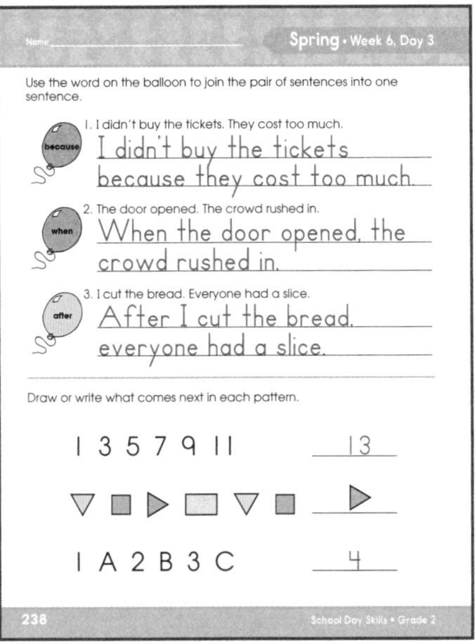

Name ___ Spring • Week 6, Day 3

Use the word on the balloon to join the pair of sentences into one sentence.

1. I didn't buy the tickets. They cost too much. (because)
I didn't buy the tickets because they cost too much.

2. The door opened. The crowd rushed in. (when)
When the door opened, the crowd rushed in.

3. I cut the bread. Everyone had a slice. (after)
After I cut the bread, everyone had a slice.

Draw or write what comes next in each pattern.

1 3 5 7 9 11 — 13

▽ ◼ ▷ ▭ ▽ ◼ — ▷

1 A 2 B 3 C — 4

238 School Day Skills • Grade 2

Page 238

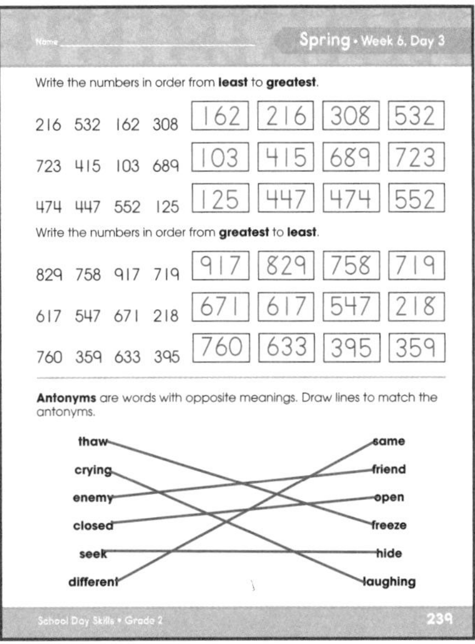

Name ___ Spring • Week 6, Day 3

Write the numbers in order from **least** to **greatest**.

216 532 162 308 — 162 216 308 532

723 415 103 689 — 103 415 689 723

474 447 552 125 — 125 447 474 552

Write the numbers in order from **greatest** to **least**.

829 758 917 719 — 917 829 758 719

617 547 671 218 — 671 617 547 218

760 359 633 395 — 760 633 395 359

Antonyms are words with opposite meanings. Draw lines to match the antonyms.

thaw — freeze
crying — laughing
enemy — friend
closed — open
seek — hide
different — same

School Day Skills • Grade 2 239

Page 239

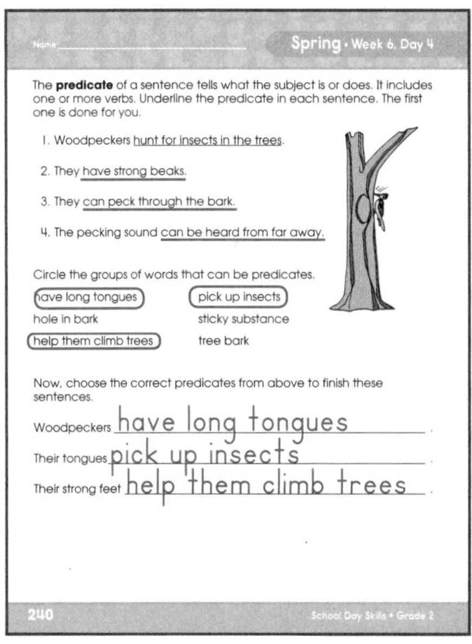

Name ___ Spring • Week 4, Day 4

The **predicate** of a sentence tells what the subject is or does. It includes one or more verbs. Underline the predicate in each sentence. The first one is done for you.

1. Woodpeckers hunt for insects in the trees.
2. They have strong beaks.
3. They can peck through the bark.
4. The pecking sound can be heard from far away.

Circle the groups of words that can be predicates.

have long tongues (circled) — pick up insects (circled)
hole in bark — sticky substance
help them climb trees (circled) — tree bark

Now, choose the correct predicates from above to finish these sentences.

Woodpeckers have long tongues.

Their tongues pick up insects.

Their strong feet help them climb trees.

240 School Day Skills • Grade 2

Page 240

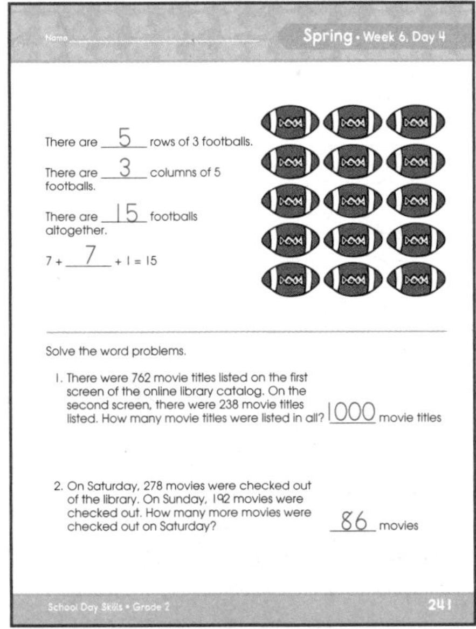

Name ___ Spring • Week 6, Day 4

There are 5 rows of 3 footballs.

There are 3 columns of 5 footballs.

There are 15 footballs altogether.

7 + 7 + 1 = 15

Solve the word problems.

1. There were 762 movie titles listed on the first screen of the online library catalog. On the second screen, there were 238 movie titles listed. How many movie titles were listed in all? 1000 movie titles

2. On Saturday, 278 movies were checked out of the library. On Sunday, 192 movies were checked out. How many more movies were checked out on Saturday? 86 movies

School Day Skills • Grade 2 241

Page 241

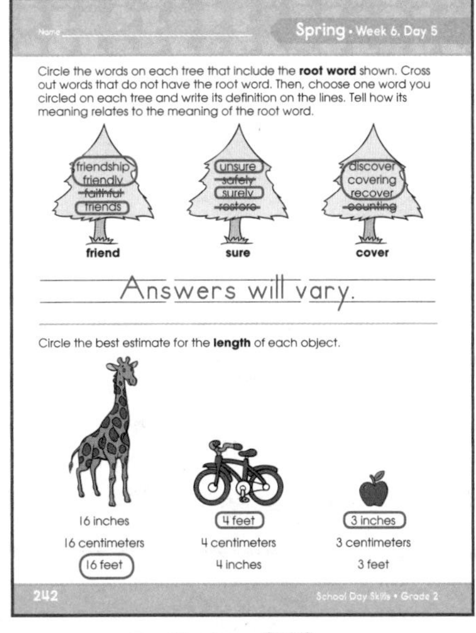

Name ___ Spring • Week 6, Day 5

Circle the words on each tree that include the **root word** shown. Cross out words that do not have the root word. Then, choose one word you circled on each tree and write its definition on the lines. Tell how its meaning relates to the meaning of the root word.

friend: friendship (circled), friendly (circled), ~~faithful~~, friends (circled)

sure: unsure (circled), ~~safely~~, surely (circled), ~~restore~~

cover: discover (circled), covering (circled), recover (circled), ~~counting~~

Answers will vary.

Circle the best estimate for the **length** of each object.

16 inches / 16 centimeters / 16 feet (circled)

4 feet (circled) / 4 centimeters / 4 inches

3 inches (circled) / 3 centimeters / 3 feet

242 School Day Skills • Grade 2

Page 242

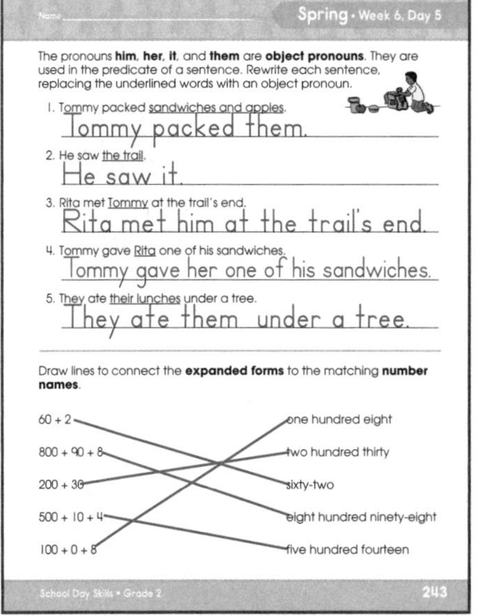

Name ___ Spring • Week 6, Day 5

The pronouns **him**, **her**, **it**, and **them** are **object pronouns**. They are used in the predicate of a sentence. Rewrite each sentence, replacing the underlined words with an object pronoun.

1. Tommy packed sandwiches and apples.
Tommy packed them.

2. He saw the trail.
He saw it.

3. Rita met Tommy at the trail's end.
Rita met him at the trail's end.

4. Tommy gave Rita one of his sandwiches.
Tommy gave her one of his sandwiches.

5. They ate their lunches under a tree.
They ate them under a tree.

Draw lines to connect the **expanded forms** to the matching **number names**.

60 + 2 — sixty-two
800 + 90 + 8 — eight hundred ninety-eight
200 + 30 — two hundred thirty
500 + 10 + 4 — five hundred fourteen
100 + 0 + 8 — one hundred eight

School Day Skills • Grade 2 243

Page 243

Answer Key

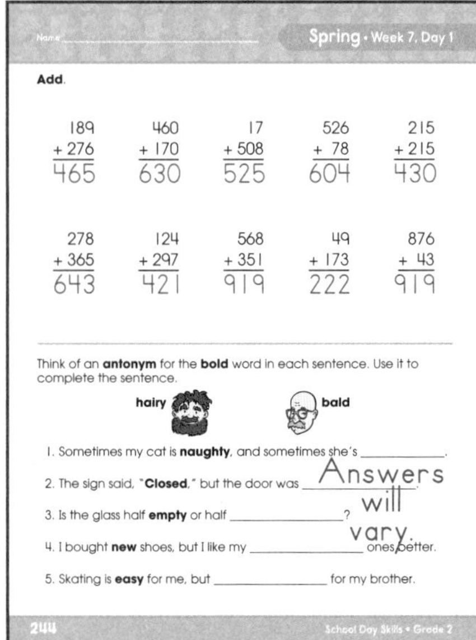

Spring • Week 7, Day 1

Add.

189	460	17	526	215
+ 276	+ 170	+ 508	+ 78	+ 215
465	630	525	604	430

278	124	568	49	876
+ 365	+ 297	+ 351	+ 173	+ 43
643	421	919	222	919

Think of an **antonym** for the **bold** word in each sentence. Use it to complete the sentence.

hairy bald

1. Sometimes my cat is **naughty**, and sometimes she's ___________.
2. The sign said, "**Closed**," but the door was ___________.
3. Is the glass half **empty** or half ___________?
4. I bought **new** shoes, but I like my ___________ ones better.
5. Skating is **easy** for me, but ___________ for my brother.

Answers will vary.

244 School Day Skills • Grade 2

Page 244

Spring • Week 7, Day 1

Rewrite the sentences. Capitalize the first word in each sentence. Capitalize **proper nouns**.

1. we celebrate thanksgiving on the fourth thursday in november.
   We celebrate Thanksgiving on the fourth Thursday in November.
2. in june, michelle and mark will go camping every friday.
   In June, Michelle and Mark will go camping every Friday.
3. on mondays in october, I will take piano lessons.
   On Mondays in October, I will take piano lessons.

Write **>** or **<** to **compare** the numbers. Make sure the open "mouth" points to the greater number.

87 (>) 4	510 (>) 500
798 (<) 814	5 (<) 75
250 (<) 275	820 (>) 768

School Day Skills • Grade 2 245

Page 245

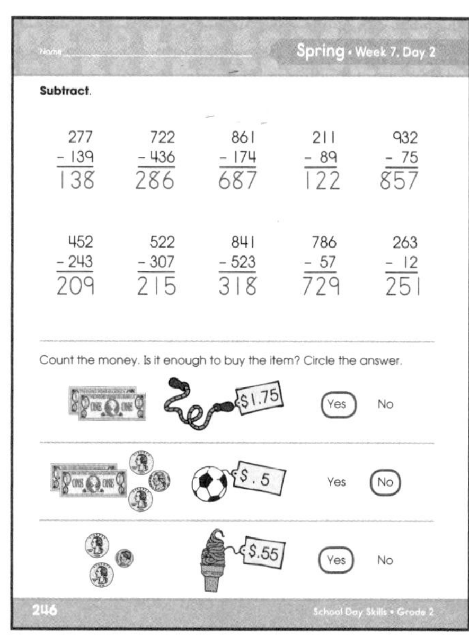

Spring • Week 7, Day 2

Subtract.

277	722	861	211	932
− 139	− 436	− 174	− 89	− 75
138	286	687	122	857

452	522	841	786	263
− 243	− 307	− 523	− 57	− 12
209	215	318	729	251

Count the money. Is it enough to buy the item? Circle the answer.

$1.75 (Yes) No

$.5 Yes (No)

$.55 (Yes) No

246 School Day Skills • Grade 2

Page 246

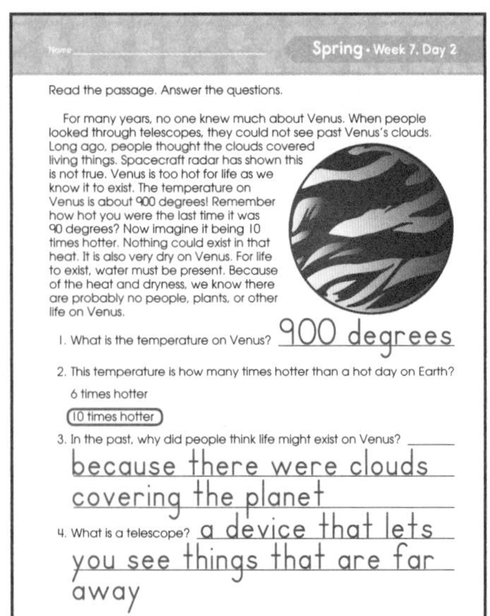

Spring • Week 7, Day 2

Read the passage. Answer the questions.

For many years, no one knew much about Venus. When people looked through telescopes, they could not see past Venus's clouds. Long ago, people thought the clouds covered living things. Spacecraft radar has shown this is not true. Venus is too hot for life as we know it to exist. The temperature on Venus is about 900 degrees! Remember how hot you were the last time it was 90 degrees? Now imagine it being 10 times hotter. Nothing could exist in that heat. It is also very dry on Venus. For life to exist, water must be present. Because of the heat and dryness, we know there are probably no people, plants, or other life on Venus.

1. What is the temperature on Venus? 900 degrees
2. This temperature is how many times hotter than a hot day on Earth?
   6 times hotter
   (10 times hotter)
3. In the past, why did people think life might exist on Venus? because there were clouds covering the planet
4. What is a telescope? a device that lets you see things that are far away

School Day Skills • Grade 2 247

Page 247

Spring • Week 7, Day 3

Circle words with the root word **pay**.

(payment) (payable) (paying) (payer)
playing (repay) (paid) replace

Write the meaning of one word you circled. Explain how it relates to the root word **pay**.

Answers will vary.

Draw lines to connect the **expanded forms** to the matching **number names**.

700 + 60 + 6	three hundred one
500 + 50 + 5	seven hundred sixty-six
80 + 6	one hundred twenty
300 + 0 + 1	eighty-six
100 + 20	five hundred fifty-five

248 School Day Skills • Grade 2

Page 248

Spring • Week 7, Day 3

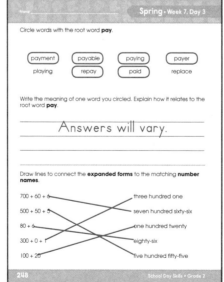

Solve mentally. Write the answers quickly.

107	107	107	455	455
− 100	+ 10	+ 100	+ 10	− 100
7	117	207	465	355

455	455	89	89	89
− 10	+ 100	+ 10	− 10	+ 100
445	555	99	79	189

Underline the **predicate** in each sentence. The first one is done for you.

1. Juan <u>looks for rocks everywhere he goes.</u>
2. He <u>has found many interesting rocks in his own backyard.</u>
3. Juan <u>showed me a piece of limestone with fossils in it.</u>
4. Limestone <u>is a kind of sedimentary rock.</u>
5. It <u>is formed underwater from the shells of animals.</u>
6. Juan <u>told me that some rocks come from deep inside Earth.</u>

School Day Skills • Grade 2 249

Page 249

Answer Key

Name_______________ Spring • Week 7, Day 4

Read the **dictionary** definitions for **note**. Write the number of the correct meaning after each sentence.

note
1. a short letter or message
2. a written explanation
3. a musical tone
4. to notice

1. Can you sing the high note in this song? 3
2. I read a book about dinosaurs and took notes. 2
3. I noted many rhyming words in the poem. 4
4. Leave a note to tell Mom where we are going. 1

Solve the word problems.

1. Cody's summer vacation was 94 days long. He spent 68 summer days at his aunt's house. How many summer days were not spent at his aunt's house? 26 days
2. Cody's summer camp cost $275. His sister Faye's camp cost $125. How much did Cody's parents spend to send the two children to camp? $400

250 School Day Skills • Grade 2

Page 250

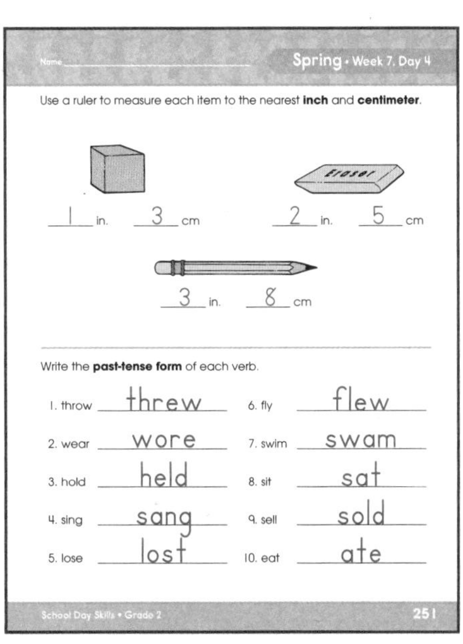
Name_______________ Spring • Week 7, Day 4

Use a ruler to measure each item to the nearest **inch** and **centimeter**.

1 in. 3 cm
2 in. 5 cm
3 in. 8 cm

Write the **past-tense form** of each verb.

1. throw threw
2. wear wore
3. hold held
4. sing sang
5. lose lost
6. fly flew
7. swim swam
8. sit sat
9. sell sold
10. eat ate

School Day Skills • Grade 2 251

Page 251

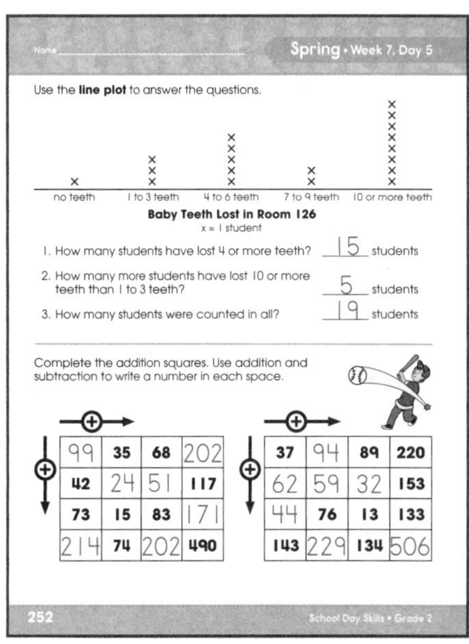
Name_______________ Spring • Week 7, Day 5

Use the **line plot** to answer the questions.

1. How many students have lost 4 or more teeth? 15 students
2. How many more students have lost 10 or more teeth than 1 to 3 teeth? 5 students
3. How many students were counted in all? 19 students

Complete the addition squares. Use addition and subtraction to write a number in each space.

99	35	68	202
42	24	51	117
73	15	83	171
214	74	202	490

37	94	89	220
62	59	32	153
44	76	13	133
143	229	134	506

252 School Day Skills • Grade 2

Page 252

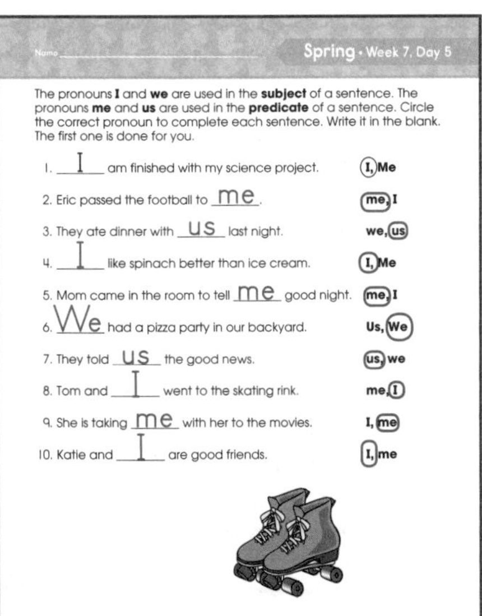
Name_______________ Spring • Week 7, Day 5

The pronouns **I** and **we** are used in the **subject** of a sentence. The pronouns **me** and **us** are used in the **predicate** of a sentence. Circle the correct pronoun to complete each sentence. Write it in the blank. The first one is done for you.

1. I am finished with my science project. I, Me
2. Eric passed the football to me. me, I
3. They ate dinner with us last night. we, us
4. I like spinach better than ice cream. I, Me
5. Mom came in the room to tell me good night. me, I
6. We had a pizza party in our backyard. Us, We
7. They told us the good news. us, we
8. Tom and I went to the skating rink. me, I
9. She is taking me with her to the movies. I, me
10. Katie and I are good friends. I, me

School Day Skills • Grade 2 253

Page 253

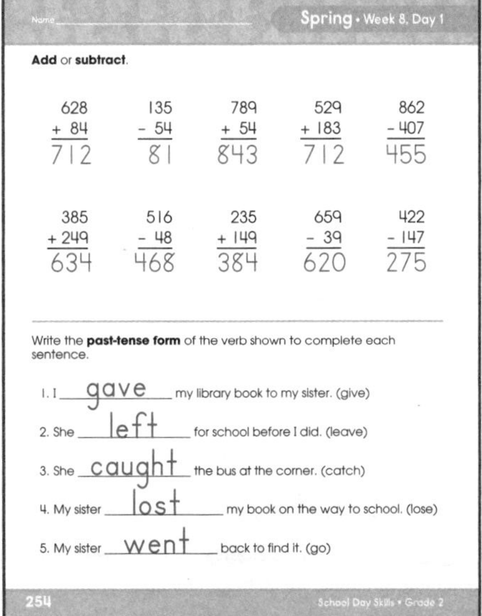
Name_______________ Spring • Week 8, Day 1

Add or **subtract**.

628 + 84 = 712
135 − 54 = 81
789 + 54 = 843
529 + 183 = 712
862 − 407 = 455
385 + 249 = 634
516 − 48 = 468
235 + 149 = 384
659 − 39 = 620
422 − 147 = 275

Write the **past-tense form** of the verb shown to complete each sentence.

1. I gave my library book to my sister. (give)
2. She left for school before I did. (leave)
3. She caught the bus at the corner. (catch)
4. My sister lost my book on the way to school. (lose)
5. My sister went back to find it. (go)

254 School Day Skills • Grade 2

Page 254

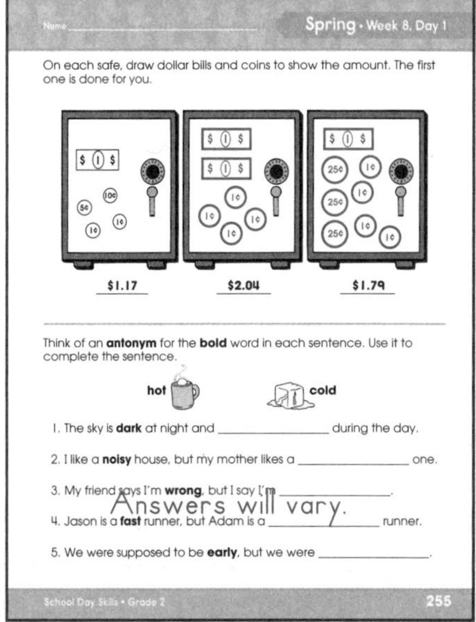
Name_______________ Spring • Week 8, Day 1

On each safe, draw dollar bills and coins to show the amount. The first one is done for you.

$1.17 $2.04 $1.79

Think of an **antonym** for the **bold** word in each sentence. Use it to complete the sentence.

hot cold

1. The sky is **dark** at night and ________ during the day.
2. I like a **noisy** house, but my mother likes a ________ one.
3. My friend says I'm **wrong**, but I say I'm ________.
4. Jason is a **fast** runner, but Adam is a ________ runner.
5. We were supposed to be **early**, but we were ________.

Answers will vary.

School Day Skills • Grade 2 255

Page 255

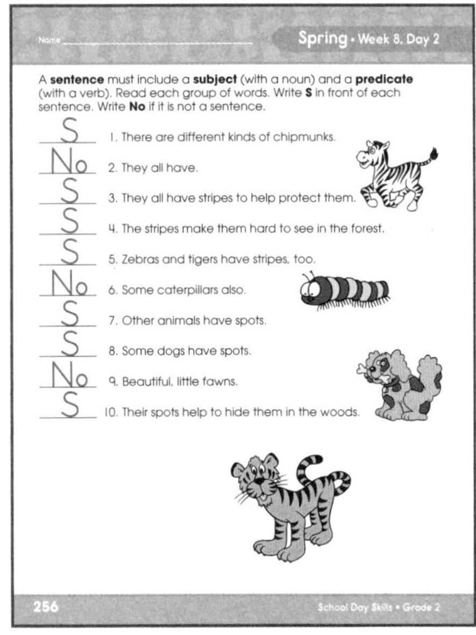

Name ______________________ **Spring** • Week 8, Day 2

A **sentence** must include a **subject** (with a noun) and a **predicate** (with a verb). Read each group of words. Write **S** in front of each sentence. Write **No** if it is not a sentence.

S 1. There are different kinds of chipmunks.
No 2. They all have.
S 3. They all have stripes to help protect them.
S 4. The stripes make them hard to see in the forest.
S 5. Zebras and tigers have stripes, too.
No 6. Some caterpillars also.
S 7. Other animals have spots.
S 8. Some dogs have spots.
No 9. Beautiful, little fawns.
S 10. Their spots help to hide them in the woods.

256 School Day Skills • Grade 2

Page 256

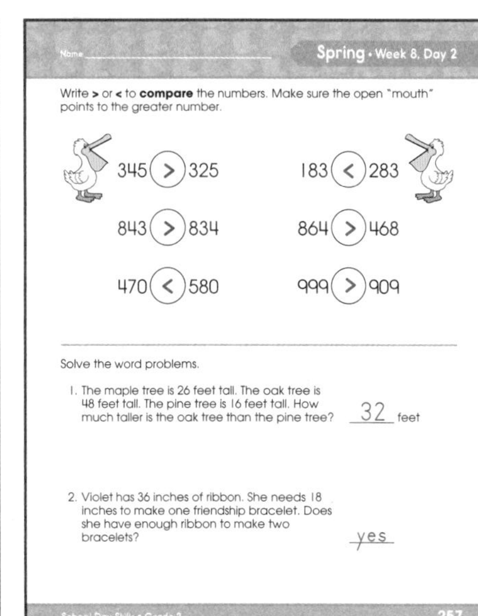

Name ______________________ **Spring** • Week 8, Day 2

Write **>** or **<** to **compare** the numbers. Make sure the open "mouth" points to the greater number.

345 > 325 183 < 283
843 > 834 864 > 468
470 < 580 999 > 909

Solve the word problems.

1. The maple tree is 26 feet tall. The oak tree is 48 feet tall. The pine tree is 16 feet tall. How much taller is the oak tree than the pine tree? 32 feet

2. Violet has 36 inches of ribbon. She needs 18 inches to make one friendship bracelet. Does she have enough ribbon to make two bracelets? yes

School Day Skills • Grade 2 257

Page 257

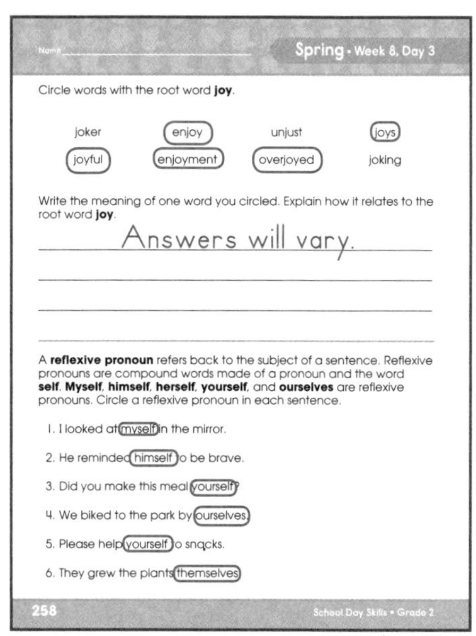

Name ______________________ **Spring** • Week 8, Day 3

Circle words with the root word **joy**.

joker (enjoy) unjust (joys)
(joyful) (enjoyment) (overjoyed) joking

Write the meaning of one word you circled. Explain how it relates to the root word **joy**.

Answers will vary.

A **reflexive pronoun** refers back to the subject of a sentence. Reflexive pronouns are compound words made of a pronoun and the word **self**. **Myself**, **himself**, **herself**, **yourself**, and **ourselves** are reflexive pronouns. Circle a reflexive pronoun in each sentence.

1. I looked at (myself) in the mirror.
2. He reminded (himself) to be brave.
3. Did you make this meal (yourself)?
4. We biked to the park by (ourselves).
5. Please help (yourself) to snacks.
6. They grew the plants (themselves).

258 School Day Skills • Grade 2

Page 258

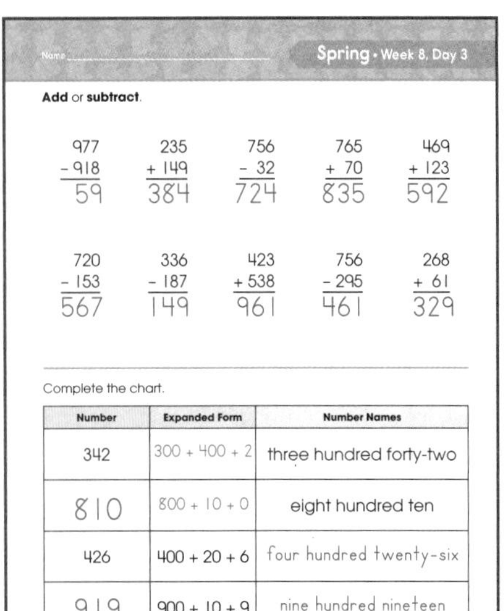

Name ______________________ **Spring** • Week 8, Day 3

Add or **subtract**.

977 − 918 = 59	235 + 149 = 384	756 − 32 = 724	765 + 70 = 835	469 + 123 = 592
720 − 153 = 567	336 − 187 = 149	423 + 538 = 961	756 − 295 = 461	268 + 61 = 329

Complete the chart.

Number	Expanded Form	Number Names
342	300 + 40 + 2	three hundred forty-two
810	800 + 10 + 0	eight hundred ten
426	400 + 20 + 6	four hundred twenty-six
919	900 + 10 + 9	nine hundred nineteen

School Day Skills • Grade 2 259

Page 259

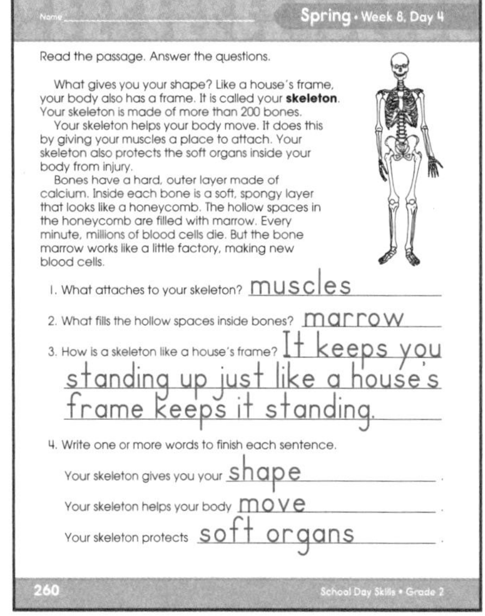

Name ______________________ **Spring** • Week 8, Day 4

Read the passage. Answer the questions.

What gives you your shape? Like a house's frame, your body also has a frame. It is called your **skeleton**. Your skeleton is made of more than 200 bones.

Your skeleton helps your body move. It does this by giving your muscles a place to attach. Your skeleton also protects the soft organs inside your body from injury.

Bones have a hard, outer layer made of calcium. Inside each bone is a soft, spongy layer that looks like a honeycomb. The hollow spaces in the honeycomb are filled with marrow. Every minute, millions of blood cells die. But the bone marrow works like a little factory, making new blood cells.

1. What attaches to your skeleton? muscles
2. What fills the hollow spaces inside bones? marrow
3. How is a skeleton like a house's frame? It keeps you standing up just like a house's frame keeps it standing.
4. Write one or more words to finish each sentence.

Your skeleton gives you your shape.
Your skeleton helps your body move.
Your skeleton protects soft organs.

260 School Day Skills • Grade 2

Page 260

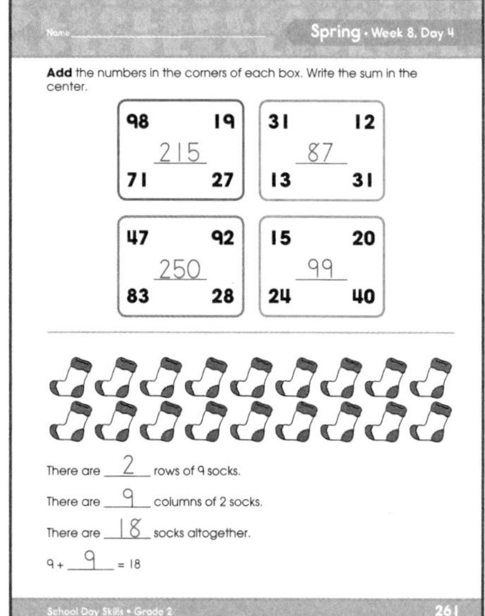

Name ______________________ **Spring** • Week 8, Day 4

Add the numbers in the corners of each box. Write the sum in the center.

Corners	Sum
98, 19, 71, 27	215
31, 12, 13, 31	87
47, 92, 83, 28	250
15, 20, 24, 40	99

There are 2 rows of 9 socks.
There are 9 columns of 2 socks.
There are 18 socks altogether.
9 + 9 = 18

School Day Skills • Grade 2 261

Page 261

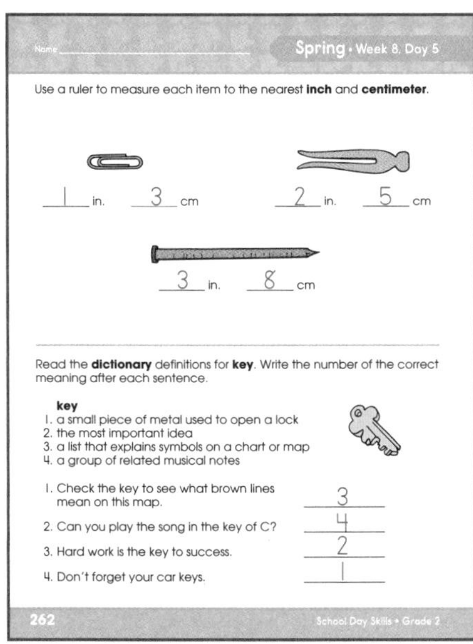

Spring • Week 8, Day 5

Use a ruler to measure each item to the nearest **inch** and **centimeter**.

1 in. 3 cm

2 in. 5 cm

3 in. 8 cm

Read the **dictionary** definitions for **key**. Write the number of the correct meaning after each sentence.

key
1. a small piece of metal used to open a lock
2. the most important idea
3. a list that explains symbols on a chart or map
4. a group of related musical notes

1. Check the key to see what brown lines mean on this map. 3
2. Can you play the song in the key of C? 4
3. Hard work is the key to success. 2
4. Don't forget your car keys. 1

262 School Day Skills • Grade 2

Page 262

Spring • Week 8, Day 5

Add or **subtract**.

137 + 329 = 466	154 − 92 = 62	329 − 85 = 244	18 + 625 = 643	436 − 242 = 194
731 − 515 = 216	379 + 102 = 481	645 + 247 = 892	371 + 38 = 409	356 − 259 = 97

A **compound predicate** has two or more predicates joined by the word **and**. Read each sentence. If it has a compound predicate, write **CP**. If it does not, write **No**. The first one is done for you.

CP 1. Abe Lincoln cut trees and chopped wood.
CP 2. Abe's family packed up and left Kentucky.
No 3. Abe's father built a new home.
CP 4. Abe's mother became sick and died.
No 5. Mr. Lincoln married again.
CP 6. Abe's new mother loved Abe and his sister and cared for them.

School Day Skills • Grade 2 263

Page 263

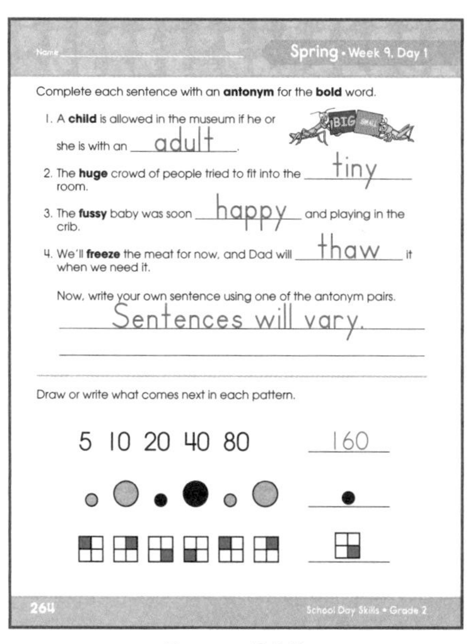

Spring • Week 9, Day 1

Complete each sentence with an **antonym** for the **bold** word.

1. A **child** is allowed in the museum if he or she is with an adult.
2. The **huge** crowd of people tried to fit into the tiny room.
3. The **fussy** baby was soon happy and playing in the crib.
4. We'll **freeze** the meat for now, and Dad will thaw it when we need it.

Now, write your own sentence using one of the antonym pairs.

Sentences will vary.

Draw or write what comes next in each pattern.

5 10 20 40 80 160

264 School Day Skills • Grade 2

Page 264

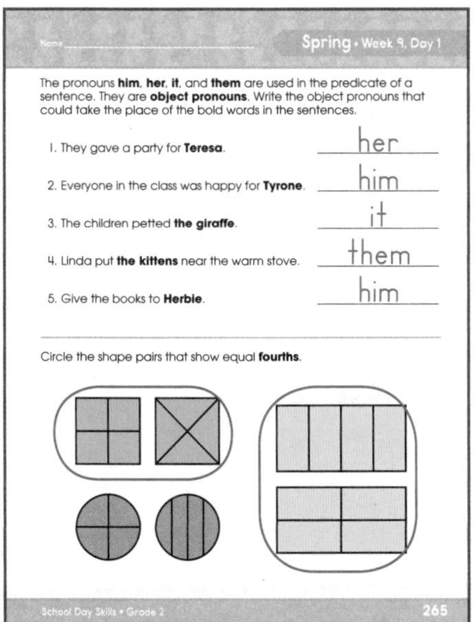

Spring • Week 9, Day 1

The pronouns **him**, **her**, **it**, and **them** are used in the predicate of a sentence. They are **object pronouns**. Write the object pronouns that could take the place of the bold words in the sentences.

1. They gave a party for **Teresa**. her
2. Everyone in the class was happy for **Tyrone**. him
3. The children petted **the giraffe**. it
4. Linda put **the kittens** near the warm stove. them
5. Give the books to **Herbie**. him

Circle the shape pairs that show equal **fourths**.

School Day Skills • Grade 2 265

Page 265

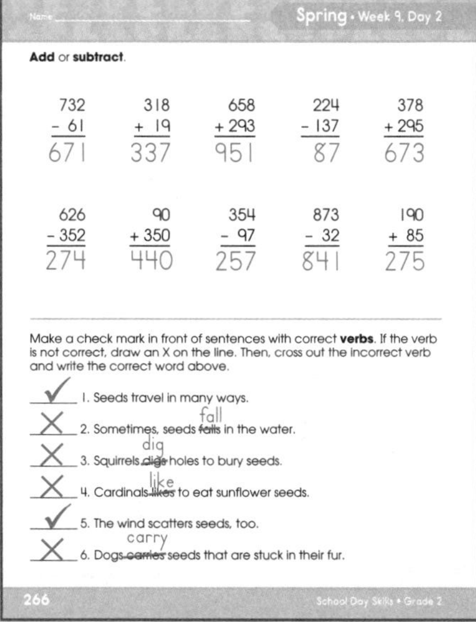

Spring • Week 9, Day 2

Add or **subtract**.

732 − 61 = 671	318 + 19 = 337	658 + 293 = 951	224 − 137 = 87	378 + 295 = 673
626 − 352 = 274	90 + 350 = 440	354 − 97 = 257	873 − 32 = 841	190 + 85 = 275

Make a check mark in front of sentences with correct **verbs**. If the verb is not correct, draw an X on the line. Then, cross out the incorrect verb and write the correct word above.

✓ 1. Seeds travel in many ways.
X 2. Sometimes, seeds ~~falls~~ fall in the water.
X 3. Squirrels ~~digs~~ dig holes to bury seeds.
X 4. Cardinals ~~likes~~ like to eat sunflower seeds.
✓ 5. The wind scatters seeds, too.
X 6. Dogs ~~carries~~ carry seeds that are stuck in their fur.

266 School Day Skills • Grade 2

Page 266

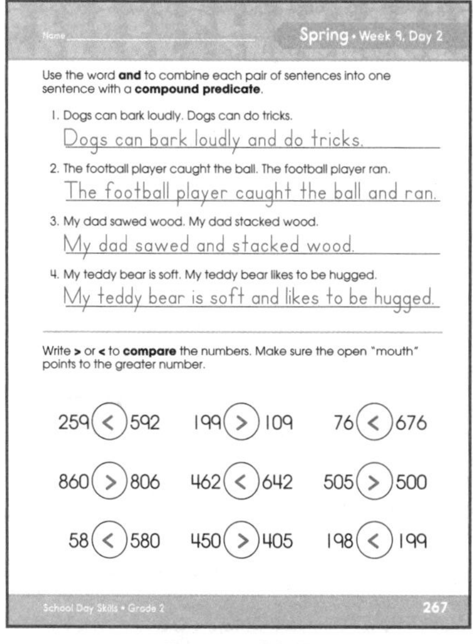

Spring • Week 9, Day 2

Use the word **and** to combine each pair of sentences into one sentence with a **compound predicate**.

1. Dogs can bark loudly. Dogs can do tricks.
Dogs can bark loudly and do tricks.
2. The football player caught the ball. The football player ran.
The football player caught the ball and ran.
3. My dad sawed wood. My dad stacked wood.
My dad sawed and stacked wood.
4. My teddy bear is soft. My teddy bear likes to be hugged.
My teddy bear is soft and likes to be hugged.

Write > or < to **compare** the numbers. Make sure the open "mouth" points to the greater number.

259 < 592	199 > 109	76 < 676
860 > 806	462 < 642	505 > 500
58 < 580	450 > 405	198 < 199

School Day Skills • Grade 2 267

Page 267

Answer Key

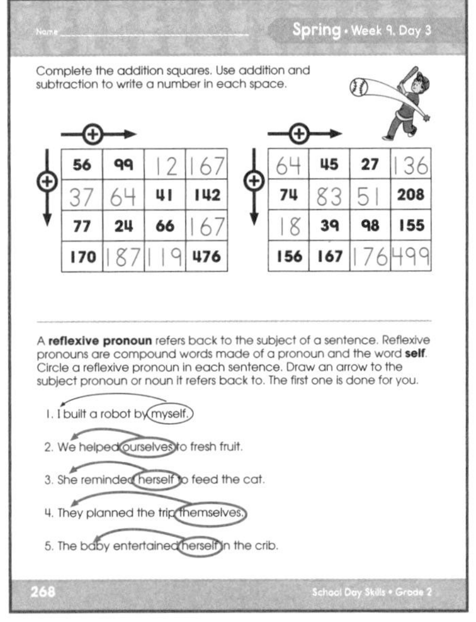

Page 268

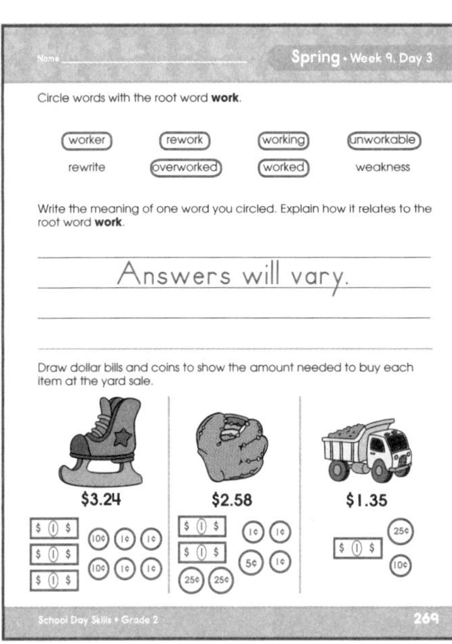

Page 269

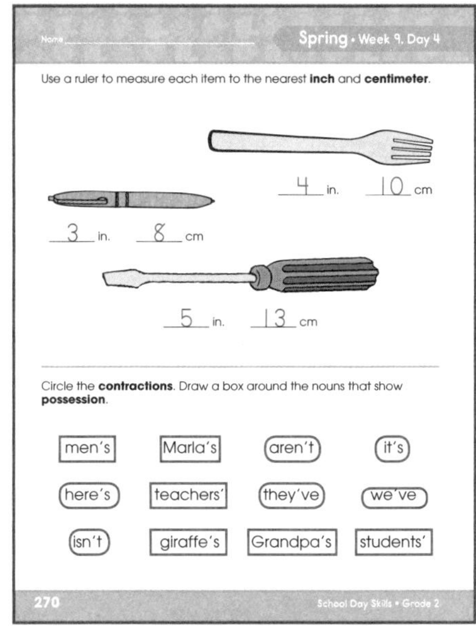

Page 270

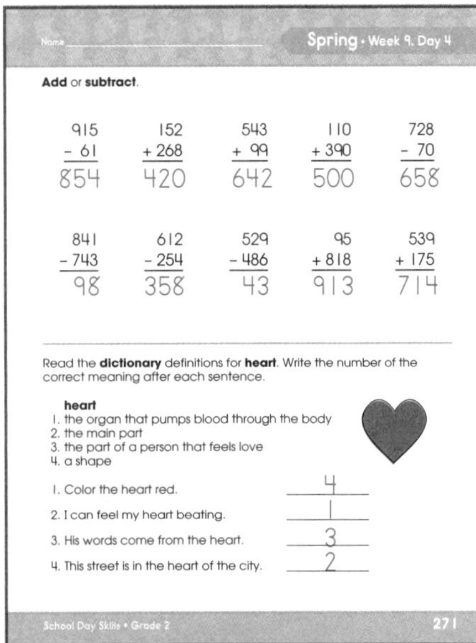

Page 271

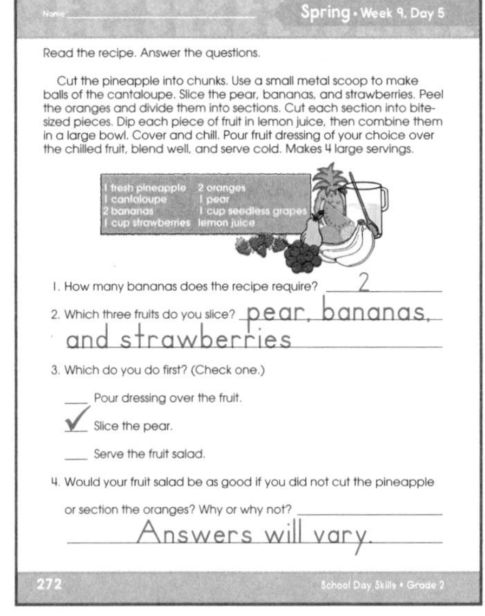

Page 272

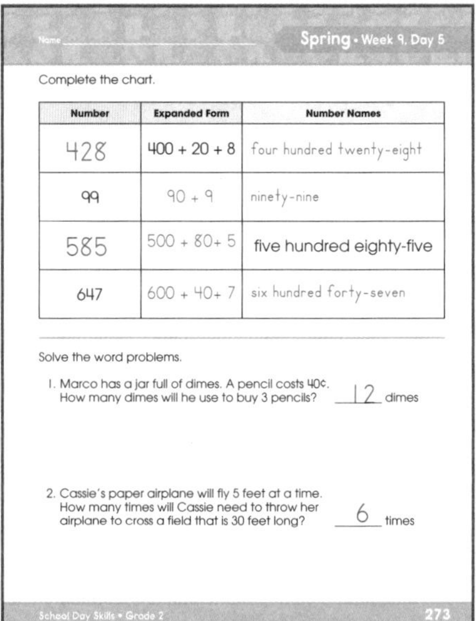

Page 273